P9-DFV-423

Differentiated Instruction

A Guide for Middle and High School Teachers

Amy Benjamin

EYE ON EDUCATION

EYE ON EDUCATION
6 DEPOT WAY WEST, SUITE 106
LARCHMONT, NY 10538
(914) 833–0551
(914) 833–0761 fax
www.eyeoneducation.com

Library of Congress Cataloging-in-Publication Data

Benjamin, Amy, 1951-
    Differentiated instruction : a guide for middle and high school teachers / by Amy Benjamin.
        p. cm.
    ISBN 1-930556-39-X
    1. Individualized instruction. 2. Cognitive styles in children. 3. Mixed ability grouping in education. 4. Middle school teaching. 5. High school teaching. I. Title.

    LB1031 .B46 2002
    373.12'52--dc21   2002019161

10 9 8 7 6 5 4 3

Editorial and production services provided by
Richard H. Adin Freelance Editorial Services
52 Oakwood Blvd., Poughkeepsie, NY 12603-4112
(845-471-3566)

Also Available from EYE ON EDUCATION

**An English Teacher's Guide to Performance
Tasks and Rubrics: High School**
by Amy Benjamin

**An English Teacher's Guide to Performance
Tasks and Rubrics: Middle School**
by Amy Benjamin

Writing in the Content Areas
by Amy Benjamin

**Social Studies:
Standards, Meaning, and Understanding**
by Barbara Slater Stern

Performance Standards and Authentic Learning
by Allan Glatthorn

**Constructivist Strategies:
Meeting Standards and Engaging Adolescent Minds**
by Foote, Vermette, and Battaglia

**Standards-Based Activities with Scoring Rubrics:
Middle and High School English
Vol. 1. Performance-Based Portfolios**
Edited by Jacqueline Glasgow

**Standards-Based Activities with Scoring Rubrics:
Middle and High School English
Vol. 2. Performance-based Projects**
Edited by Jacqueline Glasgow

**Socratic Seminars & Literature Circles
For Middle and High School English**
by Victor and Marc Moeller

High School English Teacher's Guide to Active Learning
by Victor and Marc Moeller

Middle School English Teacher's Guide to Active Learning
by Victor and Marc Moeller

**Navigating Comprehensive School Change:
A Guide for the Perplexed**
by Thomas Chenoweth and Robert Everhart

Dedication

This book is dedicated to Maggie Fontanella, who has taught me, by example, the most important things I know about teaching.

Acknowledgments

I gratefully acknowledge the mentorship of Nancy Letts, with whom I have been working for many years to understand and practice differentiated instruction. I owe much thanks to Heidi Hayes Jacobs for her continued encouragement and for the opportunities that she has given me. I thank my colleagues at the Hendrick Hudson School District for allowing me to learn from them and to grow as a professional by their example. John D'Auria and Deborah Burns offered generous and helpful comments about this manuscript and their contributions are much appreciated. And, once again, I wish to thank Robert N. Sickles, my publisher, for his continued support and faith in me as I worked on this book.

Foreword

As an instructional coach, Amy Benjamin is the ultimate professional. She is direct, fair, informed, current, and insightful. Any teacher or administrator would be fortunate to have her courtside. The practical strategies and possible plans recommended in *Differentiated Instruction* are designed to help teachers revise their classroom performance. The result of this revision is ultimately tailored to increased student productivity and to increase performance results.

In an age of standards and testing, it is easy to lose sight of the long term effect schooling can have no our learners. Every teacher knows there is a range of needs in those faces staring up at them. Certainly, we need to help our students execute assessed skill well in formal testing situations and Amy helps us here. What is impressive about her suggestions is that the teacher will enable students to see that the strategies and approaches they hone in class go beyond any test and can serve them in situations beyond the classroom. The key for the teacher is to provide what the individual student needs, to adjust classroom lessons accordingly, and to engage them in meaningful activity.

Amy Benjamin helps us see a way to take this formidable task on with intelligence and creativity.

Staff developers, curriculum writers, and instructors have much to value in these pages. Building on her previous work with Eye On Education, Amy is generating a productive set of books to coach us in this new century.

Heidi Hayes Jacobs

About the Author

My name is Amy Benjamin. I have been an English teacher at Hendrick Hudson High School in Montrose, New York, since 1973. I've taught all levels, all kinds of kids. Part of my job consists of working collaboratively with my colleagues and their classes on reading and writing in the content areas.

In addition to being a teacher, I am also, obviously, a writer of books such as this, and I run numerous workshops in New York and all around the country. Most of my workshops are about making kids better thinkers through the use of language. I've also written a couple of plays and a young adult novel. I tell you this because I know firsthand that there are different ways of being smart. When I was a student, school was a scary place, a place where I usually thought I was "doing it wrong." I'm left-handed, so I was awkward and backward at certain fine motor skills, such as handwriting and knitting. I have "my own system" of doing arithmetic. It works for me, but I thought I was cheating when I'd figure out that 26 + 8 = 34 *because* I can picture two groups of fours added to 26. I'd make patterns like that in my head to help me add and subtract. I thought that was wrong to do, but I needed to do it. If no one had told my mother that she could teach me how to tie a bow by starting with two loops, I'd be wearing velcro sneakers today. I've always been considered "creative," but, to me, "creative" was just another way of saying that I couldn't follow directions.

Oh, and I'm also a union official for my New York State United Teachers local. I am responsible for conflict resolution and seeing to it that the collective bargaining agreement as well as proper labor practices are carried out.

I tell you these things about myself because I want you to know where my voice comes from. I'm a teacher, just like you. I take attendance, keep track of grades, call angry parents (as well as some appreciative ones), eat my lunch out of a thermal bag, write out hall passes, go to staff development days, walk the talk from September to June. What I know about differentiated instruction is that:

 ♦ I've always done it, even before I knew it had a name
 ♦ I could be better at it
 ♦ It's important

I hope that you find this information and the reflections enlightening and collegial. I wish you well in your professional quest to make learning real and lasting in your classrooms.

Table of Contents

How to Use This Book

This book explains ways in which differentiated instruction can work for middle and high school teachers. We assume that readers wish to make their classrooms more responsive to the needs of individuals with a wide variety of learning styles, interests, goals, cultural backgrounds, and prior knowledge. The purpose of the text and reflections is to make you think, discuss, question, apply new strategies, share effective practices, and improve what you already do well. This book is interactive. It is best used by colleagues who have convened in a course, a workshop, a staff development day, or some other forum in which reflection and revision of practice is possible.

1

Foundations

What Is Differentiated Instruction?

Across the country, the public is expecting more from educators. With nearly every state having a standards-based curriculum, *all* students are expected to achieve at a level higher than ever before. And that's good.

It's good because the standards movement has led to better staff development for teachers and administrators. Whereas in years past we might have been able to consign certain students to low-achieving classes with euphemized names like "English for Real Life" and "Math for Everyday Living," we now must find ways to make higher achievement accessible to everyone, no matter how challenging that is for all concerned.

What do we mean by "higher achievement"? The standards are about critical thinking skills, application of information, fluent and accurate use of the English language in written and oral expression, some exposure to a second language, and familiarity with a body of knowledge referred to as cultural literacy. Out of this goal of elevating the intellectual function of all students comes the philosophy and practice of differentiated instruction (DI).

Differentiated instruction is a broad term that refers to a variety of classroom practices that accommodate differences in students' learning styles, interests, prior knowledge, socialization needs, and comfort zones. On the secondary level, it involves a balance between the content and competencies expected on the mandated assessments and various pedagogical options to maximize durable learning. The standards tell us what students need to know and to be able to do. Differentiated instruction practices help to get students there, while at the same time teaching them *how* to learn in a meaningful way.

In its modern application, a differentiated classroom is widely heterogeneous, dynamic, purposeful, and intense. The pedagogical theory that guides differentiation is constructivism: *the belief that learning happens when the learner makes meaning out of information.* That may sound too self-evident to deserve mention. Of course learning involves making meaning out of information. What else would learning involve? Well, if you've ever seen a kid memorize definitions for a list of "vocabulary words" without having the slightest idea, nor any intention, of how to use those words in context, then you know what learning is *not*: we do *not* know the meaning of a word, the significance of a historical event, the applications of a formula, just because we have memorized a set of words. That is why the first step toward differentiated instruction is knowing what understanding means.

Why now? If Rip Van Winkle were to wake up at the beginning of the 2000s and ask if there have been any changes in public education in the past generation, what would we tell him? We would probably start by telling him about the national imperative toward standardized testing. We would describe the intense pressures on administrators to produce test scores in their schools, making it appear that their schools outperform neighboring districts. These scores are going to be publicized in bar graphs in the local newspapers and even in real estate offices: The better your kids and your neighbor's kids do on the state tests, the more your house will be worth. It's that simple.

But there's good news as well. In the 1990s, knowledge about the brain and learning burgeoned. Now, we know much more than we did 20 years ago about individual learning styles, how emotions and ambient conditions affect learning, how the mind processes and memorizes information, the importance of prior knowledge, how various features of the classroom can enhance or impede learning, the role played by the teacher/student relationship, and the way certain drugs can change one's ability to concentrate. The field of neurological science has delivered information which should have transformed the look and feel of classrooms across the country.

Dispelling Some Myths About Differentiated Instruction

In the education graveyard lie the bones of myths, fads, purist fanaticism, demagoguery, shallow thinking, and silliness. Is differentiated instruction just another passing fancy? Can we just watch the carousel go by until something we like better comes along? The answer is yes, if we look at DI simplistically, if we think there's a "recipe" for it, if we think that a half-day workshop or two is going to solve all our problems. The answer is no, if we understand that DI is a complex set of beliefs and practices that take respectable, humane, and flexible principles of learning and human growth into account.

In conversations about education reform and at staff development session, we tend to hear clichés like these:

◆ *We're throwing the baby out with the bathwater*: Educators and people who care about education have a right to fear that in our zeal to make education new and interesting rather than "drill and kill," we are abandoning basic skills. By basic skills, we mean reading, writing, clear speech, and computation, as well as the facts about history, geography, and science that high school graduates are presumed to know. No one really knows what these facts are and why everyone has to know them, but we get nervous when we think too many people don't know what the capital of North Dakota is.

- *We're reinventing the wheel*: This, like many of these clichés, assumes that everything old is new again. The fact is, it's possible to make a better wheel, one that fits the kind of cars that we drive now, rather than the covered wagon wheels of yesterday. We do need to remember that not everyone is a veteran teacher. Some people, new to the field, are not reinventing the wheel, but discovering it. Some educators find no problem using the prepackaged teaching materials provided by textbook publishers. Others can't do that: they have to devise their own tests, performance tasks, lecture notes. To the former, the latter is reinventing the wheel. (It's Bismarck.)

- *We've come full circle:* We're back to where we started from. We're walking around in circles. Educators who lament that we've come full circle may think they'd have been better off just staying in the same place and waiting for the world to pass their way again. What they don't see is the value of the journey toward professionalism: to some, it may be a circle; to others, it's an upward spiral. Yes, here we are, with heterogeneous grouping instead of tracking again, or with tracking again instead of heterogeneous grouping. But, we haven't regressed unless we aren't bringing new skills and an enlightened attitude that learning is a complex process and that it isn't so easy to predict who is capable of learning what.

- *The pendulum has swung (will swing) the other way.* This either/or thinking is similar to the full-circle thinking described above. It's usually said in a tone of vindication, meaning: "See? I didn't change my ways, and now I'm back in style, just like my powder blue tuxedo that I wore to my wedding." Or, "Why should I bother changing? If I wait long enough, this, too shall pass." Actually, I don't think "it" will. We know too much about learning. I do think that the current mania for test scores won't last forever. I surely hope that the testing frenzy will abate, but I don't see Americans going back to the days when we gave up on kids as easily as we did in past generations. I don't think we're going to sort and classify kids into "college material" and "vocational school candidates" anymore. Nor do I think we will ever return to a golden age (that never existed) when kids and their parents treated the school with unquestioned deference. We're not going to reinstitute corporal punishment on a large scale. We *are* going to continue to humanize education and operate on the belief that every kid deserves to be taken seriously. If I didn't believe that, I wouldn't be doing this.

- *You can bring a horse to the water, but you can't make him drink.* This one is true enough, but it's too easy. As educators, we need to find out more about why the horse doesn't want to drink. We do have to assume that the horse might drink *eventually*, or maybe it would drink something that looked a little more appetizing. What this cliché means is that we absolve ourselves of the responsibility to do anything more than present material and give assignments. I have news for you: if that's all there is to our jobs, then we can be replaced by Web courses.

Consider the following, relative to differentiated instruction:

- What's the baby, and what's the bathwater?
- What is the wheel that keeps being reinvented?
- Where does the full circle begin and end?
- Where is the pendulum right now? In which direction is it swinging? How far do you think it will swing in this direction? What will get it to start swinging in the other direction?
- How do we get this stuff to look like something that the horse would drink?

Myth 1: Differentiated Instruction Consists of Students Doing Exercises in Self-Correcting Workbooks

When I was a young teacher in the mid 1970s, something called "individualized instruction" was the fad. Students would come into a "reading" class, go for their folders, and then work themselves through various self-correcting exercises. The teacher would work quietly with students one at a time, perhaps "going over" problematic reading comprehension questions. These questions were based on isolated passages of the sort that might be found in a content area textbook. The level of difficulty of the workbook was color-coded.

The "individualized instruction" classrooms that I observed were dreary places. There was no student-to-student talk, no interest in the text, no joy of language, no classroom dynamic, no humor. Yet, this system was considered a breakthrough improvement over full-class instruction.

I suspect that the term differentiated instruction evokes that image for many teachers, either because they once taught that way or were taught that way when they were students.

Myth 2: Differentiated Instruction Is the All-Purpose Problem Solver

The techniques that are in this book will make you a better teacher only if you use them the way you should use any pedagogy—in combination with others. No one method works all of the time for all students. Teachers have personalities, strengths and weaknesses, communication styles, and organizational habits. A particular pedagogy cannot be imposed on every teacher.

Myth 3: Differentiated Instruction Means That the Teacher Does Not Present Information

Whole class presentations are an essential part of any effective teaching plan. There's no substitute for the modeling, enthusiasm, rich knowledge of subject, anecdotes, storytelling, and shared learning experience that an excellent teacher provides. Whole class instruction sets the tone, establishes the knowledge base, and ignites the interest of students. What it usually does not do is hold the individual accountable for making meaning out of the information. Performance tasks and communication do that.

Myth 4: Differentiated Instruction Does Not Work in Classes Where Students Have to Master a Body of Information for a High-Stakes Test

Studies at reputable institutions have determined conclusively that *we can teach faster than kids can learn.* The implication here is that if we think we can "get kids through" the high-stakes test by "covering the curriculum" all by ourselves (without the help of the students), then we will find to our chagrin that we've accomplished nothing that the textbook couldn't have accomplished without us.

Myth 5: Differentiated Instruction Is Mainly for Students with Learning Deficits

This myth presumes that DI practices are strictly remedial in nature, that they can only "slow down" students without learning deficits. First of all, I doubt that *anybody* is without a learning deficit: we all have our strengths and weaknesses. When done well, DI enriches the learning of all students by engaging multiple intelligences, the arts, the emotions, and interdisciplinary connections.

Myth 6: Differentiated Instruction Means Dividing the Class into "Bluebirds" and "Redbirds"

The wise teacher does not presume who can and can't do certain things at the secondary level. By the time someone is a teenager, she has developed all kinds of interests and prior knowledge that will affect learning a particular topic. Kids who are weak performers on standardized reading tests can become enamored of very sophisticated literature for various reasons not predictable by a test score. Maybe they've seen the Disney movie of *The Hunchback of Notre Dame* and can comprehend Victor Hugo's novel because they already know the story structure and are intrigued by it. Maybe a student is an ardent watcher of the Discovery Channel and brings a storehouse of prior knowledge to a topic that you wouldn't think she knows anything about.

There are proponents of differentiated instruction who believe in sorting kids according to presumed abilities or even preassessment instruments, but I would hesitate to do that except in the short term, as for specific assignments, especially with students at the secondary level. I believe that student interest and choice should determine placement in flexible groups. If we have rigid groupings based on our perceptions about who *can* and who *can't* achieve, then we have created in-class tracking. Differentiated instruction is antithetical to tracking. If we sort kids on what we think is their ability (and this is often "determined" by a standardized test), then we must be aware that *they* are aware of exactly what we've done. Once we consign kids to "the bottom group," we have established a self-fulfilling prophesy, and we're back to where we started from when we tracked kids class by class.

Myth 7: In a Heterogeneous Class, Brighter Students Will Be "Used" to Teach the Others

I personally don't favor having students grade the papers of other students, "quiz" them orally, or be responsible to convey primary information. I don't even have a lot of faith in the "peer editing" phase of the writing process. I think there are better ways to teach revision. So, I don't believe that DI involves peer tutorials. There's a difference between cooperative learning and peer teaching. The former is based on constructing learning through socialization; the latter, in my opinion, makes an inappropriate request of students.

Values

Differentiated instruction is a practice that grows out of certain values. That is, the way we treat our students, design our curriculum, and establish rules depends upon what we think is important. Differentiated instruction requires planning, patience, organization, communication, and reflection. Consider the following statements and ask yourself if you agree with these values:

- ◆ **The value of choice**: Students who have a choice in what they learn, how they learn it, and how they show what they know are more likely to experience real learning than students for whom the teacher makes all of the decisions.

- ◆ **The value of learning how to learn**: In the process of learning your content area, students should also be learning how to learn. This implies two-tiered teaching—that is, making students aware of *how* they learn *what* they learn.

- ◆ **The value of both ritual and variety**: The best classes are those that employ both ritual and variety in structure. Ritual is important because it establishes expectations, provides security, and instills trust that the teacher is in control. Although a routine can be a rut in which every day blurs into every other day, routine can also be a structure that allows us to memorize, because the routine provides cues that trigger memory of facts. Variety is also important. Variety can bring joy and excitement to learning. But the variety must exist within a ritualized structure for the learner to feel secure.

- ◆ **The value of variety in assessments**: There are all kinds of ways to show what we know. As the teacher, you may use your discretion as to how different kinds of assessments are weighted into your final grade, but your students are likely to be more successful if your assessment system takes in a broad spectrum of abilities and modes of expression.

- **The value of collegiality**: Differentiated instruction thrives in a collegial community because you need ideas, encouragement, tips, a venue for reflection, and a wealth of sources. An increasing number of secondary classes with special education students are collaborative. Many schools use consultants to foster collegiality among teachers. Collaboration and sessions with consultants improve interrater reliability, consistency of rules, a broadening of content, and pedagogical knowledge. Collegiality, based on communication, is possible only when teachers have shared planning time. Shared planning time does not mean running into another ninth grade English teacher in the copy room and asking if she's finished with Act II of *Romeo and Juliet*. Nor does having lunch together during period 6 count as shared planning time. Shared planning time may take you away from your classroom every few weeks as you and your colleagues convene to have serious, focused, businesslike discussions about professional concerns. Ideally, these sessions are presided over by a skilled consultant.

- **The value of student talk**: Effective classrooms are often highly interactive, dynamic, and communicative. However, this is not to say that there aren't times when it's the teacher who is doing the talking as the students listen and take notes.

- **The value of open-endedness**: "Closure" is not always necessary at the end of a topic. In traditional classes, the teacher "ties it up," but some methods of teaching, such as the Socratic seminar, are purposefully left open-ended. The assumption is that thinking about the text should continue. Thinking doesn't always lead to knowing the answers. Sometimes, thinking leads to more questions.

- **The value of multiple learning modes**: The chances for durable learning are increased if there is a multiplicity of learning modes: imaginative, inquiry, facts, multisensory, technology, and socialization.

- **The value of connection**: Students need to make connections to their own experience, interests, knowledge. This is why metaphors, anecdotes, and learning logs work well to effect durable learning. In fact, *any* connectedness has a positive learning effect: the relationship between teacher and student; the sense of community (or lack thereof) that the students feel in your classroom; and the sense of connectedness that they feel to the school as a whole.

- **The value of different teaching styles**: Just as students have different learning styles, teachers have different teaching styles. Pedagogy is becoming increasingly scientific as we learn more about neurology and psychology. But it will never stop being an *art*, based on unquantifiable skills of communication, humor, intuition, hospitality, love of learning, and love of kids. You may be a teacher who relies on a textbook and a teacher's guide. Or, you may be someone who draws from a wide variety of primary sources. Your teaching style may be rich with language or rich with pictures. The point is that differentiated instruction for students does not put a crimp in the *teacher's* style. Rather, the ideas in this book offer you choices that you can adapt to your personality, beliefs, and strengths as a teacher.

Reflection:
What Does Your Class Look Like?

What *You* Are Doing:

- Writing on the board
- Explaining overhead projector transparencies
- Grading papers while the kids watch a video
- Holding conferences with individual kids
- Holding conferences with small groups of kids
- Asking questions that you know the answers to
- Asking questions that you *don't* know the answers to
- Explaining directions
- Going over homework or a test
- Collecting and distributing
- Telling personal anecdotes with direct relevance to the content
- Telling personal anecdotes with metaphorical relevance to the content
- Reading aloud
- Taking attendance and performing record-keeping tasks
- Presiding over groupwork
- Explaining what is going to be on an upcoming test
- Lecturing
- Referring to contemporary issues relevant to the content
- Explaining a visual
- Explaining and modeling a performance task
- Listening to student presentations
- Helping students plan their presentations
- Presiding over student writing
- Administering a test or quiz
- Leading a field trip
- Presiding over a library project

- Presiding over a research project involving in-class computers
- Off-task behaviors

What the *Kids* Are Doing:

- Copying notes from the board
- Watching a video
- Reading silently
- Taking a test or quiz
- Taking notes from a lecture, where notes are not provided
- Talking with peers (on task)
- Constructing something
- Presenting something
- Asking closed-ended questions
- Asking open-ended questions
- Answering closed-ended questions
- Answering open-ended questions
- Going from picture to word
- Going from word to picture
- Listening to teacher
- Listening to peers
- Being on a field trip
- Working at the computer
- Trying to put thoughts into words: written
- Trying to put thoughts into words: oral, for teacher
- Trying to put thoughts into words: oral, for peers
- Organizing information
- Working in the library
- Finding information
- Off-task behaviors

In your own way, make a profile of your class in the last week. This could be a narrative, a discussion, a bar graph or other kind of graph, notes, or anything you choose.

If you are like every other teacher in the world, you can explain why your classroom is less than what you would like it to be. These explanations have nothing to do with you, of course. They have everything to do with students, parents, administrators, and society. If only students, parents, administrators, and society would cooperate, you would be the miracle worker. These explanations are called excuses. Let's get them out of the way right now:

- The students don't have a work ethic. They don't know what it is to delay gratification, to work toward a goal, to sacrifice.

- The students watch too much TV.
- Corollary: The students don't read.
- The parents excuse their children's irresponsible behavior.
- The school is expected to function more as an institution of social work than as an institution of learning.
- Students are excessively absent. They may be absent for whole days, or late, or called out of class to go to guidance or some other office in the middle of your class. Your class may be canceled because of an assembly or other special program that is not nearly as important as your class. (Have you ever noticed that teachers who complain about assemblies *never* complain about snow days?)
- Parents and administrators make unreasonable demands.
- No one enforces rules. The school is chaotic.
- The kids get worse every year.
- The Administration doesn't give us what we need. They don't support us. They don't understand our needs. They don't care.

The reality of the above conditions is that they are only as real as you decide they are going to be. For every one of these conditions, there's another way of looking at the situation. Yes, all of these conditions are annoying. If you let them overwhelm you, then you can add "Teachers don't want to change the way they do things," to the list.

Maybe you are now wondering what you've gotten yourself into here. What does all this have to do with differentiated instruction? The relevance of the list of excuses is this: Differentiated instruction involves an attitude adjustment on *your* part. You can't change what goes on in your classroom until you clear away the excuses and do what needs to be done in spite of them. We won't accept excuses as excuses.

Learning to differentiate instruction means learning how to teach in a more informed way: a way that is open to reflection and adjustment, a way that will keep you busy enough to focus on solutions rather than problems.

This book invites you to come to a better understanding of yourself as a teacher: your style, your values, your goals, and your relationship to your subject and your students. You will think about your own uniqueness and needs, what you can do and what you can't, and what you want to do and what you don't want to do. You are the key instrument of learning in your classroom: students are affected by your beliefs and attitudes more than you may realize.

To differentiate instruction, you need to clarify what the content is (what you want students to know and be able to do), process (how students are going to go about learning the content), and product (how they will show what they know). Only when you know who you are dealing with (yourself) can you then know how you can reach your students, with their diverse needs.

2

Where Do I Start?

In this chapter, you will learn how to assess your own teaching style, attitudes, and practices to clarify how you can refine your skills. You've already started differentiating instruction. You probably already do so more than you think. How have you incorporated any of the following practices in the last month? Your workshops and collegial discussions will be about:

♦ Your habits of mind
♦ The "Big Ideas" of thinking
♦ The "Big Test"
♦ Understanding your teaching style
♦ A conversation

Teacher Habits of Mind

Differentiated instruction (DI) results from certain habits of mind about teaching and learning. These habits of mind enable the teacher to be flexible and long-sighted in how she views her role. Consider:

♦ **As a teacher, I revise and reflect**: In a differentiated classroom, teachers have the habit of mind to continuously rework, reword, and review lessons. The curriculum adheres to the demands of the "Big Test" without becoming rigid. In order for student achievement to be lasting, teachers need to constantly ask themselves:

  • Is what the kids are doing meeting the standards in terms of knowledge and skills?
  • Is my concern for individual differences working for or against my belief that students need to move outside of their comfort zones?

♦ **I encourage lots of student talk**: If DI is constructivist, which, of course, it is, then students need to talk the talk. A lot. They need to talk to each other, to the teacher, and to themselves in the language of the subject. Education reformer Heidi Hayes Jacobs urges teachers to "put words in kids' mouths." As teachers, we are initiating the novice into the professional conversation. Just as learning a foreign language demands that the learner speak the new language, learning science, math, or history is learning a new language as well.

For some secondary students, especially those from cultures other than American, the classroom is supposed to be a quiet place, where students are listening to the teacher. Such students are disturbed by the hubbub of student talk, and even think that a noisy class is chaotic. This belief in student passivity, although unfounded, is widely respected and trusted. Many teachers feel out of control amid a lot of student talk. Indeed, it is easy for study groups to get blown off course in a matter of seconds. Paradoxically, passive learning, where students are quiet receptors of teacher wisdom, is actually easier to manage than active learning. But modern DI is not the old system of "coming in and getting your folders." If learning is to be constructed, it is to be constructed noisily.

♦ **I offer choices and alternatives**: A teacher who differentiates instruction has a larger vision of content, process, and assessment than one who does not. She believes that choices will not only make the students' work more interesting, but it will make her own paperwork more varied. She believes that she can learn from her students.

♦ **I believe in reading**: When it comes to reading, like exercise, *quantity* matters. Reading plays a key role in all learning. Teachers who believe in reading are seen reading, owning and showing books, recommending books and articles, and expecting students to read. Teachers who believe in reading welcome school-wide initiatives that encourage reading, even for token periods of time. Teachers who believe in reading model the joy of reading every chance they get: they refer to what they've read, they read aloud, they give and receive books as gifts, they visit bookstores frequently, and they talk about it.

♦ **I say "This reminds me of...":** This simple but powerful statement is the beginning of teaching students to learn by making connections to prior knowledge. By modeling this habit of mind, we invite students to make sense of new information.

♦ **I am interested and curious about learning in general**: The habit of mind of "going beyond what is taught" is called generative thinking. The inspiring teacher models the behavior of the lifelong learner: visiting museums and cities, taking courses, joining discussion groups, taking part in civic affairs, etc.

♦ **I value diversity**: Someone who values diversity learns about other cultures. She refers to various traditions, languages, and lifestyles. It's not very difficult to recognize the various ethnic groups in your classes, and to ask questions, use examples, recommend readings, and refresh your curriculum to make it inclusive.

♦ **I am aware of the networks, systems, and organization of knowledge**: To have this awareness is to be constantly making connections: connections to other fields of study, connections to contemporary issues, to popular culture, to the culture of the school and community, and to the students' and the teacher's personal lives. The stronger the network, the more durable the learning.

♦ **I practice professionalism**: To qualify as a professional, you have to be enthusiastic about intellectual growth. Professionals read widely, stay informed about public affairs, have well-grounded opinions. Professionals control their emotions in the workplace, adopting an attitude of service and humility.

♦ **I understand the cumulative nature of knowledge**: Traditional educators may conceive of learning in packaged "units." Although it is important to organize information around main topics, eras, themes, or regions, we close the door on long-lasting and meaningful learning with this "unit" thinking.

Reflection

Select *one* of these habits of mind that you would like to cultivate. Give yourself three actions that will affect your classroom.

The "Big Ideas" of Thinking

Regardless of what our subject area is, we are supposed to be teaching kids how to think. We want them to think so that they can solve problems, adjust to new situations, make decisions, discern the important from the unimportant, protect themselves from those who would take advantage of them, appreciate traditions, express themselves, and understand others. The subject areas that we teach are the vehicles for improving our students' ability to think outside of our classrooms.

In this chapter, I ask you to think about how the "Big Ideas" of thinking affect differentiated instruction. When students are processing course content through the lens of the "Big Ideas," they are learning what to do with facts, just the way an artist learns what to do with colors.

There are various ways to categorize critical thinking skills. I'm naming them as follows:

♦ Comparison/contrast
♦ Connecting cause and effect
♦ Going from the generality to the specific, and back to the generality
♦ Justifying an assertion
♦ Understanding organization: arrangements, categories, subordination
♦ Description
♦ Evaluating against criteria

Comparison/Contrast

+ How are seemingly like things different? (making fine distinctions)
+ How are seemingly different things alike? (making connections)

You may never have thought of it this way before, but almost all learning involves comparison/contrast: the ability to distinguish sameness and differences. Suppose you are teaching about the Industrial Revolution. Have students generate questions that compare and contrast the Industrial Revolution, internally and externally:

+ What social factors made this period of time emerge as being different from the preceding period?
+ What technological developments made significant differences in nineteenth-century life in England?
+ Think about the contrasts that existed within English society during the Industrial Revolution. Identify as many of these contrasts in social structure as you can.
+ How is the Industrial Revolution similar to, and different from, our lives today?
+ What other periods of time are known for bringing about great change?
+ When did the Industrial Revolution end? How do we know?
+ Look at Charles Dickens' story *A Christmas Carol*. How many examples of stark contrasts can you find? What was Dickens' intent in presenting so many contrasts?

This kind of examination of similarities and differences is differentiated instruction because students are free to interpret the question in various ways, with more sophisticated students envisioning finer distinctions.

Connecting Cause and Effect

Understanding causes and effects is a sophisticated critical thinking skill. A cause and effect word bank includes: *therefore, thus, so, as a result,* and *consequently*. Have students compose sentences using this word bank to discuss events in the Industrial Revolution.

This approach to making meaning of the Industrial Revolution is differentiated instruction because not everyone's sentences are expected to be the same. Putting all of these sentences together for the class would be a powerful lesson not only about the Industrial Revolution, but also about causal factors in history.

Going from the Generality to the Specific, and Back to the Generality

This can be done through an hourglass outline:

generality: _____

    supportive detail:_____

    supportive detail:_____

    supportive detail:_____

generality: _____

The supportive details could be reasons, examples, anecdotes, statistics, and quotations. Often, supportive details come in the forms of proper nouns, numbers, and prepositional phrases. The closing generality draws a conclusion, further clarifying the opening generality.

Justifying an Assertion

An assertion can be an opinion, a claim, a generality, or anything that is set forth as truth. Novices are often at a loss for words to justify their opinion. Consider the following assertions about the Industrial Revolution:

- The Industrial Revolution was a time of great opportunity.
- The Industrial Revolution was a dangerous and cruel time.
- The Industrial Revolution has been interesting to learn about.

The third statement, being the most personalized, is the one most likely to elicit a flow of information. Asking students to compose and justify an assertion is differentiated instruction in that the field is open to their own interests, interpretations, and areas of knowledge.

Understanding Organization: Arrangements, Categories, Subordination

Finding patterns is an essential meaning-making skill. Students can express patterns in various ways: graphic organizers, outlines, paragraphs and essays, lists, or color-coded text markings. To incorporate differentiated instruction, have the students develop their own categories, rather than laying out the main headings. For the Industrial Revolution, some categories that students come up with might surprise you:

- new inventions
- famous people
- diseases and troubles
- what I like
- what I don't like
- famous events
- stories about it

Description

A good description involves precise and lively language, attention to detail, spatial organization, transitional words, and variety. Have students consider a particularly vivid and multifaceted scenario that represents the Industrial Revolution, and have them describe it in either words or pictures.

Evaluating Against Criteria

Bloom's taxonomy places evaluation at the highest level of thinking. This is because it takes in content knowledge as well as comparison/contrast, synthesis, and analysis. If you ask students to formulate questions about the Industrial Revolution, they might ask:

- Would you consider London in the nineteenth century to be a "world city"? (First, you'd have to establish criteria as to what a "world city" is.)
- The most important development of the nineteenth century was the railroad. (First, you'd have to explain the primary and secondary effects of railroads, and then show how other technological developments were dependent upon railroad travel.)
- Queen Victoria's Crystal Palace accomplished her purpose in building it. (First, you'd have to establish what the Queen's purpose was in erecting the Crystal Palace.)

Evaluating against criteria also is used in other areas, e.g., engineering. When you consider how to build a structure, you have criteria: it must withstand certain forces and stresses, serve a particular function, and meet practical limitations, such as size and cost.

Reflection

1. Use the "Big Ideas" of thinking to compose essential questions for your subject area. Consider the subject as a whole as well as the smaller units that you teach.

2. Use the "Big Ideas" of thinking to compose performance tasks.

Use these criteria to evaluate your performance tasks:

- The task depends upon the content that I want students to learn. They need to use generalities as well as details. They could not do this task if they hadn't been in my class.
- The task list provides for differentiation in terms of student choice, interests, readiness, and learning styles.
- The process of doing this task will help students to remember and apply the course content.
- By doing this task, students will learn a particular part of the course content better than they would have through a traditional test alone.

◆ Doing this task is likely to bring about better results on a traditional test.

Differentiated Instruction for the "Big Test"

We live in the day of the "Big Test." Every state in the nation (except Iowa) has Standards and Assessments (S&A's), and these S&A's typically culminate in the BTE (Big Test Experience). Whenever I work with teachers on critical thinking skills, reading and writing, and differentiated instruction, they want to connect their pedagogy to the "Big Test."

I've lived in the state of New York all my life. In New York, we've always had the Regents Exam. In New York, if something is "not on the Regents," then, well, there's no point in knowing it, is there? We don't have time to "cover" anything "not on the Regents."

It used to be that you only "took the Regents" in "Regents classes," such as "Regents Earth Science" or "Regents English 11." If you (or your guidance counselor) thought you couldn't cut it in a Regents class, you could take "Non-Regents" classes. These had titles like "Understanding the Weather Channel" or "Reading for Pleasure." (Neither of those would be a bad idea, by the way, and would probably be of more use than the Regents classes, but that's another book.)

In today's educational climate, the "Big Test" reigns supreme. No question about it. Your school district, building, department, even you as an individual teacher, are measured up (sometimes publicly) against your colleagues in terms of "how your kids did on the Big Test." You will pay dearly if you frittered away time figuring out how to get students involved, interested, engaged at the "expense" of "covering material" for the BT.

Reflection

1. Agree or disagree: The "Big Test" accurately assesses the standards in my subject area.

2. Agree or disagree: Having the "Big Test" has improved student achievement and the teaching profession.

Grading Practices and Differentiating Instruction

Many factors in our culture cause a great deal of emphasis to be placed on grades. Students, parents, and administrators demand accountability from teachers regarding grading practices and procedures. They want to know:

◆ How was the grade arrived at?

◆ Is there an appeals process?

◆ Is the teacher's grading practice presented in writing to the students and parents?

- Can students rewrite papers, retake tests, or redo projects for a higher grade?
- Is the grading policy consistent from student to student?
- Is the grading policy consistent from teacher to teacher?
- Can the student do extra credit?
- How firm are the deadlines? What is the penalty for late papers?
- What is considered homework? How much does homework count in the overall grade?
- Are there enough grades to fairly assess the student?
- Does effort play a role in the grade? If so, how is effort demonstrated?
- What constituted cheating? What are the penalties for plagiarism, unauthorized copying, having unauthorized access to the test questions, etc. Are teachers keeping tests secure from class to class and from year to year?
- Does the official grade have to be the mean? Could it be the mode or the median?
- Is a minimum grade given, so as not to make it impossible at an early point in the year for a student to pass?
- How objective is the grading process?
- How much obligation does a teacher have to deliver supplemental instruction to a struggling student?
- In collaborative teaching situations, what happens if there's a discrepancy between the teachers?
- Do administrators intervene in grading practices?
- Do teachers ever have an opportunity to discuss grading practices in a collegial forum?
- Are students and parents playing one teacher against another?
- Are teachers operating under modern theories of assessment, known as "best practice"?
- Are all of the students evaluated against the same standards?
- Is there a system of weighted grades for higher level courses? If so, is it fair? Is it regularly reviewed? By whom?
- Does the student's report card grade reasonably predict her grade on standardized tests?
- Is the teacher providing the kind of feedback that will help the student learn?
- Are there internal policies in the school, such as admittance to select courses, that depend on grades?

The competitive nature of grades and the way that grades are used can be at odds with differentiated instruction. After all, it won't take long for students to perceive differences in expectations even if we thought we were being subtle. In elementary school, it may be easier to distribute tiered performance tasks that "look the same," but high school students will spot that ruse in a second. And they will resent it. Your brighter kids will feel overburdened, and your slower ones will feel patronized.

Some of the implacable forces that militate toward the primal position of grades are standardized tests, class rankings, weighted grading systems, the college admissions process, competition for awards, litigiousness, and a culture of complaint in which our classrooms are a favorite target. No question about it: if we want to differentiate instruction, we are accountable to deliver a fair and well-articulated grading system.

What follows is an exploration of four strategies to achieve this.

The Flex Fund

Many insurance plans offer participants a certain amount of money that can be used at their discretion. You may want to put these funds toward vision care, dental, child care, or some other plan tailored to your family's needs. We can look at grades this way: we can set aside a certain number of points as a "discretionary fund" in which students may choose how they would like to earn their points. Some choices inlcude:

- **Class participation**: This assumes that the "participation" is productive, well-timed, and not overbearing. It could include reading aloud, asking productive questions, and offering responses, interpretations, or observations. What constitutes productive class participation has to be clearly distinguished from unimpressive behaviors that serve no purpose other than to be distractive to the purpose of the class. Productive class participation can be expressed in a rubric.
- **Special projects**: These could include written or oral reports on supplemental readings, displays for the classroom, investigative reports, interviews, etc. Be careful that these can't be the kind of "projects" that are clipped right off the Internet.
- **Optional test grades**: This could take the form of dropping the lowest—or doubling the highest—test grade. It could also include an optional review test or a test on a supplemental topic.
- **Close-ups**: Close-ups are reports and investigations of a subject in greater detail than what was covered in class or in the textbook. These can take the form of illustrations, lists, bibliographies, etc.
- **Notebook**: You may already check and grade notebooks. If you don't, you may want to give flex points to students whose notebooks are particularly thorough. It may even be appropriate for students to use their flex points to rewrite their notes. In doing so, they can color-code, cross-reference, flag key information, etc.

- ◆ **Leadership**: Students may earn their flex points by taking leadership roles in groups: recording, reporting out, maintaining order and focus in the group, etc.

Tiered Performance Tasks

The orthodox definition of tiered performance tasks is that they are tri-level tasks (low, middle, high) assigned to students after a preassessment is done to determine who belongs at which of the three levels. Although they call for varying degrees of depth and complexity, they are designed to "look the same" when handed out to the students. They may be color-coded.

I wouldn't count on having high school students fail to notice that the kid in the next chair is getting off easy. At the secondary level, tiered performance tasks can work, but the students should be allowed to choose their tier.

Differentiated instruction is not about having bright students do "more" or "harder" work just because they "can handle it." It works best when students who find depth and complexity in a topic or text are given the freedom to do so, while students on a less sophisticated level can work accordingly. In a tiered performance task, the content is the same. You start with a group lesson or text, and then you present the choices. Instead of matching up student to task, as might be appropriate on an elementary school level, give students time to try their hands at all three tasks before they make their choices.

What follows in Figure 2.1 is a description of an interdisciplinary tiered task that was used in an eighth-grade team. The task was assigned by all four teachers: math, English, social studies, and environmental science. The text is a children's story entitled "The Wump World" by Bill Peet (Houghton Mifflin). It is an allegory that leads us to think about endangered species. (Note that quality children's literature can be read on many levels and is accessible to students of varying abilities.)

Figure 2.1. The Endangered Species Report

Write a concise report that gives the following information about the endangered species that you have selected. Each of the headings should be bold-faced. Each section should have 1 to 3 well-developed, complete sentences. Here are your topics:

- **Species**: Give the full scientific name, as well as the vernacular name of your animal.
- **Habitat**: Describe the environment where your animal lives.
- **Why Endangered**: Explain the ecological factors that are endangering your animal.

Consider:

- **Projections**: Show how scientists project the numbers of this animal to decrease over the years. Use the formulas that you have learned this year in math to express this information.
- **Course of action to prevent extinction**: Using your knowledge of environmental science and the democratic process, suggest at least one course of action that will save this animal from extinction.
- **Consequences**: Use your knowledge of environmental science to hypothesize what might happen (and why) if and when this animal becomes extinct.

Tier II: Write to the editor of your local newspaper a letter that explains why your animal is an endangered species, why people should care about this, and what you want the government and individuals to do to prevent extinction. Use a serious and persuasive tone. Use facts and statistics.

Tier III: Act as if there is a Congressional hearing to present arguments that would protect your animal. You have two minutes to address the committee. Using notes, visuals, facts, and statistics, present your case. This is an oral report; your notes will be collected.

For all three tasks, you must submit a bibliography with at least three sources.

Contracts

Learning contracts are similar to tiered performance tasks to the extent that students have a choice in what they do. The difference is that with a learning contract, students decide on the quantity of work that they wish to do in exchange for an agreed-upon grade. The contract must be in writing, with consequences for late or unsatisfactory performance clearly spelled out.

One of the drawbacks of learning contracts is that some students will complete their contracts earlier than others, and then be unproductive and distractive in class. You can offer extra credit, supplemental readings, library time, or study hall time, but these "solutions" will not be attractive to the student who has rushed through the contract so that class time could be "free." If too many students end up with spare time, then the contract system needs to be improved. Or, the bulk of the work should be expected to be done outside of class.

Arriving at a good, functional learning contract is not as easy as it would appear.

Let's say that you set aside a week of in-class time for students to fulfill their contracts. Teenagers are not known for their disciplined time management skills. They should compose their own schedules and monitor their progress daily, with a checkoff sheet. It would be a mistake to wait until Friday to collect the final product. You need to make a plan for absences, technical glitches, absence or lack of availability of the librarian, and other obstacles that will thwart the contract. You may want to set the due date for Thursday, with Friday as a "grace" day. This method of differentiated instruction is not for the novice teacher.

Compacting

Compacting the curriculum is a strategy that works best for math, grammar, and spelling. Based on a preassessment, students are excused from "learning" material that they have demonstrated mastery on. They are accelerated to their instructional level. Often, this is where a learning contract will come in—where the advanced student works independently. It is important that these students not be "excused" from homework. They may choose homework from another source, such as a list of supplemental readings or an advanced workbook.

Not every kid who has aced the pretest jumps at the chance to do harder work. If a higher grade is not on the table, it's probably unrealistic to expect high school students to pedal harder. The reward of either higher grades or less homework has to be part of the deal.

Reflection

Teachers brainstorm and discuss all of the problematic issues concerning grading policies and procedures, such as the ones that are given in this chapter.

- ◆ **Flex**: Make a list of all of the activities that students could use for their discretionary points in your class.
- ◆ **Class participation**: Make a rubric for class participation that delineates specific manifestations of productive participation.
- ◆ **Special projects**: List five specific special projects that your students can use for their flex fund.
- ◆ **Notebook**: What would an exemplary notebook for your class look like? How would it show more than just copying from the board? Consider reflective statements, summaries, color codes, etc.
- ◆ **Leadership**: What opportunities for student leadership exist in your classroom?

- **Tiered performance tasks**: Transform a performance task into a three-tiered task. Consider the whole class lesson that the task would be based on. Evaluate your tiered performance task as follows:
  - Would the students consider each task comparable in terms of the time and effort that it would take to do them?
  - Do the tasks take into account student learning styles, interest, prior knowledge, and readiness?

Understanding Your Teaching Style: How Will Differentiated Instruction Work for You?

Teachers entering into differentiated instruction must begin by understanding their own teaching styles, learning styles, personality types, strengths, and weaknesses. They must know, as people in the investment world call it, their "tolerance for risk." By making your instruction more differentiated, you may feel that you are taking a risk. If you are used to feeling in control by knowing what everyone is doing, how they are doing it, and when and how they will show what they know, then you may have to start thinking of yourself as someone who is in control in a different way.

Consider three statements:

1. Knowledge and skills are actively created, rather than passively learned.

2. In delivering instruction and in assessing students, teachers need to consider individual differences.

3. Learning is affected by social and emotional conditions.

In order to proceed with differentiation, you need to understand what these statements mean to you and how they are reflected in your classroom. You need to consider how these statements describe your classroom right now, and how they describe the classroom that you are striving to have. And, you need to consider the needs of each course you teach this year, as well as the differences that exist from section to section.

Knowledge and Skills Are Actively Created, Rather Than Passively Learned

- Explain what this statement means to you.
- What is going on in your classroom when knowledge and skills are actively created? Give a specific example. Is this working to effect the desired learning outcomes? How do you know?
- What is going on in your classroom when students are passively learning? Is this working to effect the desired learning outcomes? How do you know?

- What are the challenges for the teacher in a class where students are actively learning? How have you been successful? What issues remain problematic for you?

In Delivering Instruction and in Assessing Students, Teachers Need to Consider Individual Differences

- Make an exhaustive list of how students might have individual differences in your classes.

Learning Is Affected by Social and Emotional Conditions

- Do you agree with this statement? If so, can you give examples from your own learning?
- What social and emotional conditions do you have control of in your classroom? What social and emotional conditions do you have no control over?

A Conversation

The participants in this conversation are Julie (teaches ninth-grade earth science); Ron (teaches special ed, all subject areas, middle school); Mary Clare (teaches eleventh-grade English); Jonathan (teaches eighth-grade social studies); and Erika (teaches Spanish, grades 9–12). I've cast myself (Amy) in the role of moderator.

Amy: Let's just open up with the first question: What does the statement about active construction mean to you? What does it look like in your classroom?

Erika: In my class, that's easy. There's no such thing as "passive learning" in a foreign language class. They are either speaking, writing, listening, or reading. I feel like I'm always engaging them. But I don't consider that differentiated instruction.

Amy: It is if the speaking is meaningful. That is, if they are speaking Spanish in order to actually communicate with you. If they are just repeating, then that wouldn't really be considered differentiating.

Erika: But a lot of language learning is repetition. They have to repeat.

Amy: Of course, and there's nothing wrong with that. It's still actively constructed learning because they are making the sounds their own. Actually, every class should be more like your Spanish class. Kids in every class are learning a new language in a way. They are learning the language of science, or social studies, or literature in those classes as well.

Jonathan: Here's where I have a problem: it feels like a lot of what I teach has to be lecture. That feels very passive to me. The kids can space out. And they do.

Amy: That's because you're so boring. Just kidding. What can you have them do to activate their listening?

Jonathan: They could take notes.

Amy: What else?

Jonathan: Well, I guess they could always ask questions, but they don't seem to do much of that—except to ask to go to the bathroom.

Ron: Or to the nurse.

Amy: Lecturing is an important part of teaching, especially in high school. You might want to integrate the note-taking into your instruction. Pause every ten minutes and have a few kids read their notes aloud. Point out the different styles of notes.

Jonathan: What do you mean by "the different styles of notes?"

Amy: Well, how do you take notes from a lecture?

Jonathan: I guess I just grab important points and write them down.

Amy: How do you know what the important points are? Let's say you listen for new terminology, for the outline format of the lecture, for introductory statements that will alert you to key points, for summary statements. You watch for the lecturer's physical cues: you are aware of when she's digressing to tell a supportive anecdote. You probably stop taking notes at that point and wait for her to return to a more intense level of information delivery.

Ron: What did you mean by "the outline format of the lecture?"

Amy: A good lecturer will stay organized and cue you as to the organizational structure of the information: She'll say things like, "I'm going to tell you three things about how the New York Stock Exchange works....."

Ron: I see what you mean. Today, most lecturers use PowerPoint. Do you think that's a good idea?

Amy: Do you?

Ron: For special ed kids, it can be good because it's visual. And it's organized. And, the teacher can give kids a written handout of the lecture.

Jonathan: Then they tune out.

Ron: If I do PowerPoint, I make the kids show me their own notes before I give them my handout, just to be sure they've listened. But I do find that you can be overly dependent on PowerPoint. Like anything else, it gets old. And it creates a distance between the information and the kids. It's too impersonal. I think, for special ed kids, anyway, it's more effective to be looking at them all the time, telling stories, relating to them on a personal level. PowerPoint gets you away from that.

Amy: That's a good example of how we have to remember that technology is only an enhancement to good teaching, not a replacement. Having everyone copying off a PowerPoint presentation is not DI. Having kids make their own presentations is more active.

Mary Clare: Yes, but then you have to be careful that they aren't so busy making it fancy that the information becomes secondary.

Amy: Let's get back to our discussion of different ways of taking notes. A lot of teachers have success with graphic organizers, which are basically flow charts that help kids make sense of the information.

Julie: I've kept kids active in the lecture by giving them a lecture guide that headlines the main points and then leaves space for their notes.

Amy: That's great because then they can see what's coming. It's very important that kids have expectations of what the information is going to be. That's part of the structure of a good lecture.

Mary Clare: I'm thinking about what my classroom looks like. I like to read aloud to the kids. I think they need to hear the literature read with expression. It gets the characters' voices right in their heads, and it also gives me a chance to stop and explain details and references. Do you consider that active or passive learning?

Amy: That's a good question. Reading used to be thought of as passive, but now we know that it is definitely an active process. I'd say that if kids are reading along, then that would be active learning. It might be active learning even if they're just listening, but...

Mary Clare: All that snoring makes it hard to hear. If they don't have their noses in their books when I'm reading, then I'm not convinced that they're listening. It has to be eyes and ears together.

Amy: Do you ever ask the kids to read aloud?

Mary Clare: I'd like to do more of that. I have to admit it makes me jittery. Impatient.

Amy: They make mistakes?

Mary Clare: They might stumble over words; they sometimes are inhibited about reading with expression. I already have enough problems with bringing the literature to life. The last thing I need is a literary executioner.

Amy: Maybe you could cultivate a cadre of dramatic readers. I'm sure some kids do it very well. They could set the example, and it could be rewarded in their grade.

Mary Clare: As part of their flex?

Amy: That's just the kind of thing the flex is for.

Julie: I have a question about differentiated content. My kids all have to take the same test. How can I decide who is going to learn what?

Amy: Kids are going to build their learning on prior knowledge and interests anyway. You can think of DI as adjusting the kinds of questions that you ask, setting up ways for kids to advance their learning on certain topics.

Julie: What happens when my scores go down?

Amy: Why do you think they will? If you're not sure about all this, why not proceed slowly. Visit some classes of colleagues that you trust. Think about what you already do to differentiate. These conversations are not about revolutionizing the way you do business overnight. They're not about throwing out what works. They are about getting us to be more reflective and to think about how we can make the best better for more kids.

Reflection

How can you use the ideas in this chapter to differentiate instruction in specific topics that you teach?

Summary

To summarize, here is a list of classroom practices that elicit differentiated instruction:

- ◆ flexible grouping
- ◆ preassessment
- ◆ interest centers
- ◆ learning contracts
- ◆ open reading choice
- ◆ learning logs
- ◆ reflective journals
- ◆ inquiry and discovery
- ◆ Socratic seminar (text-based, open-ended, student-driven discussion)
- ◆ portfolios
- ◆ inclusion of the arts
- ◆ allowing for readiness and prior knowledge
- ◆ multisensory learning opportunities
- ◆ learning opportunities that allow for multiple forms of intelligence
- ◆ allowing for socialization
- ◆ consideration of Bloom's taxonomy
- ◆ multicultural considerations

3

The Language of Differentiated Instruction

Because differentiated instruction is broad-based, much of the language used to discuss it is language heard elsewhere in educational conversation. Presented here are some thumbnail working definitions to help you navigate though this book.

Academic literacy: Academic literacy is the ability to efficiently read academic texts. Academic literacy differs from the literacy that is required to read fiction. When we read fiction, we usually do so for pleasure, looking to lose ourselves in the beauty of the language and the story. With academic readings, we need to employ strategies of reading that are directed more toward finding specific information and remembering it.

Alternative assessments (aka authentic assessments, performance tasks): Alternative assessments are ways, other than the traditional "pencil and paper" tests, for students to show what they know. Written reports can be considered alternative assessments when they are something other than traditional essays or straightforward "reports" (which are usually not good assessments anyway, since they are so easily plagiarized). Many teachers bring in the various forms of intelligence when drawing up alternative assessments. For example, in a Spanish class, an alternative assessment to the traditional test might be for a student to show correspondence with a pen pal. That pen pal could be a native speaker or another person (even a person in the class) who is learning Spanish.

Bloom's taxonomy (often referred to as "Bloom"): When educators say "Bloom," they are referring to six levels of learning, from most basic (knowledge) to most sophisticated (evaluation). Bloom's taxonomy establishes this hierarchy:

1. *Knowledge:* The learner has the information. She knows the cast of characters in her state capital.

2. *Comprehension:* The learner understands the information. She understands what her legislators and state committees can do.

3. *Application:* The learner can use the information. She can write to her state representatives, expressing her opinion or asking for assistance on appropriate matters.

4. *Analysis:* The learner can take apart and put together the information. She can identify the parts of a particular problem that could be solved by action by the state legislature. She can understand and proceed on a legislator's response.

5. *Synthesis:* The learner can bring together disparate information. Having received a response from her legislator, she can propose another solution based on information from another source. She can devise creative solutions.

6. *Evaluation:* The learner can make judgments based on criteria. She can compare and contrast various solutions, and can decide which is best in terms of cost, feasibility, popularity, environmental impact, and other factors.

Some schools agree to begin every writing or performance task with a "Bloom verb."

Brain-based learning: Also called "brain-compatible learning," this is a way of looking at how learning results from the integration of prior knowledge, emotions, physical comfort or discomfort, nutrition, attitude, patterns, frameworks, the arts, interdisciplinary thinking, habits of mind, expectations, and culture. Learning, a human activity, is the result of all that the human feels and experiences in the learning context. Teachers who are trained in brain-based learning consider how the brain memorizes and retrieves information, how we apply what we learn, and how we can enrich the ambiance so that the learning is long-lasting. For example, a biology teacher who has her students read the literary essays of Lewis Thomas is using brain-based learning theory to reinforce scientific facts and stimulate an interest in science. She understands that science is more than a collection of facts to be memorized on a test.

Chunking of information: This is a term often used to refer to the brain's search for meaningful relationships, patterns, connections. New information needs something to stick to: known information.

Clustering: Clustering is a technique of prewriting to formulate groups of related ideas that can later be developed into formal writing. Clustering can also be used as a study technique. It is an effective way of making new information stick to known information.

Compacting: Also called curriculum compacting, this term refers to eliminating from the curriculum information and skills that a student has already mastered. Based on a preassessment, the teacher advances students to their instructional level. Compacting is popularly used in math classes. The danger of this pedagogy is that we don't want advanced learners to feel that they are "being given more work." Nor do we want some students to feel that they are being sent off on their own. Compacting can work for short periods of time, when students are given choices about what to do with their class time once they have shown mastery on a given topic. For example, in a math class, the teacher may wish to preassess for mastery on rate/time/distance word problems. Upon determining who already understands the concept, the teacher can have advanced students make up their own word problems based on actual airline schedules. Teachers who use compacting often send letters home to parents explaining the rationale, procedures, and expectations.

Constructivism: Also known as active learning, this is the idea that learning is not passively received, but is actively constructed by the learner. Differentiated instruction is a constructivist practice.

Content, process, product: We often encounter these terms in the language of differentiated instruction promoted by Carol Ann Tomlinson (ASCD). Differentiating content means that students will be learning different information about the same topic. For example, a science class learning about oceanography may differentiate *content* by having four groups of students choose among four topics: measurements, tidal patterns, marine biology, and the ocean floor. Another class may have all of the students learn about ocean measurements by means of whole class instruction; then *process* is differentiated if some students make a color-coded chart, others construct a model, and others make an outline of information from the textbook chapter. To differentiate *product*, students could choose between a written report, an oral report, or a traditional short-answer test to show what they know.

Cultural capital: Cultural capital refers to the "outside of school" self. It includes dialect, socioeconomic status, family attitudes and expectations, exposure to reading material, travel, sense of safety, and well-being. Because of the importance of prior knowledge, cultural capital is an extremely important learning factor.

Curriculum components: The three components of curriculum are information (content), skills, and assessment. Another way of looking at curriculum is: *What concepts and competencies are you learning and how will you show what you know?*

Deductive reasoning: Deductive reasoning is reasoning that begins with a general rule and then goes into specifics based on that general rule. Direct instruction, where the teacher delivers a body of knowledge, usually depends upon deductive reasoning on the part of the students: The teacher gives the generality, such as a spelling rule, and the students apply it to specifics.

Depth and complexity: When we differentiate instruction for content, we think in terms of how to adjust depth (going into more or less detail in a narrower field) and complexity (having more steps, making more connections, having more interrelated parts.) For example, in a social studies class learning about the Presidency, *depth* could be achieved by investigating President Roosevelt's relationship to the Supreme Court and the Constitutional issues involved; *complexity* could involve making a graphic representation of the duties of the Presidency.

Dialectical journal: Also called a double-sided journal, the dialectical journal is the student's "conversation with herself" regarding a reading. On the left side, the student summarizes the reading. On the right side, she writes affective or interpretative responses. These can include questions, "this reminds me of..." statements, vocabulary lists, predictions, agree/disagree statements, or examples. The newspaper or student-selected outside reading works well with the dialectical journal.

Emotional intelligence: Emotional intelligence refers to a person's ability to function well in social situations, especially stress-producing ones. Emotional intelligence involves communication skills, self-control, perceiving the needs and concerns of others, self-understanding, and intuition. Timing, humor, empathy, and patience are characteristics of emotional intelligence. Contrary to outdated beliefs, emotional intelligence can be learned.

Embedded application: Embedded application occurs when a skill, such as recording measurements, is an integral part of a learning task, such as writing a lab report.

Entry points: This term comes from Howard Gardner's work on multiple intelligence. Gardner (1991, 1993) names five "entry points," or pathways, to learning a given topic. These are narrational (entering the topic via a story); logical/quantitative (entering the topic via numbers, deductive reasoning, or scientific inquiry); foundational (entering the topic via its philosophy or key words); aesthetic (entering the topic via the arts); and experiential (entering the topic via physical contact, by manipulating the objects and materials involved).

Features of differentiation: Differentiated instruction can be about any or all of the following: *pacing, degree of structure that the teacher provides, degree of independence of the learner, number of facets in the learning task, level of abstractness or concreteness, and level of depth and complexity.*

Flexible grouping: Flexible grouping is a key practice of differentiating instruction. Groups can be formed in various ways: interest, self-selection, or random. What we *don't* want is the formation of groups that are obviously ability-based. Such grouping is humiliating to the low-functioning group and breeds arrogance and a sense of entitlement in the "smart group." Cooperative learning groups work best when roles are clearly assigned. One popular method is based on "literature circles." In a literature circle, each member of the group has a job to do: word "looker-upper," metaphor-finder, illustrator, title-maker, connector, etc.

Graphic organizer: A graphic organizer, also called a concept map or web, is any kind of diagram or outline that helps the learner to arrange information visually. The Harvard outline and the sentence diagram are graphic organizers that have been around for more than a hundred years to help learners. The trouble with a graphic organizer is that it can become so complicated that it becomes its own taskmaster. Popular graphic organizers are the Venn diagram for comparison/contrast, the Frayer model for concept attainment, the KWL chart for reading comprehension, and the flowchart for sequential information.

Inclusion classes: Often called "collaboration classes," this is a model in which students with special needs are taught within the regular class, along with a special education teacher who works collaboratively with the subject area teacher. There are various models of inclusion. Sometimes, the special education teacher is present for every class; at other times, she may work with mainstream classes in two subject areas, alternating from one to the other. Sometimes, the special education teacher and her class work as a separate class most of the time, merging with the mainstream classes for appropriate projects. For collaboration to work, teachers need training, common planning time, opportunity for reflective practice, and lots of communication and administrative support.

Inductive reasoning: Inductive reasoning is reasoning that begins with the specifics and draws generalities based on them. A detective gathering information about a crime uses inductive reasoning to draw a conclusion about what happened.

Inquiry activities: Reading specialists refer to activities like the KWL chart as inquiry activities. The reader establishes overt goals for the reading, sets up expectations, makes predictions, and self-monitors her reading, aware of what she is looking for in the text.

KWL chart: This popular and effective three-column chart stands for "know, want to know, learned." Here's how it works: Before reading, the student jots down what she already knows about the subject. In the second column, she writes what she wants to know. After the reading, in the third column, she writes what she's learned. This marshals prior knowledge and focuses the reading. The KWL comports with everything we know about effective reading. It should be used in every class.

Learning centers: Learning centers are usually associated with elementary classrooms, but it's possible to have them in a middle school class. With learning centers, the room is physically arranged so that students interested in a particular type of learning can congregate. Centers can be oriented around activities, readings, topics, themes. Learning centers work well with contracts. In a seventh-grade social studies class learning about ancient Greece, students turned the classroom into a museum. The groups created stations based on philosophy, government, theater, and architecture. Each station had student-designed activities, which the class completed by rotating around the room

Learning contracts: Learning contracts are written agreements between teacher and student stipulating that certain learning tasks will be carried out by a certain time. A contract is a *negotiated agreement* between two sides. When a teacher hands out an assignment and declares that it is due by her deadline, that is *not* a learning contract. The student must have a part in drawing up the terms of the contract. In a creative writing class, the teacher and the student could discuss the nature of the writing project (making a short story out of a poem), the length, interim due dates, and criteria for evaluation.

Learning logs: A learning log is a general term for some sort of notebook in which the learner tracks her own learning. Entries can include questions, predictions, graphic organizers, summaries, mnemonic devices, connections to real life and other subject areas, diagrams, and vocabulary lists. KWL charts and dialectical journals are often part of the learning log.

Learning style: A person's learning style is her best way of processing, remembering, and using information. We usually think of learning style in terms of the senses: visual learners, auditory learners, or kinesthetic learners. Some people learn best by socializing; others, by writing; others, by talking to themselves aloud. We speak of brain laterality: the right hemisphere is the realm of intuitive learning; the left, of quantitative learning. Special education teachers are the experts in adapting information to a student's best learning style. Effective learners have a keen understanding of their own learning styles.

Microskills and macroskills: Microskills are skills in isolation, such as the skill of arranging things in order. Macroskills are microskills used in combination. Problem solving calls for macroskills.

Multiple intelligence theory: Developed by Howard Gardner, the multiple intelligence theory posits that there are eight different kinds of intelligence. These are verbal-linguistic, musical-rhythmic, logical-mathematical, interpersonal, intrapersonal (knowing of the self), bodily-kinesthetic, visual-spatial, and naturalistic (understanding the natural world). Multiple intelligence theory plays an important role in differentiated instruction.

Portfolios: Portfolios are organized collections of evidence of learning over time. There are many different types of portfolios. A portfolio differs from a folder with papers stuffed in it becasue a portfolio represents a carefully selected array of work samples that show goals, growth, and introspection. Portfolios are just as valid whether they represent an entire school year, or one particular area of study. They are an excellent way of differentiating instruction and are limited only by your imagination.

Scaffolding: As the metaphor implies, scaffolding is a support system for learning. The purpose of a scaffold device is to allow the learner to build new information upon a foundation of prior knowledge. Scaffolds can be graphic organizers, short-answer questions, dialogue, word banks, and other learning supports. For example, the social studies teacher whose students are writing a document-based essay based on a collection of Matthew Brady Civil War photographs has students answer guided questions about each photograph. The students will then use their information to compose the essay.

Schema: A schema is an organizational framework of knowledge upon which new knowledge can be built. Having a schema allows us to mentally fill in details and make assumptions about whatever it is that we are learning. The more sophisticated the learner, the more elaborate is the schema that she brings to the body of knowledge being learned. We hear a lot about schemas in differentiated instruction pedagogy. This is because any student's ability to learn new information will be based on the richness of the schema that the student brings to the subject. Assessing the detail and accuracy of a student's schema for a particular topic is one way of preassessing.

Semantic maps: Semantic maps are graphic representations of vocabulary. One kind of semantic map is the "Yes/No/Maybe" model in which the student writes the name of a concept, such as "civilizations," at the head of the paper. She then sorts various words in the yes/no/maybe columns, depending on whether they are civilizations, not civilizations, or ambiguities. Other forms of semantic maps show related words, etymology trees, synonym/antonym lists, characteristics or elements of the concept, etc. The value of the semantic map is that it calls for critical thinking about what a concept name really means.

"Show what you know" assessments: These are demonstrations of the student's knowledge in a form that is chosen by the student. The student makes a proposal, describing how her project will display her knowledge. She may offer to create a short-answer or essay test, make an oral or written report, or do a creative project. One caveat: the product cannot be something that can be taken in whole from another source. It should have enough of an in-class component that the teacher sees the product being constructed.

Socratic seminar: A Socratic seminar is a student-centered, open-ended discussion based on a text. The text may be print or nonprint. The purpose of the Socratic seminar is to invite conversation that is grounded in textual information. A Socratic seminar does not end in closure because its purpose is to stimulate independent thought rather than to come to any particular conclusion. The teacher's role in Socratic seminar is to ask questions and direct the students to focus on the text for their answers.

Textual features: Textual features are the visual cues that assist reading comprehension, especially in textbooks. Textual features that are helpful to the reading process are writing in columns, pictures, graphics, headings, bold-faced and italic type, and introductory and chapter-end questions. Textual features help the reader scan for specific information, and direct the reader's attention to key points.

Tiered assignments: Tiered assignments, usually presented on three levels, are tasks that are constructed with different levels of depth and complexity in mind. Some teachers use preassessment to determine which students are best suited to which tier. Others rely on student choice.

Think-pair-share: This is a cooperative learning strategy in which students are given a question and then asked to think about the answer, discuss their thoughts briefly with a partner, and then share the fruits of their discussion with others.

Whole-part-whole: This is a brain-compatible perspective on learning that suggests that we go from the generality to the specifics and then back to the generality.

Reflection

Working in pairs or trios with your colleagues, establish categories for the terms of differentiation listed below. Give each category a heading.

This activity serves two purpose. The first is to orient you to the language of differentiated instruction. The second is to demonstrate the process of classification.

Terms

- Academic literacy
- Alternative assessments (aka authentic assessments, performance tasks)
- Bloom's taxonomy: (often referred to as "Bloom")
- Brain-based learning
- Chunking of information
- Clustering
- Compacting
- Constructivism
- Content, process, product
- Cultural capital
- Curriculum components
- Deductive reasoning
- Depth and complexity
- Dialectical journal
- Emotional intelligence
- Embedded application
- Entry points
- Features of differentiation
- Flexible grouping
- Graphic organizer
- Inclusion classes
- Inductive reasoning
- Inquiry activities
- KWL chart
- Learning centers
- Learning contracts
- Learning logs
- Learning style
- Microskills and macroskills
- Multiple intelligence theory
- Portfolios
- Scaffolding
- Schema
- Semantic maps
- "Show what you know" assessments
- Socratic seminar
- Textual features
- Think-pair-share
- Tiered assignments
- Whole-part-whole

4

Differentiating Instruction for Reading the Textbook

This chapter shows you how to differentiate instruction to help students learn information in your textbook. You will consider:

◆ *How does your textbook fit into your teaching style?*
◆ *How learner-friendly is your textbook?*
◆ *How can you use the textbook to introduce your students to the course?*
◆ *How can you help students to carefully read a chapter?*
◆ *How can you design performance tasks that support textbook readings?*
◆ *How can you differentiate whole class instruction?*
◆ *How can you differentiate content, process and content?*

Three Teachers and a Textbook

How Does Your Textbook Fit into Your Teaching Style?

Julie, Rich, and Maura teach ninth grade earth science. All three teachers have excellent reputations, interesting classes, and exemplary results on the "Big Test." Ask yourself which of these teachers is most like you.

Julie relies heavily on the textbook and the materials provided by the publisher. She teaches out of the big binder that is stuffed with ready-made tests, review sheets, overheads, and teaching instructions. She goes in order. Julie's students get used to the routine of answering the questions at the end of each chapter. They hand their answers in for a homework grade. Julie insists that everything be carefully organized, corrected, labeled, and dated, just as she has presented it on the board. In addition to the homework grade, Julie grades lab reports and gives five tests per quarter, all of which are simulations of the "Big Test." When Julie's students go on a field trip, they have a study guide that has questions that they must answer.

Rich doesn't follow the order of the textbook. He uses the textbook for some topics; for others, he isn't satisfied with the textbook presentation. For these, he uses various authentic materials that he's collected over the years: weather maps of famous events, Internet sites, rocks and minerals, gemstones, models of geological structures, excerpts from different textbooks that he thinks are clearer than the current one. Rich does not collect notebooks, but he does give plenty of handouts for students to do in class and for homework. Rich's students need a good paperwork management system of their own. He gives approximately ten short answer quizzes each quarter, plus two major tests, each counting for 25 percent of the quarterly grade. Lab reports are graded as "satisfactory" or "unsatisfactory." When Rich's students go on a field trip, they are expected to submit logs of their observations.

Maura rarely uses that textbook in class. Her students can keep it at home and refer to it when necessary to study for tests or do projects. Maura brings in a wide variety of teacher-made and authentic materials, many of which involve art and literature related to earth science. Maura's students often learn about geological formations from the Science section of the New York Times, travel brochures, the photography of Ansel Adams, the opening chapters of James Michener's novels, and the essays of Annie Dillard. She uses these texts as ways to generate interest, to introduce terminology and concepts, and to stimulate inquiry. Maura's students keep learning journals, in which they summarize, make connections, generate ideas, ask questions, make outlines, and draw diagrams. Maura's students read assigned pages in the textbook for homework. She advises them to refer to the questions at the end of the chapters and self-test (she gives them the answers from the teacher's guide), but she expects them to self-monitor. Maura's assessments are class participation (whole class and group work), projects (oral, written, visual displays) lab reports, the learning journal, and a few tests each quarter. When Maura's students go on a field trip, they compose a creative writing piece that integrates geological terminology with an adventure story.

Reflection

1. Which of these teachers is most like you?
2. What would each of these teacher's classes look like when things are going well?
3. Discuss a profile of a student who would learn best in Julie's class.
4. Discuss a profile of a student who would learn best in Rich's class.
5. Discuss a profile of a student who would learn best in Maura's class.
6. Because he is a combination of the rigid structure of Julie and the holistic creativity of Maura, is Rich probably a better teacher?

How Learner-Friendly Is Your Textbook?

Students hate textbooks. Why shouldn't they? The textbook is not only a physical burden, it is an emotional burden as well. It contains "all that stuff" that "will be on the test." It is *work, work*. This is an unfortunate perception, because modern publishers do go to great lengths to give their textbooks "eye appeal," accessibility, ease of reading and review, and other positive textual features that conform to modern theories of learning.

Modern theories about reading instruction emphasize the importance of two things that bear on traditional textbooks: The first is the importance of prior knowledge; the second, the helpfulness of visual features of the text itself such as bold-faced print, short paragraphs, lists, pictures and captions, and overall page layout.

A Learner-Friendly Textbook

The following are the key points of Rachel Billmeyer's analysis of textbook learner-friendliness. The textbook is learner-friendly if the student:

- Sufficiently understands the vocabulary in context to make meaning from the text
- Has enough prior knowledge to make meaning from the text
- Can link new information to prior knowledge and experience
- Can learn abstract concepts by associating them with concrete examples
- Has plenty of examples, especially for new concepts
- Is not bombarded with superfluous details
- Can get a clear overview from the table of contents
- Can use chapter headings and subheadings to establish expectations
- Can use the glossary to clarify unfamiliar terms
- Can easily read the graphic information to support the textual information
- Can use the illustrations to make the textual information clearer, more memorable, and more interesting
- Considers the textbook contemporary in its depictions of people and events
- Can use textual features such as bold-faced type and italics to draw attention to key words
- Can use end-of-chapter questions to review and stimulate critical thinking
- Can easily locate introductory and summary information
- Finds enough contextual cues in the sentences surrounding new terminology

- Finds the sentence length and style neither too long (inaccessible) nor too short (condescending)
- Considers the activities and supplemental information interesting and relevant
- Is given connections to other subject areas
- Is given pictures that show an awareness of, and respect for, cultural differences
- Is given real-life application for the knowledge
- Sees colorful and attractive images
- Finds the layout easy on the eyes
- Finds that the textbook links to technology and nonprint media

Reflection

1. Evaluate your textbook in terms of the above criteria.

2. If your textbook is likely to create distance between the learner and the information, what can you do to close that gap?

3. How can you capitalize on the strengths and minimize the weaknesses of your textbook?

4. How can you use the textbook to introduce your students to the course?

For the textbook to be effective, all students must come to see that this huge tome, imposing and dense with content as it is, is trying to be nice to them In this reflection, you will learn how to help students integrate their own interests with the textbook: it does have some interesting ideas, pictures, charts, and, maybe, even whole chapters that they already know something about.

Softening the Textbook

Take a full period to introduce the textbook, to turn it from a coldhearted taskmaster to a work of art. (Hopefully, that won't make things worse.) Do this even if you are using it only supplementally, as Maura is. Although Maura is assigning only selected parts of the textbook, she would be pleasantly surprised if her students went beyond their assigned reading, if only just to look at pictures.

You soften the textbook when you give kids a chance to stroll through it before the course begins in earnest. Making time in class to overview the book can pay off in increased interest, decreased anxiety, increased connectedness, and a decreased sense of doom and gloom.
Julie might say this:

> "Think of the textbook as a museum. You don't like museums? OK, then think of the textbook as a foreign city that you are touring on vacation. You don't like touring foreign cities? OK, then think of the textbook as a theme park. Well, if you don't like theme parks, then think of the textbook as your television and that you are channel surfing. Find pictures that interest you.

Find pictures that you already know something about. Find pictures that remind you of something else. Find pictures whose colors you like, or pictures of places you'd like to go to.

Julie's students are hesitant. She's inviting them to enjoy the textbook. They are skeptical. Is this on the test?

Julie models her own enthusiasm for the subject by thumbing through the textbook and adhesive flags next to certain pages.[1] Have plenty of these on hand in class when using the textbook. The kind of teaching that Julie is doing here, modeling her own enthusiasm for the subject, has to be "in the moment." Julie knows that she can't have a premarked textbook. She has to be doing what she's asking the class to do. She asks, for example, "Did anyone pick out the picture on page 290?" (She waits for everyone to find the page.) "I love this picture of the Himalayan Mountain peaks. Did anyone ever go to a snow-capped mountain? Did anyone flag another picture of a mountain in the text?"

Julie's invitation for students to share their experiences with mountains may or may not elicit a response. If anyone offers an anecdote about skiing, or rock climbing, or seeing a movie about Mt. Everest, Julie will have a base hit that she can use to generate interest in geological formations, but if not, she is undaunted. Next, she'll tell them about the picture on page 178 of Niagara Falls. She'll ask them to locate other pictures in the text of geological formations that are tourist attractions. She'll ask them where they've been on vacation and what the geological formations were that made this place a vacation spot.

In the earth science text on Julie's podium and in her students' hands, there are hundred of pictures. Some are photographs taken from space, some are diagrams, some are panoramic views, and some are underwater photographs. Julie engages the students by asking questions such as the following:

- How do you think the photographer got the shot on page 138?
- Look at the pictures of the minerals on page 49: How do these look different from one another? How are they the same? What would you call this color? What does this pattern remind you of?
- Let's find a map, a diagram with arrows, a diagram with contour lines, a cross-sectional diagram.
- Let's find a picture that shows a historical event.
- Find a graph, chart, or table. Look at the numbers. What numbers surprise us?

Julie treats the earth science textbook in the same way a tour guide would treat a familiar city: she tells stories, both personal and historical; points out details; gives the background; supplements the plaque on the building; and can take what may look like a mundane street corner and make it come alive with tales of what it looked like at another time. Most of all, she is an expert who has

---

1   Adhesive flags are extremely useful tools for getting students to interact with text. Ask students to buy them along with their school supplies.

not lost her sense of wonder about the beauty of her subject. It remains new to her. Differentiated instruction is about that newness because, although the facts of earth science may remain the same, each students' connection to it will be unique. Julie's message to the students is this: "This textbook is interesting, and it is about you. It is *for* you."

Julie even has the students look at the bios of the authors, photographers, and editors. "All of these people had a hand in putting this textbook together. Think about the decisions that they made and what they were hoping you and I would think about their work." She takes the time to read the introductory material directed to this students. Usually, that comprises a statement of philosophy and inspiration designed to wish the students well in learning the subject and to imbue in them a sense of its importance to their lives, individually, and, collectively, as a society.

It's easy to skip over "that stuff in the beginning of the book" because it isn't going to be on the "Big Test." But Julie, a savvy teacher, recognizes that even if students learn the facts and get high grades on the "Big Test," what they learn will not stay with them, will not connect to the rest of their lives, or will not be applicable or even sensible if they don't personalize it in some way—if the textbook itself is not humanized. The difference between an adequate teacher and a great teacher is that the latter leaves a lasting impression about the love of learning.

This is not to say that Julie's class is looking at her with rapt attention, or that she has transformed the students' lives by talking about photography. What are Julie's students thinking during this third-period science class in September?

Shaun, a bright and ambitious student, buys into the program. When Julie refers to the picture of the snowcapped mountain, Shaun recalls his family's trip to Mount Rainier, and how excited he was to glimpse the summit when they were climbing up the road in their rented station wagon. He intends to do well in this class, as in all of his classes. He likes to learn. He also likes to play soccer, have a girlfriend, watch television, and go to parties where alcohol is surreptitiously consumed on the weekend. But he has a top-notch college ahead of him, along with many honors and awards to be bestowed on him over his high school years. Julie's lesson is not wasted on him: he will end up more interested in earth science than he would have been with a less imaginative teacher.

Michele hates the science that she had in middle school—too much memorization of hard terms and too many labs, with their rules and procedures. Michele doesn't like things that have to be measured and precise. And science has altogether too many numbers and formulas. What has today's lesson done for Michele? She feels a little less intimidated and turned off, because she likes the nature photographs. They are not "science-y" to her. At least this teacher lets you "like" things in science, rather than just measure them. Michele is still in her discomfort zone, and she may never be a Westinghouse winner, but by making her feel more at ease with the textbook, Julie has made earth science just a little more accessible for her. And that accessibility will pay off in better learning.

Now we come to Tiffany. Tiffany is a special ed student who panics on tests and has to have them read to her in the resource room. Even then, she usually gets grades in the 30s and 40s, and even less on the big unit tests. Science is especially hard because of all the big words. Tiffany hates big words. But today, she hasn't heard any. Even though she thinks her earth science teacher is a little loopy, she perceives that Julie is harmless, for a science teacher. Tiffany goes to her resource room teacher for period seven. Mr. Glassman asks her what she did in earth science. "Nothing," she replies. "It was stupid. We just looked at the pictures in the book." Mr. Glassman asks her to tell him about the pictures. "They were like tornadoes and lightning and stuff," she says. "It was just stupid." You can see where we're headed with this: Ted Glassman is, without too much difficulty, able to elicit from Tiffany that she has a pretty good idea of what earth science is going to be about. Julie's "stupid" lesson about the pictures in the textbook has established Tiffany's expectations for the content of the course.

Reflection

1. What has Julie done, if anything, to differentiate instruction?
2. What more could Julie do, if anything, to differentiate instruction?
3. Do you think Julie's lesson uses class time effectively?
4. How, if at all, has Julie addressed any of the following?:
   - learning styles
   - multisensory learning
   - multicultural considerations
   - visualization
   - verbalization
   - writing skills
   - reading skills
   - socialization
   - summoning prior knowledge
   - reducing student anxiety
   - storytelling
   - previewing information
   - going from picture to word/ word to picture
5. What in Julie's teaching style is similar to your own? What is different? What is outside your comfort zone?

Setting Up Expectations

That Tiffany's expectations for course content have been established is no small matter. We learn best when we understand where we are on the map. We need to know where we are going. Because new learning can only be integrated into prior knowledge, we learn best when we have one foot on familiar ground as we walk the path of new information. That is why textual organization is so important. As teachers, we need to show students how to use that organizational pattern to facilitate learning.

In a textbook, expectations are set up in the table of contents. Most people can't just "read" a table of contents, especially about a subject that they don't know much about: there are no verbs to make meaning, just nouns to name the topics. Next presented are several ways in which students can engage the table of contents of a textbook, thus establishing expectations for course content.

Table of Contents

The table of contents establishes course expectations, main ideas, and subordinate topics. The thinking skills inherent in perusing the table of contents are sorting and classifying, discerning main ideas, and using proper language tone.

What follows is a three-tiered performance task that uses the table of contents of an earth science textbook to establish expectations for course content, and to build a scaffolding of prior knowledge that will form the foundation for later learning.

This earth science textbook of around 700 pages is divided into eight units. Each unit is divided into four or five chapters. Each chapter breaks down into three, four, or five subtopics.

Whole Class Instruction

Maura asks the class what they think the units in the textbook are going to be: *"If you were to make a textbook about earth science and needed eight main topics, what would they be?"*

Here are three ways that Maura establishes course expectations through the table of contents:

1. She gives students a scrambled list of all of the unit headings, chapter headings, and subtopics. She asks them to sort and classify these.

2. She gives students the subheadings, having them supply the (more general) chapter headings. Less sophisticated students need a list of the actual headings to work with, whereas more sophisticated students are able to compose their own chapter headings. To further differentiate this task:
   - Students can compose chapter headings that use wordplay, allusion, figurative language
   - Students can express the chapter heading as a question

3. She has students transform the table of contents into a standard Harvard outline. Note that most tables of contents are almost in that form already. Students add more detail to the subtopics of each chapter.

Reflection

1. Discuss the effectiveness of Maura's lesson. How could she differentiate it further?

2. Tiered lessons can be based on preassessment. How could you preassess for Maura's lesson?

3. How can this task be assessed? How much value should it have?

4. How much time should be spent in class doing this task?

5. How would you decide which students should do which level of this task?

Make the teaching materials necessary to present this lesson on three different levels.

Reading the Chapter

How can you help students to carefully read a chapter?

Rich doesn't present his earth science curriculum in the same order that the textbook does. He likes to begin with Chapter 6, "Meteorology." He does this because of his own interest and knowledge in meteorology, and also because September is hurricane season, so the newspapers and the Weather Channel are rife with drama. To convey the information and concepts of meteorology, Rich will use both the textbook and primary sources. What follows is an example of what Rich does to facilitate the reading of the chapter.

First, Rich considers himself a teacher of reading in science. He understands that teaching kids how to read the chapter is a valuable use of teaching time if he wants them to read for understanding and be able to use what they've read to think at a higher level. So, at the beginning of the year, and periodically thereafter, Rich might say this:

> *First, we read for generalities. We "hover over" the chapter, getting the lay of the land, just as we did for the whole book. To read for generalities, we:*
>
> ◆ *"Read" the pictures*
> ◆ *Read the main chapter headings*
> ◆ *Read the Chapter Review page*
> ◆ *Take a page of notes that overviews the chapter:*
> ◆ *Exchange notes with someone else and fill in what that personr has that you don't have*
>
> *Now, we look at the questions at the end of the chapter. This is so we can keep our eyes out for important points. If you were an important point in this chapter, how would you let the reader know that you were an important point? Kids offer answers such as:*
>
> ◆ *"I'd be a heading."*
> ◆ *"I'd be a picture."*

- *"I'd repeat and rephrase myself."*
- *"I'd be a question at the end of the chapter."*
- *"I'd be in bold-faced type."*

OK, now that we have a pretty good idea what this chapter on meteorology is going to be about, we're ready read it word for word. What are some of the problems that you might have when you read this word for word?

- *"I won't understand it."*
- *"It will be boring."*
- *"I can't say the words in my head."*
- *"I don't have time to read it."*
- *"I keep thinking about other things in my head."*

The reason you might think it's boring or you can't stay focused is that you might not be giving yourself everything you need to read. Good readers do five things:

1. *Reread and self-monitor. Good readers read with an awareness of whether they are understanding and paying attention. You have to remember that* **real reading is rereading.** *I don't necessarily mean going back to the beginning after you've finished the whole chapter. That won't even help if you didn't understand it as you were going along. I mean, go back and reread sentences and paragraphs that you don't get. And don't forget to look at the pictures. They are there to help you understand.*

2. *Read because you want to know. You have to have a purpose for reading. The more you read because you want to know, the less boring it will be. Something is boring to you for only three reasons: you have decided not to care about it, you already know it, or you think it's too hard. If you've decided not to care about it, then you need to use your imagination a little. You need to ask yourself how the world will make more sense to you or be more beautiful to you if you understand this information. That's what science is all about. It's all about wanting the world to make more sense and be more beautiful. Now, if it's boring because you already know it, then skip over those parts. (But I don't think you already know this stuff.) If it's boring because you don't understand it, then you need to use the five reading strategies that I'm telling you about.*

3. *Psych out the set-up. It's much easier to understand something when we see that it forms a pattern. Science is all about finding patterns. When you read a textbook, the information will be organized into certain patterns. Here they are:*

- *Cause and effect: This shows a relationship where "this causes that." Key words would be: "this caused," "an effect of," "as a result," "therefore," "because of," and "thus." There are others. When you are in a cause-and-effect pattern, you are finding out how and why certain conditions and factors influence things to happen. You have that a lot in science.* (Having given the key words of the cause and effect pattern, Rich leaves it to the class to come up with key words for the other patterns.)

◆ *Chronological sequence: This is where things that happen are given to you in time order.*

◆ *Comparison and contrast: This is showing similarities and differences.*

◆ *Definition and examples.*

◆ *Description.*

To be a good reader, you need to develop the habit of being aware of the pattern.

4. Ambiance is everything. You'd be surprised how many people think they are reading when really they're watching television with a book in front of them. Reading can't be done on the phone, in a car with your friends, in the middle of a game (especially when you're on the field), with a headset on, while eating Cheezy Chips, or doing anything else. Reading requires your total attention. And you can't read when you're tired or if it's dark. I don't care if you read standing on your head or at your reading desk, but you need quiet, enough time, and good lights. This may seem obvious, but take a mental picture of yourself the last time you read a chapter in the textbook. How many distractions were there?

5. Visualize. Reading is what we call an active process. That means your mind has to make a movie as you read. Everything in science is visual. And you already have plenty of diagrams and pictures to show you what things look like. To learn science and to read science, you have to visualize.

Reflection

1. What has Rich done, if anything, to differentiate instruction?
2. What more could Rich do, if anything, to differentiate instruction?
3. Do you think Rich's lesson uses class time effectively?
4. What in Rich's teaching style is similar to your own? What is different? What is outside your comfort zone?

Find a textbook in a subject *outside of your comfort zone*, and read it in accordance with Rich's lesson.

Performance Tasks Based on Learning Theory

How can you design performance tasks that support textbook readings?

Rich emphasized that reading must be done for a purpose. The performance tasks here are presented as "actions" based on learning theories that are open to differentiated instruction.

Theory: *Learning must be actively constructed.*

> Action: The period 4 class makes up essay questions for the period 3 class to take. The period 7 class grades the answers, based on criteria that they establish.

Theory: *To best understand a science text, students must learn to go from picture to word and from word to picture.*

Action: Jill and Aaron are partners, playing the roles of textbook publisher and graphic artist, respectively. Jill describes the picture that she wants Aaron to create, beginning with the concept, and then getting more and more detailed. Jill and Aaron must use earth science language in their conversation. This may be done as teams, rather than as duos.

Devising Textbook-Based Performance Tasks

Devise other performance tasks for a chapter in your textbook. Base your activities on the learning theories above or on other learning theories. Consider the following principles of differentiated instruction:

- Students need to find their own access into the textbook by considering their interests and prior knowledge
- Students need to make meaning of the information in the textbook by using their best learning style
- The product is the same ("Big Test" and subtests); the content is the same; the process of internalizing the content depends upon the individual's learning style and prior knowledge

Whole Class Instruction

How can you differentiate whole class instruction?

Some people can envision differentiated instruction only as a divided class in which kids are engaged in different activities, but differentiation occurs during whole class instruction when the teacher's presentation takes learning styles into account. Here is how Rich's habits of mind as a teacher manifest in whole class instruction that takes individual needs into account:

Theory: *New information must be attached to old information.*

Action: Rich is constantly asking, "What does this remind you of? Where have you seen this before?" This habit of mind trains students to think of ways of accessing new information.

Theory: *Students need to personalize the information.*

Action: Earth science is about everything around us. Rich gets students in the habit of mind of personalizing new information by asking: "Have you ever seen this? felt this? How do you think it would feel at the equator? What would it look like? Sound like? Smell like?"

Theory: *Learning is best when it is multisensory.*

Action: Much of this information is detailed and statistical. Rich uses color-coding, encourages as much science-speak from the students as possible, insists that they write notes while he is lecturing (or immediately afterward), and provides as many visuals as he can.

Theory: *Learners are most effective when they recognize patterns.*

Action: Rich points out the patterns of the information in the chapter: cause/effect paragraphs, descriptions, chronologies, reasons and examples, and comparison/contrast.

Theory: *Metaphor is a powerful learning tool.*

Action: Rich asks for analogies, and he asks students to evaluate their accuracy: "How are the clouds like the currents of the sea? How are they different?"

Theory: *Humor is a powerful learning tool.*

Action: Although meteorology may not seem like the most amusing subject in the world, weather reports are one of the most lampoon-able genres because of their familiarity and serious tone. There's always someone in the class who would be happy to play weatherman.

Reflection

1. What has Rich done, if anything, to differentiate instruction?
2. What more could Rich do, if anything, to differentiate instruction?
3. Do you think Rich's lessons use class time effectively?
4. What in Rich's teaching style is similar to your own? What is different? What is outside your comfort zone?

How can you use learning theories about prior knowledge, personalizing information, multisensory learning, patterns, metaphor and humor to differentiate whole class instruction?

Differentiating Content, Process, and Product in the Textbook

Differentiating Content

Do students need to learn all of the information in the chapter? If they do, then we don't want to differentiate content. But before we make that blanket statement, let's consider the alternatives. Perhaps we want students to learn a few key concepts and a given list of terms. Perhaps we want their learning to be deeper and more complex on a few concepts in a chapter.

As we've seen, Maura's teaching style is amenable to differentiation. Here is how she teaches Chapter 4, "Internal Heat," and Chapter 7, "Weathering and Erosion." Maura teaches both of these chapters concurrently because she wants to put them under the thematic umbrella of *change*: how and why change happens, the results of change, and dramatic and subtle changes in the earth. Maura might say:

Chapter 4 is a dramatic chapter, all about volcanoes, tidal waves, earth-quakes, tsunamis and other big explosions that result from the earth's internal heat. What do we mean by dramatic?

Here are some student responses:

- *Things happen fast.*
- *Things that are spectacular to look at, like fire.*
- *Things are out of control.*
- *Things that you don't expect.*
- *When I think of dramatic, I think of power and danger.*

Maura: *In Chapter 7, we see dramatic changes occur, but they occur over very long periods of time. I want you to see the similarities between the forces of nature on both of these chapters.*

Maura gives the class this study guide:

Use the language of earth science to think about these questions:

- What causes change?
- How do opposing forces cause change?
- What are the results of several kinds of atmospheric change?
- What is the relationship between land, air, and water?

Reflection: Umbrella Themes

Maura wants to transform the information in the two chapters into answers to essential questions such as these. If students could answer these questions using the language and content of the chapter, would you be satisfied that they had learned the content?

Conjoin two nonconsecutive chapters in your textbook with an umbrella theme and several essential questions.

Differentiating Process

To learn the new information in this chapter, students need to find a way to integrate it with known information. Maura wants them to know a certain body of knowledge. That body of knowledge is written in the textbook, explained in her lectures, and expanded upon in supplementary teaching materials. That is where the information lies externally. How does Maura help the students make meaning out of that information?

Maura's guiding principle is this:

To learn the information in these chapters, the kids have to introduce it gradually into their brains. Most of all, they need to engage with it. They can do that using multisensory learning (hearing, seeing, writing, saying, touching), socialization (working with others in study groups, functioning as a member of a class that feels like a learning community in which the individual feels safe), inquiry (asking "what if" questions), and making con-

nections (perceiving similarities). My job is to integrate the information (content) with the learning environment (the conditions that I make possible in my class. I have to guide students in knowing that they have choices in the learning process.

Reflection

1. What has Maura done, if anything, to differentiate instruction?
2. What more could Maura do, if anything, to differentiate instruction?
3. Do you think Maura's lesson uses class time effectively?
4. What in Maura's teaching style is similar to your own? What is different? What is outside your comfort zone?

Working with your essential questions, how would you help students use their own learning styles to achieve the desired result?

Differentiating Assessment

Is a test, on which the teacher has controlled every question, the only way, or the best way, for students to show what they know? Perhaps, in addition to the traditional chapter test, students could show what they know on specific parts.

The disadvantage of traditional tests is that once they are over, no one learns anything. Yes, you can spend time reteaching, "going over" the test, but to the students, that just feels like they are holding losing lottery tickets and listening to someone tell them what numbers they should have played. It's very hard to motivate students to actively participate in the "going over the test" ritual. Those who "got number 19 right" may be enthusiastically waving their hand in the air, but what's the point? They already knew that information. They are not making progress.

Consider "show what you know" assessments. These can take a variety of forms: dramatic presentations, oral reports, written reports (be careful that these aren't snatched from the Internet or other ready-made sources), a student-written test, a mini-lesson, a three-dimensional project. The idea is to have students present the "show what you know" to the whole class, or, at least, to their study groups. "Show what you know" projects serve as constructive study guides for the presenter and the class. Thus, you don't need to make a choice between "show what you know" and a traditional test. Both work in tandem. The "show what you know" project, if especially good, could earn the student bonus points on the test, but its intrinsic value is that it results in constructed learning that should translate to a higher test grade anyway.

Reflection: Alternative Assessment

1. Compare and contrast traditional tests to alternative assessments in your subject areas.
2. How comfortable are you with alternative assessment?

3. What would you consider alternative assessment, as opposed to traditional assessment?

4. Are there cohorts in your district (parents, students, administration, Board) that favor either alternative or traditional assessment?

Devise several types of alternative assessments that hold students accountable for the information in a chapter of your textbook.

Summary Reflection: The Textbook

1. If you are a teacher like Julie, how can you differentiate instruction by using materials other than the textbook and publisher's prepared materials?

2. If you are a teacher like Maura, how can you differentiate instruction by using the textbook and publisher's prepared materials more effectively?

3. What kinds of students are likely to respond best to your approach to the textbook?

4. How are you going to help students navigate the textbook at the beginning of the course?

5. How can you, your colleagues, and your administration compensate for the shortcomings of your textbook?

5

Differentiating Instruction for Independent Reading

Reading is the key to learning. The best thing that can happen in our schools is for kids to read more. This chapter presents ideas for two kinds of independent reading programs:

- Reading the classics
- Open choice reading

Reading the Classics

Why read the classics? Is reading the classics just a concern for the English teacher? In his book, *Classics in the Classroom*, Michael Clay Thompson asserts that the classics contain unforgettable characters, thrilling stories, profound insights, history, poetic language, fanciful settings, surprising twists, deep meaning, and a noble spirit.

He speaks of "Odysseus moments," moments in which a person does what a civilized person does: reads, discusses, listens, shows regard for others, respects tradition, stands up for an ideal worth having, resists temptation, and sometimes fails to do these things and suffers the pangs of conscience.

One of the side benefits to reading the classics is the assimilation of classic vocabulary, what Thompson calls "classic words." In his miraculous little book, *Classic Words*, Thompson lays out 100 classic words. The collection of these words comprises "a minipicture of human experience." (Thompson's word list appears at the end of this chapter.) What do we learn by reading a classic? If a book has 400 pages, and there are 20 sentences on each page, that's 8,000 well-crafted sentences. If there's a new word or a word used in a new way coming up in every four sentences, that's 2,000 words taken to new places. In the classics, words are used paradoxically, metaphorically, ironically, figuratively, or just perfectly, to express the human experience. These sentences and words are absorbed into the reader's brain, forming a template for her own future thoughts. Through reading, we acquire a store of language memory that then serves as a foundation for more reading, speaking, writing, and thinking. That's what reading the classics has to do with, for example, math class.

In the classic *Peter Pan*, these are some of the words we meet: *aloof, amicable, amorous, avidly, enigma, condescend, coquettish, countenance, cipher, debonair, dejection, diffident, enigma, fastidious, hauteur, impassive, incisive, indomitable, interpose, mea culpa, miasma, miscreant, pandemonium, perfidious, phlegmatic, placid, profound, quietus, quixotic, raconteur, remonstrate, reproof, retort, sanguinary, strident, sublime, succulence, tremulous, undulate, virulent*. And this is "just a children's book."

Now consider the ideas that we meet in J.M. Barrie's *Peter Pan*: Everyone needs a mother's love; friendship requires loyalty and loyalty can entail risk; childhood is both a temporary and a permanent state.

Through the classics, we come to understand misfits: Quasimodo, Hester Prynne, Dr. Frankenstein, Huck Finn, Holden Caulfield, Esther Greenwood, Jane Eyre, Heathcliff, Bigger Thomas, Hamlet, Don Quixote, Boo Radley, Raskolnikov, the Underground Man.

By reading the classics, we develop a sense of quality. By using intelligent criteria to determine that two things are not of equal value, we engage in the highest level of thinking on Bloom's hierarchy: evaluation. Dickens, Melville, Twain, and Shakespeare are superior to car stories, teen romances, pseudo-science, and pop psychology and the thinking person who has been exposed to fine literature can explain why.

Familiarity with the classics allows us to understand allusion, even when we see it, as we often do, on The Simpsons. We enter a conversation that has been going on since the beginning of civilization when we can understand literary, mythological, and historical allusion. We "get it." If two students have read two hundred books, and one has read the classics, and the other has read only contemporary literature, who has the better education?

How do we teach students to interpret the classics? Aren't the classics too difficult, too obscure, and too long for our neediest learners? Some of them are. But if we offer a broad variety of choices, time to read, reading instruction, and a variety of assessments, all students can benefit from the classics. The list of classics included in this chapter includes children's literature. This provides choice and an opportunity to revisit books previously read. Literature provides us with the tools to its own interpretation. Look for a key quotation in the book that will unlock its entire meaning. The "answers" are right there in front of us: "There's no place like home"; "You are not the little Hobbit that you were"; "So we beat on, boats against the current, borne back ceaselessly into the past"; "It was the best of times, it was the worst of times."

A good book is good for one reading; a great book invites and rewards multiple readings. As Harold Bloom, author of *How to Read and Why*, says, the book reads *you* as much as you read *it*: you bring a certain level of understanding to the literature, and that literature can speak to at a different level once you have grown and changed with experience. Bloom tells us to first find *King Lear*, and then let *King Lear* find us. Every classic book is a model of the world, a mini-universe. If we view a book in this way, we can compare one "model of the world" to another that is presented in another book.

The trick to differentiating instruction in the classics is to help students find the pedagogical tension, sometimes referred to as the "zone of proximal development." This is the metaphorical place where the reader is challenged by the literature, but it is not so challenging as to be frustrating. If she stretches, it is within her grasp.

241 Classics: Outside Reading

Here are the directions that I give my ninth- and tenth-grade students for reading the classics (see list in Figure 5.1) in my English class:

What is a classic? A classic is a work of literature that has not gone out of style because of its meaning and quality. You may not "like" every classic that you read. You may not understand all of them. But if you focus your attention on the meaning and the quality of the overall piece, as well as the details, then you can get that classic to speak to you. Some classics, such as classic children's literature, are easy to read. Others demand patience, concentration, and an open mind. Approach the classic with *humility:* that is to say, recognize that you are in the presence of an acknowledged masterpiece.

Rules: You will read one work of literature from this list by the due date. Be prepared to discuss what you read with me, in the presence of another student. Next time, you will read a book by a different author.

Evaluation: Your discussion will be evaluated on the basis of:

- ♦ your familiarity with the generalities and specifics of the piece
- ♦ your ability to transcend the obvious
- ♦ the depth and complexity of your ideas
- ♦ your ability to make connections to other works of literature, history, your own world

IMPORTANT: You are not allowed to say the "S" word ("stupid," e.g., *"This is stupid,"* or *"I am stupid"*) in your discussion. If you do, you will fail. Same applies for the "B" word (*boring*).

Figure 5.1. List of 241 Classics

	Key Classic Codes	
K LC	Kiddie Lit Classic	These titles are considered classics in children's literature.
B	Banned	Somebody, somewhere, at some time has found these titles offensive and unacceptable for young people to read in school.
YA	Young Adult	These titles are recommended for pre-teens and young teenagers.
Pl	Play	

	Title	Author(s)	Type/Academic Use
1.	Things Fall Apart	Chinua Achebe	often used in social studies
2.	Letters	Abigail Adams	YA
3.	The Education of Henry Adams	Henry Adams	often used in social studies
4.	Watership Down	Richard Adams	YA; B
5.	The Zoo Story	Edward Albee	Pl
6.	The Bible		B; often used in social studies
7.	The Talmud		B; often used in social studies
8.	The Koran		B; often used in social studies
9.	The Bhavagad Gita		often used in social studies
10.	The Upanishads		often used in social studies
11.	Lysistrata	Aristophanes	Pl; B
12.	The Birds	Aristophanes	Pl
13.	The Clouds	Aristophanes	Pl
14.	The Frogs	Aristophanes	Pl
15.	Emma	Jane Austen	
16.	Mansfield Park	Jane Austen	
17.	Northanger Abbey	Jane Austen	

18.	*Persuasion*	Jane Austen	
19.	*Pride and Prejudice*	Jane Austen	
20.	*Sense and Sensibility*	Jane Austen	
21.	*Another Country*	James Baldwin	B
22.	*The Fire Next Time*	James Baldwin	often used in social studies
23.	*Go Tell It on the Mountain*	James Baldwin	often used in social studies
24.	*If Beale Street Could Talk*	James Baldwin	often used in social studies
25.	*Nobody Knows My Name*	James Baldwin	often used in social studies
26.	*Notes of a Native Son*	James Baldwin	often used in social studies
27.	*Cousin Bette*	Honore de Balzac	
28.	*Droll Stories*	Honore de Balzac	B
29.	*Eugenie Grandet*	Honore de Balzac	
30.	*Pere Goriot*	Honore de Balzac	
31.	*Lost Illusions*	Honore de Balzac	
32.	*Struggles and Triumphs*	P. T. Barnum	
33.	*Peter Pan*	James M. Barrie	KLC
34.	*The Wizard of Oz*	Frank Baum	KLC
35.	*Letters*	Ludwig von Beethoven	
36.	*Madeline*	Ludwig Bemelmans	KLC
37.	*Dream Songs*	John Berryman	poetry
38.	*Patterns of Culture*	Ruth Benedict	often used in social studies
39.	*Wuthering Heights*	Emily Bronte	
40.	*Jane Eyre*	Charlotte Bronte	YA
41.	*The Professor*	Anne Bronte	
42.	*Manchild in the Promised Land*	Claude Brown	B
43.	*The Secret Garden*	KLC	
44.	*The Fall*	Albert Camus	

45.	*The Myth of Sisyphus*	Albert Camus	
46.	*The Plague*	Albert Camus	
47.	*The Stranger*	Albert Camus	
48.	*Don Quixote*	Miguel de Cervantes	B
49.	*In Cold Blood*	Truman Capote	B
50.	*Silent Spring*	Rachel Carson	science
51.	*The Sea Around Us*	Rachel Carson	science
52.	*Death Comes for the Archbishop*	Willa Cather	
53.	*My Antonia*	Willa Cather	
54.	*Alice's Adventures in Wonderland/ Through the Looking Glass*	Lewis Carroll	KLC; B
55.	*The Bishop*	Anton Chekov	Pl
56.	*The Three Sisters*	Anton Chekov	Pl
57.	*The Cherry Orchard*	Anton Chekov	Pl
58.	*The Seagull*	Anton Chekov	Pl
59.	*The Awakening*	Kate Chopin	
60.	*Their Finest Hour*	Winston Churchill	often used in social studies
61.	*The Second World War*	Winston Churchill	6 volumes (read 1); often used in social studies
62.	*Orations*	Cicero	great speeches; often used in social studies
63.	*The Adventures of Pinocchio*	Carlo Collodi (Lorenzini)	KLC
64.	*The Inferno*	Dante	
65.	*The Moonstone*	Wilke Collins	
66.	*The Analects*	Confucius	often used in social studies
67.	*The Cat Who Went to Heaven*	Elizabeth Coatsworth	KLC
68.	*Madame Curie*	Eve Curie	YA

69.	The Constitution of the United States	often used in social studies	
70.	Maggie: A Girl of the Streets	Stephen Crane	
71.	The Open Boat	Stephen Crane	
72.	The Red Badge of Courage	Stephen Crane	
73.	Descent of Man	Charles Darwin	science; B
74.	Origin of Species	Charles Darwin	science; B
75.	The Voyage of the Beagle	Charles Darwin	science; B; often used in social studies
76.	Robinson Crusoe	Daniel Defoe	KCL; B
77.	Microbe Hunters	Paul de Kruif	science
78.	Bleak House	Charles Dickens	
79.	David Copperfield	Charles Dickens	
80.	Great Expectations	Charles Dickens	B
81.	The Mystery of Edwin Drood	Charles Dickens	
82.	Hard Times	Charles Dickens	
83.	Nicholas Nickleby	Charles Dickens	
84.	Our Mutual Friend	Charles Dickens	
85.	Pickwick Papers	Charles Dickens	
86.	Pilgrim at Tinker Creek	Annie Dillard	contemporary; nonfiction
87.	John Dos Passos	USA	
88.	The Life and Times of Frederick Douglass	Frederick Douglass	often used in social studies
89.	The Hound of the Baskervilles	Arthur Conon Doyle	
90.	The Brothers Karamazov	Fyodor Dostoevsky	
91.	Crime and Punishment	Fyodor Dostoevsky	
92.	The Idiot	Fyodor Dostoevsky	
93.	Notes from Underground	Fyodor Dostoevsky	
94.	Advise and Consent	Allen Drury	
95.	The Souls of Black Folk	W. E. B. DuBois	

96.	*The Meaning of Relativity*	Albert Einstein	science
97.	*The Immense Journey*	Loren Eiseley	science
98.	*"The Love Song of J. Alfred Prufrock"*	T. S. Eliot	poem
99.	*Invisible Man*	Ralph Ellison	B
100.	*Absalom, Absalom*	William Faulkner	
101.	*As I Lay Dying*	William Faulkner	
102.	*The Sound and the Fury*	William Faulkner	
103.	*So Big*	Edna Ferber	KLC
104.	*Tender is the Night*	F. Scott Fitzgerald	
105.	*The Great Gatsty*	F. Scott Fitzgerald	B
106.	*Madame Bovary*	Gustave Flaubert	B
107.	*Howard's End*	E. M. Forster	
108.	*The Slave Dancer*	Paula Fox	YA
109.	*The Diary of a Young Girl*	Anne Frank	B
110.	*Civilization and its Discontents*	Sigmund Freud	psychology
111.	*Interpretation of Dreams*	Sigmnud Freud	psychology
112.	*Where the Air is Clear*	Carlos Fuentes	
113.	*The Snow Goose*	Paul Gallico	KLC
114.	*Autobiography*	Mohandas Gandhi	often used in social studies
115.	*One Hundred Years of Solitude*	Gabriel Garcia Marquez	B
116.	*Love in the Time of Cholera*	Gabriel Garcia Marquea	B
117.	*Ellen Foster*	Kaye Gibbons	Oprah's Book Club
118.	*Dead Souls*	Nicolai Gogol	
119.	*The Lord of the Flies*	William Golding	B
120.	*In the Shadow of Man*	Jane Goodall	science
121.	*The Panda's Thumb*	Stephen Jay Gould	science
122.	*Wind in the Willows*	Kenneth Grahame	KLC
123.	*The Tin Drum*	Gunter Grass	

124.	*I, Claudius*	Robert Grames	B
125.	*Black Like Me*	John Howard Griffin	B
126.	*The Brave Little Tailor*	Jacob and Wilhelm Grimm	KLC
127.	*The Fisherman and His Wife*	Jacob and Wilhelm Grimm	KLC
128.	*Rumplestilskin*	Jacob and Wilhelm Grimm	KLC
129.	*Bound for Glory*	Woody Guthrie	
130.	*The Federalist Papers*	Hamilton, Jay, Madison	often used in social studies
131.	*Tess of the D'Urbervilles*	Thomas Hardy	B
132.	*Jude the Obscure*	Thomas Hardy	B
133.	*Catch 22*	Joseph Heller	B
134.	*The Children's Hour*	Lillian Hellman	B; Pl
135.	*Death in the Afternoon*	Ernest Hemingway	
136.	*The Old Man and the Sea*	Ernest Hemingway	
137.	*Steppenwolf*	Herman Hesse	
138.	*Siddhartha*	Herman Hesse	
139	*Kon-Tiki*	Thor Heyerdahl	
140.	*Mein Kampf*	Adolf Hitler	
141.	*The Iliad*	Homer	
142.	*Les Miserables*	Victor Hugo	
143.	*The Doll's House*	Henrick Ibsen	Play
144.	*Rip Van Winkle*	Washington Irving	KLC
145.	*The Legend of Sleepy Hollow*	Washington Irving	KLC
146.	*Declaration of Independence*	Thomas Jefferson	often used in social studies
147.	*The Metamorphosis*	Franz Kafka	
148.	*The Trial*	Franz Kafka	
149.	*Profiles in Courage*	John Fitzgerald Kennedy	often used in social studies
150.	*Dancing on My Grave*	Gelsey Kirkland	biography

151.	*Tao-te Ching*	Lao-tzu	often used in social studies
152.	*Eleanor and Franklin*	Joseph P. Lash	biography; often used in social studies
153.	*Lady Chatterley's Lover*	D. H. Lawrence	B
154.	*Elmer Gantry*	Sinclair Lewis	
155.	*Arrowsmith*	Sinclair Lewis	
156.	*Notebooks*	Leonardo da Vinci	
157.	*The Call of the Wild*	Jack London	
158.	*White Fang*	Jack London	
159.	*The Prince*	Nicolo Machiavelli	
160.	*The Fixer*	Bernard Malamud	
161.	*The Communist Manifesto*	Karl Marx	B; often used in social studies
162.	*Autobiography*	Malcolm X	B; often used in social studies
163.	*All My Sons*	Arthur Miller	Pl
164.	*Moby Dick*	Herman Melville	
165.	*The Heart is a Lonely Hunter*	Carson McCullers	
166.	*Beloved*	Toni Morrison	B
167.	*Gone with the Wind*	Margaret Mitchell	B
168.	*Lolita*	Vladimir Nabokov	B
169.	*The Octopus*	Frank Norris	
170.	*McTeague*	Frank Norris	
171.	*A Good Man is Hard to Find*	Flannery O'Connor	
172.	*The Hairy Ape*	Eugene O'Neill	Pl
173.	*The Emperor Jones*	Eugene O'Neill	Pl; B
174.	*The Scarlet Pimpernel*	Emmuska Orszy	
175.	*The Revolt of the Masses*	Ortega y Gasset	often used in social studies
176.	*Common Sense*	Thomas Paine	often used in social studies

177.	*Amelia Bedelia*	Peggy Parish	KLC
178.	*Pensees (Thoughts)*	Blaise Pascal	philosophy
179	*Doctor Zhavago*	Boris Pasternak	B
180.	*Cry the Beloved Country*	Alan Paton	
181.	*The Labyrinth of Solitude*	Octavio Paz	
182.	*The Bell Jar*	Sylvia Plath	B
183.	*Dialogues*	Plato	B
184.	*The Republic*	Plato	B
185.	*The Tale of Peter Rabbit*	Beatrix Potter	KLC
186.	*Adventures of Robin Hood*	Howard Pyle	KLC
187.	*Gargantua and Pantagruel*	Francois Rabelais	
188.	*Phaedra*	Jean Baptiste Racine	Pl
189.	*Anthem*	Ayn Rand	
190.	*All Quiet on the Western Front*	Erich Maria Remarque	
191.	*The Light in the Forest*	Conrad Richter	
192.	*How the Other Half Lives*	Jacob Riis	
193.	*Eyrano de Bergerac*	Edmond Rostand	Pl
194.	*Giants in the Earth*	O.E. Rolvaag	
195.	*The Dragons of Eden*	Carl Sagan	science
196.	*Franny and Zooey*	J.D. Salinger	
197.	*No Exit*	Jean Paul Sartre	Pl
198.	*The 500 Hats of Bartholomew Cubbins*	Dr. Seuss	KLC
199.	*Horton Hatches the Egg*	Dr. Seuss	KLC
200.	*(any play by...)*	William Shakespeare	
201.	*Pygmalion*	George Bernard Shaw	Pl
202.	*Dragon's Teeth*	Upton Sinclair	
203.	*Frankenstein*	Mary Shelley	
204.	*The Agony and the Ecstasy*	Irving Stone	
205.	*Dracula*	Bram Stoker	

206.	*Heidi*	Johanna Spyri	KLC
207.	*East of Eden*	John Steinbeck	B
208.	*Gulag Archipelago*	Aleksandr Solzhenitsyn	B
209.	*Shame of the Cities*	Lincoln Steffens	often used in social studies
210.	*Treasure Island*	Robert Louis Stevenson	KLC
211.	*Uncle Tom's Cabin*	Harriet Beecher Stowe	B
212.	*Elements of Style*	William Strunk and E.B. White	language
213.	*The Confessions of Nat Turner*	William Styron	B
214.	*The Lives of the Cell*	Lewis Thomas	science
215.	*Medusa and the Snail*	Lewis Thomas	science
216.	*Roll of Thunder, Hear My Cry*	Mildred Taylor	
217.	*Many Moons*	James Thurber	humor
218.	*The Hobbit*	J.R.R. Tolkein	
219.	*Anna Karenina*	Leo Tolstoy	
220.	*A Confederacy of Dunces*	John K. Toole	humor
221.	*The Guns of August*	Barbara Tuchman	often used in social studies
222.	*Adventures of Tom Sawyer*	Mark Twain	KLC
223.	*The Centaur*	John Updike	
224.	*Rabbit Run*	John Updike	B
225.	*All the King's Men*	Robert Penn Warren	
226.	*The Double Helix*	James Watson	science
227.	*Slaughterhouse-Five*	Kurt Vonnegut	B
228.	*Leaves of Grass*	Walt Whitman	poetry
229.	*The Island of Dr. Moreau*	H. G. Wells	
230.	*The Optimist's Daughter*	Eudora Welty	
231.	*Ethan Frome*	Edith Wharton	
232.	*Charlotte's Web*	E. B.White	KLC

233.	*Essays from the New Yorker*	E. B. White	nonfiction
234.	*One Man's Meat*	E. B. White	nonfiction
235.	*The Loved One*	Evelyn Waugh	
236.	*The Picture of Dorian Gray*	Oscar Wilde	
237.	*Look Homeward, Angel*	Thomas Wolfe	
238.	*A Room of One's Own*	Virginia Woolfe	
239.	*The Caine Mutiny*	Herman Wouk	
240.	*Native Son*	Richard Wright	B
241.	*A Vindication of the Rights of Women*	Mary Wollenscraft	often used in social studies

Interview Questions

- What other story does this one remind you of? Why?
- What do you think was the turning point?
- Tell me about some vivid descriptions of places in the story.
- Tell me about some of the most interesting characters.
- Tell me about a minor character. Why do you think the author puts this character in the book?
- How is the story about the search for:
  - honor
  - power
  - adventure
  - security
  - justice
  - friendship
- How and why does the main character change?

Other Assessments for the Classics

You may be thinking: "This all sounds very nice, but how am I supposed to design a different test for two hundred forty-one books, many of which I haven't even read myself?" To do this classics program, and also the free choice reading program, which is explained later in this chapter, you will simply have to give up the belief that you have to know everything that your students know in order to assess their understanding of a book. If you can't do that, then how will you ever do anything other than just give assigned readings? What follows are several authentic assessments for independent reading: essays, demonstrations, dialectical journals, lists, maps, and displays.

Essays

Theme: Power

Complex and meaningful stories are always about power. The power can be physical, intellectual, economic, or emotional. Discuss several ways in which the theme of power drives the action of your classic. Be sure to give specific references to characters, events, and places from various parts of your book. Refer to literary elements in your discussion such as plot, theme, characterization, irony, setting, etc.

Theme: Transformation

All classics involve a transformation of the main character. In your essay, describe the main character's transformation in terms of how and why she or he changes, the other characters and circumstances that bring about that change, why the change is difficult, and the results of the changes. Refer to specific names, places, and events.

Theme: Sense of Urgency

All classics involve a situation that creates a *sense of urgency* for the characters. In your essay, describe the sense of urgency: what causes it, why it is urgent, and how it is resolved. Refer to specific names, places, and events. Refer to literary elements such as plot, theme, characters, setting, and point of view.

Theme: Deception and Betrayal

All great stories involve deception and/or betrayal. In your essay, describe the deception or betrayal, name the characters involved and their motivation, and tell the results of the deception or betrayal. Refer to specific characters, events, and places. Refer to literary elements such as plot, theme, characters, setting, climax, and point of view.

Structured Summary (The Four-Page Treatment): Aristotle's Three-Act Structure

Aristotle gave us the story arc known as the three-act structure. This way of telling a story guides screenplay writers, who call it the four-page treatment. Here's how it works:

1 Page: Describes the opening scene
1/2 Page: Tells the general action of the first 25 percent of the book (Act I)
1 Page: Tells the "initiating event" that happens at the end of Act I, which has launched the story into "full conflict mode"
1/2 Page: Tells the action of Act II (middle 50 percent of book), specifying the confrontation that takes place at the midpoint

1/2 Page: Tells the action at the end of Act II, which propels the story into its inevitable resolution (point of no return)

1 Page: Tells the resolution

Demonstrations: The Book Box

The book box is a shoe box in which the student places various items that represent key objects in the story. The student's presentation consists of explaining the significance of these items. This differs from a plot summary in that we are not asking the students to simply retell the story. Rather, we are asking them to identify objects and show how these objects reveal the theme, characterization, setting, and other literary elements. Students usually want to decorate the box in accordance with the story. Advise students that the book box is a collection of loose objects, not a diorama.

The Pitch

You have five minutes with an influential Hollywood producer to pitch your idea for a movie based on this book. Sell it. Go.

Lists and Maps

- ◆ Props: List and explain the significance of ten hand-held items that appear in the book.
- ◆ Character Star Chart: Express the main and minor characters and their relationships to each other in the form of a chart.
- ◆ Key Verbs: List and explain ten key actions in the story. To do this, write ten key verbs (no synonyms) and explain who does each verb, to whom, when, where, and why.
- ◆ Obstacle Course: Draw an obstacle course that represents the journey of the main character.

Displays

- ◆ First and last sentence: Make an attractive and careful poster using visual images to show the story. Feature the first and the last sentence of the book. Your poster should convey a sense of the atmosphere, setting, key events, and characters.
- ◆ Multi-perceptions: Make a display that shows how a character feels about herself, how others feel about her, and how the reader feels about her. Refer to specific examples.
- ◆ Museum exhibit: Make a model of a museum exhibit that would represent this book in the Literary Museum.

Journals

Double-Sided Journal

On the left side, write the literal events. On the right side, write your interpretations, predictions, questions, reactions, and theories. This is also called a dialectical journal. The following are examples, created by different students, based on *Anna Karenina*.

Stephanie's Journal:

Anna Karenina

Events	*Reactions*
Meets Vronsky's mother on the train ride to her mother and learns everything about Vronsky's life. At her brother's house she fixes her brother's marriage. He was unfaithful to his wife, Dolly.	I knew that this was foreshadowing that Anna would fall in love with Vronsky. Anna trying to convince Dolly to forgive her brother is ironic because later on she is unfaithful to her husband.
Falls in love with Vronsky; however, she is married.	I found this to be the conflict of the story. She is in love with one man, but she is married to another and now she has to decide which one she wants.
Vronsky reads her palm and her husband, Alexy, sees.	This made me mad because Alexy found nothing wrong with this; however he did not realize that his wife was falling in love with this man.
Sneaks off to Vronsky's house and gets pregnant.	This event pushes her to tell her husband about Vronsky. I think that if she did not get pregnant she would not have had the motivation to tell her husband that she was having an affair.
Decides she is going to tell her husband about the baby and Vronsky and then wants to run away, but she does not want to leave her son, which is the second conflict.	This is another conflict. Anna would leave; however she is not allowed to take her son with her. Now she has to pick to be with her eight-year-old son, or Vronsky, which is very hard for her.
Vronsky falls off his horse in a horse race and she runs to him. Her husband sees and gets all upset. She tells him that she hates him and loves Vronsky.	This event made me realize how unhappy Anna was with Alexy. I knew she would rather be with Vronsky, but I did not know that she hated Alexy.

Adrienne's Journal:

Anna

Action: Anna takes a train to Moscow to visit her brother Stiva, in the hope of helping him to reconcile his marriage. On the train she sits next to Count Vronsky's mother, who helps her cope with her guilt at having left her son for a few days. As Anna gets off the train in Moscow, she is introduced to Count Vronsky by his mother and then meets him again at a ball in Moscow.

Reaction: When Anna meets Vronsky, that is the beginning of the conflict of the story. It's obvious that she is going to fall in love with him and since she is married, that is the problem.

Christopher's Journal

Anna Journal

Important Events	Observations, Reactions, Effect on Other Characters, etc.
Anna meets Vronsky on the train, because she sits with his mother.	It is apparent that there is an attraction between them.
Anna dances with Vronsky at a party.	This upsets Kitty, because she is in love with Vronsky.
Anna goes to Vronsky's house and spends the night with him. She continues having an affair with him.	This devastates her husband, but he only wants her to continue to be his wife so it will look good to other people.
Anna gets pregnant with Vronsky's child.	This complicates everything, and Anna's husband says that they will have to say that the child is his.

As you can see, these three students have variant levels of literary sophistication. The double-sided journal is excellent for sorting out plot from other literary elements. These journals do tend to get lengthy. You might want to limit them to selected chapters.

Character Journal

Write journal entries from several characters, or from one character at several points in the story. Go beyond just telling what is happening. Express the reasoning of the character, her choices, her emotions, and mixed feelings.

List of One Hundred Classic Words

High School Students

1. countenance	26. abate	51. abject	76. imperious
2. profound	27. undulate	52. austere	77. derision
3. serene	28. traverse	53. rebuke	78. profuse
4. manifest	29. repose	54. dejection	79. apprehension
5. languor	30. wistful	55. vivacious	80. ardent
6. acute	31. palpable	56. despondent	81. myriad
7. prodigious	32. pallor	57. importune	82. droll
8. grotesque	33. superfluous	58. incendiary	83. resolute
9. sublime	34. lurid	59. pensive	84. insensible
10. allude	35. furtive	60. impend	85. drudgery
11. boorish	36. subtle	61. preemptory	86. reproof
12. condescend	37. clandestine	62. doleful	87. reprieve
13. clamor	38. austere	63. aloof	88. listless
14. singular	39. remonstrate	64. tedious	89. wan
15. placid	40. stolid	65. tangible	90. morose
16. incredulous	41. audible	66. magnanimous	91. physiognomy
17. tremulous	42. somber	67. indolent	92. dissipate
18. odious	43. prostrate	68. retort	93. ignominy
19. visage	44. vex	69. inexorable	94. malevolence
20. venerate	45. abyss	70. benevolence	95. abash
21. amiable	46. pervade	71. procure	96. felicity
22. vivid	47. sallow	72. expostulate	97. jovial
23. sagacity	48. genial	73. ostentatious	98. affable
24. vulgar	49. portent	74. obsequious	99. oppress
25. melancholy	50. torpid	75. eccentric	100. fain

Middle School Students

1. drastic
2. enchanted
3. gallows
4. retrieve
5. appellation
6. expedient
7. rectory
8. hamlet
9. apothecary
10. infusion
11. transcribe
12. vexed
13. melancholy
14. frugal
15. tenacious
16. rueful
17. decisive
18. innocuous
19. disoriented
20. furtive
21. incredulous
22. formidable
23. unrelenting
24. repose
25. disdain

26. sheepish
27. strident
28. ostentatious
29. abated
30. plucky
31. incantation
32. guffaw
33. garb
34. copious
35. pate
36. wistful
37. recluse
38. meddlesome
39. miserly
40. wrench
41. dappled
42. bewildered
43. wrathful
44. fanciful
45. singular
(meaning *odd*)
46. apprehension
47. scoff
48. cataract
49. reverence
50. whence

51. disposition
52. serviceable
53. mournful
54. bestow
55. malice
56. communion
57. console
58. wrought
59. naught
60. conjecture
61. precipice
62. endeavor
63. irksome
64. iridescent
65. allure
66. contrive
67. barbarity
68. henceforth
69. tyrant
70. wretched
71. entreat
72. suffer (meaning *allow*)
73. fruitless
74. apparatus
75. merciless

76. recollection
77. loathe
78. revive
79. inclination
80. tranquility
81. massacre
82. endure
83. impending
84. torment
85. elude
86. agitation
87. inscription
88. perseverance
89. invigorate
90. anguish
91. persecutor
92. encompass
93. surpass
94. paramount
95. borne
96. fleeting
97. unbounded
98. remorse
99. lapse
100. concealment

Using the Lists For Differentiating Reading Instruction

As you can see, many of your students will already know the meanings of many of these words. Even so, they can use their knowledge of the words to deepen their understanding of what they read. Instruct students to identify words that they already know, as well as a few others that they are unsure of or would like to know. Then, have them be on the lookout for these words in their classic. (If they can't find any of these words, which is unlikely, then they should "share" someone else's book to find a word; if all else fails, they should nominate another word as an "honorary" classic word.) Now, for the reading comprehension piece, have students explain the power of this particular word in its context. Would a synonym have exactly the same flavor? What would we have to substitute if this word did not exist? How would that change the sentence in meaning? implication? sound? rhythm? A single word can open the door to a lot of meaning in a text.

Encourage students to be neutral about the number of words that they already know or don't know on the classics list. Even if they "know" all or most of them already, they can still use the words in different forms, identify relatives, use the word in their own language, or find the etymology of the word. And if they know only a few, they can still use what they know about words to learn more words. The idea is simply to learn more about words, from wherever the student's starting point is.

Raise awareness about the literary quality of words: some words are seldom used anymore in modern spoken language. They've gone out of style. Why? Are these words for nouns, such as *rapier*, that we seldom speak of? Are they words with a formal, legalistic tone, such as *henceforth*? What is the effect of these words on the reader? Do they invite you in or keep you out?

Free Choice Reading

An effective literacy promotion program also includes free choice reading. What the research tells us is that when it comes to improving reading fluency, stamina, speed, and comprehension, *quanity counts.* In his article, "Improving the Reading Skills of Adolescents"(Educational Leadership, October 1999), John H. Holloway cites a 1996 study by Nancy Collins. Collins determined three characteristics of adolescents who are deficient readers: poor motivation, lack of experience, and egocentricity.

Motivation comes out of having an interest in content and learning for its own sake. Motivation tends to attenuate in the middle school years, but teachers can sometimes breathe life into the dying reader by finding connections between reading and real life. That's where free choice reading and differentiated instruction comes in. When students are invited to read whatever they want for given periods of time, and when they can find their own ways to show what they know, then we have a fighting chance to keep them in the reading game.

Nancy Farnan (1996) concludes from her studies of middle school readers that reading skills will thrive under the following conditions:

♦ literature leaves lasting impressions

♦ students learn to monitor their own understanding, reread accordingly, and apply strategies based on their own effective learning styles

♦ students read to learn more about themselves and others, reading from a variety of sources

♦ students view reading as an enjoyable experience

All of this speaks to the importance of wide availability of all kinds of reading material, especially material that is easily accessible, contemporary, personalized, and adolescent-centered. That means Young Adult (YA) literature, but also magazines, and, yes, tabloids.

Getting kids to love reading may not be for the faint of heart.

Ten Effective Schoolwide Reading Initiatives

1. Make it possible for kids to own books: Book ownership makes a big difference in how kids feel about reading. Have book clubs and book exchanges. Get grants to put money in kids' pockets for a shopping spree at a well-stocked bookstore.

2. Show kids that the adults in their school value reading: if you have your nose in a book when the class files in, someone is bound to ask you what you are reading. Take it from there.

3. Ritualize reading: Set aside time for schoolwide sustained silent reading. Some places call this DEAR, for "drop everything and read." Another effective program is "Get Caught Reading," sponsored by the American Association of Publishers.

4. Read aloud to kids. Teenagers are not too old or too sophisticated to be read to. They need to hear the dialect and rhythm of literature.

5. Include reading for pleasure in all classes—reading isn't just for English class. One of the loudest, most persistent laments of content-area teachers is that "these kids can't read," yet many, if not most, content-area teachers don't think of themselves as reading teachers.

6. Use every possible media opportunity to promote reading: Make book reviews a part of morning announcements, bulletin board displays in the halls, newsletters, and school newspapers. Get your local newspaper to run a column of book reviews written by students.

7. Institutionalize reading conversation: Use small group conversation as an alternative assessment to the written book report or book test.

8. Keep plenty of high-interest reading materials around: Do whatever you can to bring kids together with the kinds of materials they'd like to read.

9. Have the big kids read to the little kids. Hook up with an elementary school teacher and invite her class to visit yours for a reading session now and then.

10. Train teachers in the importance of reading: Reading is not a fad. All teachers need to understand modern reading theory and the role that not only reading, but language in general, plays in learning their subject area. Teachers who believe that reading is a distraction, rather than a boost, to their classroom procedures need to be exposed to the research that consistently shows otherwise. For example, a well-respected and replicated study done in 1996 by the National Association of Secondary Principals reveals that 40 percent of the errors on mathematics exams are reading errors.

We don't have to choose between the classics and free choice. The free choice reading, for those with reading deficits, makes possible the skills— fluency, speed, stamina, flexibility—that will enable the reading of more demanding material.

Neuroscientists and neurolinguists like Stephen Pinker tell us that whereas language is instinctive, reading is not. Reading is learned. It comes from the language center of the brain, but there is no "reading center" per se in the brain. The richer the person's language, the more possible it will be to learn to read and to want to read.

Reflection

1. What does your school do to promote recreational reading? What could you do more of? How might you make more reading happen in your school?

2. What is your opinion about reading the classics versus free choice reading?

3. Do some research into the following programs: Get Caught Reading (American Association of Publishers), DEAR (Drop Everything and Read), and Junior Great Books.

4. What is your opinion about including children's books in the list of classics?

5. What is your opinion about including historical documents in the list of classics?

6

Differentiating Instruction for Learning New Words

Consider the role of learning new words in your subject:

♦ How many new words will your students encounter in a given day? week? month?

♦ What are the built-in systems of reinforcing these new words? How are the words repeated and revisited?

♦ What opportunities do you provide for students to manipulate and use these new words?

The achievement gap is a language gap. The language gap is a vocabulary gap. This chapter shows you how to differentiate instruction in vocabulary, based on sound pedagogy. We learn vocabulary most effectively when:

♦ New words are repeated, reviewed, revisited.

♦ New words are presented in meaningful contexts.

♦ New words are modeled enthusiastically.

♦ New words are used in various forms.

♦ New words are connected to word families.

♦ Students have opportunities to practice new words.

Three Categories of Vocabulary

Words that students need to learn may be divided into three categories: *vernacular, academic, subject-specific.* To effectively improve our students' language, we need to work on all three areas simultaneously. We don't learn one word at a time. Words are always learned in context. They may be *taught* in isolation, as on a "vocabulary list," but unless they are learned in a real (live) context, they will remain outside the students' lexicon like an uninvited party guest.

Vernacular

We all lament the paucity of our students' vernacular. That is to say, we shake our heads in disappointment that they don't know the meaning of *lament* or *paucity* in the previous sentence. Maybe they "got it right" on last Friday's vocabulary quiz in English class, but that doesn't mean that they "know" it in the sense that they can use it. After all, they might not hear it anyplace else but in English class, and even then, they may never be hearing it in a real context, but only in the vocabulary exercises, which may only be in written form. They may never even hear the words *lament* and *paucity* pronounced. Talk about a paucity of instruction!

When Liz Daniels, who teaches social studies, decided to get serious about improving her students' vocabulary, she went around to the English teachers of her ninth-grade students and picked up their vocabulary lists. She chose 50 words that she thought fit well into her own speech when she spoke about social studies. Calling these 50 words "The Hot List," she posted them in her classroom. And then she used them in the course of her teaching. She encouraged her students to use them. She kept them posted. She rewarded students for using these words (correctly and naturally) in their essays. Liz's list (see Figure 6.1) was realistic, practical, and limited to 50 words.

Figure 6.1. The Hot List

abhorrent	animus	apogee	benevolent	bilateral
cadence	carnage	chronicle	comportment	contiguous
cudgel	diatribe	dichotomy	effusion	equivocate
epithet	forego	genesis	hierarchy	invective
lament	magnate	malevolent	nexus	nefarious
omnipotent	paucity	polyglot	recant	replete (with)
renounce	rectify	supplicate	synergy	syndrome
superfluous	supersede	subjugate	symposium	tenacious
transpose	transient	truculent	urbane	unilateral
vacuous	vivacious	vociferous	xenophobia	zenith

Liz believed that if her students expanded their vernacular, they would be better thinkers in social studies. We can consider this to be differentiated instruction because:

♦ Students integrate the words into their own vocabulary at their own pace.
♦ Students have opportunities to learn the words via various learning styles. They have the auditory reinforcement of the words as they hear Liz and their peers use them in context; they have the visual reinforcement of the words because they are posted; they have the so-

cial interaction with their peers and teacher as the words are used; and they write the words in their notes and essays.

♦ Advanced learners in the ninth grade can use the Hot List in challenging ways: variant forms, sophisticated sentences, or words with the same root. Average and needier learners in the ninth grade should be able to grab onto at least some of these words and will benefit from the reinforcement of the words that they are expected to know in English class.

♦ The Hot List is useful to all speakers, regardless of dialect and language style.

Academic

Now we come to academic vocabulary. By this, we mean those words that are useful in the kind of language that we use across the curriculum. These words fall into two categories: *connectors* and *anchors*.

Connectors are words that allow us to show comparison or contrast, link cause to effect, justify an assertion, and give examples. Here are some connectors:

therefore	thus
whereas	because
hence	consequently
following	consisting (of)
comprise (ed, ing)	except
however	even though
although	

Although these words are already in the students' vocabulary, the students don't necessarily call them into service effectively. Connectors are tools for thinking. As with any tool, the user needs to learn how to wield these tools, and to choose the right one for a given purpose.

Anchors are those words that appear again and again in academic discourse. Like connectors, anchors are likely to already be in the students' vocabulary, but students need some training in their use. Most anchors are words with a Latin root. When we learn a word with a Latin root, we have the perfect opportunity to learn other words with that root. Lengthy lists of Latinate words and roots are easily found. Figure 6.2 presents a brief list of twenty common words that can open doors to greater word-learning and deeper thinking.

Figure 6.2. Common Words with Latin Roots

Word	Root	Relatives
agent act	agere: to act, do, drive	activate, inactive, exact, inexact, react, trans-act,actual, agent
incident	cadere: to fall also cad, cas, cid	accident, casualty, cadaver, deciduous, case, coincidence, coincide, occasion
receive	capere: to seize, lay hold of, contain	deceive, conceive, perceive, deception, con-ception, reception, perception. accept, except
conclude	claudere: to shut, close	exclude, preclude, include, enclose, seclude
essence	esse: to be, exist	absent, consent, resent, essential, quintessen-tial, assent, present, represent, presence
facet	facere: to make, to do	factory, manufacture, faculty, facility, affect, effect, perfect
infer	fer: to bring, to bear	defer, refer, transfer, proliferate, prefer, suffer
fluid	fluere: to flow	influence, confluence, affluent, superfluous, flush
reform	forma: shape	deform, conform, formal, informal, informa-tion, transform
general	genus: race, kind	gene, generalize, genesis, generic, regenerate, degenerate
progress	grad, gress: to step	congress, digress, regress, transgress, aggres-sive, grade, gradient, degrade, graduate, gradual, retrograde
report	port: to carry	deport, portable, portal, purport, important, opportunity, comportment, import, export, porter, rapport, transport
appeal	pel: to drive	repel, compel, impel, dispel, expel, propel, re-peal, pulse
emit	mittere: to sendmise, miss, mit, mitt	remit, commission, commit, admit, compro-mise, permission, omit, unremitting, transmit, surmise, submit
isolate	insula: islandsol, sula	insulate, island, insular, peninsula
elevate	levare: to lighten, to lift	levity, leaven, relevant, irrelevant, lever, le-verage
legislate	leg, lex: law	legitimate, legislative, privilege, legal, paralegal
temporary	tempus: time	contemporary, extemporaneous
descend	scandere: to climb, to leap scen, scend	condescend, ascend, descendant, ascendancy, transcend

Academic language is anchored in Latinate words, but ordinary speech is mostly Anglo-Saxon. That is to say, the novice needs to learn how to use Latinate words, whereas Anglo-Saxon words come naturally to the native speaker. The more comfortable one is in the academic world, the more easily one uses Latinate words. The good news is that Latinate words have so many relatives: linking new knowledge to prior knowledge is easy once we understand how words are related through roots and affixes.

To differentiate instruction based on this word theory, we can have students keep word cards with Latinate roots and add to the cards as they use new words. Students can color-code their Latinate roots in their notes and sentences. They can establish individual goals as to how many new Latinate words they intend to use in a given semester.

Understanding how Latinate words work (prefix, root, suffix) can make spelling much easier for those who learn by rules. Unlike Anglo-Saxon and Greek words, which tend to have more unvoiced letters, Latinate words are phonetic. Their prefixes and suffixes conform to rules.

Subject-Specific Terminology

The third category, subject-specific terminology, consists of the technical terms that makes possible the communication of specialized information. Subject area teachers are in the business of giving this language away, training the novice in its use. Subject-specific terms come in two categories: technical terms that are not used anyplace else, and technical terms that have a different meaning in lay speech. In both categories, we are speaking not necessarily of individual words, but also of phrases. That is why we refer to subject-specific vocabulary as *terminology* or *terms* rather than *words*.

In the first category are terms such as photosynthesis, divine right of kings, Methodism, isotherm, algorithm, radioactivity, osmosis, and metaphor. Many of these terms have Greek or Latin roots, and the learner can find relatives from which to make hypotheses. In the second category are words that have another meaning in lay speech, such as culture, diffusion, offensive, restoration. Such terms offer the teachable moment for showing how words change and adapt to context.

Consider the difference between teaching technical vocabulary and teaching lay vocabulary:

Technical Vocabulary Teaching	Lay Vocabulary Teaching
The meaning of the word is the theme of the lesson. We can't teach a word such as photosynthesis through context. The learners don't yet have a context, because the concept is unfamiliar.	The concept of the word is already familiar. The new word is a refinement or a renaming of what we already know. When we teach a word such as sojourn, we already know what its concept means. We are learning a new name for known information.
The word probably does not have a synonym, and is rigid in its meaning.	The word probably does have a synonym, and much flexibility.
The word is probably part of a cluster: chlorophyll, chloroplast, blastocyst.	The word may or may not be part of a cluster.
The word probably has a stable meaning.	The word probably has a meaning that is nuanced by context and purpose.

Traditional Vocabulary Teaching: English Class

For years, Judy Evans taught vocabulary to high school students using a workbook. The workbook was divided into chapters and units, with each chapter presenting a list of 25 unrelated words and definitions. On Monday, Judy pronounced the words for the students and had them read the definitions aloud. Monday, Tuesday, and Wednesday night's homework was to fill in the exercises in the workbook—sentence blanks and matching, analogies. Every class would begin with a brief vocabulary review of last night's homework. On Friday there would be a test on the week's words; every few weeks there would be a cumulative test.

Ellen Bloom used vocabulary taken from readings. She would write a list of words on the board that students would supposedly be encountering in their assigned reading. Students were required to write dictionary definitions of these words, compose original sentences using those words, and know the words for the unit test on the assigned reading.

Judy and Ellen found no surprises in their students' performance on their vocabulary tests: good students usually did well; weak students usually did poorly. One thing was certain: no one was really improving their vocabulary in speech or writing because there was little to no crossover between the words the students studied and the words they used.

After some training in differentiating instruction, Judy and Ellen improved their vocabulary instruction. That is to say, their students began showing an interest in the words, using them in speech and writing, and remembering them.

Judy wanted to hold on to her vocabulary workbook. She liked the built-in reinforcement and homework. She knew that students would have to spend more time with the words, but she couldn't spare more class time and didn't want more paperwork for herself. Ellen wanted to continue to use words encountered in the literature. Like Judy, she didn't want to devote more class time to vocabulary instruction. Here is how Judy and Ellen used the pedagogy of differentiated instruction to make vocabulary instruction more robust and durable:

- *Less is more:* Judy asked students to pick out 10 of the 25 words in each chapter to learn for the week. She suggested that they select words that they had heard of, but never actually used. Ellen asked students to scan the literature on the lookout for 10 "interesting" words. Students then used sticky flags to mark these words.

- *Context:* A dictionary or glossary definition is bloodless. A word has to breathe, stretch, and jump around in real time. Judy and Ellen made a conscious effort to teach vocabulary just by using the words and encouraging kids to use them. They reminded kids whenever a "word opportunity" came up in their speech. Those words were written on the board, just waiting to be pressed into service. Doing this, they used the words metaphorically, in various grammatical situations, in various forms. They also asked for "word sightings," times in which "our words" were heard in other classes, on television, or in the movies.

- *Visuals:* Instead of doing matching columns, Judy's students were asked to draw pictures in their notebooks to represent the words, especially the nouns. She would spend just a few minutes at the start of class having students draw their diagrams on the board or post them in the vocabulary center

- *Vocabulary Center:* In a prominent place in the classroom, Judy and Ellen set up posters, visuals, model sentences, and other displays to remind students of their words.

- *Personalizing:* Judy and Ellen asked students to write brief statements about their own lives, incorporating the new words.

- *Storytelling:* Judy and Ellen had students retell familiar stories and fairy tales, using the words that they were learning.

Levels of "Word Knowing"

- I use this word in my speech and writing
- I know what this word means, but I've never used it myself.
- I've heard of this word, I have some idea what it means,

- and I'm interested in it
- but I'm not interested in it.
  ◆ I've never heard of this word,
  - but I'm interested in it.
  - and I'm not interested in it.

Exercises that can deepen students' knowledge of words include: sorting lists of words and deciding upon the categories; making semantic maps with lists either provided by the teacher or generated by the learners; generating derivatives, inflections, synonyms and antonyms of a word; making trees that show the relationships between superordinates, coordinates, and specific examples; identifying or generating associated words; combining phrases from several columns; matching parts of collocations using two columns; and completing

Three Ways to Learn New Words

The work of Allan Hunt and David Beglar divides vocabulary learning into three categories:

1. *Incidental learning:* Incidental learning of new words happens when students are exposed to extensive reading and listening to language at their instructional level. Teachers can support incidental learning by making it a habit to elevate their language level by defining words in context when speaking to students.

2. *Explicit instruction:* Explicit instruction happens when teachers present and analyze new words for students, helping them to understand etymology, suffixes and prefixes. Explicit instruction involves expanding on a dictionary definition by assisting students with using the word in context in its different forms, providing practice in usage and pronunciation, and building a learning environment in which new words are nurtured.

3. *Independent strategy development:* Independent strategy development should be the goal of explicit instruction, in which students learn how to learn new words through contextual clues, dictionary and glossary use, etymology, and maximizing personal learning styles such as visualization, memorization, and categorization.

Effective vocabulary instruction for native speakers involves the interweaving of these three pathways. This means that teachers exploit teachable moments to teach word roots, synonyms, antonyms, and nuances as new words appear in context. Many teachers do this by reading aloud, stopping along the way to teach what is likely to be a new word to most students. Even high school students can benefit from more sophisticated dictionary training, focusing on secondary definitions, grammatical notations (such as whether a verb is transitive or intransitive and what that means in terms of how the verb is used in a sentence), and etymology.

Remember that vocabulary teaching involves not only words, but also phrases and figures of speech and common expressions and metaphors. To enrich your students' vocabulary, expand your concept of what a *word* is.

What follows are adaptations of the principles of word-learning proposed by Hunt and Beglar:

- Incidental learning of new words is all about exposure: Read, read, read. The more students read, no matter what they read, the more they are building stamina and fluency. Even if they choose to read low-level materials, they are still incidentally learning much about language structure, spelling, syntax, suffixes, prefixes, and word roots.

- Concentrate on high-frequency words: When giving explicit instruction, use your common sense and word experience to prioritize words. What words are students most likely to use, hear, and read? Remember that even though students may be able to deliver a dictionary definition of a word, they may not tend to use that word in their own vocabulary. Such words are worthy of explicit instruction, because the idea is to expand the students' actual deployment of more words.

- Nurture new words: We need to provide opportunities and reminders for students to use new words purposefully. Although incidental (contextual) learning is the most natural and effective way to learn new words, we can expand our students' word knowledge by explicit instruction. Explicit word-teaching is most effective when the word is used in meaningful contexts; it is least effective when words are isolated, such as on a matching column. Giving students isolated words does not show them how to fit the word grammatically into a sentence, how to change its form, or how its meaning is shaded.

  If you are using a list, ask students to make cards for each word. That way, they can arrange the cards in an order that best suits their needs. The process of sorting and categorizing is itself instructional. To differentiate instruction, students can add information to the cards, such as synonyms, antonyms, etymological information, related words, mnemonic devices. etc.

  The paradox of word-learning is that the best way to improve vocabulary is by exposure to reading and listening, but the learner needs a certain level of language in order to understand what she's reading or hearing in the first place. Thus, we need to supplement incidental learning with explicit teaching. This paradox is especially applicable to English language learners.

- Be deliberate in how you cluster words: Learning one word is an opportunity to learn its family and friends. Present words in clusters based on semantics (synonyms, antonyms), etymology (prefixes, suffixes, roots), If words are similar in form but semantically unrelated, it can be confusing to learn them together. This is the danger of teaching words alphabetically: just because words look alike doesn't mean that they are semantically similar, although very often there is a relation between look-alike words.

♦ It's best to learn a few words thoroughly over time than to try to learn many words over a short spurt of time. The largest window of forgetting happens just after new information is learned. Deeper mental processing and retention are more likely to take place if you practice repetition and review of fewer words. Try teaching 5 to 7 words per week rather than 20 to 30. To get more mileage out of the 5 to 7 words, teach them along with related words.

♦ Provide opportunities for elaborating on word knowledge: Knowing a word means a great deal more than just being able to recite its dictionary definition. To know a word, you have to know its guises: How can it be adapted to fit different grammatical forms? What affixes does it take? You have to know its neighborhood, where it hangs out: What are its connotations? associations? nuances? We speak of receptive knowledge, i.e., being able to recognize the word when it is used by others, and of productive knowledge, i.e., using the word in one's own speech and writing. The latter requires a deeper understanding and more practice than the former. Teaching a word for deep understanding means providing opportunities for practice, placing the word in original contexts, using the word both literally and figuratively. Is this a word that is likely to be found in ordinary speech or is it a technical term? Does this word carry emotional baggage or is it neutral? How fixed or flexible is its definition?

♦ Work toward fluency: To work toward fluency with new words, we need to integrate the new with the known vocabulary. Where will the new words find a place in one's own language? Conversational practice is essential. Here, again, extensive reading and listening to elevated vocabulary in meaningful contexts works toward fluency. Fluent readers don't read individual words, but groups of words—a habit that can be learned and practiced. One effective way to improve reading fluency is timed readings: readers practice timed reading on passages that they have already read, increasing their speed with each reading and monitoring their reading techniques as the do so.

♦ Learning to guess: Strategic guessing at the meaning of unfamiliar words is an independent reading strategy. However, to guess from context, the learner has to already know 95 percent of the words. We can't expect a student who is reading above her head to be very good at guessing through context. SAT scores attest to this. Guessing from context is more effective for the high-level student, and this is something to remember as we differentiate vocabulary instruction.

The following is a procedure for guessing from context. First, decide whether the word is important enough to learn: is it repeated? does it seem essential to meaning? This decision itself is a reading skill. Then, determine the function of the word in the sentence: What is its grammatical job? Then, simplify the sentence by bracketing unnecessary words. Then, examine the immediate vicinity of the word. At this point, make an educated guess as to the meaning of the word and check with a dictionary, glossary, or, better yet, the teacher. Be sure that the guess is in the same part of speech as the target word. Use affixes as clues. This strategy is best when used instructionally, i.e., demonstrated by the teacher. Teachers provide richer and more memorable definitions than dictionaries.

◆ Learning to use dictionaries and glossaries: Don't assume that kids can already do this effectively. Chances are, your neediest learners are just grabbing the first definition and copying or memorizing it verbatim. Chances are they are not using the grammatical or etymological information at all. Although using a dictionary is not the best way to achieve deep understanding of a word, there are times when we need to look up words. Students with language deficiencies benefit from electronic dictionaries with multimedia annotations. It's a lot easier to use a computerized dictionary than a paper one if you're already at the word processor or on-line. *The New Oxford Picture Dictionary CD-ROM (1997)* links entries to visual images. One of the most important dictionary skills, especially for language-deficient learners is knowing how to check the word's original context carefully to make sure that the correct entry for that context has been chosen.

Teachers need to plan a wide array of activities, exercises, conversational contexts, and reinforcements in order to effectively teach students to learn new words. The instructional plan must embrace incidental learning, explicit instruction, and independent learning strategies. Vocabulary learning must be contextual, enthusiastic, purposeful, and gradual if it is to be lasting. Students need to read and listen extensively, elaborate, connect, guess from context, use dictionaries efficiently and thoroughly, and have lavish opportunities for practice with their new words.

Assessment: Beyond the Vocabulary Quiz

Ben Trellised gives every kid in his English classes their own vocabulary quiz, based on the words they decided to learn. Does he go home and make up 112 different quizzes? No. All he does is give the kids a sheet that has ten blank spaces on the left hand side, with ten blank spaces corresponding on the right hand side. The day before the quiz, Ben's students write down the words that they want to be quizzed on. They write these words down the left hand column. They've taken these words from their readings in the literature or from the newspaper. The next day, he hands them back their own quizzes, and has them fill in definitions in the right hand column.

Ben's students keep a vocabulary journal. They select a certain number of words per week. Each word is written in the center of their journal page. The page is then filled in with definitions, related words, roots and affixes, other forms of the word, original sentences and phrases, synonyms, and antonyms.

Exploiting Context

Rave Beirut's way of teaching vocabulary is to make the most of what students already know, using the book, *A Way With Words*. Here is a sample from this book:

The Emperor's New Vestments

Words You Will Meet:

despotic	autocratic
narcissistic	garb
exigencies	mundane

Paragraph 1:

> Once upon a time, there lived a *despotic* and *autocratic* Emperor who had a *narcissistic* streak a mile wide. So taken was he with symbolic *garb* that he scarcely had time to tend to the *exigencies* of the *mundane* tasks of running a kingdom.

Learn and Remember

Vestments is a formal, literary and archaic word meaning *clothing*. We say *vestments* instead of *clothing* when referring to ceremonial robes, headdresses, and other symbolic *garb*. What are some occasions when vestments are worn?

Despotic and *autocratic* both mean *ruling like a monarch; domineering; bossy; tyrannical*. In history class, you will learn about the *benevolent despots* of the Age of Enlightenment, who ruled less autocratically. Who was one of the benevolent despots?

Narcissistic means *self-infatuated, loving oneself (especially one's appearance) excessively, extremely egotistical*. A narcissistic person is a narcissist. This word comes from Greek mythology: Narcissus was an egotistical young man who liked to admire himself in the water's reflection. He was turned into a flower (called the narcissus), which grows by the waterside. What is the story of Narcissus and Echo?

Exigencies are *pressing needs, chores, demands.* Another word for *exigencies* is *vicissitudes.* What are the vicissitudes of running a kingdom?

Mundane means *ordinary, everyday, unexciting.* In French, the word *la monde* means world. Thus, *mundane* means *of the world,* or *ordinary.* What is the word for *world* in Spanish? Italian?

Practice

1. Would a candidate for the Presidency of the United States boast that she intended to be autocratic?

2. Would a narcissistic person carry a mirror in her purse?

3. Would you want to hire a person who paid attention to daily exigencies?

4. What kind of garb world you wear to your graduation from college?

5. Would travel agencies feature brochures of mundane places?

6. When your mother picks up your socks from the bathroom floor, is she doing something that is *autocratic, narcissistic,* or *mundane?*

7. Would you consider doing homework one of the *exigencies* of your life?

8. Sylvia is searching for Mr. Wonderful in the personal ads. Would any of the words in this section attract her?

9. Father Joseph is donning his vestments for Saturday evening mass. What do you picture him doing?

Picture the Words

Draw a picture of:

Audrey the Autocrat	Dave the Despot
Norman the Narcissist	Vincent the Vestment Vendor

Reflection

What are all of the learning styles that come into play in *A Way With Words*?

Other Word-Learning Performance Tasks

Building a Glossary

Arah Nachum has students build a glossary in their notebooks. Students are given a list of 100 words, from which they are to select 20 each quarter. Arah suggests that they select words that they have heard of, but the meanings of which they are not certain. To further differentiate, he uses three lists in increasing order of sophistication. Arah has arranged these three lists so that they don't appear obviously leveled: The "easiest" list doesn't necessarily contain short words, nor does the most sophisticated list contain polysyllabic words.

In their glossaries, students must do five things with each word: *define, describe, explain, exemplify,* and *expand.*

- *Define:* Write a dictionary definition in your own words
- *Describe:* Use words that give a visual image that help you understand the word
- *Explain:* Use words that give more information about how this word is used
- *Exemplify:* Use the word in a meaningful sentence that clearly expresses its meaning.
- *Expand:* Give several forms of this word

Juicy Sentences

Tim McMillan grew frustrated with the empty sentences that his students would deliver when asked to use their new words in a sentence. Here is how he instructs students to write meaningful sentences:

Please save these directions for future reference.

This week's writing task is to write 10 (juicy) sentences that feature vocabulary from our literature. Your sentences should be written according to the following specifications:

- *Substance:* Each sentence must consist of at least 20 words.
- *Context:* Each sentence must use one of our words in a natural-sounding context. Boldface the featured word. In another part of the sentence, use a synonym or brief definition. *Italicize this part.* Do not just "stick in" the synonym/brief definition in a redundant way. Work it into the natural context of meaning. Your sentence may or may not be about the literature that we are reading.
- *Action:* Your sentence should tell a story. It should have action verbs and descriptive detail.

- *Grammatical Principles:* In any two sentences, feature the grammatical principles that we have learned and identify them. For example, one of your sentences could demonstrate your understanding of the use of who/whom and another could demonstrate your understanding of parallel structure. Asterisk these two sentences and write the grammatical principle (briefly) in parentheses after the sentence.
- *Format:* Double space (or 1.5 space); number all sentences

Example

Note how the synonym or definition is in the same part of speech as the key word:

> Claude Frollo, who secretly studied alchemy, scrutinized the portal of Notre Dame, thinking that the secret of turning base metal into gold was encoded in the intricate carvings on its *great door.* (comma to set off nonessential element) (who/whom).

> He glowered at me as if I'd just spilled hot coffee all over his laptop and knocked folders out of his hands, so I *frowned* back. (parallel structure).

Clustering

Clustering is a technique in which you consider how words are alike and different. From the word list, form several categories, each consisting of at least five words. Use your imagination to form the categories: connotation (positive, negative, neutral), parts of speech, structure, visuals/non-visuals, etc. Not all of the words in the group have to fit into your categories. Feel free to change the form of the words. You may have a few leftovers.

Spelling

Spelling comes into the conversation about vocabulary for two reasons: the spelling of a word gives us clues to its meaning, and we are more likely to use a word in writing if we are confident about its spelling. But like the weather, spelling is one of those things that everybody talks about, but nobody does much about it. Don't we all expect kids to "already know how to spell" by the time we get them?

If you're not an English teacher, you may say, when asked, that "spelling doesn't count," but it's got to distract you when kids butcher key terms in your subject area. To know a word is to know how to spell it. Anyone can overlook a minor spelling lapse, especially of a tricky word. But gross and persistent spelling errors diminish credibility and distract from the writer's purpose.

What do you hear when you bring up the subject of teaching spelling? That some people just can't spell to save their lives. That kids should have learned how to spell long ago. "Forget it, it's too late now." "Whatever happened to the Friday spelling test?" That spelling isn't important anymore now that we have spellcheckers. That we need to be interested in "higher-level thinking" rather than something so mundane and beneath us as spelling. Yet, spelling is one of the strongest outward signs of literacy. And the public expects the educated person to be a reasonably good speller, especially of the terms that one uses most in one's trade.

Actually, spelling is one of the most teachable skills, and one of the easiest to differentiate instruction for. Mirroring its diverse speakers, English is a complex, amalgamated language. It is much more systematic and predictable than we give it credit for. In the following materials, I address two myths of spelling instruction: that English is a crazy language, and that you can't teach a bad speller.

The following are various ways to improve spelling:

- *Intellectualizing:* "I need to know why." Contrary to belief, the English language is largely sensible if you know how to group words. People who learn by intellectualizing should learn the rules of dropping and doubling letters. They should also learn patterns and groupings, for example, that *ght* words are Anglo Saxon in derivation, whereas words with a "y" as the second letter are Greek. Teach intellectualizers how to use the etymological information in the dictionary to understand more about the *why* of spelling. Think of words as the archeologist would: a word's history gives clues to its construction. Prefixes are simply tacked on to the beginning of a word, whereas suffixes are added in accordance with certain fairly reliable rules.

- *Repetition:* "I need to go over and over it." Learners with a strong musical sense can learn to spell through finding the rhythm of the words. This involves spelling the words out loud, in groups, and tapping out the rhythm. Mnemonics often rely on rhythm, such as "Climb the ladder of success: s-u-c-c-e-s-s."

- *Kinesthetics:* "I need to know it in my hands." "Air writing" works well for many learners. Many people can't spell in their heads. They need to actually write the word, either on paper or in the air. Perhaps this is a combination of the kinesthetic and the visual.

- *Visuals:* "I need to see it."Most people are strong visual learners. Posting words around the room is a powerful reinforcer. Some people visually exaggerate the danger zone of the word.

- *Multisensory combinations:* "I need the whole body spelling experience." The see-say-write method has proven useful for special education students.

Learning to spell is all about metacognition: learning how to learn. Effective lessons are ongoing, integrated, exploitative of the teachable moment, and enthusiastic. But whatever you do to teach spelling, please don't ever present the misspelled word next to the correct word and ask the student which one is correct. What that does is to reinforce the negative, tricking the brain into thinking that wrong is right. Never take the chance that the learner's brain won't decide to latch on to the misspelled word, taking the incorrect mental snapshot.

Reflection

In social studies, vocabulary is often referred to as "Terms To Know." How would you use the ideas in this chapter to differentiate vocabulary instruction for the following terms:

- usurp
- industrialization
- natural resource
- coup d'etat
- Divine Right of Kings
- legacy
- merchant class
- heresy
- city-state
- exploitation

1. What can students learn about words from the dictionary? Establish a continuum from basic to complex showing how to differentiate instruction for dictionary use.

2. Explain how and why any of the ideas in this chapter will change the way students learn new words in your class.

3. Add other strategies for differentiating vocabulary instruction.

4. How could you use the following gimmicks to stimulate interest in word-learning:

- ice cream sticks
- a beach ball with velcro strips
- a deck of cards
- construction paper
- colored markers
- small assignment pads
- index cards

7

Differentiating Instruction Through the Arts

Any discussion of differentiated instruction, learning styles, brain-based learning, multicultural education, educating for social justice, and multiple forms of intelligence must include the arts. In her article entitled "Gaining the Arts Literacy Advantage" (Educational Leadership, October 1999), Laura Longley reminds us that the world we live in and are creating for the future is

> ...beyond global. More Complex. Faster. Ambiguous. Visual. Virtual...Tomorrow's world will demand a quick mind. Focus. Discipline. Imagination. Grasp of the big picture. Attention to detail. Teamwork. Knowing good work from bad...How will we educate our students to thrive in such a world? Through the arts.

Technical proficiency does not suffice to build leaders and people adaptable to change. The young people that we graduate need divergent and convergent thinking. When they learn the arts, they think verbally and nonverbally, symbolically and literally.

Integrated arts education has brain-based learning research behind it. It is through multisensory experience that we remember things, make them real. Through the arts, we can assess students in multiple ways, accommodating diverse learning needs. Through the arts, we make connections, remember what we've learned, extend our thinking. The arts teach us not only how to communicate complex ideas, but also how to formulate them.

Here are descriptions of what various districts are doing to integrate the arts to differentiate instruction:[1]

- ◆ Las Cruces, New Mexico: Bonnie Hosie is an elementary visual arts teacher. When she wanted to teach kindergarten children about the color wheel, she had them mix colors in finger paint. She tells of one child's revelation when, looking at his orange hands, he "got it!": red

---

1 Longley, Laura. "Gaining the Arts Literacy Advantage." *Educational Leadership*, October 1999.

and yellow actually and literally and miraculously *make orange!* She would see this little five-year-old look at his hands weeks later, remembering the color wheel. What a wondrous example this is of literally having learning in your own hands.

♦ Miami-Dade County, Florida: In a school district that integrates the arts into reading, writing, and mathematics learning strategies, fifth graders use a sketchbook/journal to work out their ideas. For example, the children went on a field trip to an art museum, where they viewed works related to the First and Second World Wars. This was in the context of a unit on conflict and resolution. The children then learned about conflict and resolution through interviews with adults, stories, and historical events. All the while, they used their sketchbook/journals to express what they thought about and what they knew. These sketchbooks were such a powerful artifact attesting to what children think about human relations, that the Wolfsonian museum actually purchased them and put them on display in its permanent collection!

♦ Milwaukee, Wisconsin: Twenty-five private and parochial schools and the Milwaukee Symphony Orchestra have an education partnership called Arts in Community Education (ACE). The partnership seeks to advance every student's learning through a series of culturally diverse arts presentations and experiences. These presentations and experiences center around a theme at each grade level, K–12. The program includes problem solving, science and the arts, the blending of cultural influences as seen in the arts, and local and global community-formation through the arts.

♦ Maine Township, Illinois: Park Ridge High School believes in the performing arts and creative writing. They offer a wide array of courses in speech, drama, broadcasting, creative writing, art, photography, and music. Here is what their curriculum guide says:

"[The arts] teach students where to look and what to look for in gathering support for an idea. They also help students learn to give, to accept, and to follow constructive criticism; listen courteously and critically as others speak; become more logical, more direct, and more creative in organizing thoughts for presentation; learn to control the fear of speaking of performing before an audience, and, as a result, become a more confident person. (President's Committee on the Arts, 1999, p. 61). At Park Ridge, they include the arts in their assessments of all seniors, requiring exit tests in one field.

Art is about big projects with a lot of moving parts: producing a play, presenting a concert or dance recital, constructing a visual arts portfolio, or writing a book. Such projects encompass emotional and intuitive as well as academic intelligence. Students involved in the arts learn about coherence, cause and effect, critical thinking, decision making, self-understanding, and communication with others.

Here are the comments of Hewlett-Packard's Doug Sessions after his visit to the new School for Arts and Academics in Vancouver, Washington:

> ...the interdisciplinary approach to instruction, the project-oriented focus, the sense that students are working in teams, collaborating, and, too, the high expectations in terms of the core subject areas, that's something that comes through. You know, you don't have to be here very long to see that there's an ethic of high performance. It's kind of an unusual place for Hewlett-Packard to look for math and science achievement, but the whole package is here. That's what we want. That's the way *our* employees work. (President's Committee on the Arts, 1999, p. 33).

The term "whole package" is the key to realizing the importance of integrating the arts into the school day. The arts bring in communication, culture, cognition, and creativity. This chapter suggests integration of the arts, not merely as an add-on after school programs or "enrichment" time in the arts. The arts have tremendous potential for maximizing learning in a differentiated classroom. The proven benefits of arts integration far outweigh budgetary objections. We need to prioritize what works.

Hendrick Hudson High School, where I am an English teacher, had an interdisciplinary arts program that worked like this: Two teachers, Paula Correale and Jennifer Morrissey, were assigned to four classes per day rather than the contractual five. With the extra period, they hooked up with teachers in various disciplines: science, English, social studies, and foreign language, and brought the arts into the subject area classrooms for special projects. One of these projects was:

♦ Illuminated manuscripts: My students were reading *The Hunchback of Notre Dame*. To fully appreciate this book, readers need a sense of the Gothic cathedral and the monastic lifestyle. My students spent three days in Paula's art classroom, where she and I gave them lecture and hands-on experience on the history of manuscript illumination. Students selected from the book a quotation that interested them. Then, having taking a vow of silence (that was the best part of this project), we cranked up the Gregorian chants and they expressed their quotation as an illuminated manuscript. One pleasant surprise was that the students had to use extreme care in the punctuation, spelling, and capitalization of their quotation. When the sentences were completed and displayed, Paula and I pointed out how characteristics of art such as motif, balance and symmetry, contrast, and subtlety also bear upon a well-crafted, sophisticated sentence, such as the ones they had selected from Hugo's masterpiece.

Other interdisciplinary projects were:
- ♦ Clay models of cellular structure
- ♦ Lectures on Spanish painters
- ♦ The Van Gogh Project
- ♦ Literary sock puppets

In addition to the obvious benefits of deepening students' understanding of academics, this collaboration has the hidden benefit of evoking creativity in teachers.

Eleven Ways to Facilitate Arts Integration

1. Do the research that shows the importance of the arts
2. Garner community support
3. Use that community support to educate the BOE and administration
4. Institute block scheduling
5. Write grants
6. Be prepared to show proven results
7. Connect the arts to social justice and violence prevention
8. Enlighten your school community about multiple intelligence theory
9. Showcase the arts
10. Hire teachers who have a background in the arts
11. Encourage, fund, and facilitate field trips to museums and concerts

It is through the arts that we make the emotional connections so important to learning. The arts offer opportunities for interdisciplinary problem solving, verbal and nonverbal communication, and socialization.

We know that healthy brains flourish in an environment rich with sensory input, beauty, and rhythm. The arts strengthen memory, critical thinking, and neurological synapses. The arts are manipulative, cognitive, emotional, and social. Creating a work of art requires decision making, revision, reflection, patience, knowledge of traditions, and technique. The artist needs to know physics, mathematics, and engineering. Through the arts, we travel, know other cultures, and understand the past and how it prologues the present. That which can't be expressed in words can be expressed through the arts.

Humor and the Arts

There's a reason why the words "humor" and "human" are sound-alikes. To the Greeks, "humours" of the body referred to various internal fluids. We don't have to go into detail here about these fluids and what each was associated with. We just have to think about how human it is to have humor, how essential humor is to being human.

The arts offer lavish opportunities to bring humor into the classroom. And the reason we should want to do so is simply this: levity enhances learning. Laughter promotes fellowship, reduces stress, and induces trust. It may even increase the body's production of neurotransmitters that sharpen alertness and memory. The following are some media or activities that integrate the arts with humor:

- Videos
- Role-playing
- Cartoons
- Satire
- Music
- Games

The ability to make people laugh is an intuitive blessing. People who are funny can't help being that way. It's their worldview that others find surprising, outrageous, ironic, incongruous. You can't order or assign students to be funny, but you can enable them to have fun and to learn through humor. Gary Larsson was a biology teacher. One way that he had of teaching biology was by making zany cartoons. These developed into *The Far Side*. All those amoebas and protozoans, those guys in lab coats bending over specimens, those multi-tentacled sea creatures struck Larsson as absurdly funny, given the right context.

Six Reasons to Bring the Arts to Your Classroom

1. The arts help students understand, remember, and construct information.
2. The arts are about science; science is about the arts.
3. The arts can be used to make academic information real for students.
4. The more interdisciplinary connections students can make, the better they will retain and value their learning.
5. The arts allow for multisensory learning.
6. The arts bring multicultural education to academics.

Advertising, Arts, and Academics

We should not overlook advertising as a hub for various art forms: poetry, music, visual arts, and drama. Advertising is accessible to students. It's their common cultural touchstone and we can exploit that common knowledge.

For example, consider slogans. Everyone knows that slogans are memorable and durable. When we learn history, we learn lots of slogans and metaphors that have poetic qualities: *Operation Desert Storm, Operation Infinite Justice, the Dust Bowl, the Cold War, the red scare, yellow journalism*, etc. Consider the connotations of the language in these slogans: America: Love It or Leave It; Fifty-Four Forty or Bust; The Buck Stops Here; It's Morning in America; Four More Years; etc.

What about slogans in science? Here are some examples: An object in motion tends to stay in motion; ontogeny recapitulates phylogeny; for every action, there is an equal and opposite reaction. We think of these as principles, and they are, but they are also slogans. We remember them because of their poetic qualities. Suppose students were to dramatize a science commercial ending with an voice-over of one of their slogans. Using props, dialogue that uses the language of science, and demonstrating a principle, they would not only be learning themselves but they would instill a memorable visual and auditory image in others.

How is using slogans to learn science or history a way of differentiating instruction? Use of slogans enables students to connect new knowledge to prior knowledge, making sense of the unfamiliar by means of the familiar. It validates the cultural capital that they bring to the classroom. Not everyone will do the same thing with the same information in the same way. That's differentiated instruction.

Sometimes we scoff at the demands that we "make learning fun." We get frustrated with this idea because we know that learning a complex body of information can't always be fun. We are teachers, not recreational directors. Besides, "fun" gets old fast, and then it's up to us to come up with more "fun." Meanwhile, there's a "Big Test" out there, and it isn't going to be any fun to take it. True enough. But that doesn't mean that we should trivialize the importance—the *educational* importance—of enlisting pop culture on the side of conveying information.

Advertising involves music. Music is memorable. We often remark that students who can't remember basic tenets of biology have no trouble with song lyrics. Maybe they could remember the steps in the process of cell division if they set it to the tune of a familiar song. In any case, the time spent trying to do that would be time spent in close contact with the information about the cell.

Reflection

1. Your students bring to your class a great deal of information based on advertising. How can you use this information to strengthen learning in your subject?

2. How do slogans play a part in learning in your subject? How can you make more use of slogans?

3. How do you already integrate the arts?

4. What are some ways in which you can strengthen learning in your subject by integrating arts education?

Arts and Critical Thinking

- Biographies, profiles, and obituaries of artists and musicians: Who or what influenced this artist? How was she both a maverick and a follower of artistic tradition? What professional risks and personal sacrifices did this artist make?

- Interview successful artists and musicians in your school.
- Music reviews: How does the writer use language to help us hear the music? On which criteria is the reviewer basing her opinion? Compare the use of language in reviews of different types of music.
- The word "artist" is used generically to refer to various people who create things of beauty and power. Make a concept map to show the various kinds of "artists" and their relationship to each other.
- Theater and movie reviews: What are the implied criteria for excellence that this reviewer is going by?
- Cultural issues in the news: These might include articles about funding for the arts; art and music that make people angry; or censorship issues. Why do some performances evoke actual riots?
- Think about what Hamlet says: "I have heard/ that guilty creatures sitting at a play/Have/By the very cunning of the scene,/Been struck so to the soul that presently/They have confessed their malefactions." What does this mean? Why would this be so?
- Find out about some interesting cases where the arts evoked a violent reaction: The Astor Place Riot in New York; the debut of Stravinsky's *Rites of Spring*; the publication of Salmon Rushdie's *Satanic Verses*; and the photography of Robert Mapplethorpe.
- Role-play "The Censorship Committee": Have students pretend that they are the Censors General in a totalitarian nation. They should literally cut out all "objectionable material" from the arts section.
- Consider the issues surrounding the financial support of artists, museums, and arts education.
- Make a concept map that shows as many categories of the arts as you can think of, and the relationship among them.
- The official language of ballet is French; the official language of music is Italian. Make a poster that illustrates some commonly used terms.
- Try to express in words why you don't like your parents' music and why they don't like yours.
- Compare classical music to rock music.
- Make a concept map for all the different kinds of rock music that you know and the relationship among them.
- Compare watching a movie at a movie theatre to watching a movie at home.
- Suggest a classic tale as a Disney movie.

- Think about rock stars who have remained popular for more than one generation of teenagers. Why do you think they have retained their popularity?
- Compare several reviews of a popular movie.
- Nominate a movie for "Best of the Decade." Explain your criteria.
- Explain why photography is an art.
- Explain the relationship between art and science.
- Think of 10 movies. Decide which of these give a positive, and which a negative, view of American life. Divide them into as many categories as you can think of. Which of these make a social statement? What is that social statement? Consider the use of the English language in these movies. Which of these movies features regional dialect?
- Make a scrapbook of photographs that represent the past year in America.
- Think of an idea for a movie that would be an excellent movie, but probably would not make much money. Explain why its excellence would not be widely attractive.
- What does a photographer need to know about math?
- How does music bring people together, inspire people, or comfort people? How does music drive people apart? degrade people? disturb people?
- Interview someone who was born in another country. Ask her what she misses most about that culture. Ask her if, or how, she experiences her home culture in America.
- Think about great cities of the arts: Paris, Rome, Florence, New York, Vienna, and Hollywood. Think of several ways in which one of these cities is "odd man out."
- Although cities are necessarily centers for the arts, much great art is associated with rural life. What are some paintings of American and European rural life?
- What are the most famous museums and concert halls in the world?
- Think of several ways in which the arts can foster peace and social justice.
- And, finally, how has the September 11 disaster affected the arts in New York and in the world?

Reflection

How do the above activities invite critical thinking?

8

Differentiating Instruction for English Language Learners

I am the best of them that speaks this speech/Were I but where 'tis spoken.
Shakespeare—*The Tempest*, Act 1, Scene 2

One of our biggest challenges in differentiating instruction is teaching students whose native language is not English. These students range from those who enter our schools with no English at all, to those whose speech is proficient, but whose writing lacks the fluency of a native speaker. Unless you have been trained in Teaching English to Speakers of Other Languages (TESOL), you probably don't know much about how to address the needs of these students. This chapter considers four questions:

1. What do you need to know about your ESL (English as a Second Language) students?
2. How are other languages different from English?
3. How do differences in dialect affect learning?
4. How can you help?

What Do You Need to Know About Your ESL Students?

To work with students who are learning the English language, we first need to understand some rudiments of second language learning. Then, we need to consider some basic facts in comparative linguistics. The purpose of this chapter is to help you make your English language learners more at ease and better able to communicate with you. Here are some questions about individual students:

♦ How closely is her native language related to English? English is a Germanic language with Latinate and Greek influences. It is cousin to the Romance languages: Spanish, Portuguese, French, Italian, and Romanian. The ESL student whose native tongue is a Romance language will find many cognates that open doors to English words. On the other hand, Asian languages have much less common ground in terms of sentence structure, word order, formation of plurals, and the sounds themselves. Asian languages have very few cognates for the student to hang her hat on.

♦ What is her functional level as a speaker of English? In the best of circumstances, your school will have an ESL specialist who will evaluate the English proficiency of your students and give you an accurate report.

♦ How old is she? The older one is, the harder it is to assimilate a new language. Before puberty, language is learned intuitively, in the left hemisphere of the brain. After puberty, we lose the ability to learn language intuitively, and language learning becomes a right hemisphere function that is more difficult to keep in long-term memory.

♦ Is she socializing with English speakers? What is the language of her socialization? Anything you can do to encourage socialization in English would be helpful. If you've ever been in a country where you don't speak the language, you know how lonely and frustrating it can feel. Schools that care about their ESL students arrange for social opportunities such as clubs, buddy systems, breakfasts, and invitations to events. They see to it that their community welcomes newcomers and has a place for them. Teachers who care about their ESL students express an active interest in their culture and language, offering opportunities for them to communicate and make friends, making sure everyone in the class knows how to pronounce their names, and presiding over an atmosphere of invitation and inclusion.

♦ Is she happy to be here? Affective factors play an important role in second language learning. Aversion to a culture, not wanting to be here, and longing for home and family, can impede learning English. These students need adults in the school to look after them. Sad to say, sometimes our ESL students are exploited as laborers and not given time and opportunity to study.

The first and best way to differentiate instruction for your ESL students is to be a gracious host or hostess to them in your classroom. The other students will follow your example. Learn all you can about their interests, their level of proficiency, their family situation, their culture, and their language. Doing so will make the situation less frustrating and more rewarding for everyone involved.

Finally, a word about the word "foreign." If you lived in a place and went to school there, would you want to be considered a "foreigner"? "Foreign" and "foreigner" are words that should be consigned to the list of archaic and misguided epithets that we don't use anymore in polite society. Spanish, for example, is hardly "foreign" in the United States. It is one of many languages spoken in a society where English is the predominant language.

How Are Other Languages Different from English?

Some of the following information may be too specific and grammatical for your needs. The purpose of this section is to show you some basic differences in structure between English and several other languages: Spanish, Hmong, Vietnamese, Cantonese, and just a dash of Japanese and Korean. This information is not meant as a crash course in six languages. It is hoped that by knowing some of the ways in which your ESL student is struggling to make sense of English, you can better support her.

Spanish

Perhaps the most glaring difference between Spanish and the other Romance languages and English is that the Romance languages genderize their nouns. A Spanish-speaking student may take a while to get the hang of using the neutral pronoun for inanimate objects. Additionally, English nouns don't necessarily take an article (*a, an, the*), whereas Spanish nouns usually do. Spanish speakers may want to insert an article before nouns that don't take articles in English, and this may sound very odd to us.

In Spanish, as in many other languages, the adjective usually comes after the noun. In English the adjective is usually in the pre-noun position, but it can also be a predicate nominative, that is, a word that follows a conjugation of the verb *to be*—for example, *Martha is silly.* In English, the adjective means the same thing whether it is in the pre-noun position or the predicate nominative position. However, in Spanish, the adjective changes its meaning when it appears in the prenoun position (which is seldom). In English, we don't pluralize our adjectives; in Spanish, we do pluralize adjectives.

Don't be surprised if your Spanish speakers conflate the prepositions *in, on,* or *at.* They are accustomed to using one preposition (*a*) for all of these meanings. You'll hear your Spanish speakers use *that* when you expect *who* or *which.* That is because Spanish uses the word *que* to refer to *that, who* and *which.*

Spanish speakers don't like to end a sentence with a verb. You might hear them switch the subject and verb in a sentence that comes out sounding awkward in English. Instead of *I know what she is thinking*, you may hear or read *What she is thinking I know*, or *She is thinking I know what.*

English has only one verb for the *to be* concept, but Spanish has two be verbs: *ser*, for permanent circumstances, and *estar*, for temporary ones. In English, the direct object comes after the verb, but in Spanish, the direct object comes before the verb. English places the indirect object between the verb and the direct object. *Jack sent Jill a pail of water.* Spanish places the indirect object between the subject and the verb: *Jack Jill sent a pail of water.*

In English, when we refer to a person, we use the same language whether that person is present or absent. But Spanish speakers use the article to refer to an absent person. In English, that would sound like this: *I saw the Mrs. Benjamin in the grocery store.*

You may hear Spanish speakers refer to the word *people* in the singular rather than the plural. This is because *la gente* is singular in Spanish.

Spanish expresses the person that the verb refers to by manipulating the ends of the verb. This is called inflection, and it is a hallmark of the Romance languages. Because the person (first person, second person, or third person) is implied by the verb inflection, Spanish speakers are free to omit the pronoun altogether. We never do this in English. Your Spanish-speaking ESL student may think it is acceptable to omit the pronoun in English.

In English, we express possession in one of two ways: we use the possessive apostrophe or the *of phrase*. The Romance languages use only the *of phrase*. Considering how much trouble native speakers have with the possessive apostrophe, you can imagine how much trouble a Spanish or French speaker would have with it.

Hmong

Hmong, a language spoken in Southeast Asia, has a complicated system of noun classifiers to introduce nouns. In English, we use very few noun classifiers: *a*, *an*, *the*, and some possessive pronouns.. In Hmong, there are hundreds of classifiers, and each has to match a particular classification of noun. Hmong speakers may insert superfluous noun classifiers in English.

Because Hmong speakers form the possessive by using a noun classifier that is not available in English, they may be confused by the possessive apostrophes. They may also be confused by the apostrophe in English contractions.

The passive voice of the verb is not available in the Hmong language. Verbs are always expressed in the active voice. This may present problems in reading and listening comprehension because the student may wrongly interpret an English sentence in the passive voice, thinking that whoever is meant to receive the action is actually performing the action of the sentence.

Hmong speakers are used to keeping the form of the pronoun the same, whether it is in the subjective or objective position. In English, the pronoun changes from subjective case (*she*) to objective case (*her*) depending on its relationship to the verb.

Another area of confusion for Hmong speakers may be the use of *what* in question formation. Hmong speakers employ the word *puas* to form a question; they do not use end punctuation to mark a question.

Hmong speakers don't use the verb *to be* when using a predicate adjective in a sentence such as *"He is cute."* They would say: *"He cute."*

Finally, the Hmong language pluralizes by inserting *cov* before the noun. The practice of pluralizing by adding s to the end of the noun will be unfamiliar.

Vietnamese

As in Spanish, the Vietnamese adjective is placed after the noun.

Vietnamese does not have the *be* verb. You can expect your Vietnamese students to need help inserting the correct form of *be* in statements and questions.

A writer of a sentence in Vietnamese will usually place a transitional word between the introductory clause and the main clause. In English, this sounds awkward:

Because she likes to sing, therefore she joined the choir.

Vietnamese, like English, uses the subject/verb/object order. However, Vietnamese omits *it* when referring to weather, distance, and time. There are no neuter pronouns in Vietnamese.

In English, we express comparison by adding *er* to the adjective (*bigger*). In Vietnamese, the concept of *more* is expressed by adding the word for *more* after the adjective. *The truck big more than the bus.*

The vowel sounds in the words *hit*, *bad*, *shower*, and *hire* are not heard in the Vietnamese language. This accounts for why the Vietnamese speaker may confuse words that sound like words that have these vowels.

Expect your Vietnamese students to have some trouble with tense. Vietnamese does not use the same system of expressing events in time. You might hear and read: *We take a trip to Sacramento last summer.* This speaker is using context clues in the sentence to convey the tense, rather than transforming the verb, which is what we do in English, but not in Vietnamese.

Cantonese

Cantonese speakers are not accustomed to using helping verbs for questions or negatives. They may be particularly baffled by the English use of *do* in questions and negatives. You may hear this: *How much money this cost?* When we speak English using the helping verb, we usually don't stress that helping verb, so it would be hard for a native Cantonese speaker to hear it. You may want to stress the use of the helping verb *do* in questions and negatives.

Cantonese speakers are likely to be confused by the use of prepositions in English because Cantonese does not use many prepositions. Prepositional use in English is so idiomatic that it may even seem to be random. For example, why do we ride *in* a car but *on* a train? Why do we park *in* the parking lot? Why do we hang a picture *on* a wall, rather than *against* a wall? Your Cantonese speakers may need you to emphasize prepositions in your speech, to help them hear the conventions.

You'll hear your Cantonese speakers placing all of their modifiers up front in the sentence, before the verb: *For her mother on her birthday on Saturday, we gave her a surprise party.*

Cantonese speakers tend to leave off plurals in English. This is because of the nature of the Cantonese grammar, and also because of the difficulty in pronouncing the final *s*.

Cantonese speakers may have trouble with pronouns. They are used to a language with fewer pronouns, many of which are dropped.

A, an, and *the* are not used in Cantonese. That is why Cantonese students may erroneously omit the article, as in: *I have dog.* They may also insert the article erroneously, as in: *I have the pets.*

Korean

In Korean, pronouns don't have gender, so you might hear Korean-speaking students referring to males and females using the gender-neutral pronoun *it.*

Japanese

In Japanese, pronouns don't have to match their nouns in terms of singular or plural, so you might have to show them how to use *we, us, they* and *them.*

General Strategies for ESL Students

Students whose native language is not English don't automatically know how much English depends on word order for meaning. Although you take for granted that *The dog bit the man* conveys a different meaning from *The man bit the dog,* an English language learner might not think that is so obvious. English is a subject/verb/object language. Japanese and Korean are subject/object/verb languages. Arabic is a verb/subject/object language. Knowing this difference may help you decipher your students' intended meanings as they learn English.

Because English is a word-order language, it's important to understand what a direct object does. A direct object receives the action of the action verb. In the English sentence *Claudia loves Ramon,* Claudia, the subject, is giving the love; Ramon, the object, is receiving it. This is what we mean by the SVO (subject/verb/object) pattern.

In English, we expect the subject to be stated (except in the case of commands, where the subject is "you (understood)." Many other languages do not require the subject to be stated outright, but expressed through the verb ending. You may have to remind students that in English, the subject must be first. English language learners need to stick to simple SVO sentences.

One more thing about verbs: the most common verbs in English are the irregulars, a fact that is not convenient for fledgling speakers.

In English, we place the preposition before its object. That's why it's called a *pre*position. Other languages don't necessarily have this placement. Sometimes, the object comes before the preposition.

Talking about transportation is often a puzzlement for English language learners because of the prepositions *in* and *on*. When the vehicle carries only one person, or, when it carries more than a handful of people, we use *on*: *on* a bicycle, *on* an ocean liner, *on* a train. When a small number of people ride in a conveyance, we use *in*: *in* a rowboat, *in* a car.

English language learners may need some help understanding the meanings of conjunctions, so you might have to explain the difference between *and* and *but*.

In English, it's easy to form the past and past participle, because both forms are the same for regular verbs. All we do is add *have* or *has* to the past tense to form the past participle. Not all languages work this way.

English is rich in metaphors, idioms, and figurative language. You can imagine how these nonliteral expressions would bewilder the novice. An idiom such as *used to* is famous for mystifying newcomers to English.

Remember that conventions for capitalization differ from language to language. Nationalities are not capitalized in Spanish, Romanian, Russian, or Portuguese. The second word of a geographical place name (*Hudson River*) is not capitalized in Serbo-Croatian and Vietnamese. Not all languages capitalize days of the week or months of the year. And Cantonese does not use any capital letters to indicate a proper noun.

Not all punctuation looks like English punctuation. Some languages use inverted questions marks, circles, vertical lines, series of dots, and other markings Commas don't always appear the way they do in English. In some languages, the comma is inverted, raised, or reversed.

Not all languages have the same rules as English does regarding the joining of independent clauses. Whereas English does not permit two independent clauses to be joined by a comma, such joinings are permissible in Persian, Arabic, Russian, and Turkish.

English spelling drives native speakers crazy. Imagine what it must be like for speakers of other languages, such as Spanish and Vietnamese, which have much more consistency. Your ESL students will run into difficulties that you don't expect, because their pronunciation conventions may differ from those of English speakers. For example, in some languages, the final consonant is not pronounced. If a speaker of such a language carries that practice into English, she will be likely to drop the final consonant in spelling, as well as in speech, of English words.

In English, we have lots of affixes. Other languages, such as many Asian languages, do not add affixes to words very often. The notion of a word root, which has meaning although it does not function as a complete word, is unfamiliar.

Your non-native speakers will have problems enough with the irregularities of English spelling. You can help them learn spelling by working with them on their pronunciation. Doing this doesn't always necessitate correcting them. Simply exaggerating your own pronunciation of tricky words will be helpful.

Chinese and Vietnamese do not pluralize words. These languages convey the plural in the context of the sentence. Romance language do have plurals, but the plurals are formed according to rules which are much more consistent than the rules in English. Be aware that ESL students may find English plurals difficult.

Homonyms, words that sound alike but have different, often unrelated meanings, don't exist in all languages.

Finally, we need to keep in mind that the nonverbal cues of communication differ from culture to culture. Most Americans expect the person to whom they are speaking to make eye contact. Not to do so is considered a sign of disrespect. In some cultures, making eye contact is a sign of confrontation; downcasting one's eyes when an authority is speaking signifies proper deference.

Summary of Differences Between English and Other Languages

Here are some of the ways that languages can differ from English:

- The nouns can be genderized.
- Plurals may be formed by adding words or syllables to the sentence, or by giving context clues in the sentence to indicate that there is more than one.
- The word order may not follow the familiar subject/verb/object pattern.
- The pronoun may not have to agree in gender or number with its antecedent.
- Other languages may have fewer prepositions, making it confusing for the novice to know which preposition to use in English. Also, the preposition may not precede its object.
- There are differences in inflection and pacing.
- There are differences in written conventions, such as punctuation and capitalization.
- Nonverbal communications, such as gesture, eye contact, silences, and what people do to indicate that they understand, differ from culture to culture.

How Do Differences in Dialect Affect Learning?

One of the goals of education should be to make every high school graduate bidialectical. What this means is that everyone has a dialect. By dialect, we mean speech patterns that are at variance with the homogenized style of public discourse. We can think of this as "private speech" and "public speech." Some linguists refer to "private speech" as "the language of the family." You may also think of bidialecticalism as "informal" and "formal" language.

Enlightened educators appreciate and value all of the many forms of spoken English, and recognize the various voices of informal written English. At the same time, it is incumbent upon us as educators to help our students communicate in a way that will not put them at risk of being thought unsophisticated when they travel from place to place or from level to level in the business world.

This is a sensitive area. Nothing is more personal to us than our language and the language of our family, loved ones, ethnic group, and community. It is imperative that we show and feel a genuine respect for dialect. It also behooves us to know something about the grammatical structures of the dialects that we hear in the communities in which we teach.

One of the most controversial English language variants is AAVE (African American Vernacular English). In *Understanding English Grammar*, Martha Kolln and Robert Funk explain the use of the *to be* verb in AAVE. The way the *to be* verb functions in AAVE is actually more refined than in so-called Standard English, because AAVE distinguishes between present action which is going on now (*He eat.*) and habitual action (*He be eating.*). Before we judge a dialectical variant as "substandard" we need to know more about its grammatical structure.

We suppress dialect at our peril, because our suppression feeds a sense of alienation from education and public discourse—the last thing any educator wants. The classroom task is to establish the relationship between voice and audience.

In English, social studies, and language classes, we can differentiate instruction by acknowledging dialect in authentic literature and documents. We can show changes in the language over regions and time.

How Can You Help?

- ◆ To help ESL students learn how to use nouns and adjectives, have them write descriptions.
- ◆ To help ESL students learn how to use pronouns, have them write narratives about themselves and their friends.
- ◆ To help all students become more sophisticated about dialect, avoid using terms such as "substandard," "wrong," "broken English," "illiterate," and other pejorative terms that discount the value of linguistic variation. Instead, use terms such as "colloquial," "informal," "regional," "dialectical," and "inappropriate for this context." Stress the importance of using the language tone geared for a particular audience and situation.
- ◆ To help all students learn more about languages, point out cognates and Latin roots. This will also help native English speakers to learn and remember new words.

- Find as many ways as possible to reword complex statements.
- Use visuals, but explain them verbally.
- Be responsive to the affective needs of new students.
- Be aware of the effects of your speech. Speak more slowly than you ordinarily would. Gesture and use facial expressions to exaggerate your meaning. Use the active voice and positive statements. Speak in short sentences.
- Be aware of context, and include definitions of unfamiliar terms within your sentences.
- Be aware that the English language is full of idioms that baffle the novice.
- Organize your message around key words and use these frequently.
- Model a positive, open-minded attitude about language variations. Doing so is one of the most powerful ways that you can teach for social justice.

Reflection

1. How many ESL students have you had in your class in the last five years? What challenges have you encountered? What are your successes?

2. Think of five specific ways in which you can assist your English language learners.

3. Find examples of idioms, metaphors, and figurative language in this chapter. How would you explain these to an ESL student?

9

Administrative Support for Differentiated Instruction

Case Studies

This chapter presents composite case studies that offer insight about how secondary administrators were successful in instituting, motivating, and sustaining differentiated instruction in their schools. They faced the same problems that you face in your school: funding, reluctance to change, the tyranny of the "Big Test," lack of time, and rigidity in scheduling. They attribute their successes to the following:

♦ Long range planning and patience with change:

♦ Cultivating a positive school climate

♦ Effective use of consultants

♦ An attitude of professional encouragement and communication

Meg Whitman of McCleary Middle School: Rx: Reading

In the second year of her leadership at McCleary, Meg Whitman set the goal of improving reading performance across the curriculum. She wanted to see kids doing more reading on their own, and she wanted them to know more about how to read academic information that would help them study and retain.

Meg envisioned her success:

♦ Kids would show an active interest in books: they would purchase their own books, exchange books with others, talk about books, and read for pleasure. Anyone walking into McCleary would be able to feel, see, and hear reading in the air.

♦ Kids would show behaviors of purposeful reading in their textbooks. They would know how to skim, scan, peruse, take notes, and review.

- Kids would have a variety of reading strategies. They would improve their reading fluency, stamina, patience, and comprehension. What's more, they would understand themselves as readers, knowing how to adjust their reading rates and when to reread.
- Kids would have a better vocabulary and sense of written language, which would make them better writers.

Meg needed funding for new and used paperbacks and magazines, classroom bookshelves, a top-notch consultant, and released time for teachers. She knew that, although everyone gave lip service to the importance of reading, making actual changes in the school would be another story. Changes always cost money, and are always, to some degree, suspect: "How do we know that this will work?" Meg knew that she'd need research to support her theory as well as quantitative and qualitative evidence that her ideas about reading had worked to improve student performance.

Meg decided to call her vision "Rx: Reading." This name was inspired by the American Bookseller's Association's "Prescription for Reading," a program that uses children's visits to their pediatrician's office to encourage reading at an early age. Meg believed that giving her plan a catchy name would unify its components and facilitate publicity. She hoped that the publicity might generate funding and enthusiasm.

After nosing around for some sources of research on the long-term benefits of reading for pleasure, Meg decided to rely on two main sources: NCTE's *Reading for Understanding* (Schoenback, Greenleaf, Cziko, and Hurwitz, 1999) and the American Booksellers Association's "Get Caught Reading" Web site (www. bookweb.org).

Armed with a name, clear goals, and two frameworks (the book and the Web site), Meg put the call out for a task force. She roped in two of her best English teachers and a parent who was active in the parent organization, and a BOE (Board of Education) member.

Meg and her task force established the following components of Rx: Reading:

Preassessment

The preassessment consisted of three parts: a standardized reading test (Degrees of Reading Power), a standardized vocabulary test, and a survey about reading behaviors. The survey asked these questions:

1. How much time do you spend per week reading on your own?
2. How much time do you spend per week reading for schoolwork?
3. Do you have reading material for your own enjoyment in your room at home?
4. The last time that you took a long trip or had to wait for a long time outside of home, did you read to pass the time?

5. Have you recommended any reading material to your friends in the last month?

Sustained Silent Reading Time

The task force wanted to habituate and ritualize reading for pleasure on a daily basis. Beginning modestly, Meg adjusted the schedule to allow for 10 to 20 minutes once a week, working up to 10 to 20 minutes of pleasure reading per day. These set-aside times for reading in some schools are called "DEAR," an acronym for "Drop everything and read."

The Sustained Silent Reading (SSR) time in the adjusted schedule was not without controversy. There were teachers who ignored it. Realizing that not everyone would be on board for SSR, Meg's schedule rotated the SSR time around each day. That way, a kid whose math teacher kept right on teaching math instead of observing SSR would at least be able to get some reading in the next day, when the SSR time took place during a different period.

Meg ran into other objections to the SSR time: Some teachers protested that kids were "doing English homework" in "their" classes; others were nervous because of the nature of the reading material that students brought in: "What if a parent objects that the kid is reading a book with objectional material?" Still others objected to the material themselves, insisting that kids should not be allowed to read "trash" in school. They wanted to have kids do assigned reading during SSR, reading that related to their subject matter. Because this was a matter of academic freedom, Meg couldn't impose the "read whatever you want" philolsophy on teachers. She knew, going into Rx: Reading, that it wouldn't work in all classrooms. She persevered without pushing. Meg kept the faith that, eventually, reading would sell itself.

Book Ownership and Availability

The task force came up with several ways to get more books into the hands of more kids:
  - ◆ Make it possible for kids to exchange books by collecting paperbacks in the library.
  - ◆ Provide as many classes as possible with small bookshelves filled with paperbacks and magazines for SSR.
  - ◆ Take kids to a local bookstore and give them a book allowance. Meg thought the purpose of this would be obvious: to familiarize kids with the culture of a good bookstore, to encourage them to visit bookstores in their leisure time, and to spark book-talking among peers. The task force was unpleasantly surprised by the negative comments of many teachers who considered the book store outing to be a frivolous "shopping trip." Some teachers, administrators, and board members remarked that students clearly had plenty of discre-

tionary income. Why hand them money to purchase books? These kids weren't poor.

- ◆ Supply all offices with reading material.

Modeling

- ◆ Meg knew that it was essential for teachers to model reading behaviors during SSR. She didn't want teachers using the time to grade papers or do classroom chores while the kids were reading. She wanted them to read something of their choice in front of the kids. Meg modeled this behavior herself, welcoming the chance to read during the day. She always had her current book out on her desk for kids to see when they were in her office.

- ◆ Meg arranged for teachers to receive inservice credit for participation in literary discussion groups. Each group met for 15 hours (three hour sessions for five weeks) after school at the public library. The 15 hours consisted of two segments. The fiction segment was divided into literature for adults and young adult literature. The nonfiction segment was divided into general nonfiction and books related to social issues in education. The manager of the local bookstore, delighted with Rx: Reading, even offered a discount on the books for the inservice teachers.

- ◆ Rx: Reading set up a bulletin board outside the gym. Posted on the board were photographs of adults and kids in the school reading, open comments about books, and recommendations.

Training

Using released time out of class, teachers had three sessions with a top-notch consultant in the field of reading education. The consultant guided teachers through the "Reading Apprenticeship Program" described in *Reading for Understanding*. Briefly, this book shows teachers and administrators how to make kids better subject area readers.

Share Success

Meg made time at every faculty meeting for teachers to share their successes with Rx: Reading. These were *very brief reports*, not opportunities to complain or look for training. Meg saw to it that every teacher received a written summary of the success stories.

Post-Test and Evaluation

The post-test reflected the preassessment instruments, along with anecdotal reports from the teachers.

Reflection

1. Discuss what you think would be some of Meg's problems in reaching her goals. How would Rx: Reading work in your school? Would all or part of it be worth trying?

2. Discuss how Rx: Reading is differentiating instruction.

3. How well did Meg use the four principles given in the beginning of this chapter?

Greg Freeman of Parkville High School: Advanced Placement Enrollment

When Greg Freeman was hired as principal of Parkville High School, the Board and Central Administration made it clear to him that they wanted more kids taking Advanced Placement (AP) classes. Greg envisioned his success. He had a two-year plan: he would introduce at least two more Advanced Placement courses, increase the number of staff members qualified to teach Advanced Placement classes by at least two, and attract 20 percent more students to Advanced Placement courses over the next two years.

To make this happen, Greg sought to restructure the honors program in grades nine and ten at Parkville. Traditionally, students applied for acceptance in the honors classes by taking an entrance test. The teachers selected students on the basis of this test, grades in the subject, teacher recommendation, and standardized test information. Many parents whose children were rejected wanted further information. Some were aggressive in wanting their kids placed in honors classes. The popular thinking in the community was that "Your kids can get a good education at Parkville only if they are in the honors classes." Several parents each year chose private schools when their kids failed to quality for the honors program. Middle school teachers tended to "over recommend" students into the honors program, for various reasons. This led to more emphasis on the entrance test.

The only teachers at Parkville who were really happy with this selection process were those who taught honors classes. Many of the other teachers felt the absence of the "cream." And the teachers of the honors classes were growing weary of the pressures and threats of litigation by parents who wanted their kids "to get in." Greg decided that the time was right to change the system.

As a result of several goal-setting meetings, and after much soul-searching and negotiating, Parkville launched the "honors option" program for ninth-grade English and social studies classes. It was decided that the other departments were not ready to move forward at this time. The "honors option" program would work as follows: In a nine period day, all ninth graders would take a heterogeneous English and social studies class. In addition to that, they would have a special "honors option" class every other day, alternating English and social studies. The honors option class would not introduce new material.

Rather, it would expand upon the regular curriculum by going into more depth and complexity. When the students were reading *Romeo and Juliet* in their regular English classes, they would be going into more detail and doing more performance work in the honors class. In social studies, they would be reading more primary documents and having more Socratic seminars. *The honors option class would be open to anyone.*

The honors option plan was welcomed by the teachers for several reasons. First, they had fashioned it collaboratively, so they felt ownership. Second, those teachers who had never taught the honors classes anyway saw the advantages of having truly heterogeneous classes, rather than pseudo-heterogeneity with the top lopped off. Third, the teachers who had been doing the screening were relieved not to have to do it anymore

But there were vociferous objections by the community. Because their kids hadn't been screened, everyone assumed that their kids would have been accepted, especially because the grading system at the middle school favored high grades. Many parents and students were miffed that the honors classes were no longer selective. They feared that the heterogeneity would dumb down the classes. But the largest objection was over the workload: "Why should our kids be punished with more work just because they're smart?" was the outcry.

The parents who objected to the restructured honors plan were organized and determined. They formed committees and held meetings at people's homes, wrote letters to the editor, were interviewed by the media, delivered oratory at BOE meetings, signed petitions, and networked at the sidelines of the sports teams that their kids played on. They used every legal means at their disposal to exert enough pressure to defeat the new program. They used inflammatory language: *dumbing down, going backwards, pandering, etc.* Two BOE members were firmly on their side. The other five were willing to give the new program a chance.

Greg's program was a major career risk. All eyes were on the honors option program, most of them hoping that the program would fail so that they could go back to the good old days of selecting students on the basis of an entrance test. Greg's vision was expensive on the face of it, but it also had unanticipated expenses. Although the social studies classes followed more or less the same sequence, the ninth-grade English classes did not. The English teachers proposed that they align their curriculum around five main works of literature that would be taught at approximately the same time:

1. First quarter: *Fahrenheit 451* (Bradbury)
2. Second Quarter: *The Odyssey* (Homer)
3. Edith Hamilton's *Mythology*
4. Third Quarter: *Romeo and Juliet* (Shakespeare)
5. Fourth Quarter: *A Raisin in the Sun* (Hansbury)

This alignment incurred substantial costs because all students needed to be supplied with the same book at the same time. Ordinarily, Parkville English teachers rotated the books, sharing class sets.

As a result of all this politicking, some of the students entered Parkville High School with more than the usual trepidation. They felt singled out for "more work." Had the honors option program gone the wrong way, they'd have been the first to declare that the regular classes were beneath them but that the honor option class overburdened them. They wanted the status of the honors class, but without the increased demands. Parents were not shy about complaining about whatever they could: the summer reading contained inappropriate sexual material, papers weren't being returned fast enough, their students were stressed, etc. Greg's phone rang off the hook for the first few weeks.

It may seem as though any program would falter under such a barrage of criticism. But the honors option program was a success. There were a few refugees early on, but once the school year got underway, very few students dropped out of their honors option classes. Some even decided to come on board mid-year. When all was said and done, students said that they enjoyed the class, enhanced their skills, and expanded their learning.

There is no question that the determining factor in this success story was the excellence of the teaching. The teachers in both the English and social studies departments delivered on their promise to make the heterogeneous classes more interesting as well as more democratic. In the honors option class, students were indeed brought to a level that would not have been possible under the former system.

Not all students in the honors option classes excelled. Some struggled, some even failed, but all benefitted by being in a challenging class. Parkville would have continued the honors option classes into the tenth grade, but doing so would have disallowed students from taking electives in other departments. In the tenth grade, all students were invited into the honors classes, doubling what the enrollment had been under the old system.

Teachers were part of the process from the beginning. They did have the support of a consultant who specializes in differentiated instruction and cooperative learning. Common planning time among the teachers was not available, and this proved to be a problem, because the honors option teachers felt that they were operating blind sometimes, not knowing what the other classes were doing. Teachers made the best of it, but common planning time would have tightened the timing of the curriculum.

Greg instituted Advanced Placement classes in the eleventh grade in English and social studies: he added AP Language and Composition to the English department, and AP American History to the social studies department. To do this, the Board had to entice teachers to take the graduate level courses that prepares teachers to teach Advanced Placement. They offered a stipend in addition to the salary credits that teachers accrue for taking graduate courses.

Greg's goal was to have more AP and honors courses at Parkville. He was not deterred by the fact that many students taking these courses would not get excellent grades. The philosophy was never about grades. It was about opportunities.

Reflection

1. Discuss what you think would be some of Greg's problems in reaching his goals. How would the honors option program work in your school? Would all or part of it be worth trying?

2. Discuss how the honors option program is differentiating instruction.

3. How well did Greg use the four principles given in the beginning of this chapter?

Graciela Rodriquez of Meadowbrook High School: Improving Instruction

As a long-term principal facing considerable staff turnover, Graciela wanted to see better classroom management and differentiated instruction strategies among her new and veteran teachers. She wasn't seeing the kinds of student-centered classrooms at Meadowbrook that indicated that differentiated instruction was going on. A tour of her school revealed students sitting in rows, with the teacher doing most of the talking at the board or podium. Graciela wanted to see more students at the podium and at the board. She wanted more student talk in the classrooms.

At Meadowbrook, many teachers were frustrated and stressed because of classroom management problems. Attendance, overall, was poor—a sign of low morale. Kids were regularly ejected from class because of recalcitrance; far too many kids were "hall puppies," chronic roamers and lurkers. Cutting and tardiness were so rampant that by the fourth quarter, the pile of referral slips far outran the manpower to attend to them. Kids, teachers, and administrators walked around with a "no joy in Mudville" attitude, and Graciela knew that was not good for education.

Graciela envisioned her success: At the end of two years, she would see more Socratic seminars, student presentations, cooperative learning groups, and collaborative teaching. Her teachers would base their practice on sound modern pedagogy, mixing traditional "stand-up" delivery with multisensory learning, constructivism, differentiated instruction, and brain-based learning strategies. She was convinced that a change in the instructional approach would invigorate the learning atmosphere at Meadowbrook, resulting in fewer disciplinary problems as well as better academic performance.

She wanted to begin with a focus group of teachers But before she convened them, Graciela and her assistant principal for curriculum and instruction, Michael Greer, strategized: They knew that the project needed a name so that it would have form and shape, but the name couldn't be anything that could be stigmatized, such as "classroom management improvement." They also knew how reluctant many teachers at Meadowbrook were to welcome changes initiated by administration. Graciela and Michael decided that "Differentiating Instruction" was the most neutral name for their vision.

They soon found that differentiating instruction had two connotations: special education and elementary school. They familiarized themselves with the work of Carol Ann Tomlinson to learn more about how differentiated instruction worked in middle schools, but they felt that they were blazing a trail in trying to differentiate instruction in a high school.

They put out a call for the focus group, and, to no one's surprise, they received only two responses. Undaunted, they met with the two brave teachers who had come forward, and asked those teachers how they thought other people could be enticed to join. A little thinking about human nature led to an offer of lunch. What did anyone have to lose? The district was willing to foot the bill for a catered lunch and the focus group attracted a handful of people who were released from their afternoon classes. It was a start.

At that first meeting of the focus group, Michael and Graciela had three core questions:

1. What do you already do to differentiate instruction?
2. Would you like to do more of that?
3. What is stopping you from doing more differentiated instruction?

Teachers were doing many things which differentiated instruction, but they were not thinking of these things as such. The popular notion of differentiated instruction was that it consisted of lowering expectations for less able students while laying more work on the brighter kids. The teachers were uncomfortable with having kids in the same class responsible for different products, foreseeing complaints from parents, kids, and, ultimately, administrators. Graciela and Mark could see that their own attitudes about what an active class should look like were going to be crucial in helping teachers to take risks.

Some of the teachers' comments that interested Graciela were about control:

Teacher: "If I'm up in front of the room, I feel in control."
Graciela: "Do you feel in control if that kid in the back row has his head on the desk while you're talking?"
Teacher: "Whenever you have kids working in groups, they start talking and getting off-track."
Graciela: "Have you tried giving the groups a deadline of, say, 10 minutes? They don't have to have the task completed in ten minutes, but they do have to give a progress report."
Teacher: "I don't like groupwork. It seems so inefficient. It takes much longer for kids to learn that way."
Graciela: "You could always give the factual information as a lecture, and then do the groupwork to reinforce and use that information. Think of it the way science teachers do: they have lecture and lab. The lab is to *apply* the information in the lecture."
Teacher: "When these kids go to college, they're not going to have groupwork. They're going to have lecture. We have to get them used to that."

Graciela: "What kind of learning do you like to have when you take a graduate or inservice course? Do you ever like to talk with your colleagues about the learning?"

Theoretically, the focus group should have come up with an action plan for receiving training in differentiated instruction. But Graciela was afraid to give them carte blanche, because she knew there was a limited budget. It was not going to be possible to hire a national consultant or to send a group of teachers off to a major conference. So she offered visitations to other schools with follow-up discussion after school (for compensation).

She also instituted a teacher leadership component to her monthly faculty meetings. For no more than 15 minutes, teachers would present strategies in differentiated instruction that had worked in their classrooms. Along with the presentation, the teachers presented samples of student work and lesson plans. Why would teachers volunteer to present? Because Meadowbrook's untenured teachers needed to build a portfolio, so these presentations were advantageous to them. Graciela was also able to offer inservice credits to teachers who submitted year-end portfolios based on evidence of differentiated instruction.

Graciela's was a gradual and subtle plan. Teachers who took a risk on more cooperative learning, student choices, alternative assessment, and student-centered classrooms worked against the status quo of passive learning. They needed patience, support, training, and flexibility. They also needed to get out of Meadowbrook and be inspired by speakers, conferences, and outside workshops.

Reflection

1. Discuss what you think would be some of Graciela's problems in reaching her goals. How would the differentiated instruction focus group work in your school? Would all or part of it be worth trying?

2. How well did Graciela use the four principles given in the beginning of this chapter?

3. How could Graciela evaluate her plan for improving instruction at Meadowbrook?

Art Jaffe of LaSalle Central Schools: Paradigm Shift—Social Studies Instruction

Art taught social studies at a suburban high school for 13 years before taking a position as K–12 department chair at LaSalle. In his third year, Art established the goal of having his teachers be more concept-oriented, rather than detail-oriented, in their approach to instruction in social studies. Although Art valued specific knowledge of dates and facts, he wanted students at LaSalle to be better at recognizing the patterns of history and geography. He also wanted students to make connections to today's world and to be better critical thinkers.

Art's social studies department was informally led by three veteran teachers who were known for their "hard tests" and fact-based curriculum. These teachers had earned wide respect from colleagues, students, and parents. Their students did well on high-stakes tests. "What's the problem? Why intervene?" Art was asked. Art believed that the commendable grades and even the stellar reputations of the teachers and their programs did not tell the whole story of what students could be getting out of social studies classes. He respected the work that the veteran teachers were doing, but he felt that his younger teachers had more to offer and that he could encourage them to come into their own.

Art envisioned his success: At the end of two years, he would see more literary readings being done in social studies classes, more use of graphic organizers to express concepts, more performance tasks involving contemporary issues connected to historical events, and more reading of newspapers and news magazines, with students tracking issues over long periods of time. He wanted to see portfolio work based on themes, collections of key quotations and how they could be applied to more than one historical event, and comparison/contrast of leaders. Finally, Art envisioned a change in the informal leadership of his department, such that the cadre of teachers who were less traditional would rise in the esteem of their colleagues.

He decided to begin by making it possible for more teachers to attend both major and smaller conferences. Art was not surprised at the teachers who came forward to attend these conferences, which he also attended. Following the conferences, he set aside time in the school day for the teachers to work on a presentation for their colleagues about what they learned. These presentations were followed up by samples of student work being shared with department colleagues at subsequent monthly meetings.

Art also encouraged and facilitated visitations from one teacher to another, along with time for follow-up collegial discussion. Again, Art was not surprised by which teachers volunteered to do this. Teachers began to exchange ideas and take risks. Art was not surprised that some teachers rolled their eyes and glanced at each other sarcastically during meetings when new work and student samples were featured. He was not surprised to hear the "Yes, but...." responses:

> *This is very nice, but how are these kids going to do on the common final?*
> *All these newspapers are fine, but how are you going to cover the textbook?*
> *Yes, but what about knowing the facts?*

Art countered with his own questions:

> *Knowing the facts is very nice, but how can you remember them if they don't connect to your own world? All these dates and treaties are fine, but what do they mean? Why do they learn them in the first place if they aren't related to anything else? Yes, but without the connections, patterns, and relationships, how do you inspire kids to care about history?*

Two tenth grade teachers, Cara Finlay and Susan Corsa, decided to focus on four themes of civilization:

1. Technology
2. Leadership
3. Geographical features
4. Religion

In Cara Finlay's class, students were given the following directions for a portfolio project:

The Technology Portfolio Project

You will make a portfolio containing information, opinions of authorities, and personal responses to the following theme statement:

Technology changes history in both positive and negative ways. When major new technology comes about, the following social phenomenon occurs:

- Controversy
- Changes in lifestyles
- Changes in major social structures, such as government, education, exchange of information, economics, etc.

For your portfolio, choose two historical events from different regions of the world. For each event, include the following entries:

- A paraphrase of the information in your textbook which explains the event.
- A timeline of the 50 years before and after the event.
- A one-page narrative explaining the timeline.
- An explanation of how technology effected the event.
- An explanation of how this technology went on to effect the historical period following the event.
- A (fictitious) letter written by an ordinary citizen who experienced this event.
- A (fictitious) letter written by a political leader who held power during the event.
- A copy of a primary document relating to this event.
- An explanation of the significance of this primary document.
- An explanation of why the technology related to this event was controversial. Explain each side of the controversy.
- An explanation of how this event and its technology changed lifestyles of ordinary people.
- An explanation of how this event and its technology changed a major social institution.

Note: Your portfolio entries must contain specific information: dates, names, places, documents.

♦ In addition to the above, paste in at least 10 newspaper or news magazine articles that remind you of this event. For each article, write a one-paragraph explanation of the connection between your article and the event.

Students in Mrs. Finlay's class were given 10 weeks to complete their portfolios. Here is what she says about the success of this project:

This was differentiated instruction because the students followed their own interests. They chose events that were related to various weapons (the longbow, the atom bomb, the guillotine, gunpowder), as well as inventions affecting transportation, communication, and industry.

The key to the success of the portfolio was having kids learn how to manage their time. They had to hand in time budget reports every week, indicating what they had accomplished, what they expected to accomplish for the coming week, and how long they anticipated that would take. Using a staggered schedule, I collected and checked their work every two weeks. I couldn't have handled all of the work at once. And I couldn't have graded the whole portfolio at once. What I did was to give interim grades as I went along, and then, when the project was completed, I averaged those for the total grade. Although this project sounds monumental, each entry is rather short, so it was less overwhelming to grade as it might sound.

I didn't allow rewrites once a particular segment was graded. This is because I wanted the kids to know that they were accountable for the work that they submitted when it was due. I wasn't going to let the whole thing snowball. What a nightmare that would have been. Of course, I had students and parents clamoring for a chance to write a segment that they were careless on. I'd just tell them, "learn from your mistakes and you'll get a better grade on the next segment."

Susan Corsa used literature to introduce concepts and themes. Her students read *Brave New World* to extend their understanding of technology, leadership, and religion. Instead of doing the obvious, considering *Brave New World* in the context of the twentieth century, Susan shifted the focus to the Renaissance as the brave new world. Her students created charts on which students showed how the features of the Huxley novel connected to the features of the late Middle Ages as it transitioned into the Renaissance.

Susan said:

This project was much harder for the kids than I thought it would be. First of all, they didn't read the book. A lot of them were operating on very little information. I still believe in the general concept, though, of using a novel to make connections to history, but next time, I think I'll give them a novel that is more closely related to the period that we're learning. We missed a big step here, trying to go from one century to another. That was my mistake.

Ninth-grade teacher Raphael Stephano used a thematic approach to teaching the relationship between geographical features and ways of life. Using verbs, he helped students to see what geographical features do:

- Mountains *isolate, block, prevent*.
- Rivers *facilitate* transportation and communication.
- Bodies of water *provide* a means of transportation, fishing, and cultural exchange. They can also *isolate*.

Mr. Stephano's class spent one week just considering geographical features and what they do. They brainstormed a list of geographical features and generated a list of verbs. This was kept in their notebooks on pages labeled "Geographical Features Inventory." As the year progressed, the geographical features essay popped up in every unit of the text. Raph said:

> The geographical features inventory was very useful to the students for writing essays, the kind of essays that you see on the end-of-year test all the time. I intend to do the same kind of thing for the other topics: The Religion Inventory, The Technology Inventory, and The Leadership Inventory." Once the kids get the verbs right, their thinking about the concept falls right into place for them. Verbs are the key to thinking. The inventories provide that.

As for the veteran teachers, two of them remained loyal to the lecture style of teaching the details. Art remained satisfied with one of these teachers, Mr. Clothilde, whose delivery was dynamic enough to sustain student interest. As for the other teacher, Art felt that his energies as a supervisor were better spent on teachers who were more open to change rather than with a resister. No significant test score statistics could justify or refute Art's efforts. Anecdotal evidence from students and teachers spoke favorably of the changes in pedagogy that Art had facilitated: both students and teachers reported that the concept-oriented approach was more interesting and memorable than the fact-oriented approach to social studies.

Reflection

1. Discuss what you think would be some of Art's problems in reaching his goals. How would Art's plan work in your school? Would all or part of it be worth trying?

2. Discuss how or if the teachers in Art's social studies department are differentiating instruction. How could their pedagogy be more differentiated?

3. How well did Art use the four principles given in the beginning of this chapter?

Maureen Phillips of
Somerville Middle School: Inclusion

Maureen's goal was to implement inclusion classes at Somerville Middle School. Although almost all schools have instituted inclusion classes, Somerville still had self-contained classes for special education students in each department on the sixth-, seventh-, and eighth-grade levels. Somerville had an unusually high proportion of its students classified as special ed. Many of these students were in regular classes, supplementing their learning with resource room support. A good percentage of other special ed students were in self-contained classes, and these classes grew larger (never smaller) as the year progressed and the regular ed teachers felt that the special ed kids "couldn't handle" the work.

Relations between regular education and special education classes were prickly at Somerville. Many outspoken regular education teachers resented the constant demands for paperwork, requests for homework, late papers, and disciplinary problems posed by the special education students and their teachers. It seemed to the regular ed teachers that here they were, burdened with classes of 25 to 30 students, and without the assistance of an aide. Meanwhile, down the hall was a special ed teacher with either a self-contained or resource room class of eight kids, an aide, and a private telephone line. When the special aide would appear at the beginning of a class to request homework or to ask for an extension on a task, the regular ed teacher would comment later in the faculty lounge that she wished she had her own messenger service. Such was the level of collegial tension at Somerville.

And the resentments ran the other way as well. It was common to hear special ed teachers complain that "no one wants our kids. They just make it hard for them so they'll come back to us in self-contained."

Into this hostility comes inclusion, where a special ed teacher will work collaboratively with a regular ed teacher in a heterogeneous class consisting of most of the special ed kids who would formerly have been in self-contained classes. (One multilevel class would be formed for students who couldn't handle mainstream classes, even with a special ed teacher present.). You can imagine how the idea of inclusion classes was received by both camps.

Convinced that inclusion was a better way to go than self-contained classes for special education students, Maureen envisioned her success:

- The inclusion model would result in more differentiated instruction for all students.
- The inclusion model would invigorate teachers with a sense of collegiality

She operated in accordance with the following guidelnes:

- Start slowly; proceed carefully.
- Invite interested teachers to learn about inclusion.

- Make it clear that teachers will have support and training, and then follow through.
- Provide common planning time.

After meeting with several teachers and researching what other schools did with their inclusion programs, Maureen and the teachers on her task force developed an inclusion plan that looked like this: There would be two inclusion classes at each grade level, each with five special education students who would otherwise have been in self contained classes. In these classes, there would not be other special education students over and above the "targeted" five. A special education teacher would work collaboratively with English and social studies classes every other day. On alternating days, there would be an aide in the classroom to assist with classroom management. The English and social studies teachers would have common planning time with the special education teacher, so that they could meet several times a week. In other words, if the inclusion classes met during periods 1 and 2, then period 3 would be a common planning time for the special ed, English, and social studies teachers to use as needed. In addition, Maureen secured the services of a special education consultant who would run a summer workshop and also consult with the teachers at intervals over the year. Teachers were given visitation days and conference days. Other teachers were given released time from classes to visit the inclusion classes.

Maureen had a great deal invested in those teachers who had volunteered to lead the way to inclusion at Somerville. She knew that they would need to feel appreciated for their efforts and that credit was due to them for their success. Should this venture fail in the eyes of these teachers, it would be extremely difficult to enlist other teachers to work collaboratively. Forcing teachers to do so would be surefire disaster. Maureen's veteran teachers, if they felt forced to teach in a manner that they did not believe would work, would not hesitate to politicize the issue, igniting parents with negative rhetoric.

Maureen had faith in her teachers and faith in her ability to support them in a structure that she believed was best for kids. With an open mind and encouraging hand, she led her school into the controversial model of inclusion.

Reflection

1. Discuss what you think would be some of Maureen's problems in reaching her goals. How would Maureen's inclusion plan work in your school? Would all or part of it be worth trying?

2. How well did Maureen use the four principles given in the beginning of this chapter?

Joanna Brandon of Sandiford Middle School: Personal Decision Making

Joanna Brandon's background as a high school guidance counselor gave her a keen awareness of the need for middle school students to be good decision makers. Joanna believed strongly that the adults in a young teenager's life can make a difference in how that teenager makes choices. Her vision was to integrate issues of personal decision making across the curriculum. Joanna anticipated that many of her teachers would view this notion cynically, considering it "touchy-feely" and a diversion from valuable academic time.

Joanna envisioned her success:

- Students would understand the dynamics of personal decision making: evaluating pros and cons, considering consequences, delaying gratification, and interpersonal and intrapersonal communication
- Students would understand the components of goal setting: setting realistic goals, making an action plan, self-monitoring, rallying support, and delaying gratification

Joanna invited a group of teachers and counselors to a working lunch in which she presented a broad outline of her vision. She hoped that each of these five teachers and counselors would invite at least one colleague to join the task force for positive decision making. The task force gathered eight members and they assisted Joanna with a request to the Superintendent that Sandiford be given one school-wide conference day to explore how issues of decision making could be integrated into the curriculum.

The conference day began with a keynote by a specialist in brain-based learning. Teachers heard about the research that supports the pedagogy of connecting personal responses to academic information. Teachers then met in break-out groups to brainstorm ways in which students could see how what they were learning in school could help them make positive decisions that would help them to reach their own goals. Ideas consisted of:

- journalizing
- personal response writing
- free reading
- raising awareness about cause and effect
- holding parenting groups
- strengthening the parent/faculty organization
- bringing in motivational speakers
- reevaluating extracurriculars
- reevaluating the sports programs
- classroom poster contests
- inspirational morning announcements (made by students)
- discussions of current events in *all* classes

- understanding philosophical paradigms: *ethos, logos, pathos*
- Socratic seminars
- considering personal decision making on issues of science and technology
- letter writing and other communication
- participation in government
- understanding argumentation
- critical thinking, reading, writing
- open-ended questions arising from academic information
- linking academic information to current controversies

Teachers also discussed some possible pitfalls of the above:

- students often specify names in open discussions
- discussions about personal issues easily go off-track
- sensitivities regarding sexuality issues
- overall lack of teacher control
- teachers can be considered instrusive, meddlesome, overreaching
- discussions of personal matters detract from academics

As Johanna expected, some teachers wanted nothing to do with bringing personal issues into the classroom. Others felt that they could use what students were already thinking and problem solving about to make connections into literature, history, physical education and health, as well as overall learning attitudes.

Joanna visited several classrooms to lead and participate in discussions. She enjoyed the interaction with kids, a welcome break from the disciplinary interventions that usually formed the basis of the relationship between her and them. She felt that she reconnected to her days as a guidance counselor, a field she greatly loved.

Reflection

1. Do you consider Joanna's "personal decision making" vision to be differentiated instruction?

2. Could a plan such as this be evaluated? What would the evaluation entail?

3. Could any of the ideas in Joanna's plan work in your school?

10

Case Studies

This part of the book provides you with a variety of lesson models for secondary classrooms. Most of these lessons are interdisciplinary, involve reading, and call for critical thinking.

Think about ways in which these lessons can be differentiated for your students. Consider the following models for differentiation (these are overlapping):

- ◆ Depth and complexity
- ◆ Readiness, prior knowledge, and interest
- ◆ Learning styles and multiple intelligence
- ◆ Brain-based learning theory (multisensory, emotions, graphics and visuals, metaphor, humor, and simultaneous processing)
- ◆ Introspection: reflection, self-monitoring, and metacognition
- ◆ Communication and socialization

Consider groupings: whole class, subgroups, and pairs. How will the class develop the sense of connectedness that will make the learning meaningful, memorable and durable? Consider reinforcement: lab exercises, case studies, and hands-on construction. Consider real-life applications: field work, service learning, and communications through technology.

In his inspiring book, *The Courage to Teach: Exploring the Inner Landscape of a Teacher's Life,* Parker J. Palmer describes the "subject-centered classroom." In a teacher-centered classroom, all knowledge emanates from the authority of the teacher. The teacher could just as well be an information-dispensing electronic device, and often is. In a student-centered classroom, you have the cliche of the blind leading the blind. I've had students who declare that a poem means whatever they say it means, textual evidence and author's intent notwithstanding. As you read these case studies, you will see how master teachers placed the *subject* in the center, with the learners, one of whom is the teacher, feeding their own experience into it and drawing knowledge out of it.

Case I: The Bible

Discussion Questions

The Learning Context: Mrs. Daniels' tenth-grade students have read the selections from the Old and New Testaments that appear in their literature anthology. They have read these selections aloud, as a whole class. Mrs. Daniels has emphasized the poetic qualities of the literature: how its sound evokes meaning, rhythmic qualities, metaphor, and unity.

At first, the students were a little surprised that they would be reading Biblical literature. "Isn't that illegal?" they asked. Mrs. Daniels, expecting their response, explained the Supreme Court Lemon ruling to them, asking them to be mindful of whether or not their reading the Bible in class served a secular or a religious purpose. In so doing, she established criteria for evaluative thinking at the outset. She asked, "What would it look like if we were reading these selections for religious purposes? What would it look like for secular purposes? She asked what other literature with a religious theme was in the anthology. Students noted that they read Greek and Roman mythology and stories in which characters experienced religious epiphanies. Mrs. Daniels used the word "epiphany" to show how many words that appear on vocabulary lists have religious meanings. Out of the positive, respectful, inquisitive tone of her class came evocative questions that invited critical thinking.

Directions to the Students: We will organize groups randomly today. Each group will choose a discussion question from the list. You will have 20 minutes to carry on your discussion, and then we will report out.

Here is how to organize your group:

- ◆ Assign a group leader. This person will move the group along and keep everyone focussed on the agenda
- ◆ Assign a recorder: This person will take notes on the progress of the discussion. These notes will be collected.
- ◆ Assign a speaker: This person will report to the class.

(Mrs. Daniels encourages the use of the democratic process to assign roles, but she monitors the groups to make sure time is not being wasted doing so. When groups are inefficient in deciding roles, Mrs. Daniels intervenes, shuffling people into other groups, assigning the roles herself, assigning new roles, or doubling up the students so that everyone is engaged.)

Choose one of the following discussion questions:

1. What does it mean to be reading the Bible "as literature" in a humanities course as opposed to reading the Bible as a means of religious understanding? What aspects of the text do we notice, discuss, and focus on when we read the Bible as literature? How would the questions that you would ask in English class be different from the ones that you would ask in a Sunday school class? How would the questions that you would ask in English class be different from those of a social studies class?

2. Compare/contrast the psalms to the stories. How do you personally respond to the psalms as opposed to the stories? Which brings a closer or more interesting meaning to you? Why? How would you characterize the language in the psalms as opposed to the language of the stories? How does language play a role in your response to each?

3. Literature, especially poetry, relies heavily on *contrast* to create dramatic interest. Find as many examples as you can of contrast in the selections that we have read. How do these contrasts operate to enhance or clarify the meaning?

4. When we wrote our poems and descriptions, we learned how to apply various language concepts. Find specific examples from our readings that apply these concepts:

- Specificity (noun sharpening)
- Anglo-Saxon verbs
- Metaphor
- Rhythm/refrain
- Onomatopoeia
- Minimizing modifiers
- Unified mood

Reflection

Assessment: Mrs. Daniels assessed this activity in a generalized way, based on observation of the students: simply, were they participating earnestly, or were they distracted and disengaged? She did not assign a specific grade to each student or to the group. This assessment went into the hopper of "the class participation grade" and was not discretely recorded.

Mrs. Daniels's reason for this casual assessment is that she believes that not everything students do and learn is subject to specific evaluation. Doing so compromises the communication and inquiry that makes discussion authentic.

> *Do you agree with Mrs. Daniels? Students spend two days, one on the discussion and one on the reporting, on this activity. Do you think this time should be reflected in a number grade? Are there other ways to assess what students have learned here?*

Differentiation: Mrs. Daniels would say that she has differentiated instruction here by offering students choices in the discussion topics, and then leaving them open for commentary. She notes that the questions lead straight into students' own experience, inviting them to integrate the new with the known.

Where it is *not* differentiated is that everyone has read the same text, although students certainly come to these readings with a varying levels of prior knowledge. Incidentally, one student, Nate, the only African-American student in this class and one of the few in this school, found his moment in the spotlight in this lesson. Because he attended a Baptist church regularly, his knowledge of the Bible was far greater than that of the other students, most of whom were

Catholics and Jews. Mrs. Daniels was very gratified to see Nate's high level of participation and the astonishment of his classmates when he could rattle off Biblical text, something no one else in the class, including Mrs. Daniels, could do.

> *Does this lesson effectively differentiate for depth and complexity? What, if anything, could you do to accommodate learning styles in this lesson? What would you say to a parent, student, or administrator who objected to the content of the lesson?*

Case II: Research Paper— Sports and Society

The Learning Context: Mr. Marsh teaches a college prep elective called "Social Issues." The course is targeted to 11th and 12th graders who may have some difficulties in a competitive four-year college, and who need to integrate study skills (reading, writing, research, time management) into the content areas.

Mr. Marsh's class is mixed, but many of these students have a negative attitude toward academics, even though most are headed toward college. His goal is to equip them with the habits of mind that will ease that transition, giving them the confidence they need to carry an academic task through to conclusion without a major breakdown. He uses the newspaper and Internet heavily, trying to interest students in controversies about science and technology, censorship, privacy, civic rights and responsibilities affecting young people, and issues surrounding cars. He tries to interest students in *The New York Times* and other scholarly publications, but he's satisfied when they read popular weekly news magazines.

Mr. Marsh has recently become aware of the importance of graphic information as it relates to reading factual material. He is trying to get his students to integrate information found in graphics with narrative information: "Go from the picture to the words, from the words to the picture." Because sports is a topic involving numbers, graphs, and charts, this topic seemed to lend itself to learning from a multiplicity of information sources.

Directions to the Students: You will write a research paper of 5 to 7 pages that answers *your own question* about some aspect of sports in society. You may consider the following ideas:

- ◆ Athletes as heroes and role models
- ◆ Fame issues
- ◆ Sportsmanship issues
- ◆ Economic influences of sports
- ◆ Sports and racial issues
- ◆ Student athlete issues
- ◆ Young athletes and parents
- ◆ Sports and gender issues

- Violence in sports
- Sports, records, statistics
- Sports and language
- Sports and medicine
- Sports and technology
- Sports reporting

Your central question should meet the following criteria:

- You don't already know the answer.
- The answer is complicated.
- The question is researchable.
- The question is significant and worth knowing about.
- The question will take 5 to 7 pages to discuss.
- The question requires several different sources of information.
- The answer will combine fact and opinion.

Components of your paper:

Abstract: You paper should open with an abstract, labeled as such. An abstract is a one-paragraph summary of your purpose and findings.

Outline: This should be handed in as a separate piece. The outline is a working document. That is to say, you need an outline before you begin, but it may change as you proceed. You should find yourself going back and forth with your outline as you proceed.

The following components should be worked in to your paper, in an order that you decide:

- *Anecdote:* A little story involving a real person
- *Analysis of statistics:* Your paper should contain at least one chart or graph of statistics. This material should be cited, the same as a quotation would be. You should include an analysis and/or commentary of this information.
- *Description:* At some point, you should have a descriptive paragraph, consisting of visual detail. This can be part of your anecdote.
- *Extended definition:* An extended definition is an explanation of a key concept. It differs from a dictionary definition because it operates in your particular context. For example: if you are writing about *gender equity*, you should explain what that means.
- *Block quotation:* This is a lengthy quotation (of several sentences) which gets set off from the text by wider margins and single spacing. It is introduced by a colon, and followed by a parenthetical citation, unless the citation is presented in the text.
- *At least two sides of the issue:* This is a research paper, not a persuasive essay. Although you may express your opinion, be sure to present opposing sides as objectively as possible.
- *Conclusion:* A paragraph at the end that sums up your paper.

- *Bibliography:* You need at least five sources

We will have in-class lessons on the following:

- Format/ Documentation techniques
- Paraphrasing/plagiarizing
- Identifying propaganda
- Bibliography

Dates:

Monday, March 13: Submit your question

Monday, March 20: Submit a tentative bibliography (*format doesn't have to be correct at this point.*)

Monday, March 27: Submit a working outline

Monday, April 3: Submit your abstract

Monday, April 10: Submit two pages of the paper

Monday, April 24: Paper is due

Organizing Theme: The culture of sports permeates our society and offers many opportunities for reflection about issues of all kinds: economic, medical, educational, and social. By examining various issues surrounding sports, we can gain insight into ourselves as individuals, as communities, and as Americans.

Essential Questions:
1. What are the positive and negative ramificaitons of sports?
2. What questions are raised in your mind regarding sports in society?
3. What are the social consequences of our love affair with sports?

Reflection

Assessment: Mr. Marsh will assess the final product against a rubric that the students have in advance. The rubric evaluates for:

- *Meaning:* The extent to which you've done what you were asked to do
- *Development:* The extent to which you've provided detail: facts, figures, names, places, events, reasons, examples, and cause/effect statements
- *Organization:* The extent to which your reader can follow the flow of your ideas
- *Language:* The extent to which you've used appropriate words
- *Presentation:* The extent to which your paper shows respect for the conventions of the English language; the extent to which your paper is neat and carefully put together

In addition, Mr. Marsh keeps a check-off list for all interim work on this project. He deducts points for lateness or incompleteness on these interim assignments.

Differentiation: Mr. Marsh would say that this project represents differentiated instruction because students get to formulate their own question and because the topic is diverse and open to choice. Where it is *not* differentiated is that everyone has to write a research paper under extremely controlled specifications. Mr. Marsh sets these specs up because he finds that the students in his Social Issues class have one big problem when it comes to writing: they don't know what to say. Mr. Marsh has given them the components; now, they just need the facts.

This case study is an example of differentiating content. The process, writing a research paper with certain components, is the same for all students. The product is essentially the same. It's the content of the paper that is differentiated.

1. Discuss the pros and cons of Mr. Marsh's "Sports and Society" project. How can it be extended to include more communication, technology, and community interaction?

2. Suppose you wanted to have students do a similar research project on "Music in Society." How could you adapt Mr. Marsh's project?

3. How could you adapt this lesson to include other genres besides writing?

Case III: Mathematics Portfolio

The Learning Context: Ms. Mosier, a seventh grade math teacher, has her students create a mathematics portfolio. The portfolio is a display of the student's best work in solving a broad range of mathematical problems, as well as introspective "How I Learned" statements. The pieces in the portfolio must represent the following properties of mathematics:

♦ Pattern-finding

♦ Calculation and measurement

♦ Symmetry

♦ Proportion

♦ Extrapolation

Ms. Mosier teaches her students to be mindful of the mental processes of mathematics. She begins by asking them what a good problem solver does, and makes a list of verbs:

♦ observe

♦ record

♦ rework

♦ monitor

♦ hypothesize

♦ apply

♦ measure

♦ calculate

♦ balance

♦ add, subtract, multiply, divide

- follow directions
- follow procedures
- research
- communicate
- lay out
- test
- check

The students have to use these verbs in their "How I Learned" statements. Ms. Mosier also raises awareness about what she calls the Attitude Equipment that a problem solver must have:

- Patience
- Curiosity
- Motivation
- Organization
- Optimism
- Perseverance
- Listening skills

The portfolios are indirectly related to the class lessons. Ms. Mosier has it this way deliberately. She doesn't want the portfolios to just be another form of homework in which students practice discrete skills. Rather, the portfolio represents real-life applications, such as the following:

- Erika took pictures of, and named, polygonal *patterns* that she found in her home.
- Steven made a graph representing the number of miles he walked during the week, as opposed to the weekends, over a one-month period.
- Caroline described the symmetry in composition of a song that she liked.
- George constructed a miniature of his house and property.
- Maddie composed a formula for guessing the number of jelly beans in a jar.

Directions to the Students: Your portfolio is a chance for you to show what you know and can do in mathematics. You should begin by noticing mathematics all around you. Think about your own interests and the problems that you have to figure out every day. Select problems that show that you understand what we've learned in class, what you've learned before in math, what you've learned in other classes, and what you've learned outside of school.

I will check your portfolio every six weeks, on a rotating basis. I expect to see progress from one checkpoint to the next. Your work will be graded based on the following:

- *Complexity:* Does your problem have many parts and steps?

- *Accuracy and Efficiency:* Are your procedures and numbers correct and do they follow the best path to knowledge?
- *Understanding:* Are you showing that you understand the topic (patterns, measurement and calculation, symmetry, proportion, extrapolation)
- *Presentation:* Is your problem presented in a way that is neat, clear, and easy on the viewer?

Here are some problems that you can solve:

- What would it cost to wallpaper your room?
- How much will you have to spend on gerbil food for a year if you have two gerbils, and they have offspring?
- If you forgot two numbers of your locker combination, but you knew that they were odd numbers, how many combinations would you have to try?
- How much land could you cover if you walked from dawn to dusk on your birthday? How about in your half-birthday?
- Make a mathematical representation that shows the astrological signs of the people in our math class.

Reflection

Differentiation: Ms. Mosier's portfolio takes into account that students have different needs and interests regarding mathematics. We know that ethnicity, language, cultural identification, gender, and life experience all play into one's approach to mathematics. This diversity can account for the time it takes a student to solve a problem, how or if she needs to communicate about it, how she expresses what she knows, and whether she cares about the problem at all.

Ms. Mosier seeks to increase the relevance of mathematics for her students by connecting it to their real lives. She allows them to learn in the way that they learn best: by stories, by visuals, by trial and error, by manipulatives, by language, and by abstractions.

Differentiating instruction in mathematics means:

- finding ways in which to create a context of mathematics within the students' life and environment.
- inviting students to think of mathematics as connected to what they know, what they care about, who they are, and how they think.
- asking students to explain their thinking
- inviting alternative methods to problem-solving

Ms. Mosier found that certain features of her students' lives influenced the way that they approched problems. Once the abstract math problems were placed in a real -ife context, answers became more open-ended. As she understood her students' reasoning, she came to realize that there were more factors influencing their answers than she might have thought of herself. For example, she might ask students to comparison shop, looking for the best prices on particular items. But real factors in problem solving, such as travel expenses, intervened in the "purity" of the arithmetic. In real life, a bargain is not a bargain if it cost you two bus fares to get it.

Case IV: Math and Stories

The Learning Context: Mr. James Beverly teaches practical business math to high school students. Most of his students have had difficulty with the higher levels of abstract math. Many, if not most, of Mr. Beverly's students come to him with negative attitudes about math and their ability to do math. One of the ways in which he makes math more accessible is to have students write their own "story problems." Aware of the relationship between language and thinking, Mr. Beverly helps students clarify abstractions by putting them into words. Learners need to know that they can use their language to proceed through a math problem: saying it aloud, explaining it to someone else, verbalizing their thinking as they go, and using graphic organizers.

The following are the pedagogical principles on which student-generated math stories are based:

◆ students learn best when "a friendly context" is established

◆ students learn best when they are given a chance to internalize the learning, making it real to them in their own world

◆ language is not only a way to express what one knows, but also a way to learn how to learn

Because part of Mr. Beverly's strategy is to socialize math, he uses flexible grouping. Students may work in pairs, with each one figuring the other's problem. They may work as teams, producing a complex problem and then giving it to another team to solve. Groups may be divided in accordance with the type of math function to be used in the story problem: fractions, multiplication, division, etc. Or, they may compose story problems based on a particular scenario: travel problems, merchandise problems, money problems, etc.

Directions to Students: In class, we have been learning about tax deductions for depreciation of assets. Arrange yourselves into random groups of three. One person will play the role of the CEO; the other two are the Loyal Employees. The CEO has asked the Loyal Employees to find information and make a joint report on the following question: Should our company lease our cars or should we purchase them? Your group must submit the following:

◆ *Action Plan:* This is a step-by-step division of labor report: who has to do what to solve the problem?

◆ *Findings:* This is a clear report that makes the recommendation and shows the facts and figures that support it.

◆ *Evaluation:* This is the CEO's response to the report: Is it complete and satisfactory? If additional information is necessary, explain what and why. Is the report entirely clear and convincing? Write a memo to your Loyal Employees giving them your response to their work.

Extension: Students Write Their Own Business Math Stories

Mr. Beverly eventually wants his students to be able to compose their own problem-solving scenarios. He has devised three levels:

Level 1: Simple fact-finding and calculation: In a Level 1 problem, all the problem solver has to do is go out and gather up appropriate numbers, present them clearly, and then do whatever the calculations are to solve the problem. Example: Using an amortization chart, you are making a report comparing the mortgages on several homes.

Level 2: Substitutions: In a Level 2 problem, you have to substitute some information for other information and then recalculate. You may have to decide what variables have to be substituted to solve the problem. Example: You are figuring out how your monthly payments would change if you changed the term of a loan.

Level 3: Pros and cons: In the "pros and cons" scenario, your problem requires you to evaluate alternatives. Each of these alternatives must have several variables. Some of these variables must be uncertain. Example: You are weighing the pros and cons of purchasing stocks, as opposed to bonds.

Reflection

Assessment: This is a research project that will involve trips to the library or computer room. Mr. Beverly will assess the students based on

- ◆ Fact-finding behavior: Are the students on task, displaying a serious attitude, keeping records appropriately, and communicating in the language of business math?
- ◆ Written reports: Are the reports presentable in a business format? Is the information clear and accurate?

Differentiation: Here, the product and content are constant; the process is open to differentiation. Consider the following about Mr. Beverly's role-playing task:

1. How do cultural differences play into this task? Will these differences hamper or advance the learning?
2. Do you think this role-play represents time well spent in learning about the topic?
3. What collateral learning is likely to take place here?
4. How much should the teacher intervene in this task?
5. Could this pedagogy be applied to the more abstract math courses?

Case V: Math, Reading, and Visuals

The Learning Context: Mrs. McMillan teaches practical math to special education students, grades 9–12. Her students come to her with significant reading deficits. What we term "practical math" or "business math" is largely reading. Mrs. McMillan teaches her students to manage the reading material by offering students the following strategies:

- Reword the problem. Say it in your own words.
- Show what the problem looks like: Make a diagram. Use colors.
- Make a "to do" list to help you approach the problem step by step.
- Estimate, to get a ballpark figure of where you are going. Then, go back and use the exact numbers.
- Put yourself in the problem. Tell the problem in the first person.
- Learn how to make tables, charts, and graphs to help you visualize and organize the information in the business problem.
- Talk to yourself as you work through a problem.

Mrs. McMillan knows that effective readers do three things, which effective math readers need to do as well: *visualize, mark the text,* and *self-monitor.* She also knows that as a business math teacher, she is a vocabulary teacher. That means that she has to explain word roots and go over pronunciation and spelling. The root, pronunciation, and spelling of a word are all strong cues to its meaning.

Case VI: Creative Writing

The Learning Context

This case study is based on my Creative Writing (CW) elective (half year) at Hendrick Hudson High School. The class consists of 15 students in the 11th and 12th grades. It is a mixed class, comprising mostly high achieving students, with a few mid-achievers.. All have good academic gpa's and are highly motivated to learn. There are no special ed students in this class.

Although I've taught creative writing as an elective for many years, I always find assessment problematic. Rather than assign a grade to a piece, I prefer that students learn to self evaluate. More importantly, I want them to think of writing and storytelling as a means of communication, rather than something that is handed in for a grade. I suspect that reliance on grades discourages the necessary risk taking that goes along with my goals for creative writing. Also, many teenagers write about personal experiences and feelings, and I'd rather not assign a grade to such expressions. There's a certain amount of trust involved with personal writing, and I feel that a negative grade violates that trust.

Each creative writing class is unique for two reasons. One is the mix of students. Sometimes, I get a rowdy group dominated by students who don't take writing seriously. Sometimes, I get an extremely diverse group, ranging from future Ivy Leaguers to kids who come to me out of self-contained special ed classes. The former are there because they actually have the potential to make a living as writers; the latter, perhaps because there was "no where else to put him" and "he says he likes to write poetry." No matter what the circumstances, doling out grades for creative writing never has felt quite right to me.

Another reason why each creative writing class is unique has to do with my own evolution as a teacher—what I am "into" at the time. It may be that I've taken a screenplay-writing class and am thinking about story structure. I may be in a grammatical frame of mind and be pushing grace and style in syntax. I may be hooked on a particular author. Or on a newspaper kick. Or a poetry binge. I keep my folders with my notes from year to year, but, I have to admit, I rarely reuse anything from one creative writing class to the next. So, my assessment system is always different.

This year, I'm thinking a lot about speech and its function in the classroom as a means of assessment. If we consider assessment a judgment of evidence of learning, then speech in the classroom certainly applies. When I attended Heidi Jacobs' two-day institute in Boston on language and learning, I reshaped my thinking about student talk. I've always known that students are supposed to talk a lot in an English class. Now, I'm coming to see even more the importance of student talk. When it comes to creative writing, the stories begin with the talking. The telling of stories itself becomes the class: it's a better creative writing class if we broaden the word "writing" to include "storytelling" through verbal means as well.

All of this may sound wonderful, and it is…or, it *would* be if not for the pesky little detail that I have to grade this stuff. It's hard enough to grade a kid's written description of her first day of school. How can I possibly put a grade on her oral rendition of it? And, what about kids whose nature it is to be shy? Or those of an ethnic background that encourages quietness in a classroom? Assessment in creative writing feels fluid and intuitive to me. I know that there are educational theorists who believe that there's a rubric for everything, but I never could function that way.

This I know: for kids to write from the heart and share their writing, they have to feel safe. That means, much time must be spent cultivating a comfort zone. This comfort zone, in my class, is fashioned out of anecdotes, laughter, and the sharing of stories about family, friends, and growing up. I have to set the example that it is safe to share stories, by telling stories of my own life.

What all of this has to do with differentiated instruction is simple: In Stephen King's recent memoir about the writing life, he tells how the writer doesn't go to some sort of "story warehouse" to pull ideas off a shelf. The writer doesn't make up stories, he *recognizes* them. So, what I try to do is to get students to recognize the stories that already exist in their lives. To do that, we tell stories. Our own stories. Stories about what happened on the playground in the third grade, or the time we were the new kid. My goal is to help kids recognize that they *already have* stories worth telling, stories with introductions, point of view, attitude and voice, setting, climax, irony, ambiguity, and denouement.

Procedures

I always start off by saying that the creative writing class will consist of four parts:

1. Direct instruction: I will teach a particular writing technique, such as point of view, and explain the writing task in detail.

2. Modeling: I will present a piece of exemplary professional or student-written literature and show how it demonstrates excellent use of the technique.

3. Lab: Students will write, either in the classroom, or in the computer room.

4. Sharing and postmortem: One way or another (reading aloud, writing key sentences on the board, exchanging papers, reproducing class sets, etc.), students will read each other's work.

Somehow, every time, my best intentions go awry almost immediately, and all four discrete steps get mushed together. Steps 1 and 2 may go fine, but when we get to the "students will write" part, I find myself in the position of Writing Warden, a role that I absolutely hate. There's something extremely artificial and wrong about telling people that they must all write and not talk to each other. It just doesn't work in my class, probably because I'm usually the first one to break the silence, even if I'm doing the task myself, which I'm not always disciplined enough to do.

So, that brings me to what I decided to do this year to differentiate instruction and properly assess: I decided to have students submit a portfolio of specific kinds of writing. (See the directions below.) We would tell stories, discuss technique, and read models in class. On their own, they would write the designated pieces, and hand in the portfolio at the end of the quarter.

Results

The results were mixed, yet predictable. Diana and Kyle were absent and did not hand in their portfolios until after vacation.. Three or four students handed in disappointing work, even though they were ordinarily conscientious in a traditional class structure. We had one near nervous breakdown: It seems that Colleen was on the noneligibility list for failing multiple courses at mid-quarter. In order to get back on the team, she needed the signature of all of her teachers, indicating that she had everything handed in. She stuck her sign-off sheet under my nose and demanded my initials at the start of class. I asked her to produce her portfolio. She reported cheerfully that she'd have it just as soon as I gave her a pass to go down to the computer room and print it out. I balked, saying that if it wasn't ready to be handed in, then it was late and therefore I would not sign her sheet. She dissolved into tears of despair at her desk, protesting that she had it, or would have it, just as soon as I gave her a pass to print it out. Colleen and I had words in the hall about our disagreement over the definition of a deadline. Finally, I relented. When I returned to class, they were glum. They "felt stressed" over the "amount of work" I had laid upon them.

This was the teachable moment about the writer's life. I told them that all
work is seasonal, that everyone has busy times of the year. I also told them that
about meeting deadlines. Now they could understand
about writing. Many of them had procrastinated and their
had not done their best, and were ready to blame me for
horter deadlines.

he due date as the last day of the quarter, so that there
s. They could, of course, have handed in the portfolio ear-
hen they complained that there was too much work in the
s, I reminded them that those stipulations were to get a
was simply to make the perfectly acceptable choice to get
. *Ah, but we don't want a "low grade." We want that 95; we just*

do more than anything else in creative writing class is to
sponsibility for their own progress. What this discussion
hat many of these students are not ready for long term
t I decided to do: I told them that, for the fourth quarter,
tween two plans. The High School plan would be a tradi-
rly short works due every few days. These would be
ased on how well they demonstrated an understanding
lesson. The College Plan would be the portfolio assess-
ould hand in a completed story and a screenplay, along
e end of the quarter.

instruction model presented here works well for creative
ng to my goals. It accomplishes two purposes:

1. Students get to write freely, based on their life experiences, without
being controlled by a grade.

2. Students practice the important life skill of time management and
self-discipline.

Summary: A high school creative writing class has an inherent tension: we
sacrifice spontaneity and risk taking if we are too judgmental about the grade.
Also, students will vary widely in their talent for writing and in their expectations for the course. On the other hand, we sacrifice a certain amount of control
and accountability when we play it too liberally with the grades. Contracts are
one way to even the tension, but even these do have pitfalls. Creative writing
classes are characterized by long-term projects, personal narratives, rewrites,
experimentation, and the kind of writing doesn't lend itself to traditional evaluation.

Directions

Here is what I gave my CW class, including directions, to explain the grading system for the fourth quarter:

1. Writing Stories
2. Writing Screenplays

Please select one of the following plans for your fourth quarter grade:

♦ High School Plan: You will be given a specific writing assignment to hand in every few days. You will get a numerical grade on each piece that reflects how well it demonstrates skill in the given writing technique.

♦ College Plan: A few days before the end of the quarter, you will hand in a portfolio containing the following:

  • One completed story of at least 5 pages.
  • One completed screenplay of at least 10 pages.

Each of the above pieces must be accompanied by:

♦ a story board or story map

♦ a reflective piece, explaining your writing process (what you did, how you did it, what you were trying to do, how well your story expresses your intended purpose)

Case VII: Maps—A Tiered Assignment

The Learning Context: Miss Lyons teaches ninth grade Global History and Geography. She always begins the course with assessing students' map-reading skills. She spends the first two weeks of school on the tiered assignment described here. The field of the maps is Europe, North Africa, and the Middle East.

Miss Lyons has a shrewd plan. Not only does she want students to improve their map skills, but she also wants them to improve their reading skills by perusing the textbook in doing this task. To find the needed information, they will be giving themselves an overview of the whole book.

Level I: The Lay of the Land: These are students whose preassessment shows that they really don't know where key geographical features and national borders are in the field. The cognitive skills for this level are familiarity and recognition. Students need to learn by labeling, color coding, and reconstructing.

Level II: Geography is Destiny: These students know their basic geography of the field. They are ready to do some inferential thinking about how particular geographical features have determined key historical events. They need to consider why cities developed where they did, the economic value of certain geographical features and why that changed, military implications of geographical features, trade routes, etc. These students need to learn by tracing, categorizing, linking cause and effect, and comparing maps from various eras.

Level III: Telling the Story: These students are ready to narrate historical events based on map information, going from picture to word and from word to picture. They are also ready to process many kinds of map information simultaneously, and integrate that information into their story. These students need to learn by sequencing, linking cause to effect, generalizing, and finding supportive evidence for generalizations.

For the preassessment, Miss Lyons gives the class the following Level II task:

> Look at the map on page 377 of your text. Label all of the geographical features that you know. Make an educated guess about the following and mark the places on the map accordingly:
>
> - A major trading center (mark with dollar signs)
> - A great vacation spot (mark with a smiley face)
> - A place that probably gets invaded by its neighbors (mark with an arrow)
> - A place that is difficult to invade (mark with a heavy border)
> - A place that has an inhospitable climate (mark with a frowning face)
> - Mark the most expedient routes between three pairs of major cities (use arrowed lines)
> - The most populous city (mark with dots)
> - Explain your answer, using language that shows what you understand about geography.

All students need to:

- Practice spelling the place names
- Reduce the field into smaller and smaller geographical units
- Increase their ability to associate places with events
- Understand those features on the map that are constant and those that change with history
- Understand the kinds of information that can be conveyed on a map
- Express map information in words
- Express verbal information about geography in the form of a map

Directions to the Students: (After sorting students into one of three levels based on the preassessment, Miss Lyons gives them written directions.) You may work in pairs or on your own. Both you and your partner must hand in your own work, in your own handwriting. We will do these tasks in class, but you are expected to do some of the work at home so that you finish by the deadline. Don't rely on your partner to bring in materials. Your partner's absence will not be an excuse for you to be unprepared.

Everyone must complete Level I and Level II. If you start out with Level II, you should do the Level III or the Optional Map Challenge. If you start with Level III, you must choose one of the Optional Map Challenges.

(Optional Map Challenges: The purpose of the optional map challenge tasks is so that students at Level III will have as much to work with as students in Levels I and II. Also, the optional tasks provides for extra credit for students who finish in time to do another task. And, students at Level II are offeredd the choice between doing the Level III or one of the optional tasks.)

- Optional Map Challenge A: Comparison/Contrast:
- Find two maps of the same place at two different points in history. Make a two-column chart that shows every difference that you notice between the two maps.
- Optional Map Challenge B: Borderlines

Find a map of a country in Europe that shows the divisions within that country. Make educated guesses as to why the country is divided the way it is: what geographical features account for border divisions?

Reflection

Assessment: Because students are working together on these tasks, Miss Lyons will employ an additional assessment, based on individual performance. She has made up a short answer test for Level I, and a constructed response test for Levels II and III.

Differentiation: Typically, tiered tasks are differentiated on the basis of a pre-assessment and differentiated for content, process, and product. Map interpretation can involve very interesting and varied ways of learning. Jigsaw puzzles offer manipulatives, visuals, and reinforcement through repetition. Coloring with crayons can reinforce the image of the map. Labeling can reinforce spelling and memorization. Beyond the literal level of map interpretation are math skills (proportion, extrapolation, calculation), logic (cause and effect, pattern-finding), relationships, and symbolism.

1. How are maps used in other subject areas?

2. How can you use local maps in your instruction about the kinds of maps found int he textbook?

3. How can you apply Miss Lyons's tiered assignment to learning about time lines?

4. How can you use maps found in newspapers to reinforce learning at various levels?

5. What advantages and disadvantages do you see in Miss Lyons's tiered assignment?

Case VIII: Shakespeare for the Moment

Learning Context: It has been said that no one has ever understood the human heart in all of its manifestations better than Shakespeare. After the disaster of September 11, I, like every other teacher, struggled to find words with which to face my students, not to explain the unexplainable, or to console the inconsolable, but just to help them name their response. I thought of Prospero's speech in Act V of *The Tempest*, as well as some other lines from Shakespeare plays:

> The cloud-capp'd towers, the gorgeous palaces,
>
> The solemn temples, the great globe itself,
>
> Yea, all which it inherit, shall dissolve,

And like this insubstantial pageant faded

Leave not a rack behind.

(The Tempest, V)

Some are born great. Some achieve greatness. Some have greatness thrust upon them.

(Twelfth Night)

Our legions are brimful. Our cause is ripe.

The enemy increaseth every day.

There is a tide in the affairs of men,

Which, taken at the flood, leads on to fortune.

Omitted, all the voyage of our lives

Are bound in shallows and in misery.

On such a full sea are we now afloat,

And we must take the current when it serves,

Or else lose our ventures.

(Julius Caesar, V)

Cry Havoc! and let slip the dogs of war.

(Julius Caesar, III)

The readiness is all.

(Hamlet, V)

There's providence in the fall of every sparrow.

(Hamlet, V)

Our revels now are ended.

(The Tempest, V)

We few, we happy few, we band of brothers,

For he today that sheds his blood with me

Shall be my brother, be he ne'er so vile

This day shall gentle his condition;

And gentlemen in England, now a-bed,

Shall think themselves accurs'd they were not here,

And hold their manhoods cheap whiles any speaks

That fought with us upon Saint Crispin's day.

(Henry V, IV)

When I teach a full Shakespearean play, I go over every word, line, and speech as closely as I can. But there are additional ways to let students find Shakespeare: let Shakespeare find *them.*

Directions to Students: Think of a powerful event in your life, or in history, or in a book or movie. Select something that you really feel a strong emotional response to. In class, we have many Shakespearean plays available for you to look through. See if you can find lines that speak for you about this event. All you have to do is copy out the lines into your writing journal. (At this point, I explain the conventions used to quote from a play.)

Reflection

Differentiation: This activity yields amazing results in terms of how students internalize Shakespeare. They begin to look at Shakespearean text for what it is: the most eloquent expression of human experience in the English language. They are able to look past the archaic grammar and unfamiliar nouns and read with eyes of the heart.

This simple but powerful activity is differentiated instruction because each student is finding meaning for her own self-selected experience. There's no assessment. Students are just invited to stroll though the plays in class, taking what they want for their own.

If you try this activity, expect some students to reject it. Not all students are ready to connect to a powerful emotional experience on demand. If students are "not getting it," I sometimes suggest that they just pick out lines that appeal to them, for whatever reason.

Like a hologram, any Shakespearean play is a slice of the whole collection. You can do this activity with a single play if you choose. I always find it regrettable that we don't find time to go back to the literature, especially the Shakespeare, of previous years. The usual sequence is *Romeo and Juliet* in grade 9; *Julius Caesar* in grade 10, *Macbeth* in grade 11, and *Hamlet* in grade 12. I'm suggesting that, as each new play is introduced, the others be brought back for an encore.

1. What kind of classroom climate would be necessary to make this activity effective? How can this climate be achieved?

2. Do you consider this activity too emotionally laden to be appropriate? What advantages and disadvantages do you find?

3. What other ways can you think of for having kids connect to Shakespeare on an emotional level?

Case IX: Investigative Report—The SAT's

The Learning Context: This performance task can be given to English, social studies, or math classes at the high school level. The description that follows was given to my tenth grade English classes. It can be adapted to social studies or math classes.

Directions to the Students: Your task for this investigative report is to pose a question about the SAT's that you can answer by doing various kinds of research. You will write a paper of 8 to 12 pages (1.5 spaced) that explores your question and uses standard research paper conventions. Your question may be of one of the following types:

- Your opinion about the SAT's and how they are used
- The history of the SAT's
- The relationship between the SAT's and high school and college achievement
- An explanation of how and why the SAT's are used
- An explanation of controversial issues about the SAT's
- Anything else that is answerable by research
- Test preparation

What is research? Research is the process of searching for, collecting, organizing, and analyzing information.

What forms can research information take in a research paper? Your research may be presented in any of the following forms:

- Direct quotations
- Indirect quotations and paraphrase
- Charts and graphs
- Statistical information
- Anecdotes (personal stories) and interviews
- Primary source material (The actual SAT's)

What should I use as a model for what an investigative report looks like? You will find investigative reports in *The New York Times.* Often, these are serialized over several days.

Reflection

Assessment: The rubric assessing the final paper has the following attributes:

- *Meaning:* The extent to which you've followed the directions.
- *Development:* The extent to which you've provided sufficient information: examples, reasons, cause/effect, facts and figures.
- *Organization:* The extent to which you've presented your information in a logical sequence with proper transition.
- *Language:* The extent to which your word choice and sentence structure convey knowledge and a serious attitude.
- *Conventions:* The extent to which you've used proper spelling, punctuation, capitalization; the extent to which your research format follows the style guide; and the extent to which your paper shows care and seriousness in presentation

I also had various interim dates at which students had to give me the question that they devised, a few of the sources that they found, and a few pages of a rough draft. These items were graded on a pass/fail basis.

Differentiation: This performance task differentiates for content. Everyone is following more or less the same process of doing an investigative report, so whole class instruction is possible, to show students what an investigative report looks like, and what the steps are in doing one. You could say that the product, a research paper based on an investigative report, is the same, although everyone's content is individualized.

1. How could this performance task be adapted to a math class?
2. In what way(s) does this task call for critical thinking?

Case X: *The New York Times* Quotation Project

The Learning Context: This performance task may be used for English or social studies classes. I used it in my tenth-grade English class, but it could easily be adapted for middle school students. I used *The New York Times,* but a local newspaper could also be used for middle school students. News magazines designed for classroom use, such as *Scholastic Update,* are also appropriate.

Directions to the Students: Cut and paste headlines/lead paragraphs of articles that illustrate the following quotations. In one sentence, explain how each article illustrates the quotation.

Presentation: Cut the article out *neatly* and tape it on a piece of paper.

Development: Where the quotation is self explanatory, you do not have to explain it. Where the quotation requires explanation, explain it in one sentence *and* specify what criteria a news item would have to have in order to satisfy the quotation.

Selections: You may select news items because they illustrate the quotation directly, or because they illustrate it *ironically, br representing the opposite.*

> It was the best of times, it was the worst of times.—Charles Dickens, 1859

> The test of our progress is not whether we add more to the abundance of those who have much; it is whether we provide enough for those who have too little.—Franklin Delano Roosevelt

> There is no kind of dishonesty into which otherwise good people more easily and frequently fall than that of defrauding the government.—Benjamin Franklin

> If I were asked to what the singular prosperity and growing strength of the Americans ought mainly to be attributed, I should reply: To the superiority of their women.—Alexis de Tocqueville

Upon the soundness and integrity of public opinion depends the destiny of our democracy.—Robert M. LaFollette

A wonderful fact to reflect upon, that every human creature is constituted to be that profound secret and mystery to every other.—Charles Dickens

Corporation: An ingenious device for obtaining individual profit without individual responsibility.—Ambrose Bierce

Reflection

Assessment: The connections that students make between the quotation and the articles that they select may not always be clear to you. I assessed this project more on whether they could explain their connections than whether their connections were readily apparent to me. I graded this task on three levels: P (Pass); PD (Pass with Distinction) and I (Insufficient).

To receive "pass with distinction" students had to demonstrate any two of the following:

- Connections which are subtle, yet clearly explainable
- Articles taken from various sections of the newspaper
- A collection of articles on a specific theme. A theme is different from a subject.
- Articles that are connected to the quotation ironically
- The inclusion of a written report that explains the connections of the articles to the quotation (optional).
- Transcend the obvious

Differentiation: To receive "pass with distinction," students have to treat the topic with depth and complexity. Students at lower levels of sophistication will select the most obvious quotations, and then find the most obvious articles. If they do that, they will receive a passing grade, and they still will have learned something about what's going on in the world, and how these events are connected to a meaningful statement.

How could a social studies teacher link The Quotations Project to the study of history?

Case XI: *The New York Times* Review Project

The Learning Context: This performance task may be used in English, social studies, music appreciation, and art classes. This is a critical thinking task because students have to discern what criteria the reviewer used to evaluate the piece.

Directions to the Students: Read one of the following types of reviews:

- Books
- Film

- ◆ Television
- ◆ Music

1. Read the review.
2. What did the reviewer like/dislike about the piece being reviewed?
3. Based on this review, what would you say are the reviewer's criteria for excellence?

A Matter of Taste: The following *task choices* require you to justify your opinion about the arts. In answering these questions, focus on *why* you hold a particular opinion. Don't dwell on telling your feelings or opinion without *justifying it.* Responses should be one well-developed paragraph in length.

Choose One:

I   Describe how your tastes in movies and/or music have changed over the past few years. Why has your taste changed? Do you expect that the next several years will see a further change in your cultural tastes? Explain why you think these changes may come about and why your tastes have changed in the past.

II Select a film from your childhood that had a particularly strong impact on you, and analyze why it had such a strong effect and, perhaps, why it continues to.

III Describe the effect that seeing or hearing something that you thought was beautiful had on you.

Reflection

How could the Review Project be used as a tiered assignment?

Case XII: *The New York Times—* Front Page and News Summary

The Learning Context: The followings discussion guide can be used in English or social studies classes. It may be used to generate whole class discussion, small group discussion and reporting out, journal writing, or essay writing.

Discussion Guide

- ◆ Is there any news in today's *Times* that directly or indirectly affects your life or your family's?
- ◆ Why do you think each front page story is put on the front page? If the *Times* were to receive a news story that must replace one or two front-page articles, which ones would you move to a less prominent page?
- ◆ What kind of research did the reporter have to do for a particular article?

Is there anything in today's *Times* that relates to what you are learning in one of your classes?

- Which *Times* stories about local, state, or national politics and government do you think might have never been printed if people in power could have called up and said, "I know you're planning to print that story. Don't print it."?
- Judging from the news in today's *Times*, is the world today (no matter how slightly) better or worse than it was yesterday?
- What changes in another country indicate economic, political, scientific, or social *progress?*
- What changes in another country indicate economic, political, scientific, or social *regression?*
- Censor the *Times*: If you were in charge of censoring any material that "someone" could find insulting, dangerous, subversive, or disturbing, what stories would you censor in today's *Times*?
- What examples are there in today's *Times* of people behaving honorably, heroically, courageously, or nobly? Who is your "hero of the day" today?
- What examples are there in today's *Times* of people behaving dishonorably? Who is your "villain of the day" today?
- "The Past is Prologue": History and current events blend in *Times* articles all the time. What connections do you see between past and present in today's news? What historical background do you need in order to understand today's news?

Differentiation: Students have varying degrees of experience and prior knowledge about news events. Those who are at "entry level," are likely to shy away from discussion, happy to let the more sophisticated students take over. In discussions of news events, we often see two or three students in a display of ostentatious bluster, shouting everyone else down, as if they were on a Sunday morning news-talk show. Everyone else slinks down in their seats, or does math homework. To bring more students into the discussion, and to have them feel safe, you might want to have students self-select into the following groups:

- Novices
- Dabblers
- Hounds

Each group selects a moderator, known as Law and Order. This moderator reads off the list. If three people in the group say "pass," then the group moves on to the next item until they find a consensus on a question for discussion. *Assessment:* You can't go around and assess every student in the class in terms of how they well they are contributing to the discussion. Negative behaviors that show a lack of seriousness are likely to attract your attention. These negative behaviors may be overt or subtle: habitually asking to leave the room, having off-task side conversations, tipping back on the chair, looking elsewhere, doing paperwork, conversing with members of other groups, or just biding time.

The teacher might say this:

> If I take a picture of your group, what are you doing in the picture? Are you looking at the front page for evidence? looking at the speaker? being the speaker? I can't hear what each of you is saying, but I can see with my eyes if you are communicating, listening, and reading. If I see that, then I know you are learning. If I see something else, then I assume you are not

Reflection

Do you think small group discussions about news events can be assessed?

Case XIII: *Edith Hamilton Mythology* and *The Odyssey*—The Hero and the Goddess

Collaborative Ninth Grade English Class

The Learning Context: These are Mrs. Kate Bryson's tiered lessons for her ninth grade English class. Here is how the collaborative model works at Kate's school: Ten special ed students are in this model. The model consists of three periods: English, social studies, and resource room. These meet during periods 2, 3, and 7, respectively. A block of five of these special ed students are in Mrs. Bryson's period 2 class, and then in Mr. Leighton's period 3 social studies class. This setup is mirror-imaged, so that the other five students are in Leighton's period 2 social studies class, and Bryson's period. 3 English class. The special ed teacher is present in each class on alternating days. His presence is mirror-imaged by that of an aide. In other words, Bryson and Leighton always have a second pair of hands, whether that be the special ed teacher or an aide. During resource room, period 7, the special ed teacher meets every day with the 10 students. He is able to provide very specific and targeted support, because he has been in the classroom, observing the learning.

Mrs. Bryson's English class consists of students of all ability levels. She administers the following preassessment:

♦ Do you like to read fantasy adventure stories? If you have read at least five fantasy adventure stories, write their titles.

(Commentary: This is to determine interest, experience, and prior knowledge. Students with a flair for the fantasy adventure genre are in a position to find patterns and make comparisons. They will be familiar with the story structure and language of mythology.)

♦ Circle the words below that are unfamiliar to you:
  • Oracle
  • Trojan War
  • Odysseus
  • Achilles heel
  • Athena

- Zeus
- Apollo
- Helen of Troy
- Ithaca
- Penelope
- Lotus Eaters
- Cyclops
- Circe

(*Commentary:* Students usually come into the ninth grade with some background on mythology, but the language may still be intimidating to them.)

♦ *Reading comprehension:* Kate has prepared 10 reading comprehension questions based on passages from the texts. The questions break down as follows:

1 to 3: Literal level

4 to 6: Vocabulary and idiom in context

7 to 10: Interpretative and inferential

Kate uses this preassessment to help students make their choice about which group to go into. She does not use the pre-test to sort and assign students to certain groups. She might say this:

Some of us remember a lot about the mythology that we learned in earlier grades. Some of us liked the stories and the names of the people and the places that we learned about before. Mythology may still be new to some of us. Pick your group based on what you know and like about mythology.

Four Mythology Groups:

1. Philosophers: Be in this group if you remember a lot about mythology, if the pre-test was easy for you, if you like saying and reading the words of mythology. This group will think about themes, compare the myths to other stories that they know, find current situations that remind us of the myths.

2. Poets: Be in this group if you like to figure out what words mean, and you like to read aloud.

3. Travelers: Be in this group if you like maps and places, and if you like to visualize stories.

4. Crew: Be in this group if you don't remember much about mythology, and you would like to get the basics of the stories.

5. Warriors: Be in this group if you like the action scenes.

Tiered Assignments

Students work together. Individuals submit reports for themselves. Reports may be in any form that answers the question: *notes, paragraph,* or *diagram*

How it works: Give students the following thematic statements about *The Odyssey*.

- ◆ Philosophers compare these themes to other stories and/or to their own life story. They also answer thematic questions, such as "Why is this episode included?"
- ◆ Poets collect words, phrases, and sentences that capture the themes. They also find key passages to read aloud.
- ◆ Travelers make maps of the literal and thematic territory.
- ◆ Warriors express the conflicts between groups and within the individual (Odysseus, Penelope, Telemachus).

Episodes

The Lotus Eaters: The episode about the lotus eaters is one of the most famous episodes in *The Odyssey*, yet it is only one paragraph long. Why do you think it is so famous? Why do you think it is so short?

Cave of the Cyclops: The episode that takes us to the cave of the Cyclops is said to represent the "realm of mythic space" where the comforts of familiar space are removed: deserts, wilderness, the high seas. But the cave of the Cyclops can represent places in our own lives, individually or as a society. Compare the war on terrorism to the cave of the Cyclops. Be sure to use specific references to *The Odyssey*.

Understanding the pattern: First, the hero embarks upon the road of trials. This is a pathway that is fraught with many dangers, as well as some unexpected pleasures. The hero begins his journey for reasons of business, curiosity, or just plain happenstance. Sometimes, he is a reluctant traveler. When he finally reaches a doorway, he must confront a threshhold guardian, guard of the entranceway to the deeper world. He must prove himself worthy to make the passage into this realm. Then, he must fall into the belly of the whale, a dark and deadly place that swallows him up. He undergoes a period of great interior searching, before being yielded back up into the world. Explain how this pattern operates in another fantasy adventure story.

Winds: In the Aeolus episode, Odysseus's goal is in sight and he sabotages it. He lets his guard down at the critical moment. Consider the symbolism of the wind: inflation followed by deflation. Odysseus and his men represent the divided self. While he sleeps, his weaker selves go into motion, undermining the stronger self. After the debacle of the winds, Odysseus may consider himself an enemy of the gods. But he is willing to learn from his mistakes, and becomes open to deeper teachings.

The Feminine Powers: Odysseus's first adventure at the hands of the feminine powers is the exact opposite of the last, that with princess Nausicaa. In both, there is a meeting with a young girl at a source of running water; in both, there is an immediate referral to the queen, the girl's mother. This experience ends in devouring destruction at the hands of the female powers.

Divestiture: Note how, as Odysseus travels, he has less and less (loses his ship and his men).

The Island of Circe: Circe is the "Initiator as Temptress": she lures men to experience the Mysteries of regression in the service of transformation; woman as source of magical/creative life; she selects a man of unusual powers, and shares some of her magic with him.

Circe: the transformational goddess: singing and weaving (hair is woven into braided tresses); the Triple Goddess (Circe, Calypso, Penelope) are the weaving goddesses: they hold things together (Charlotte's Web).

Pig Mystique: Pigs played an important role in ancient rites; pig sacrifice, offered as a symbol of death and rebirth, healing and renewal; in Celtic cultures, pigs were associated with flying goddess who would drop piglets down from the sky; pigs seem to have mysterious knowledge of the earth (rooting); associated with the underworld of death and the underworld of the psyche; scarring by the boar's tusk was considered the marking of the king (Odysseus is scarred in the thigh by a boar, and that scar is how he is recognized by the servant Euraclea upon his return to Ithaca).

Descent into the Underworld

Tiresias: he once saw two snakes mating; he wounded them with his staff and so became a woman for eight years, had a great time as a woman; then he saw two snakes mating again, did the same thing, and was turned back into a man; so, Tiresias became a marriage counselor; Tiresias has deep "inner sight" although blind.

Blindness: Tiresias and Odysseus: Tiresias is literally blind; Odysseus is metaphorically blind (Odysseus falls asleep at critical times); ironically, Tiresias is Odysseus' guide; Tiresias has androgynous knowledge.

Mothers of the Underworld: The irony of the meeting of the mothers in the underworld is that mothers give life. The Realm of the Mothers is the eternal life force: beauty but no passion; realm of no change; once the hero enters the Realm of the Mothers, he is gifted with inner knowledge of the patterns of things, the workings of the cosmos; many of the mothers reveal to their children that Zeus was their real father, and so they have special powers; Odysseus' mother, Anticleia, reveals that she died in grief of him; Odysseus' name means *trouble*; he brings trouble to those who love him.

The Mythology Project

This is a bi-leveled task. Students who choose the "challenge" do so in addition to the basic task. Successful completion of the challenge levels is rewarded by additional points.

Choose One:

- ◆ Brutality and Savagery: Give at least 20 examples of acts of brutality/savagery/barbarism. For each one, tell the characters involved, the nature of the brutality, the reason for it, and the result. You may set these up in sentence form (single spaced within each entry; double spaced between entries) or in chart (table) form.

Challenge: Explain in one or two sentence how ten of these acts of brutality and savagery are committed for one of the following reasons:

- Self-Defense (in response to a threat)
- Domination (to control others who pose no threat)
- Nobility (service to others)

♦ Headlines: Write 20 headlines and lead paragraphs for various mythological events. The events do not have to be related. Write your headlines and lead paragraphs in journalistic form: *clipped language for the headlines; straightforward, informational style for the lead paragraph.*

Examples: Odysseus Cleans House; Atalanta Finishes Last: Oedipus Blinds Self

Challenge: Write three articles (200 words each), using journalistic format (presenting events in descending order of importance).

♦ Women of Myth: Consider the women of mythology. What categories do they fall into? Decide on three categories and make a list of women for each. Explain briefly why each woman belongs in the given category. Mention at least 20 women. Include groups of women (harpies, graces, maenads, etc.)

Challenge: Explain what qualities the Greeks seemed to admire in women, and what qualities they condemned.

♦ Suffering in Mythology: Give one example of each of the following: *terror, shock, alienation, loneliness, separation, loss, torture, hunger, disease, pain, uncertainty,* or *fatigue.* For each type of suffering, name the characters, the reason for the suffering, and how the suffering changed the character.

Challenge: Agree or disagree, providing supportive examples from the myths: Suffering brings about strength, compassion, and nobility in the sufferer.

♦ Mythology Clippings: Clip and display at least 20 references to mythology in the newspaper (the Arts section is best) and magazine ads. This project requires no further explanation. Your display must be neat and attractive. Also, find at least 20 words in the English language that derive from mythology and list/define them.

Challenge: Propose a mythological name for a new product. Explain why the name would be memorable and would entice people to purchase the product.

Mythology: In Class Follow-Up

◆ Hubris: Give three examples of hubris, and how it is punished.

◆ Nobility: Develop a definition: *selflessness, courage, modesty, loyalty,* and *truth.* Explain why a particular character in mythology is noble, according to your definition.

◆ Trickery: How does a trick work? What conditions have to be present in order for a trick to work?

  Give three examples of tricks in mythology and why they work. Mention the circumstances, the skill of the trickster, and the vulnerability of the victim. How do both luck and skill come in to play?

◆ Women: Consider 30 women (trios or groups of women count as one). Place them into three or four categories.

◆ Compare the mythologies of two different cultures. Consider *monsters, tricks, women, power, nature, nobility,* and *hubris.*

Follow-up: Hand in your mythology folder with *at least five pieces* developed: neatly presented or typed, each at least one page.

Case XIV: Grade Eight—Bridges

Bess Ettinger's eight-grade history students are starting the textbook chapter about the Great Immigration Period of the nineteenth century. She will be using bridges as her theme. The bridges will be both real and metaphorical: showing connections among various cultures and the relationship between the old and new worlds. The Brooklyn Bridge, as the technological marvel of its time, stands as a great symbol of connections during the late nineteenth century. Bess believes that students can develop an understanding of the day-to-day life of urban America by learning about the construction of the bridge, what it meant to the society at the time, and the changes that it brought about, both physically and patriotically. Underlying the Brooklyn Bridge, and the bridges that soon followed it, was a belief system in the capabilities of engineering that would change the way Americans viewed the world and the way the world viewed Americans. It is a metaphor for the connection into the modern age.

Bess starts off with whole class instruction about the great immigration wave that took place in the mid-1800s. Using monographs, slides, Web sites, and other teaching materials available from Ellis Island, she sketches out what life was like during this time period. She stresses the economic and social conditions in Europe and America, the expectations and realities of life for these immigrants, and the connections to today's immigrants. Whole class instruction takes three days and is rich in terminology, names, places, events, and visuals. Key concepts are how economics affects demographics, how technology affects lifestyles, and the problems faced by immigrants, then and now.

Prior to, and then following, whole class instruction, Bess asks students to write or draw and explain a journal entry of an immigrant to an American city in the 1860s. On the basis of the depth and complexity of the journal entries, she makes an assessment of whether the whole class is ready to move on to differentiated instruction. She asks several students to read parts of their journals aloud.

Students will have a choice of five bridge projects. They may work alone or with a partner. If they work with a partner, they must submit a written "division of labor" plan that must pass her preapproval. Students must complete the following for their projects:

1. Annotated bibliography of at least five sources
2. A presentation of how the bridge affected both the rich and the poor levels of society. This presentation may be in paragraph or graphic organizer form.
3. A written explanation of a visual. This visual may be a cartoon, a photograph, or a diagram.
4. A fact and figure sheet: This may be a chart or graph containing relevant statistics
5. An oral presentation to the class.

The students may integrate items 2, 3, and 4 into the project itself. Or, they may submit these as separate items.

Here are the essentials of Bess Ettinger's choices of bridge projects. (Note that students may choose a bridge other than the Brooklyn Bridge, although that is the bridge for which the most abundant information's available.)

- Extra, Extra: Write several kinds of newspaper articles for various points in the process of building the bridge. Some ideas are feature articles, editorials, obituaries, headlines, cartoons, quotes of the day, science reports, or letters to the editor.

- A Day in the Lives: In any sort of written form, express the daily lives of two people at different ends of the economic scale of the time that the bridge was erected. Each person's life must be connected to the building of the bridge in some way. Your people may be real or fictitious.

- Beauty and Function: Using the terminology of art and engineering, explain how the bridge that you select attractive to the eye. Find and clip several images of your bridge. Then, explain why the elements that make the bridge beautiful to look at also make it strong and functional.

- Before and After: Make a side-by-side list that shows how your bridge changed the world.

- Comparison: Compare two major bridges in as many ways as you can think of.

- Your Own Idea. You may write a written proposal of your own idea. You must have it approved by me.

Bess will take her classes to the library for three days to work on this project. She doesn't expect it to be hard for them to find information. Her main concern is that students will pull information straight off the Internet without processing it in their own words. To encourage against this, she will ask students to submit a handwritten outline or graphic organizer of key points.

If each student, or pair, were to make an oral report to the whole class, Bess would have to spend more time on this topic than she can afford. In the interest of time efficiency, the oral reports will be done within subgroups.

What Bess is doing is taking a broad historical topic, immigration, and connecting it to a (literally) concrete object: a bridge. Students received a rubric at the beginning of the project that specified the following expectations:

- ◆ You have handed in all parts of the project on time.
- ◆ You show an understanding of what we learned in class about immigration.
- ◆ You show the connection between the bridge and how it affected history.
- ◆ Your information is accurate, thorough, and relevant.
- ◆ You have shown thinking about the "Big Ideas."
- ◆ Your presentation is attractive and carefully constructed.

Tamara, a student with information processing deficits, worked with her resource room teacher, Lia Kranz. Lia walked Tamara through the choices, encouraging her to do the one that was most interesting to her. Tamara, not at all interested in the time period or bridges, settled on *Days in the Lives*. At Mrs. Kranz's suggestion, Tamara made an hour-by-hour schedule of a man who worked in a caisson and a well-to-do society lady whose town-house window faced construction on the Brooklyn side.

Stephanie, an honor roll student, loves history, especially stories. She is facile with words and is an avid reader. She compiled a Brooklyn Bridge scrapbook that displayed the various stages of construction. Stephanie's scrapbook included the facts and figures and the explanation of the visual(s), but not the comparison of rich and poor. For that, she used the concept of a Venn diagram, presented as a bridge, with the differences between rich and poor listed on either side and their commonalities listed on the bridge span.

Both Tamara and Stephanie learned about the immigration period at a level appropriate for their skills. Each of these projects connects the micro (individual lives) to the macro (technology affects history).

Reflection

How does Bess Ettinger's bridge project connect to the "Big Ideas":
- ◆ Comparison/contrast
- ◆ Connecting cause and effect
- ◆ Going from the generality to the specific, and back to the generality
- ◆ Justifying an assertion

- Understanding organization: arrangements, categories, subordination

The Unpleasant Surprises

What unpleasant surprises might Bess encounter?
- It took longer than I thought.
- The results were shallow.
- It was much harder to assess then I thought.
- Kids finished at much different rates.
- Everyone chose the easiest route.
- The kids were unproductive in class. They kept saying they would "do it at home." Of course, they didn't, and then they'd come in unprepared.
- We ran into facilities problems: the library and computer labs were unavailable
- Absenteeism wrecked the cooperative learning piece.
- The class felt like a factory. I felt more like a floor supervisor than a teacher.
- They copied their reports right off the (fill in the blank).

After reading a list like this, you might want to just forget it. However, remember that your own skills at DI are cumulative. Start small. Have a backup plan.

Anticipating the Problems

1. Brainstorm ways in which the above problems can be *prevented*.
2. Brainstorm ways in which the above problems, once they start, can be *minimized.*

Conclusion

I hope you've seen that learning to differentiate instruction is not a simplistic "plan in a can" process. It is an approach to teaching that requires us to reflect on what we want students to know (content), how we can help them learn it (process), and how they can show us what they've learned (product).

Differentiated instruction thrives in a school climate rich in collegial communication. We need to know how students function in other classes with other teachers.

Although differentiated instruction is often accomplished in flexible groupings, it does not necessarily have to "look" a certain way. A teacher who is presiding over whole class instruction may very well be differentiating. In the course of her explanations, the teacher can be addressing various learning styles, showing students how to make meaning by connecting new information to old information, using multisensory references, or redefining her terminology in context as she speaks.

Three is not a magic number. We should get away from thinking of differentiated instruction as though we are buying sweatshirts in small, medium, or large sizes. What students are capable of learning and doing is more subtle than that, far less predictable, and not nearly so neat and clean. Assume that your students can do more than their standardized test scores would indicate.

Differentiated instruction is an outgrowth of humanistic and constructivist pedagogies. That translates into student choice, flexible groupings, use of prior knowledge to make meaning, integration of the arts, respect for students' culture and language, and lots of student talk.

I wish you well in your workshops and collegial discussion groups.

TRAIN TIME

TRAIN TIME

Railroads and the Imminent Reshaping
of the United States Landscape

JOHN R. STILGOE

University of Virginia Press

CHARLOTTESVILLE AND LONDON

University of Virginia Press
© 2007 by the Rector and Visitors of the University of Virginia
All rights reserved
Printed in the United States of America on acid-free paper

First published 2007

1 3 5 7 9 8 6 4 2

LIBRARY OF CONGRESS CATALOGING-IN-PUBLICATION DATA

Stilgoe, John R., 1949–
Train time : railroads and the imminent reshaping of the United States
landscape / John R. Stilgoe.
p.   cm.
Includes bibliographical references and index.
ISBN 978-0-8139-2668-1 (cloth : alk. paper)
1. Railroads—United States—History. 2. Landscape—United States.
3. Railroads—United States—Traffic. 4. Railroads—United States—Freight.
5. Railroads—Social aspects—United States—History. I. Title.
HE2751.S683 2007
385.0973—dc22
2007008232

ALL PHOTOGRAPHS BY THE AUTHOR

For Stephen Bartlett and Russell Briggs

CONTENTS

PREFACE

Rumbling faintly in the distance, trains return as the key shaper of the United States built environment. From near oblivion, from a past too long romanticized or simply ignored, trains roll into the attention of those who know how to pause, look around, listen carefully, and see how present events skew the near future. While politicians debate the future of Amtrak and the public reads little of an industry ordinarily newsworthy only when trains derail, consulting firms, real estate developers, and other for-profit enterprises scramble to analyze an industry of once-massive corollary impact.

Unlike so many United States industries, railroads have a fundamental and often ferocious attachment to American soil and to particular regions. Along their tracks, events are unfolding rapidly, generally unnoticed except by rail experts and a cognoscenti attuned to imminent landscape and cultural change.

Away from the coasts, booming freight traffic raises a number of questions about the national economy. Hundreds of trains carry containers emblazoned with the names of Asian shipping companies or Asian manufacturers, mixed now and then with containers labeled in Spanish. In the old Rust Belt, across the High Plains, along the entire Mexican border, across the upland South, rolling freight trains are a reminder that much manufacturing and many assembly-line jobs have moved to the Far East, the Philippines, Mexico, and other foreign countries. This impression is bolstered by Department of Labor calculations that in the 1990s the United States lost 1.5 million manufacturing jobs to China alone.

It might even be said that freight trains swayed the 2004 presidential election. In the American heartland, voters chose a Republican candidate determined to "protect" the nation, not only from containers filled with terrorist explosive or chemical weapons, but—of even more pressing concern to the electorate—from long-term economic dislocation. The growing manufacturing muscle of China so evident in mile-long freight trains conjures images of a

Chinese-dominated automobile industry, a potential economic disruption exceeding any threat posed by the Japanese in the world industrial marketplace. Trains deliver, and increasingly what they deliver rides in boxes obviously from Asia, Mexico, and elsewhere. Those living in United States coastal areas rarely see the long trains that slither inland from ports nowadays isolated, even fenced off from casual observation. High-tech ports opening on world trade, such as Kalama, Washington, are rarely discussed; many otherwise well-informed Americans cannot even locate it, despite its Pacific Rim importance. Yet Kalama and other ports service hundreds of freight trains bound into and across a red-state heartland growing ever more concerned about "homeland security" in ways that are economically protectionist.

Kalama, Halifax in Nova Scotia, perhaps especially Prince Rupert in British Columbia, offer railroad companies exquisitely modern, jam-free access to ocean trade. From Halifax, trains of containers roll west and south across Canada and the northern United States. Halifax now threatens the shipping primacy of Boston, Portland, Maine, and even the clogged, shallow-water wharves of Perth Amboy and Elizabeth in New Jersey. New Jersey has completed a new freight railroad linking its wharves to transcontinental rail lines, partly to lessen truck congestion at the southern end of the George Washington Bridge, but chiefly to avoid the fate of such traffic-vexed Pacific Coast cities as Seattle and Los Angeles. Far to the north, at Prince Rupert, a port city a few hours' steamship time nearer Asia than its California competitors, ultramodern wharves now draw cargo from the Mississippi Valley over a long-decrepit track speculators built a century ago.

Freight trains are at the core of the change analyzed here, but there are other elements involved. Part of the future begins to reveal itself in coastal cities and other urban areas where freight trains share rails with existing and planned passenger service. Manhattan rail commuters cannot fail to notice the lengthening freight trains snaking around new passenger stations at Secaucus and elsewhere. In the harbor itself, the great barges of the New York Cross Harbor Railroad Terminal Corporation float freight cars between New Jersey and Brooklyn. Between 2002 and 2005 car-float traffic has doubled from four thousand to eight thousand cars, as connecting railroads hurried priority cars around jammed yards squeezed by routes already dedicated to passenger service. While New York and New Jersey politicians confront the growing necessity for a freight railroad tunnel under the harbor, a project that already threatens to fracture the Port Authority of New York and New Jersey by shifting transshipment activity back to Brooklyn, commuter rail authorities despair of adding more trains along routes jammed with freight trains. And in rural areas far from New York, Los Angeles, and other ports, burgeoning freight traffic impedes hopes and plans for new passenger service envisioned on New York models. This is already evident in coastal cities and other cities in which freight trains must share rails with new passenger trains.

In late 2004 New Mexico state officials ordered ten new bi-level commuter railcars. Costing $2.2 million each, the cars are intended to serve commuters riding back and forth between Belen and Bernalillo, small communities officials now identify as part of greater Albuquerque. Wealthy people live north and south of the sprawling city, in places that 1970s tourists found quaint and inexpensive villages. Fast commuter service over existing high-quality rails hitherto carrying only long-distance freight trains means that exurbanites will whisk past inner suburbs, truck traffic, and rush-hour traffic jams. Albuquerque might seem an unlikely city to institute commuter rail service, but some of the most aggressive railroad reincarnation happens where city councils suddenly abandon hope in highways. In Atlanta, St. Louis, and other automobile-centric cities, politicians are initiating feasibility studies and rail-equipment manufacturers are soliciting orders. The train is returning, an economic and cultural tsunami about to transform the United States.

A casual survey of railroads and areas where railroads once operated produces multiple discoveries, not all particularly reassuring to observers rooted in highway-based shopping mall culture. Parking lots that once served long-demolished passenger and freight stations host lengthy visits by deep-pocket real estate developers who stare speculatively at adjacent stores and roads, spread old maps across automobile hoods, and make notes on laptop computers. Elsewhere, surveyors park their SUVs next to access points along abandoned tracks converted to nature trails. Sometimes fragments of plastic tape mark their activity, but often surveyors measure adjacent property almost clandestinely. Here and there, usually at rush hour, retail-marketing experts scrutinize the behavior of commuters boarding and exiting trains, walking across retail streets, or driving to and from parking lots; these observers leave no trace either. Around modern warehouses served by rail, logistics engineers test the movement of specialized freight cars or robotic unloading systems. Watching people who watch railroads reveals a new analytical energy, something quiet but brutally powerful happening along railroad alignments. Energy and long-term investment are beginning to gravitate from roads and highways, from suburban and rural land adjacent only to asphalt, and from automobile manufacturers.

Inspectors of grassy, disused railroad tracks often provide the first quasi-public indication that a long-idle mine or manufacturing plant will reopen, or that rail traffic will shift onto a near-abandoned route. Something is about to happen near Etowah and Copperhill in Tennessee, but right now the close-lipped examiners of an overgrown track are the only clue to impending reinvestment. Change less massive but equally indicative of a larger reorientation begins to reshape a bit of western Pennsylvania, where the Rosebud Mining Company, after spending a million dollars in 2004 to repair local roads damaged by its coal-hauling trucks, now debates not only buying the Kiski Junction Railroad but extending it to its Logansport mines. Sharp-eyed observers of landscape note the surveyors, and occasionally, alert local journalists realize something might be about to happen, often in areas where much happened decades ago, before rusting into oblivion.

Everywhere local newspapers record fragments of a larger story seldom reported in the likes of the *Wall Street Journal.* Just as the Wal-Mart and Dollar General retail chains originated and matured almost unnoticed in the Tennessee-Arkansas cradle of Tyson Foods, J. B. Hunt Trucking, and other now-powerful firms reshaping national business and landscape, so railroads and railroad-related industries begin to flex economic muscle, but usually away from coastal areas. Wal-Mart transformed the context of small-store Main Street, shopping malls, and dozens of regional discount department-store chains, and Tyson Foods morphed the agricultural landscape into a well-nigh industrialized zone. Coastal media miss the great changes recently wrought by railroads away from coastal regions.

Anyone who looks carefully will find people studying railroads, both indoors and out. Archivists and librarians note the rising interest in historical railroad documents, from the dustiest and driest of reports dealing with sixteen-hour passenger service between Chicago and New York to information on fast freight operation between New Orleans and Kansas City. Stockbrokers and investment analysts note an upsurge in interest among would-be investors in railroads: the Conrail stock that went on sale in 1987 for $28 a share sold in 1997 at $115. But investment experts often know nothing about profitable companies that serve the railroad industry or that intend to profit from the coming railroad boom. In an age of online stock trading, many investors lack any introduction to the nascent reinvestment already evident in rising railroad company share prices. In 2005, when the first freight train rolled into Dallas over the long-derelict tracks of the former St. Louis, Mexico & Orient, only local newspapers reported the event. Texas Pacifico, Ferroccarril Mexicano, and other subsidiary corporate names suggest the internationalizing of the post-NAFTA border country, but no national news media noted the creation of an integrated transcontinental route between Dallas and Topolobampo.

High-tech industries already serving railroads are sometimes poised to transform them. Rail Power Technologies, a British Columbia builder of locomotives, furnishes low-polluting, fuel-efficient, quiet-switching locomotives especially adapted to urban areas. Its Green Goat prototype heralds a transformation in locomotive design, and its stock prices reflect investor confidence. Other companies, especially those manufacturing railroad cars and making railroad ties from recycled plastic or concrete, surprise even seasoned investors. Shareholders in J. B. Hunt express confidence and satisfaction too, but only those who read annual reports thoroughly know what farm children learn simply by watching speeding freight trains west of St. Louis. J. B. Hunt prospers by moving trailers by rail, not over interstate highways.

Railroad industry annual reports only hint at the much larger subject of this book, the discerning of landscape and cultural change just beginning to occur. The best way of formulating an idea of how the United States landscape will change in the immediate future is to watch the subtle but rapid change so evident around so many active railroad lines. Scrutinizing that change heightens awareness of imminent social, cultural, and economic change otherwise not easily noticed, and usually not noted by news media. Extrapolation is not design, nor is it planning; but it now drives present investment that reflects change and produces change.

Few Americans take notice of developments in the rail industries. Even fewer *realize* them. Comparatively few people ride Amtrak long-haul trains, and often freight trains move in corridors difficult to reach by car. For decades railroads have operated through the skid row sections of cities, skirting the parts of town where middle-income people rarely venture. One train seems much like another. Now and then a freight train stops traffic for a few minutes, but few delayed motorists notice anything particular about the string of specialized railcars rumbling across the road. Tourists in remote areas are likely to express surprise when an Amtrak express flashes across a bridge or emerges from a mountain valley. Urban intellectuals shrug when they learn that trains will return to the abandoned line between Etowah and Copperhill in Tennessee or to the old tracks linking Dallas and Topolobampo or to dozens of other long-quiet routes. Only rarely do they ponder such activity as the effect of wealth transferred geographically and from one set of industries to another. All too rarely, change in rail-centered industries causes change in landscape that passes as unnoticed as a train in the far distance. Making sense of that change describes a scenario of events moving as fast as any express train.

Now a train is often only a whistle heard far off on a sleepless night. But romantic or foreboding or empowering, the whistle announces both return and change to those who listen.

ACKNOWLEDGMENTS

My former students are many now, and the imminent change wrought by railroads intrigues many of them. I began lecturing on railroad-corridor landscapes thirty years ago at Harvard University, and I am grateful for the observations, suspicions, and hunches of alumni who learned to watch the rails. Anonymity often cloaks the enterprise of would-be real estate investors and others; here I maintain the obscurity of people intending to profit from change-in-the-making. Thomas Armstrong, Robert Belyea, Fletcher Hall, Donald House, and Harold Tuttle have all offered valuable insights. Stephen Bartlett and Russell Briggs helped especially acutely, and I am grateful for their friendship and viewpoints. I commend my editor, Boyd Zenner, for her confidence in a book about potential futures. My wife, Debra, deserves more credit than I have words. Not only does she smile when I follow railroads across the country, driving down rutted roads and small-town alleys and into regions lacking good motels, she often notices much I have missed.

TRAIN TIME

Long trains racing over well-maintained tracks everywhere in rural America lure capital investment away from decaying highways and trucks dependent on them.

INTRODUCTION

Only birds skitter along the high-level platform at Bethel, Maine. Weeds grow among the rails and ties of the track it abuts, and the station behind it sits more quietly even than the quiet town. No automobiles park in the station lot. No passenger trains stop at the platform. No expresses hasten past it. Only one or two daily freight trains rumble along the shiny rails beyond the platform track, linking Portland and Quebec while serving dozens of trackside industries in rural Maine and northeast New Hampshire. The stop at Bethel might be any one of thousands of similar points along United States railroads, except for one thing. The passenger station, the high-level platform, the station track, even the parking lot are all brand new and waiting.

Maine voters and politicians intend that passenger trains will return, and soon. The rationale for the new structures at Bethel proves simple. Three miles away, the spectacular resort of Sunday River offers superb skiing and other snow sports in winter, year-round mountain and forest recreation, and conference facilities. But getting to Sunday River from anywhere, even Portland, can be difficult. Travelers arriving at Portland by air find what all motorists find: two-lane roads winding up hill and down. Neither the Portland airport nor the rural highway system entices visitors to Sunday River, or to Bethel, for that matter. The resort famed for the best skiing in New England deserves something better, and the people of Maine know what: a passenger train.

So with little difficulty, in 2001 the state prevailed upon Amtrak to inaugurate several daily trains between Boston and Portland over upgraded tracks owned by a freight railroad. All the trains, called Downeasters, cover the 116-mile route in about two and a half hours, and all immediately exceeded ridership estimates. At first operating at sixty miles per hour and then at seventy-nine, the trains make commuting between Portland and Boston possible, and between southern Maine and New Hampshire towns and Boston a pleasure. But the Downeasters have a meaning deeper than commuting.

At seventy-nine miles per hour Sunday River is about forty minutes beyond Portland. The state of Maine built a platform, station, and parking lot in anticipation of the start of Amtrak service to Portland continuing under state subsidy sixty-five miles further to Bethel. Such planning and construction are part of a larger transportation vision in a rural state usually considered highway focused but acutely aware that it attracts ever larger numbers of Europeans enjoying six-week vacations and many New Yorkers and southern New Englanders weary of road traffic. In the fall of 2006, buoyed by data indicating that the 330,000 Downeaster passengers represented a 31 percent increase in ridership over the previous year, the governor of Maine issued an executive order to expand service far to the north and west of Portland. In a public address accompanying the order, he emphasized the speed with which the passenger trains had boosted investment in every town in which they stopped.

Few Americans know much about the renaissance of railroads suddenly shaping high-power politics of real estate development, industrial location, and population parameters. Population growth shapes the thinking of decision makers. In 2055 the United States will be home to 417 million people, up 129 million from its current population of 302 million. Most government transportation planning remains based in circa-1960 assumptions derived from a population of about 150 million people. Almost all the anticipated population growth will occur in metropolitan regions already choked with motor vehicle and airliner traffic. As 13D Research emphasized in a private, August 17, 2006, report to institutional investors, "Another Solution to the Energy Crisis: Railroad Equipment," population growth in restricted areas suggests a very strong future for railroads.

Despite feel-good advertising by the automobile, trucking, and airline lobbies, by 1970 most planners knew the futility of building more and wider highways, especially at urban choke points. Almost certainly, advisers to John F. Kennedy understood the futility years earlier. On April 5, 1962, Kennedy sent a terse "Message on Transportation" to Congress, stating what nowadays seems extraordinary for a Democrat of that era. "I am convinced that less Federal regulation and subsidization is in the long run a prime requisite of a healthy intercity transportation network," Kennedy asserted. Moreover, he insisted that until the federal government had solid data reflecting the relationships among transport types, Congress should resist any further tinkering with a transportation industry involving both public rights-of-way, especially interstate highways, and private ones. At some point in the near future, Kennedy concluded, users of taxpayer-subsidized rights-of-way must begin covering the costs of repair and periodic rebuilding, and in the meantime no federal initiative should restrict the innate technological advantages of one transportation type to subsidize another. In the midst of crises involving agriculture, urban renewal, racial integration, Medicare, and the steel industry—but just before the Cuban missile crisis—Kennedy made clear in sixteen typewritten pages that physical realities must henceforth shape federal transportation policy, and that hard data, including demographics, might forecast forces affecting physical realities.

Numbers meant much to Kennedy for reasons nowadays forgotten. The 1960 presidential election proved not only the closest up to that time but the first accurately predicted by computer. Despite a substantial early lead by Nixon, the NBC computer named Kennedy the winner at 8:20 EST, and other network computers followed. After NBC had approached RCA in early 1960 about using one of its mainframe computers to predict the election, RCA quickly divined that election prediction resembled many industrial problems. By 1962 RCA had discerned the simplicity of predicting elections compared with predicting the outcome changes in and among industries, and had become adept at programming scenarios involving electoral effects of issues developing late in political campaigns. But sinister currents swirled beneath much popular reporting of computer-based election prediction because news media experts knew corporations already used computers to predict and analyze trends.

Some of the most respected journalists in the United States, including Eric Sevareid and David Brinkley, insisted that computer-driven scenario analysis might destroy elections. In a 1964 *Popular*

Mechanics article, Clifford B. Hicks outlined journalist fears and then explained the technology RCA used. Before anyone voted in the 1960 election the RCA computer had predicted the outcome almost exactly, based on analysis of polls and regional "political comment."

No one knew better than Kennedy the importance of numbers and scenario prediction, but he glimpsed something more. In pushing the post office to analyze automation, Kennedy envisioned the digitizing of geographic information in ways far more subtle than those used by the Bureau of the Census. In the summer of 1963 the zip code was launched as a way of speeding mail delivery and coding demographic and geographic data. Long before the public learned much about computers predicting elections, astute venture capitalists were using zip-code-based data to track production and consumption flows and to predict the best companies and locations in which to invest.

Computer-driven predictions using zip code and other data merged with other inventions in the early 1960s. In a Baltimore home basement, three freelance inventors won the race to create the videocassette recorder, and by 1965 they were besieged by television network executives and scores of other interested professionals, including school superintendents and golfers anxious for instant video feedback. As Mark R. Levy points out in *The VCR Age,* behind the throng quietly moved another group. Venture capitalists saw not only a massive market for renting video tapes played through television sets, even imagining the tapes rented at specialized stores or delivered and returned by mail, but the splintering of television network hegemony that hired election-result computers. At first, they discerned market areas based on zip code analysis, but quickly at least a few envisioned interactive telephone/teletype/television services linked by cable in ways that presaged the Web and Internet. By 1979 Fotomat had begun renting cassettes from each of its three thousand stores, and within three years a national proliferation of videocassette rental stores proved the correctness of mid-1970s data-driven investment scenarios. Such private-sector scenarios depended on government-collected data, but at first scenario prediction did little to sway federal transportation policy following the Cuban missile crisis.

Foreign policy issues, then assassination, deflected federal interest away from rigorous, scenario-based analysis of transportation issues and from prediction grounded in technological invention. The administration of Lyndon Baines Johnson, mired in both the Vietnam War and expensive antipoverty efforts, avoided the realpolitik Kennedy expressed, perhaps realizing that its social welfare policies could not survive computer-based scenario inspection developed by defense analysts. Just as early computer software required users to type perfectly and in standard English, so late-1960s mainframe-based computer analysis of large-scale, nuanced issues produced results unpalatable to politicians in both parties. Building more urban highways produced a measurable need for more parking garages, for example, and would eventually produce downtowns consisting largely of multistory garages. Retrospect suggests that the Johnson administration devastated not only transportation analysis and planning but urban renewal and rural development despite spending billions of dollars; it ignored the Kennedy understanding that as prediction software became more sophisticated it would shape all public works projects. Its bumbling begat the fast-sprawling metropolitan growth that dwarfed 1950s suburban development, and, more importantly, it stymied efforts by public researchers to predict facets of the growth over time.

Paralyzed by political inaction—especially in large-population states having one or more dense cities sprawling rapidly toward each other—and by fear of angering voters enamored of private motorcars as the key to suburban living, planners said little about the physical impossibility of accommodating tens of millions more automobiles, especially in the vicinity of large airports and harbors. The energy crises of 1973 and 1978 ought to have alerted federal, state, and local planning experts to the futility Kennedy descried, but the official record suggests otherwise. This may be one reason that many left the planning profession for greener pastures in the far more tough-minded private sectors of marketing, real estate development, and site analysis.

In the Nixon, Ford, Carter, and Reagan administrations, federal experts moved slowly toward the deregulation point of view Kennedy espoused years earlier but which the Johnson administration ignored. The most casual investigation of the historical narrative reveals instances of seeming confusion and paradox. The Nixon administration privatized the post office while making rail passenger service the responsibility of the quasi-public Amtrak. The Staggers Act of 1980 effectively removed much railroad industry regulation and produced a far more profitable industry that pleased Carter administration experts and stockholders alike while dismaying labor unions, but railroad deregulation efforts failed to solve the deepening crisis in a national transportation policy still focused on highways. Beyond the radar of government planners, some Americans began moving toward a new vision of railroad-based industrial, commercial, and residential investment. Just as the poultry-farming initiatives of Perdue and Tyson perplexed rural planners, and the spreading of Wal-Mart and Dollar General stores puzzled small-town and then urban planners, the efforts of investors in a railroad-based future now moving from obscurity puzzle and irritate government planners. But remarkably little public discussion focuses on their efforts. The investors might as well be the inventors of the VCR or early investors in Blockbuster Video or Netflix, for they are nearly anonymous and nearly removed from government oversight.

Americans now live in what appears to be the final, sickly sweet blossoming of the automobile and airliner, and the related real estate development. A frantic energy masks the desperation of real estate developers terrified that people will not buy the last of the structures built according to automobile thinking. Recently the California Historic Resources Commission reversed itself by declaring a 7.5-mile stretch of railroad running between National City and Imperial of so little value that it may be built upon. Despite citizen opposition, the commission, under pressure from the governor, stripped the corridor of its Historic Register status in order to expedite residential real estate development favored by the Chula Vista and San Diego Unified Port District Authority. Part of a 21.5-mile portion of the San Diego and Arizona Eastern Railway, which ran from downtown San Diego through Imperial Beach to Coronado, the 7.5-mile stretch raised the specter of a nonautomobile route to downtown. Not often are spaces entered into Historic Registers excised, but in a state still enamored of the motorcar, every existing rail route worries real estate developers still committed to an automobile-focused development model.

That model begins to crumble. In September 2005 national media reported studies suggesting that freight traffic had to move from urban highways to railroads to avoid gridlock. Newspapers tended to frame the scenarios only in local terms. The *Boston Herald* emphasized that shifting a quarter of truck freight to rail by 2025 would save an average of $513 and 32.3 hours a year per metropolitan commuter and reduce Boston-area air pollution by 12,300 tons and fuel consumption by 247 million gallons annually. Few articles note the significance of averages: suburban and exurban commuters would save far more money and time than urban residents. Even fewer noted that the first metropolitan regions to shift to rail freight would increase their competitive advantages significantly or that, in national terms, the scenarios necessitate new models for real estate development.

The argument that follows here rides atop steel rails, sometimes smooth, sometimes rusted and uneven; and what underlies it may surprise, irritate, or anger. At some point soon, many middle-income Americans will no longer be able to afford to live as they live now. They will face difficult choices, including those pitting automobile against home ownership. At present, many find desirable affordable housing only in far outer suburbs. Commuting long distances exacts a toll on automobiles, of course, but it consumes time too—sometimes so much time that it proves unaffordable. Gasoline prices figure in domestic budgeting, but the significant equation involves commuting time and house finance.

Mortgage costs have risen seventy times faster than a worker's income over the past generation, according to authors of the 2001 Consumer Bankruptcy Project. Many married couples, even well-educated ones, now find that both partners must work to earn enough to buy housing in high-quality school districts. However counterintuitive they may be, the findings of Elizabeth Warren and

9

Amelia Warren Tyagi reported in *The Two-Income Trap* seem clear: seemingly successful couples face a far higher likelihood of filing bankruptcy than couples in which only the man works. In 2001 a greater number of people filed for bankruptcy than graduated from college or filed for divorce, and Warren and Tyagi predict that one in seven children will live through a bankruptcy before 2010. What many middle-income couples vaguely feel proves true: even with both people working, often at well-paying jobs, they have less discretionary income than did their parents. Gigantic mortgage costs, spiraling health-insurance premiums, and costs of child care and nursery-school tuition contradict traditional wisdom about success, the good life, and the American dream. As Warren and Tyagi argue, neither news media nor most young or middle-aged adults care to hear that feminism, computerization, and commuting may have contributed to the impoverishment of two generations. Few American families can sustain the actual costs of owning two cars, or of replacing a roof as the oldest child enters college. Despite owning one or more personal computers, almost none can predict their short- and long-term financial circumstances. Many worry about making ends meet, sending children to college, the offshoring of white-collar jobs, and the persistent rumors of Social Security bankruptcy. No politician of any party wants to tell such people that nothing can be done to salvage their lifestyles, and the advertising industry always encourages further consumption. Credit-card indebtedness and middle-class bankruptcy now loom exactly as highway congestion loomed before planners in the early 1970s. What worries middle-income families paralyzes politicians into silence, for the politicians understand the force of scenario analysis.

At some point soon, the grittiness of commuting time, mortgage costs, and rising parallel expenses, including gasoline prices, will reverse suburban sprawl permanently and accelerate staggering spatial and cultural change.

Such change provides opportunity to the forewarned. Some Americans can and do use computers to predict, though running detailed scenarios depends on access to top-notch computer hardware and software, masses of databases, and experts skilled in crunching numbers in geographic context. It requires some knowledge of history too. It was for-profit firm consultants rummaging for that knowledge in the Baker Library at the Harvard Business School and the Loeb Library at the Harvard Graduate School of Design who first alerted me to the tremendous force about to change the United States built environment.

Implicit conspiracy ballasts this book. Conspiracy theorists imagine evil men in office towers or government bunkers manipulating the public or media or economy. Implicit conspiracy requires another sort of imagining. Without active effort, often without knowing each other, individuals—and corporations—may allow something massive to happen because a small part of it benefits them. As Mancur Olson argues in *The Logic of Collective Action,* such unorganized activity often proves immensely powerful but extremely difficult to trace. However forcefully politicians condemned 1960s urban riots, violence and arson produced windfall profits for fencing suppliers, burglar and fire alarm installers, private security firms, and especially for developers of suburban shopping malls, office complexes, industrial parks, and—above all—housing. No one suggests that any of those firms or investors conspired to spark riots or impede efforts to end and prevent civil disturbance. But hindsight offers glimpses of how they and others profited quietly from urban disinvestment and other crises still labeled *urban,* never *metropolitan.*

Implicit or tacit conspiracy often involves nothing more than recognizing a good investment opportunity when it arises and keeping silent about it. Across much of the United States, railroads attract little public scrutiny, let alone sustained historical analysis. In some places—say near North Platte, Nebraska, where the Union Pacific operates a fiercely busy three-track transcontinental main line—rail activity impresses coastal state tourists who chance upon it. Elsewhere, however, railroads seem slightly down-at-the-heels— not quaint exactly, but not high tech. Magisterial works like Carl Condit's *The Port of New York* and Joseph Schwieterman's *When the Railroad Leaves Town* seem pure history. But such books interest investors, management consultants, developers, and others in ways I discovered after I published my *Metropolitan Corridor: Railroads and the American Scene* in 1983. Quietly, always politely, but often intensely, came inquirers. I began fielding questions about the period on which I had focused a scholarly book, roughly that between 1885 and 1939. At first the questions struck me as harmless, the sort every university faculty member routinely receives from the public, usually by telephone. Someone wanted to know about sixteen-hour train service between New York and Chicago. Someone else inquired about express package service. An alumnus, sharp-eyed as an undergraduate and now a venture capitalist, wondered about bright-yellow boxcars with two doors on each side. Another alumnus asked about freight distribution practices across the South in the 1930s, thanked me, and then asked if I would mind not mentioning his inquiry to anyone. Slowly I realized that something other than historical curiosity drove the inquiries, and I began quietly questioning my former students in real estate development. Deep-pocket, long-term investors had begun to think of replicating fragments of the railroad-run past.

In their thinking, and throughout this book, past will be prologue. In the fifty years following 1900 the population of New York City grew from about 3.4 million to 7.9 million. The population of Manhattan scarcely changed, but Brooklyn more than doubled to 2.7 million. As William D. Middleton points out in *Metropolitan Railways: Rapid Transit in America,* almost all New York City growth occurred in the formerly undeveloped sections of Queens, the Bronx, and Brooklyn made accessible by new elevated lines and subways. Added to Condit's impeccable analysis of New York suburban railroad building, Middleton's work becomes a portal through which visionaries might peer. Schwieterman explains what happened when railroads abandoned cities and small towns. What follows here examines what will happen when railroads come back.

When Alvin Toffler published *Future Shock* in 1970, Americans had grown jittery from rapid change, especially the changes in social mores emphasized by news and entertainment media. Free love, political protest, illicit drug use, and other issues now preoccupy most analysts of the 1960s. But retrospect makes clear that much 1960s change worked in subtractive ways: Americans lost many options and opportunities.

In the early 1960s, for example, the Hudson & Manhattan Railroad Company rumbled along in postbankruptcy dirtiness and noise. Its 19th Street station stood abandoned, and few passengers used its stations at 14th and 23rd Streets; its more frequented stations appeared nearly derelict. Commuters between New Jersey and lower Manhattan expected service to cease as other commuter rail service already had, imminently and perhaps with no advance warning. Only an obscure group of visionaries glimpsed the potential in the 12.5 miles of tunnels beneath the Hudson River. Transferring ownership of the rickety system to the Port Authority, which rebuilt and extended it into a swift, reliable railroad, made the World Trade Center towers financially feasible as private development. Analyzing that quiet envisioning of a creaky, derelict, underutilized short-line railroad operating mostly in tunnels as the generator of real estate development across lower Manhattan proves maddeningly frustrating now. In the middle 1960s New Yorkers were scarcely aware of the Hudson & Manhattan trains and tunnels, much less did they think about their potential. But the transformation of the Hudson & Manhattan is only one example from the now-ignored 1960s that demonstrates how much the future shocks when it arrives ahead of schedule. In the wake of 9/11, architectural, urban, and social historians understandably focus on the World Trade Center complex, especially the Twin Towers; but the complex itself depended on the discovery and reinvention of the Hudson & Manhattan commuter railroad, which eventually enabled the concentration of population at the lower end of Manhattan.

Railroads concentrate population. Automobiles and airliners distribute it. Once understood, that simple dichotomy explains not just the new station at Bethel but a spatial revolution in the making, one that is accelerating as many Americans face economic uncertainty and strain.

Railroads will return along routes abandoned to hikers and nature lovers fifty years ago. Already some trails have reverted to railroads again, jarring people who thought abandonment permanent. Since 1997 the Commonwealth of Massachusetts has replaced three entire trail systems with three commuter railroads stretching far south of Boston. Few notice abandoned railroad rights-of-way snaking through the landscape, and fewer still realize the potential of these as transportation corridors. But since the 1950s, as the first chapter will show, some groups have anticipated that the train will come again. Dismissed as nostalgic or cranky by all but deep-pocket, long-term investors, their foresight now shakes the very foundations of politics and economics. *When* the railroad returns, not *if,* it will not only transform the half-forgotten jewels that lie along the nation's obscure operating railroad routes but also re-shape regions far from existing tracks. Return will alter everyday life more dramatically than the arrival of personal computers, In-ternet connections, or cell phones. Return will remake the United States economy in ways that private-sector savants already antici-pate. However difficult it is to imagine a grass-grown railroad track becoming a high-speed, heavily trafficked route, it is still more dif-ficult to imagine grass growing through the pavement of interstate highways. But at least some people with imagination have made the intellectual leap. The built landscape just now is entering a transfor-mation of unprecedented proportions, one as little noticed as the rise of Wal-Mart, the invention of the VCR, or the use of computers to make predictions.

Whether or not they know it, millions of Americans live in an economy waiting for the train. Outsourcing, the offshoring of computer-based jobs, and rising energy prices deflect media inter-est from a shift in intellectual and financial investment that anyone who looks around can notice and begin to study without much ac-cess to research university libraries or think-tank reports.

Small cities, the middle rings of metropolitan regions, very small towns, and much of rural America reward future-focused analysis best. In the 1970s railroads began abandoning their big-city freight yards, selling the acreage for real estate development, and ripping up tracks. In an honest, open way they enlarged existing classifica-tion yards in land-cheap locations far from center cities and in-terstate highways. Low land-use taxes in rural counties prompted railroads to store infrequently used cars on sidetracks along rusty branch lines, and sometimes on the branch lines themselves. Few tourists drive along the dirt roads southeast of Bonne Terre, Mis-souri, but those who do find strings of automobile-transport cars bisecting farm fields on rarely used track. Decades ago transconti-nental travelers would have seen the new yards and stored cars from the windows of passenger trains. Nowadays few travelers see them at all, and few locals think much about them. Far from the gaze of most Americans blooms a railroad industry about to reshape national life and culture. Only recently have national newspapers glimpsed the broad-based economic good times evident in Sioux Falls, Fargo, Rapid City, Iowa City, and other rural cities. As Joel Kotkin argues in an August 2006 *Wall Street Journal* article, "The Great Plains," old images of dying towns, aging populations, and failing ranches remain popular with eastern journalists despite being wrong.

Nothing more definitely indicates mass misperception than the enduring presence of steam locomotives in books and other media aimed at children. The little engine that could still chugs and puffs its way uphill, Thomas the Tank Engine rumbles about Victorian Great Britain, and the whoooooeeeeee of the steam locomotive whistles the longevity of early twentieth-century railroading in contemporary cartoons and music. But only in museums is modern American railroading romantic, smelling of coal smoke, steam, and hot valve oil. Elsewhere it is serious business, far more high-tech than most outside the industry recognize and far more powerful—and capable of rapid change—than almost anyone in or out of the industry is willing to mention in public. In 2005 the General Electric Company ran full-page ads in the *Wall Street Journal* touting its fuel-efficient, low-polluting Evolution Series locomotives as the new "engine that could." In its 2005 annual report, Norfolk Southern told shareholders about its pioneering use of LEADER, Locomotive Engineer Assist Display and Event Recorder, a computer-powered system that advises engineers on the optimum fuel-efficient speed for their trains based on tonnage, topography, and other real-time factors. Children's books, popular music, even railroad museums reflect and encourage a sort of mass nostalgia rooted in the distant past, to the exclusion of contemporary activity and potential.

After World War II, automobiles, trucks, highways, and airliners transformed both landscape and culture, producing the metropolitan sprawl so many Americans condemn while enjoying its amenities. Now, in an era of rising fuel costs and intractable highway congestion, burgeoning metropolitan and diminishing rural population, post-NAFTA manufacturing growth in Canada and Mexico, and perhaps above all a global shift in manufacturing away from the United States, railroads begin to drive spatial and cultural change about to disconcert Americans, especially middle-income people far too comfortable inside their cars. In *Outside Lies Magic: Regaining History and Awareness in Everyday Places,* I counsel Americans to walk acutely, look around, and discover what news media often ignore. Here I suggest they scrutinize railroads to glimpse the signs of large-scale landscape change.

History rides everywhere in the pages that follow, but this book focuses on the near future, not even the near past Richard Saunders brilliantly recounts in *Main Lines: Rebirth of the North American Railroads, 1970–2002.* It emphasizes how subtle change forces more change, despite public outcry or political cravenness. It stresses that physical constraints wield far more power than politicians and media moguls alike, and it emphasizes contemporary change shaped by discerning, future-minded people, often very wealthy ones, who speed such change for their own ends, and only sometimes for the public good. It sketches what will happen in an era when public and private resources prove too scanty to fund alternatives. It glances backward frequently, simply because remnants of past landscapes now function as capital in the plans of people already in the know about future landscapes.

Scenario analysis underlies this book. Such analysis asks a simple question of complex issues and data, and of change: What if? Glimpsing *the* future preoccupies few scenario analysts. Instead they descry possible futures, not so much parallel ones as ones diverging and interlocking, in ways locomotive engineers perhaps see tracks and switches stretching ahead of trains.

Sometimes technical innovation forestalls anticipated technical progress. Technical innovation demands and rewards retrospective scrutiny within any scenario-analysis context. Diesel-electric locomotives use far less fuel now than they did in 1980, a change that dramatically reduced the fuel-saving advantage of electric locomotives operating beneath overhead wires (although widening the competitive gap between trains and long-haul trucks). Railroad locomotives account for only about 1 percent of the national oil consumption, so electrifying tracks has only scant national energy-independence value either. Moreover, locomotive manufacturers actively experiment with liquid fuels derived from coal; such fuel proves uneconomical unless oil moves and remains above forty dollars a barrel. Constructing electrical catenary above existing tracks might interfere with tall freight cars moving new automobiles, double-stacked ocean-shipping containers, and other high cargo; it also might require adjusting the height of bridges and tunnels. But post-1980 electrification experiments have proceeded too, on the Black Mesa & Lake Powell and other little-known short lines, and the nuclear-power industry moves in this realm actively if quietly. The Amtrak Boston–Washington corridor electrification uses ordinary high-voltage electricity from the consumer grid with a success level that pleased electric utilities who envision railroads as new customers. Riders enjoying Amtrak high-speed Acela service know the silent swiftness of electric power, but probably only industry experts and scenario analysts have pondered a 1920 General Electric report authored by A. H. Armstrong, *The Future of Our Railways,* that anticipated Acela and raised an issue ignored for decades.

Armstrong emphasized that electrification sharply reduces rail traffic congestion, since electric-powered locomotives accelerate and decelerate far more rapidly than any others, pull more tonnage at higher speeds, and require little maintenance. Electrification matters not so much when the cost of diesel fuel rises, but rather when railroads reach traffic capacity, as they have *now.* Scenario analysts understand electrification in technological context, in what might be termed "a magic moment," that is, when technological and economic restraints and opportunities coincide, when some decisions are implemented but not others, when computers analyze data and determine only some choices remain, events happen, usually in quickening sequence.

In this book, the magic moment is now. At some point a railroad company must decide to double-track its main line or lose business to a competing line or to trucks, but almost certainly it will not electrify a single-track route. Nevertheless, the first railroad from the Mississippi to the Pacific that electrifies will enjoy a decisive advantage over its rail competitors, and certainly over the long-haul trucking industry, especially if it has already double- or triple-tracked its route. Industry executives know that, and weigh electrification against other variables, including the fact that many ships are too large for the Panama Canal, and the increasing danger that poor maintenance may cause that canal to fail, thus thrusting massive traffic demands on already stretched railroads. They also notice the overtures of the nuclear-power electric industry, which sees the railroad industry as a powerful potential ally in reversing its decline. Might global warming mean more windy days, and higher winds on windy days, producing the sheer that closes small airports? Might inventory- and package-tracing software drive a desire for next-day express shipment service impossible to achieve by truck and highly expensive to manage by air, but tricky to manage even on double-track diesel-powered railroads? Always industry personnel wonder about the rising cost of fuel, the price of real estate along main lines, and ponder the likelihood that automatic train operation may reduce railroad costs below anything highway and airline competitors can manage. In the immediate aftermath of 9/11, one bit of encouraging data emerged: Amtrak handled surging ridership with aplomb. The past partly determines the parameters of any magic moment, and lately the past receives much scrutiny from forward-looking analysts.

At the very close of World War II, just as the federal government began its massive defense-driven subsidizing of the airline industry, railroads contemplated a variety of innovations, especially 110-miles-per-hour passenger trains. In his 1945 *A Railroad for Tomorrow,* Edward Hungerford presciently outlined the intentions. By 1965 only railroad fans recalled the book, and even they paid it little attention: aficionados looked backward, at near-vanished coal smoke. But *A Railroad for Tomorrow* is the sort of book that underlies this one, and puts Jennifer S. Light's *From Warfare to Welfare: Defense Intellectuals and Urban Problems in Cold War America,* Steven W. Usselman's *Regulating Railroad Innovation: Business, Technology, and Politics in America, 1840–1920,* and other new scholarly works into built-environment scenario-analysis perspective. Most of the sources on which this book is founded are available to anyone, but the chief source is the same basic outdoor observation that enriches real estate developers and their consultants. As my Harvard Business School colleague William J. Poorvu points out in *The Real Estate Game: The Intelligent Guide to Decision-Making and Investment,* disciplined looking around reveals a great deal about the context of real estate activity in general, and observation refined by a specific agenda usually leads to profitable discoveries.

Consider an Amtrak Acela rider racing or creeping south from Boston. If the rider holds only an Amtrak timetable, he sees his train in a simple time-space framework: Acela is either on time or late wherever it happens to be. But if the rider holds schedules for the Massachusetts Bay Transportation Authority, Metro North, New Jersey Transit, Southeastern Pennsylvania Transit Authority, and Maryland Area Regional Transit trains, an Acela trip becomes markedly more informative. Even between New York and Washington, the four-track main line operates almost exactly at capacity, especially at rush hour, when trains move on 90-second headways. The inside express tracks require Acela to switch to local-service tracks to make station stops at Metropark, New Carrollton, and other lesser way stations. Switching slows speed considerably, so the high-speed train rarely stops at certain intermediate stations. Analyzing the Amtrak timetable makes it clear that Acela exists chiefly to serve well-heeled business travelers: its intermediate stops vary not only from weekday to weekend but by time of day. Acela races through New Haven but stops in Stamford, and often it scarcely gets up to speed south of Baltimore before stopping at BWI Airport. Acela trains serve both Metropark and BWI, but not both in any one trip; more northbound trips stop at BWI in the morning than in the afternoon (when more southbound trains stop), and southbound Acelas stop often in Metropark in the morning while northbound ones stop frequently in late afternoon. Amtrak timetables demonstrate that Acela targets business travelers and suggest that some people commute via Acela, something Hungerford and others predicted a half-century ago.

On the other hand, very frequently Acela creeps for miles, and any rider holding a regional transit authority schedule soon figures out that Amtrak's premiere train follows a commuter express. Any observer equipped with a watch, several timetables, and a window seat soon realizes that very fast trains pose serious problems to dispatchers overseeing all trains, even on multitrack routes. Regular Acela riders can anticipate the location of delays and thus predict late arrival times with some accuracy. Experience may therefore deflect would-be passengers from Friday afternoon, Monday morning, and holiday trips, or cause them to hop a transit authority express.

Of course, simply watching corridor trains demonstrates how frequently Acela moves slowly, especially between New York and New Haven, and how often it follows a commuter express. Nor is this the case only along the busy Northeast Corridor. Between Walker and Shawnee Junction, Wyoming, the Burlington Northern Santa Fe recently added another eight miles of triple track to its freight line, bringing the route near its planned goal of sixty triple-track miles. Tracks are busy near Baltimore, but busy around Walker too, but far fewer people visit Walker or connect the triple-track route with the rising price of shares. To recognize that overhead electric catenary reaches where the rich and powerful commute, one must first recognize catenary in the built environment. The choice of a rural location may well be influenced by the realization that Walker and other small towns enjoy frequent high-speed international freight service. Deep-pocket investors have no reason to share their hard-won data with anyone, and often corporate annual reports simply ignore the corollary impacts of explicitly mentioned items. Interested observers must notice with care, with the scrutiny of a prospective investor or spy, and then find archival sources that frame what is noticed.

Europeans immediately recognize Acela as different from high-speed British, German, and French trains, but often they cannot specify exactly how they differ. Acela is vastly heavier—something suggested by its locomotive on each end and definitely something apparent in its ride. Federal regulators crafted Acela with a particular wreck in mind, the 1987 collision of two freight locomotives with Amtrak's Colonial in northern Maryland. The conventional express had reached 128 miles per hour when it hit the errant locomotives. The express performed splendidly, in point of fact: the wreck killed 16 and injured 175 of the 622 aboard the ruggedly built cars. But

American passenger trains share rails with very heavy, long freight trains, and engineers have always designed them for potential collisions with freight trains far heavier than any operating in Europe, crafting massive passenger trains that move more slowly than foreign ones. The Colonial wreck shaped the design of Acela, which remains a slow train by European standards. Acela often moves more slowly than the traditional Colonial did in 1987—a fact that may spur investors to consider 128-miles-per-hour "traditional" service to a satellite municipality in which they have interests. The design of Acela indirectly illuminates the rarely mentioned electrification of New Jersey Transit commuter lines and other recent innovations. Acela is not merely an American-design high-speed passenger train intended to operate over tracks once in a while used by freight trains. It is the prototype of trains intended to cruise at 145 miles per hour down long stretches of straight track regularly used by massive coal and other freight trains. Conventional electric passenger trains like the old Colonial will serve metropolitan regions; the successors of Acela will serve the High Plains.

The 1987 wreck accomplished something more dramatic, albeit far from Amtrak tracks. Conrail moved all but local industry freight trains off Amtrak's Northeast Corridor. The old Reading and Lehigh Valley lines became the main Conrail route from the south to metropolitan New York, specifically to a place few white-collar people know, Oak Island Yard, near Newark and harbor wharves. More and more freight trains moved north from Hagerstown in Maryland through Harrisburg, Reading, Allentown, Bethlehem, and Easton, Pennsylvania, and then on through Flemington into Newark, New Jersey. The wreck at Gunpow, Maryland, shifted a massive amount of capital investment away from the Amtrak main line between Washington and New York and refocused it on a weedy route connecting worn-out factories. After Conrail rebuilt the track, abutting factories and warehouses suddenly became valuable. Improved freight train service worked its own magic in Reading, Bethlehem, and other gritty cities. Manufacturing and warehousing enjoyed an infusion of money, service, and, most importantly, multiple potential futures arising from being on a main freight line from New York to the south and west. So many freight trains now roll into the Rutherford yard near Reading that railroad officials have begun considering restoring the double track between Harrisburg and Hagerstown. The wide bridges remain from 1950s double-track passenger train days, making such an improvement financially feasible. Any Amtrak passenger notices the derelict factories and warehouses along the Northeast Corridor, but few see the new structures lining a freight-only route. Few designers or planners identify the rebuilt freight line as the generator of urban design and real estate investment, but it is the equivalent of a new interstate highway slicing a truck-thronged metropolitan region.

Not everything that follows here makes pleasant reading. *What if?* proves hard to face sometimes. Consider the fate of many Americans who own homes near long-abandoned railroad rights-of-way, perhaps routes now converted to nature trails. As traffic increases congestion on active tracks located some distance away, railroads, shippers, and commuters may demand that the nature trail become a rail route once again. Abutters may scream, "Not in my back yard!" just as so many abutters now complain about increased train traffic—and especially grade-crossing whistle noises—but in the end the "greater public good" may demand rail restoration.

But what if only passenger train service operates on the restored rails? Then the municipalities already crossed by the active railroad may find themselves served only by freight trains. Canny real estate developers must analyze such scenarios endlessly: What if most long-abandoned but rail-banked rights-of-way emerge as passenger routes, a sort of parallel rail grid controlled not by a dismembered or vanquished Amtrak but by regional transit authorities manipulated by local politicians? What if they emerge as freight-only routes and passenger trains serve the deteriorated cores of small satellite cities, making them dormitories for big-city service employees? Developers and speculators understand the subtleties of leaving freight trains where they operate now and putting passenger trains where affluent people live—adjacent to nature trails. The well-to-do people will commute swiftly and cheaply, perhaps no longer needing the Chinese-built automobiles freight trains will move inland from ports. On the other hand, moving freight trains from satellite-city downtowns can mean revitalizing and converting much run-down residential and commercial space if passenger trains link the down-towns with center cities.

All that follows here concerns a spatial future emerging subtly, but recognized by many individuals in and close to the railroad industry. *Railway Age* and other railroad industry magazines offer an immediate glimpse into recognition equally apparent in *Modern Materials Handling, Commercial Investment Real Estate,* and similar warehousing, logistics systems, and land-development journals. Chapter 1 analyzes the information sources and the viewpoint that prompted investors to reorient their thinking in the late 1970s. Chapter 2 explains the potential significance of cities like Lynchburg, Virginia—cities now difficult to reach but long ago at the junction of multiple passenger train routes. Chapter 3 deals with the politics that sidetracked the railroad industry in the 1960s, and the creation of Amtrak when "driverless automobile" and other urban transit experiments failed. Chapter 4 explains the myopic view of passenger trains as intercity transportation, then places future passenger service in wilderness recreation areas already populated by the wealthy. Chapter 5 examines luxury train travel in historical perspective as a way the elite strengthened personal and family links and solidified their hold on United States society—something the present-day elite not only remembers or rediscovers but now reinvents. Chapter 6 focuses on how mail and package express shipments once moved extremely quickly, and how such service will return as more and more trains operate above eighty miles an hour. Chapter 7 concerns freight that nowadays moves faster than many mail trains did in the 1950s, and examines the new intermodal cargoes so visible along most major rail lines: boxlike ocean-shipping containers and trucking company trailers. Chapter 8 deals with slow freight trains moving bulk grain, coal, petroleum products, and other commodities in ways that already transform port cities and rural United States regions, and that threaten the hegemony of the Interstate Highway System. Chapter 9 analyzes the failure of government and urban business communities to grasp the imminent urban and suburban difficulties planners recognized as implicit in much 1930s data—data that now suggest that the resurgence of railroads in wilderness and rural locations will transform cities already choked with truck traffic. The final chapter traces the short history of contemporary urban light-rail transit systems built by many cities on disused railroad alignments soon to be needed for regional and long-distance passenger and freight service.

Always the focus here is spatial, not technological and not financial. Railroads now skew landscape change, and the potential of that change forms the core of the argument that follows. Retrospect in landscape studies ordinarily means studying extant artifacts, even entire or fractured landscapes. Looking forward differs from both planning and design. It requires shielding the eye and the mind from distractions without any certain definition of distraction, and it requires a willingness to trust visual apprehension in the absence of quantitative and other sources. It requires seeing what is not in the scene as well as what is, and identifying what is changing even as one looks.

SOURCES: Armstrong, *The Future of Our Railways;* A. Black, *The Story of Tunnels;* General Electric Company, "Can Technology and the Environment Peacefully Coexist?"; Harley, "U.S. Railway Freight Electrification"; Hicks, "They'll Tell You How You'll Vote"; Hungerford, *A Railroad for Tomorrow;* Kotkin, "The Great Plains"; Levy, *The VCR Age;* Light, *From Warfare to Welfare;* Middleton, *Metropolitan Railways;* Norfolk Southern Corporation, *Annual Report 2005;* Olson, *The Logic of Collective Action;* Poorvu, *The Real Estate Game;* Schwieterman, *When the Railroad Leaves Town;* Usselman, *Regulating Railroad Innovation;* Warren and Tyagi, *The Two-Income Trap.*

WHISPER

Greenbush waits quietly now. Building after building stands empty. Asphalt and gravel parking lots catch the autumn sun but house no cars. Blue and red machinery stands abandoned, and here and there birds fly in and out open doors and windows. Temporary metal fencing snakes around some lots, its gates punctuated by modest white signs lettered in black. Across the adjacent salt marsh seagulls soar, their movement enlivening the fringes of a district so quiet that their cries echo from inland. Only a rare car cruises Driftway Street. Sunlight strikes deep into the woods at the heart of the industrial area. Much of the undergrowth has been slashed down. Mature trees remain, but for the first time in decades daylight blasts beneath the demolished highway overpass, revealing the soot-smudged granite blocks of its abutments. Old sofas, piles of shingles, lawnmower engines, pallets, and bottles poke above the fallen branches; the boatyard is bereft of boats. Slanting sunlight and frost-dropped leaves reveal paths winding toward the coffee shop, liquor store, and post office beyond the littered woods. The white signs announce condemnation and imminent destruction. The railroad is coming. The railroad is coming back.

Opened almost tentatively in the 1840s, the coastal route of the Old Colony Railroad served towns settled two centuries earlier. Steam locomotion technology supplanted the little packet vessels that connected Hingham, Scituate, Marshfield, Duxbury, and Plymouth with Boston, and it soon supplanted the tiny steamboat too. The parallel coach line along the former highway likewise succumbed, although modest competitors began short-distance, right-angle service linking inland villages with the coast-hugging railroad. Regular rail service altered everyday life, and in time the landscape focused on the tracks. Businesses moved from harbors and estuary wharves to trackside, and as shipping withered, the railroad opened its many drawbridges less and less frequently. By 1900 fishermen growled about spans permanently down, and farmers knew the salt-marsh-crossing railroad as a dike protecting inland fields from gale-driven tides. The railroad seemed almighty, carrying not only commuters and summertime tourists to Cape Cod but almost all the mail and freight that moved along the coast. Its route was more enduring than any public road: it was the *permanent* way.

Twenty years later the railroad company had begun to suffer from the widespread use of automobiles moving along paved roads, and by 1939 it had abandoned the track south of the marsh, ripped up ties and rails, and turned over the weed-grown remnant of permanent way to abutters and municipal government. Greenbush became a terminal, not a way station. The New York, New Haven & Hartford Railroad Company, having acquired the Old Colony by merger, erected a roundhouse, turntable, water tank, and other facilities for turning, storing, and servicing steam locomotives, and built a coach yard south of the overpass it had already installed to alleviate grade-crossing danger. Every evening the yard filled with long trains of dark-green coaches, soon pulled by diesel-electric locomotives that made the expensive roundhouse and most other service facilities superfluous. As late-1950s commuters chose to drive to Boston over newly built highways, the company struggled to maintain track, trains, and profit. When vandals burned an estuary trestle in 1959, the company gave up for good, abandoning passenger service the very next morning. A day or two later the passenger trains rumbled away from Greenbush, making their way to Boston by a roundabout route south and west of the smoldering trestle. For a while a weekly freight train arrived to serve the Greenbush feed mill and a handful of other bulk-commodity industries, before it too disappeared, never to return. No ceremonies marked the abandonment of railroad service.

Weeds and scrub and finally trees masked the railroad right-of-way. Small manufacturing businesses located on the former train yard after the roundhouse burned, but beyond the concrete-block structures and parking lots the trees grew taller by the year. The railroad right-of-way shrank from coach yard and roundhouse site to a narrow strip of land running across the municipality of Scituate and other townships too.

Town governments did nothing with the land acquired by de-

Railroad restoration often begins beneath aging highway bridges, when contractors arrive to start replacement efforts.

fault. Hikers and shortcutting teenagers made a narrow footpath down the center of it, almost precisely halfway between the locations of the long-gone rails. In the early 1980s intrepid mountain-bike riders discovered the right-of-way as a secret route free of interruption and connected with gigantic Wampatuck State Park, itself a former naval ammunition depot once serviced by a spur of the Greenbush route. Cross-county skiers followed the mountain bikers in winter, and joined with bicyclists and hikers to remove the occasional fallen tree that blocked the narrow path. The detritus of railroad operations—switch stands, twisted rails, signal boxes, and other debris—they skirted, and they took special care crossing bridges officialdom neglected. A ribbon of woods ran all the way to East Weymouth, where an active railroad rematerialized at the junction of Conrail and the Fore River Railroad, the latter a short line serving the city of Quincy. At this junction the woods ended, and hiking became trespassing, and dangerous too.

No English word properly designates the overgrowing of the abandoned right-of-way. Such a word might help explain why even users of the right-of-way did not truly see it in a way that made and makes it real. Neither *wilderness* nor *bewilderment* connotes a place overcome by wilderness. Because English lacks the concept Germans know as *Ortsbewüstung,* meaning the re-wildering of a specific place long before shaped by people, the users—and abutters and casual crossers too—did not *realize* the right-of-way any more than did local government authorities. It existed merely as a trail through leaves, somehow distinct from all space and structure through which it sliced, yet also a part of the larger scene.

As memory of the train faded, the path became as well used as the rocky landing in a nearby salt marsh built in the eighteenth century by the prosperous owner of a sailing packet. The packet is long gone from human memory and figures only in obscure local history pamphlets, but the packet landing is now a pleasant fishing and picnicking spot almost universally accepted as "natural." Only the experienced mariner, fisherman, or longshoreman sees its piled rocks as a perfectly sited docking spot, or notices that the tiny pile-driver barge and tug still working the estuaries tie up at it despite its lack of wharf equipment. The packet landing is a good place to touch a workboat to shore, as pleasure boaters sometimes learn when they see a workboat there, or when they need to touch land themselves without problems of tide and current. But so overgrown is the landing that it masquerades as a natural hummock linking estuary, salt marsh, and abutting woodland.

The overgrown right-of-way is bewildered, if one translates the German starkly. *Ortsbewüstung* designates the bewildering of a place, something that jars English speakers accustomed to thinking of people as bewildered by all sorts of circumstances, including being lost in wilderness. Almost certainly a product of the Black Death, the mid-fourteenth-century plagues that killed up to two-thirds of the population in many German-speaking regions, the concept involves nature slowly overwhelming land abandoned by people. Whole villages returned to forest, grass grew in desolate city streets, and well-traveled roads became greenways, used enough to keep down brush but not enough to destroy grass. Generations of

Germans after the Black Death understood nature, and especially forest, as something that only continuous effort keeps at bay. They expected to find ruins deep in forest, and their folk tales often involve children and other wanderers discovering a decrepit cottage or gingerbread house or castle surrounded by dense woods. Despite a terrific death toll from the plagues themselves, the English never formalized a similar understanding. North American colonists accepted the notion that settlement meant carving landscape from wilderness, and that wilderness never overwhelmed the carvers.

Twenty-first-century Americans prove prone to thinking of wilderness in national park terms, or else as something "good" endangered by people. Simple visual encounters sometimes disturb such casual thinking, but rarely for long. Everywhere east of the Appalachians, hikers find stone walls in woods and sometimes cellar holes or still-standing stone and brick chimneys. Obviously people once lived where the hikers hike, but many hikers fail to grasp that the remnants are the detritus of abandoned agricultural enterprise. No one builds stone walls in woods. The walls took form as linear rock piles made by people clearing land for plowing, and proved secondarily useful as fencing. Modern farmers hiking or hunting across such regions can look at the base of the walls and tell from the mounding of soil which side of the wall faced the field plowed last. But most explorers in the woods are not farmers, and they pay no more attention to the mounding of soil along walls than they do to the age and species of trees in the forests, the way brooks flow along channels dug two centuries earlier, or to the traces of a road abandoned a century ago. They cannot even find the well on a long-bewildered farm.

Landscape historians and foresters characterize such territory as afforested, not reforested, meaning that the woods appeared out of neglect rather than by deliberate planting. In the final analysis, however, most Americans care little for such nuance. Only at sundown on a winter night, when the afternoon walk has lasted a bit too long, do the darkening woods take on a wilderness aspect. When big, cat-nourished coyotes appear at the edge of the suburban woodlot, people stare at a raw wildness they decide belongs in some national forest. Genuine wilderness exists everywhere away from the great agricultural regions of the Midwest and High Plains, even if it is wilderness returned.

When pushed, most Americans grudgingly admit they distinguish between woods and forest: the one is defined by well-known surrounding roads and is pedestrian in scale, while the other is amorphous in shape, vast, and penetrable only by well-equipped hikers. They may know that a dense swamp lies beside the interstate highway, but they neither trek across the swamp nor know much about its constituent elements, including the homeless people rumored to inhabit it. Americans tend to think of wilderness in terms of remote national parks; it is unlikely that many spend much time pondering the sharks in urban harbors, or the fact that the eastern states were 80 percent open land two centuries ago and three-quarters afforested now. They do, however, know a gentle walk when they walk it, and railroad rights-of-way, usually almost dead level, make for relaxing walking indeed. In the middle of the nineteenth century, Thoreau commented that he crossed active railroads as though they were cart paths in the woods. By 2000 the Greenbush line had become less wide than even a cart path, and it had become its own woods to boot. Its crossing gates and signals long removed, its highway-crossing rails buried in asphalt, it appeared as a momentary blur of green to motorists speeding across it. Except for old-timers and for a few active walkers, runners, and bicyclists, the right-of-way merged with other forested land, becoming green scenery.

But no municipality designated the Greenbush line as conservation land, recreational space, or anything else. Legally, the right-of-way, all its trees, and the path along its centerline were nonexistent. Abutters encroached upon it, dumping brush and rubbish there, but sometimes extending lawns and gardens into it and even erecting buildings upon it. Municipal authorities, when apprised of such activity, acted suitably if not always aggressively; after all, they knew that the ill-bounded right-of-way was municipal property, if property held for unspecified use. But most of the time, no one but hikers noticed the encroachments into the ribbon of woods, and if they did, few knew the precise boundaries of the old right-of-way.

However, occasionally there walked, among the bikers and hikers and skiers, people enamored of railroad history. Almost always male, usually but not always middle-aged or older, the men often walked in pairs, printed or sketched maps in hand. Their cars left behind at some former grade crossing, or the parking lot of a train station converted into a liquor store or hair-styling salon, they walked slowly, searching for the ruins of the railroad itself.

Everywhere they found them. Some stood out so clearly as to be unmistakable. For example, the salvage companies never removed the six-foot-high metal relay boxes that sheltered signal mechanisms. Spaced at what appeared to be random distances from each other, the silver boxes seemed impervious to rust, and made good landmarks for walkers negotiating the green tunnel. Other ruins lay underfoot. On some, hikers stubbed toes: lengths of rail escaped removal, as did thousands of rail spikes and steel tie plates. Anyone scuffing the leaves on either side of the footwide path almost immediately uncovered something metal, often something heavy sinking into the soil around it. Downslope from the embankment snaking through swamps lay rotting wooden ties escaped from the tie-removal machine, and forty-foot lengths of rail mislaid in the early nineteenth-century track renovation. Skewed at all sorts of angles were fallen telegraph poles, some toppled by the Great Hurricane of 1938 and never retrieved by repair crews erecting new ones. Anyone walking the right-of-way was bound to see some artifacts of rail road.

But only the discerning few noted other ruins. Far out in the salt marsh, where the right-of-way is merely a narrow embankment crowned with poison ivy and other halophytes, the concrete bases of the drawbridge signals remain, swathed in vines. In the dense swamps, the right-of-way embankment broadens where it once supported two parallel tracks, and a few feet from the path lies ballast pitched slightly differently from that a few feet away. In a woods a mile north of the swamps, a massive switch stand lies toppled away from the path, almost invisible in fifty years' worth of fallen leaves. Such ruins attracted the scrutiny of railroad buffs looking for evidence of sidetracks to long-gone industries or junctions with branch lines.

These ruins offered information available elsewhere only in fragmented format. Unlike that compiled by government agencies, railroad company information was and is largely private, and railroad companies—especially those collapsing into bankruptcy, reorganization, and nullity—have no legal obligation to keep much of their documentation. Between the 1920s and about 1980, railroad abandonment and bankruptcy often meant the immediate destruction of masses of documentation. Long after such destruction, inquirers found themselves examining physical evidence for answers to questions originating in simple curiosity sparked by bits of information in old newspaper clippings, photographs, or local tradition. Audubon Society folk enjoyed watching birds along the abandoned right-of-way, and delighted in piecing together some understanding of ecosystems, especially avian ones. The railroad historians walking among them enjoyed a similar pleasure, one focused on gaining a broader understanding of how the railroad actually worked.

Railroad historians bifurcated in the 1920s. By far the more powerful group continued work begun in the 1860s, perhaps even earlier. Largely academic and grounded in business schools and departments of economics, it dealt almost exclusively with the financial end of railroading or with the juxtaposition of railroad finance and government regulation. This group battled within itself, some scholars arguing in favor of increased government regulation and others attempting to demonstrate that regulation led to higher rates, lower profits, and poor service. The group split in other ways as some writers focused on regional matters, some emphasized the history of individual railroad companies, and others attempted to draw international comparisons. Today, economic historians mine the work the group produced. Almost without exception, however, the business-focused group ignored the other group, which coalesced in 1921 as the Railway and Locomotive Historical Society.

Technological transformation of railroad equipment, physical plant, and operations occurred so rapidly in the years just before World War I that a group of interested observers determined to preserve the early technical history of the industry. At first the loose-knit group focused on the early steam locomotives supplanted not just by more massive successors but by electric-powered engines. But then the society quickly began to assemble documents pertaining to the nascent everyday operation of railroads, especially during the Civil War. Within a few years it had extended its focus to railroad building west of the Mississippi and had begun classifying railroad operating information. Around 1930 it began analyzing both technical innovation and operating procedures.

Until after World War II, the newer group worked essentially academically too. The society accepted new members only upon submission of a monograph on some phase of railroad history and two photographs of steam locomotives. But during the Depression it began to attract a spectrum of other railroad-industry-focused people ranging from photographers, to collectors of lanterns, telegraph instruments, and other industrial antiques, to those determined to preserve entire pieces of rolling stock. By the time the New York, New Haven & Hartford Railroad Company abandoned the line south of Greenbush in 1939, the society had become a powerful force in preserving documents and artifacts from Depression-era bankruptcies.

The supplanting of steam locomotives by diesel-electrics in the 1950s brought the second group to national prominence simply by expanding its numbers. However staid and methodical its core membership might have been, the society welcomed a burgeoning group characterized as "rail fans." Nostalgia for vanishing steam locomotives suffused these newcomers, almost entirely men who saw the demise of steam-powered railroading as the end of an era in which they had come of age. Aficionados may have seen the steam locomotive as symbolizing values—especially the freedom to travel—for which they had fought in World War II. The diesel-electric locomotive often seemed a product of a rapidly changing economy and a harbinger of excruciating changes in mining, heavy manufacturing, and other traditionally male-dominated industries. Thousands of men joined the rail fans in stopping the family car at grade crossings and dragging little children up to the tracks when a steam locomotive chugged or blasted past.

The children, especially boys, fit into the larger concatenation of hope and nostalgia and worry as consumers of toy trains, especially those made by Lionel and American Flyer. For boys of the 1950s, an electric train set was the premiere Christmas present, but only retrospect reveals the striking division so apparent in 1950s catalogs of toy train manufacturers. Every autumn new catalogs featured not only the latest miniature copies of modern diesel-electric locomotives but the most powerful of steam locomotives, albeit ones developed twenty or thirty years earlier. The entire 1950s panoply of toy trains—the basic train set, the additional cars, the complexities of track and switches, the structures and signal systems, the scenery and the electrical components—all existed perhaps as much for parents (especially fathers) as for children (especially sons). Many of the sons became rail fans themselves, some deeply interested in museum-piece steam locomotives, but most intrigued by the latest permutation of diesel-electric locomotives.

At the beginning of the twenty-first century, the rail fan movement supports multiple magazines, a video industry, perhaps two hundred historical societies focused on extant and long-vanished railroads, and a tour effort that now shapes economic development priorities in remote towns adjacent to high-interest railroad history or contemporary activity. It drives the proliferation of railroad museums and tourist railroads, and even the private ownership of railroad equipment. And it merges with another railroad-focused group, the scale-model railroaders.

Adults who decades ago played with toy trains form the core of the scale-model hobby, a multi-billion-dollar effort that prizes the building and collecting of superb models and their operation in prototypical fashion. Model railroading is more than railroad-model building, although many of its adherents specialize in historically accurate detailing as much as do the modelers of eighteenth-century sailing ships. The operation of models shapes the hobby, which focuses on the layout as the central facet. In clubs and in hundreds of thousands of garages, basements, and special-purpose backyard buildings, model railroaders build layouts that represent a particular piece of railroad at a particular moment, usually the late 1940s steam-to-diesel transition period. They support many of the magazines, artifact-acquisition fund-raising, tours, and other efforts of the rail fans, but since the 1930s have accumulated their own magazines, national organizations, and even museums. Allied with collectors of antique toy trains, and with the burgeoning group of married couples who build large-scale outdoor garden railroad layouts, traditional model railroaders fuel an increasingly intense effort to understand prototypical but long-vanished railroading.

While difficult to measure, the greater railroad enthusiast movement is one of the more muscular popular history phenomena. Perhaps only a half-million families operate layouts: hobby manufacturer associations have uncertain data beyond sales and repeat-sales figures. Each of the larger magazines reaches about a quarter-million readers a month, but many enthusiasts read only special-interest magazines focused on Rocky Mountain narrow-gauge steam-era railroading, or East Coast trolley cars, or contemporary Southern California rail operations. Railroad museums welcome increasing numbers of visitors, but have no way of distinguishing real enthusiasts from general-interest visitors. Surveys suggest that the movement is a cross section of the population, but some components of it, especially the scale-model railroaders, are distinguished by graduate degrees, professional occupations, and high income. Some surveys interpret income in the context of discretionary time: building a model railroad takes decades, and joining a tour to abandoned Rocky Mountain railroad tunnels or Alaskan narrow-gauge rights-of-way takes weeks. In an era when media focus popular attention on sports, all hobbies move beneath most media radar, and even thriving hobbies like those related to the railroad industry get surprisingly little attention.

Railroad hobbyists scarcely intrigued by modeling but rather by collecting photographs, timetables, and other ephemera, or by teasing out the history of a type of rolling stock, a junction, or some stretch of main line or branch track, work almost invisibly. They support journals ranging from national ones such as *Railroad History* to regional ones published by the Terminal Railroad Association of St. Louis Historical and Technical Society and dozens of other quasi-scholarly societies. Moreover, they fuel a very healthy specialized industry that increasingly publishes books by scholars and industry archivists as well as enthusiasts.

Academics and sometimes even railroad industry consultants admire the enthusiast effort and often contribute to it. Sophisticated scholarly work often appears first in *Trains* and competing enthusiast magazines. Michael Bezilla of the University of Pennsylvania and author of *Electric Traction on the Pennsylvania Railroad*—a meticulous history of technological innovation within a business

35

enterprise—explained in a 1978 *Trains* article how diesel fuel prices might cause railroad investors to extend existing electrification beyond Harrisburg to Pittsburgh. Like Civil War, logging, and marine amateur historians, railroad historians enjoy open-air effort. In the 1970s their low-cost hobby blossomed. Magazines began publishing sophisticated and lengthy outdoor-exploration-based articles that in turn engendered others. One on the geology of the Canadian Shield—the 1.8 million sq. mi. rocky, forested region east of Winnipeg—sparked many others analyzing railroad routing and construction nuances forced by topography and geology. An article on the route of the New York, Ontario & Western Railway from Oswego on Lake Ontario south to Cornwall, New York—where it operated over another line into Weehawken, New Jersey—pushed writers to examine how the abandonment of that company subsequently denied specialized rail service to Scranton and to Rome, Utica, and other New York cities. In the 1978 article "The Fun of Finding Yesterday," one *Railroad Model Craftsman* columnist praised the exploration and research effort for producing "feelings of archeological purpose and worth." In the late 1970s, the National Trust for Historic Preservation began advertising in *Railroad Model Craftsman,* having discovered that railroad enthusiasts had a deep interest in material history. Learning about ghost railroads meant stretching mental and physical muscles both, and perhaps producing historical information of some value to succeeding generations. Recently articles have appeared in the *Chicago Tribune* and other large newspapers reporting the strength of the enthusiast movement and linking it to real estate development and other potential change along active and abandoned rights-of-way.

A handful of the men walking the Old Colony right-of-way after 1959 searched for the reality of vanished railroad operation. Understanding the dedicated model railroader as someone every bit as determined as the historical geographer or landscape historian to uncover landscape artifacts or long-hidden documents takes a bit of doing. But a glance at *Mainline Modeler* or *Narrow Gauge and Short-Line Gazette* reveals in-depth articles illustrated with period photographs often assembled over decades, many written by attorneys, physicians, and other professionals. *Railroad History,* published by the Railway and Locomotive Historical Society, remains a scholarly journal, but even its scholar-authors acknowledge the accomplishments of amateurs, especially those who devote decades to chasing paperwork trails. How did it work? Scholars and hobbyists alike often struggle to answer the same question, and sometimes hobbyists trump academics. Determining how a railroad worked in a particular period demands more than skill at archival research: often it requires on-site examination and deep background understanding.

Vanished railroad companies leave behind paperwork. Reports lodged with federal and state regulatory agencies explain financial issues, albeit often in skewed ways. Buried in the mass of regulatory agency documentation, the sheer volume of which deters many academics, amateur researchers tease out arcane data, like the number of trains that arrived late in 1891, or the cost of operating freight service in 1933, or the persistence of United States Post Office distrust of airmail in the 1960s. Much of the research focuses on the collision of engineering miscalculation and subsequent financial disaster. Railroad bridges collapsed repeatedly in the 1890s as locomotives became much heavier; strengthening or replacing thousands of bridges emptied railroad company coffers.

In the 1960s the Pennsylvania, New York Central, and other northeast railroad companies invested heavily in gondola, hopper, and specialty cars serving the steel industry. Within several years that industry collapsed like a bad bridge before moving to Asia, leaving behind a superb but sidetracked fleet of cars eventually sold to China at knockdown prices. From the 1910s through the 1930s, some railroads experimented with electrification. Scholars have difficulty analyzing streetcars that accelerated faster than a contemporary Porsche, let alone hydroelectric-powered locomotives incorrectly dismissed in the 1970s as less efficient than diesel-electrics. While business and economic historians and analysts make some sense of period documentation, other experts explore the realities implicit in working railroads. Their explorations involve the physical artifacts enthusiasts love and sometimes reproduce in miniature, and that frequently lead to on-site examination.

Some exploration leads to fantasies academics might condemn

but investors, especially scenario analysts in large consulting firms, encourage, for speculation by civil engineers, Realtors, and other enthusiasts often begins in data about which professional experts know little. Suppose a railroad company drained of its capital by financial chicanery had instead double-tracked its main line as its earlier ownership intended and announced, and then electrified it. The broader effects of such improvements might have transformed a region. Industries might have expanded owing to more efficient shipping, or suburban growth might have extended along a high-speed, high-capacity route. Such questions intrigue enthusiasts and academics willing to shift contemporary scenario-based spatial analysis away from ecological issues and toward historical ones. Questions about increased speed, frequency of service, and the development of long-distance routing dependent on new motive power beguile inquirers who discover that in 1925 or 1960 railroad management confronted alternate futures. The walkers along the Greenbush line descry more than remnants birders miss. Sometimes they encounter a point where a junction might have been built connecting a planned but never-completed track with another main line: they note the preliminary grading and the lack of any subsequent work. They discern where an extra passing sidetrack might have increased rush-hour capacity by two additional trains that would have cut 1940 commutes by twenty minutes. From such observation, it is possible to imagine alternative futures now shrouded in mature trees.

Beginning in the early 1970s enthusiasts glimpsed something looming ahead, but not around the curve of the overgrown footpath. Most journalists laughed at their predictions of the tracks returning to the coastal region south of Boston, but a handful of journalists listened and reported on what might be. Since the railroad stopped operating in 1959, the coastal region had become hard to access, especially at rush hour and on summer weekends. The 1960s-era divided highway, so choked with traffic as to become a statewide joke, stymied commuters, Cape Cod–bound tourists, and truckers. While development west and north of Boston mushroomed, the environmentally sensitive rural coastal region to the south enjoyed an eerie peace. Difficult highway access engendered perceptual vagueness: many residents in eastern Massachusetts knew little about the region bordered by the interstate-like highway connecting Boston and Cape Cod. Local residents, especially a new breed working from home offices and rarely visiting Boston, confronted highway engineers vexed by salt marshes, estuaries, swamps, and other half-wild areas that stymied road building, and voiced their disapproval of proposed roads. But in the 1980s archival sources and on-site examination merged into a scenario suddenly viable.

At public hearing after public hearing between 1985 and 1995, all sorts of people began reading aloud railroad timetables from the 1920s, something regional newspapers reported. In 1929 steam locomotives pulled commuter trains at eighty miles an hour. At that speed, living in an environmentally sensitive, beautiful area forty miles from South Station in Boston means a very short commute indeed, scarcely time to read the morning paper. Eighty miles an hour transcends all highway travel: the speed is illegal and, in any metropolitan area at rush hour, a fond fantasy only. But at one public hearing after another, especially those held along the coast and inland near the ends of the proposed revitalized lines, the data from railroad enthusiasts shaped public policy reality almost overnight.

With accelerating speed, the Massachusetts Bay Transportation Authority began rebuilding decrepit freight-only tracks southwest of Boston. Two lines reopened in the late 1990s as state-of-the-art commuter train routes linking Plymouth, Kingston, Middleboro, and intermediate stations with South Station, the Boston terminus undergoing pre-Acela electrification. Ridership exceeded all analyst prognostication. So many passengers thronged the trains north of South Weymouth that conductors could not move through the cars to collect tickets or glance at passes. The transit authority added more coaches, and almost at once they filled. Double-deck passenger cars, the immediate solution to the problem of passengers standing in aisles, seemed at best a stopgap measure.

Transit authority experts admit that adding more trains is tricky without double-tracking the existing lines, but so far that idea has fallen on deaf ears. Within the city of Boston, the single track parallels an interstate highway built on the former six-track railroad main line. Slicing a lane or two from the vehicle-choked Southeast Expressway remains heresy. Perhaps electrification would expedite train movements; perhaps not. But more trains cannot be added now to the renovated routes simply because trains operating from Greenbush will increase traffic to capacity on the single urban track.

At one end of the route, planned for full operation by early 2008, lies a railroad track already maniacally busy at rush hour. Train after train, many with double-deck cars, all carrying standees, sizzle past sometimes as close as five minutes apart, slowed by proximity to terminal platforms. At the other end is only a pregnant stillness interrupted by earth-moving equipment. In Greenbush buildings stand abandoned. Brush cutters have felled sight lines for surveyors, and here and there the wilderness footpath widens into a trail for pickup trucks filled with civil engineers.

No one along the Greenbush right-of-way doubts the trains are coming back. No one any longer believes that restoration of railroad service will please anyone. Abutters who lived for decades next to overgrown walking paths, especially newcomers who bought houses decades ago and paid the rusted rails little attention, often protest and organize against restoration. But their efforts produce mostly blunt response: "When the woman in Hingham moved in sixteen years ago, was she wearing blinders?" asked one 2004 letter to the editor about a still-vocal protestor. "Didn't she see the tracks? Didn't she ask questions?" As early as 1974, the *Boston Globe* published a brief story suggesting the promise in what only railroad aficionados advocated. "The South Shore—200,000 People Within 10 Minutes of an Unused Rail Line" focused on a set of routes reaching far into Cape Cod, and it blew the first faint warning whistle heard by anyone other than railroad enthusiasts. Trains would eventually return because no other form of transportation, even monorails and other science-fiction devices, promised any solution to population growth in environmentally sensitive areas or to rush-hour and summertime traffic jams. But not for ten years did abutters see the first surveyors hiking along the long-abandoned tracks. Only when stakes and orange spray paint appeared in the woods behind backyards did the protests begin.

Elsewhere across the United States, a return of passenger train service strikes most people as folly. But south and southwest of

Boston, observers are beginning to realize something that railroad enthusiasts and railroad historians knew in the 1960s. Underneath nostalgia about glamorous 1930s passenger trains, lonesome steam whistles echoing at midnight, and Lionel toy trains rumbles something vastly more important: the landscape that people created around the railroad may have been better than the sprawl the automobile engenders. Excellent railroad service may enhance our quality of life by reducing commuting time and local road traffic congestion, and by reshaping residential and commercial landscape. A sensible railroad system is a common good, but defining *sensible* is not easy. Replicating the past is foolish, but the possibility of welding the best of the past to the most-choice components of the present makes the study of places like Greenbush well worthwhile.

Real estate developers and investors, and investment analysts, study Greenbush very carefully, not only by examining municipal documents but by speaking with abutters, often asking how to contact property owners who refuse to answer their mail or who might be party to a blind realty trust. The walker trudging inland from the salt marshes on a winter afternoon realizes that the two men looking around so carefully stand near a rental automobile, exactly as Poorvu sketches in *The Real Estate Game*. A few words exchanged about the weather prove enough to verify the hunch. Two Texans stand in the silence of Greenbush, looking for themselves at the face of change. All the walker need do then is remark on how the area functioned when the trains last operated. Then the cross-examination begins, the subtle and not-so-subtle questions that reveal that the visitors work for no railroad or transit authority but for people who intend to profit when the railroad returns to some communities far away from the Atlantic Coast.

SOURCES: Bezilla, "The Electrification That Might Have Been"; Borrone, "Sparking the Globalized Trade and Transportation Connection"; Carstens, "The Shawangunk Carrier"; Ewing, Pendall, and Chen, "Measuring Sprawl and Its Transportation Impacts"; Fifer, "Transcontinental"; Koester, "The Fun of Finding Yesterday"; Menzies, "The South Shore"; Nelson, "Look Again"; Swain, "Scenery of the Canadian Shield"; Wurst, "On Rail's Trails."

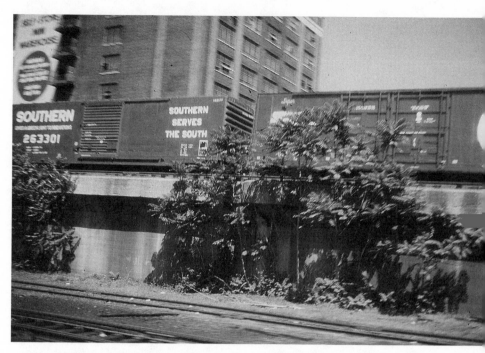

In many cities, only freight trains roll where passenger trains once did; too few Americans visualize passenger service supplementing freight service and making downtowns far more vibrant.

NECKLACE

No new regional airport better exemplifies the problems bedeviling small-city airline service than the Lynchburg Regional Airport smack in the center of Virginia. Opened in 1992, the terminal structure faces a 5,799-foot-long runway capable of accommodating midsized jet airliners. But jets no longer serve Lynchburg. Instead a handful of tiny, propeller-driven aircraft flutter back and forth from Charlotte, Pittsburgh, and Washington, D.C. Ostensibly, jet service disappeared in the wake of nationwide financial problems, but something less complex seems a more likely reason.

The new airport is simply too close to other airports. Roanoke Regional is only 57 miles away, Charlottesville is about 60 miles, Piedmont Triad (in Greensboro, N.C.) is 120 miles, and Richmond is not much farther, at 142. Only slightly farther off are two major airports, Washington Dulles and Reagan National, at 166 and 182 miles. Just as nineteenth-century railroad companies once played off one city against another, so now do airlines squeeze Lynchburg. The remaining small-aircraft flights frequently do not operate, especially the last one of the day leaving Charlotte for Lynchburg. Repeated missed connections make Lynchburg residents wary and infuriate regular fliers from distant places.

Lynchburg's 96,000 people form the core of a much larger rural population living in a region known for its spectacular scenic beauty. Lynchburg has a rich history, a multitude of cultural institutions including five colleges; a sumptuous, active downtown of gorgeous period buildings; and a diverse economy based on a sophisticated, prosperous industrial and commercial base. Appomattox Court House National Historic Site, eighteen miles to the east along a state highway, attracts many tourists to the region.

Lynchburg blooms away from interstate highways. I-81 and its parallel cousin, the Blue Ridge Parkway, lie about thirty-five miles west, running north–south. At Charlottesville, some sixty miles north, I-64 runs northwest from Richmond to its T-junction interchange with I-81 at Staunton. Other north–south interstate highways run far to the southeast (I-85) and southwest (I-77), but angle away from Lynchburg toward Charlotte and other large North Carolina cities. Long-distance motorists simply bypass not only Lynchburg but the entire region that surrounds the city. Lynchburg residents enjoy their distance from dense highway traffic, especially long-haul truck traffic, but they realize the evolving difficulties of driving to airports other than their own. Traffic in Roanoke and Richmond, increasingly heavy and sporadically stopped, makes time-to-airport estimates mere guesswork. The Roanoke Airport is now at least a half-hour longer drive from Lynchburg than it was in 1990.

Highway atlases distort the geographic perspective of travelers and people planning vacation trips. They convert entire regions like the one focused on Lynchburg into perceptual gores, places avoided by interstate routes. Only locals move about on the secondary and tertiary roads removed from interstate highways, and only motorists with reasons for penetrating such regions do so. Long-distance motorists are no more likely to wind up in Lynchburg for lunch or for the night than are long-distance truckers. Far more crucially, the road-map mentality blinds most Americans to the long-ago importance of cities like Lynchburg in nonhighway topographical and transportation contexts.

Lynchburg lies far enough west and south in Virginia that highway atlas cartographers depict it in terms of both North Carolina and West Virginia. In most atlases, North Carolina appears only as a quarter-inch-wide yellow margin below the two-page Virginia map, and West Virginia, simply because of the diagonal state boundary, proves an excellent place to insert a half-dozen small maps showing Virginia cities against a pale yellow background. No highway atlas attempts to show Lynchburg in relation to the Allegheny or Appalachian mountains, or explains why the Piedmont region is called—in French—"the foothills," let alone makes clear the importance of the Shenandoah Valley. No highway atlas explains the relation of Lynchburg to Charleston or Wheeling in West Virginia, or helps anyone understand why Lynchburg Airport has nonstop service to Pittsburgh and Charlotte but not Philadelphia. Highway atlases may be the best-selling annual publications in the country, but they do nothing to suggest, much less explain, why so much population growth remains concentrated in certain areas increasingly choked with automobile traffic.

In 1929 Lynchburg lay about halfway along a direct high-speed rail route between New York and New Orleans. Operated by several cooperating railroads, the Washington, Chattanooga, New Orleans Limited slipped out of New York's Pennsylvania Station every afternoon at 4:50. It arrived in Lynchburg at 3:55 the following morning, bound for Knoxville, Chattanooga, Birmingham, and Meridian. Four hours later, a slower but nonetheless first-class train, No. 25, left New York along the same route, reaching Lynchburg at 8:00 AM. The opposing trains left Lynchburg daily at 1:50 AM and 7:20 PM, arriving in New York at 12:30 PM and 6:40 AM. While not the most convenient service, sleeping cars provided a chance for a good night's rest, even for passengers headed to Washington, where night trains detached Pullman cars so passengers could sleep undisturbed until awakened at 7:15. Trains No. 41, 42, 25, and 26, while not especially luxurious, carried dining cars, drawing-room sleeping cars, and other amenities. They competed, after all, with the Crescent Limited.

That train carried special sleeping cars, a club car, an observation car, and other luxuries, including maid and valet service, showers, and a woman's lounge. It left New York at 8:40 every evening and arrived in Lynchburg at 6:52 the following morning; its opposite number left Lynchburg at 8:45 in the evening and arrived in New York at 10:50 AM. A so-called candy train, it offered luxury travel not only between large cities like New York, Washington, Atlanta, and New Orleans, but between much smaller cities like Charlotte, Spartanburg, Auburn, Montgomery, Pensacola, Mobile—and, of course, Lynchburg. The Crescent Limited touched fortunate small cities with big-city glamour twice a day.

It was not necessarily the fastest way to go, of course, nor was it the longest-mileage train. Twice a day the United States Fast Mail paused in Lynchburg, at 11:00 AM heading toward New Orleans and at 3:50 PM toward New York. Carrying sleepers and a dining car, it offered passengers a first-class if slightly rough ride, for it existed chiefly to hurry car upon car of first-class mail. The Piedmont Limited, the Boston–New Orleans train, paused in Lynchburg too, toward New Orleans at 2:50 AM and toward Boston at 8:45 PM. It too was invested with some urban glamour, but included among its ordinary sleeping cars a special, low-priced "tourist" version operating on to Los Angeles. All joint projects of the Pennsylvania, the Southern, the Norfolk & Western (N&W), and other great railroad companies, the trains operated over tracks of shorter and subsidiary lines carefully noted in master timetables. Cooperation by the Atlanta and West Point Rail Road Company, the Western Railway of Alabama, and the Georgia Railroad made possible the stream of long-distance trains stopping in Lynchburg.

In an east–west direction flowed another set of first-class trains, mostly operating over the N&W, known as the Aristocrats. Advertised as connecting the Midwest with "the Virginias and the Carolinas," the trains originated and terminated in Norfolk, Virginia, and in Cincinnati, where connecting sleeping cars switched onto them for runs west. Pausing in Lynchburg regularly every day and night, the trains connected Winston-Salem, Abingdon, Ironton, and other small cities along a route that opened not only on seashore vacations but on central Midwest connections. All stopped in Lynchburg, in part so that passengers might connect with north–south trains and with the trains operated by the Chesapeake & Ohio Railway.

The C&O trains—the Pocahontas, the Cavalier, and others known by mere numbers—linked Lynchburg and other small cities, and even some towns, with the two east–west C&O main lines running west from Old Point Comfort on the seashore through Norfolk and Richmond to Louisville, Cincinnati, Chicago, and on to St. Louis. The northern main line ran through Charlottesville to Clifton Forge in Virginia, where it joined the southern east–west main line from Richmond that passed through Lynchburg; passengers could choose either route for the same fare. Astride the great lozenge-shaped east–west system linking the nation's capital with West Virginia mountain resorts like White Sulphur Springs and Greenbrier and with major cities farther west, Lynchburg prospered as a junction for transcontinental travel.

It prospered too as a branch-line terminal. Radiating from

Lynchburg stretched secondary tracks that meandered through the hills, sometimes paralleling main tracks a dozen miles away. The C&O operated a curving route from Richmond to Lynchburg by way of Bremo, Warren, and other hamlets, and a northwest-running line to Natural Bridge, a scenic wonder that attracted tourists. The N&W branch line stretched thirty-four miles southeast to Brookneal (where it crossed the Virginian Railroad, a major coal hauler that operated a handful of fast passenger trains too); thirty miles farther on it reached South Boston, a junction on a Southern secondary line, before terminating at Durham in North Carolina. No name trains raced along the branches. But twice a day, at 8:15 AM and 2:20 PM, a train left Lynchburg for Durham, stopping at Rustburg, Gladys, Halifax, and Denniston; the opposing trains arrived in Lynchburg daily at 3:35 and 8:35 PM. Unlike the main-line name trains, especially the United States Fast Mail, the branch-line trains clicked along at about thirty to thirty-five miles an hour. But despite their slowness they made Lynchburg not only a way station on long-distance routes but the hub of a secondary system. And they let long-distance travelers transfer at Lynchburg for trains to Natural Bridge and other tourist destinations.

Twenty-fours a day, seven days a week, a stream of trains paused at Lynchburg, offering residents of the city and its environs a sumptuous choice of destinations and arrival and departure times. For well-to-do riders, the day trains boasted club cars and fine dining service, and the night trains offered multiple choices not only in sleeping accommodations—berths, bedrooms, drawing rooms, and so on—but in ways of spending sleep time. One might board early and rise early at one's destination, or dine late, board late, and sleep late as the train reached New York or Mobile. When the Pullman Company operated most sleeping cars on United States railroads, it functioned as the largest hotel corporation in the country.

Railroad connections mark Lynchburg still. Any visitor to the city marvels at the architectural beauty of its downtown, perhaps especially at the grace of period styles. Something of big-city style suffuses Lynchburg, and not merely in architecture. The Maier Museum of Art has been hosting symposia by New York artists for a century, and the city's historic preservation program rivals anything in Washington, D.C. Yet Lynchburg culture is profoundly regional too: the city is a treasure trove of Piedmont antiquities seasoned somehow by both the Deep South and the sea. Scrutinizing and probing reveals an enduring cosmopolitanism prized by many Lynchburg citizens, belied by the city's lackluster airline service.

Airlines cannot stop cities and counties from building new airports, but in an age of government deregulation they can serve some airports in ways that make them well-nigh useless, while concentrating flights, and hopefully profits, at a handful of others. But perhaps more mysterious forces intend Lynchburg to be isolated.

Cold War worries caused the federal government to build the structure that now houses the Maier Museum of Art at the Randolph Macon College for Woman. Intended as a safe repository for the collection of the National Gallery, the structure opened in 1952 as the college art museum. But behind the single gallery lay rows of sliding metal racks on which curators would hang the national collection evacuated from Washington in time of nuclear threat. Lynchburg lies on the direct route to the Greenbrier, West Virginia, bunkers built to shelter Congress from nuclear attack. Perhaps Congress intended art to arrive by train, for the Military and Interstate Highway System avoids Lynchburg totally. Perhaps Congress intended the Lynchburg and Greenbrier regions to be free of panicked motorists fleeing the East Coast, and so angled highways away from them. But perhaps only bad luck kept the highways from Lynchburg. Or perhaps good luck.

Highways are not air routes, and Lynchburg now pays a heavy price for its honest audacity in building a spectacular airport. Airlines simply expect Lynchburg people to drive one to three hours to airports they consider nearby. Unless one's trip originates in Charlotte or Pittsburgh, almost any flight from anywhere means changing planes at Charlotte or Pittsburgh to fly the seventy-five minutes or so into Lynchburg. Flying to Lynchburg from almost any place within a thousand-mile radius consumes most of a day, even if one lives adjacent to a major airport. Someone who lives an hour or so from a major airport probably spends almost an entire day flying to Lynchburg, given time spent in traffic and security lines. Flying into Roanoke, which has more frequent service, offers little gained time, since one must still drive to Lynchburg. Almost all the flying happens by daylight: by eleven at night the Lynchburg Airport is closed. Savvy travelers and Lynchburg citizens alike now and then wonder about the days when one boarded a fast train in Lynchburg, ate a pleasant meal in the dining car, slept in one's personal bedroom, and awoke outside New York to a shower and breakfast. For that matter, the same people wonder about the fast trains that raced to Washington and stopped in Charlottesville and Arlington.

Lynchburg blossomed as a junction. For a time one of the wealthiest cities in the United States, it prospered as what air travel now calls a hub. Other cities prospered simply because they lay along railroad lines having international significance, as any deep reading of *The Official Guide of the Railways and Steam Navigation Lines of the United States, Porto Rico, Canada, Mexico, and Cuba, Also the Table of Railroads in Central America* demonstrates. In small towns and large, stationmasters and ticket agents thumbed through the 1,800-page tome and figured out how to get prospective passengers to Hamburg, Tokyo, and Havana. For decades, Cuba and the rest of the Caribbean preoccupied station agents in the wee hours of the morning, when only the telegraph sounder clicked for company and they determined how a customer might best enjoy a vacation. Station agents once acted as travel agents, and used the *Official Guide* as their bible.

As the Illinois Central System boldly announced above the pages devoted to its Panama Limited, it saw some of its trains operating "To Foreign Lands Nearby: Cuba, Nassau, Canal Zone, Central and South America." The Panama Limited moved in the company imagination as something like a ship, not only named but operating figuratively across the Caribbean. While railroad employees knew it as No. 7, passengers and onlookers down the Mississippi Valley knew it by name, and knew it carried a ladies' maid, barber and valets, bathtubs, a fine dining car, and only Pullmans, never coaches. Leaving Chicago at 12:30 every afternoon, it raced southward, stopping at a handful of cities only to pick up passengers booked for Memphis and beyond. Only at Memphis did it pause for long: five minutes, to switch out Pullmans bound for Mobile. At 5:40 the following morning it paused for one minute in Jackson, Mississippi, and at

9:30 pulled into New Orleans, 921.2 miles from Chicago. Averaging only forty-four miles an hour, No. 7 ran faster than the New Orleans Special but nowhere near as fast as the Daily Fast Mail, a train that attracted businessmen in a hurry. The Panama Limited existed not for speed but for luxury. Its patrons paid for the privilege of having a buffet car open continuously, and a dining car serving gourmet meals. Such people wanted hot baths before breakfast, and compared forty-four miles an hour with twelve knots.

Buried in the *Official Guide* are secrets that delight careful readers willing to jettison computer software quickness for a far slower mode of analysis. Facts stick to other facts as one consults timetable after timetable, and serendipity shapes inquiries into the history of cities like Lynchburg, Mobile, and Cairo.

While the Panama Limited discharged no passengers at Cairo on its roll southward, other Illinois Central trains, including the Daily Fast Mail, did. An abbreviated timetable in the Illinois Central section advertises a connecting service that made Mobile twenty-three and a half hours from Chicago, via a Mobile & Ohio train, the Gulf Coast Special, operating on the M&O main line between St. Louis and Mobile. At 3:40 every morning, a Pullman filled with sleeping passengers was switched from the New Orleans Limited onto the Gulf Coast Special. Fast freights carrying bananas crossed at Cairo en route from New Orleans and Mobile toward Chicago and St. Louis, but only locals noticed their hurried movements. While frazzled businessmen murmured in their sleep as a switcher moved their Pullmans from one train to another, vacationers bound from St. Louis to New Orleans murmured as the little locomotive plucked their Pullmans from the Mobile-bound train. The banana trains indicated something vague about maritime activity to the south, but the Pullman movements carried explanation printed in timetables and on railroad depot posters.

The railroad companies worked hand in hand with steamship companies, especially the United Fruit Company, which owned the "Great White Fleet." Operating as far north as St. John's, Halifax, and Boston, linking New York, Philadelphia, and Baltimore with Havana, Kingston, and Cristobal, and even connecting San Francisco with Cristobal, the firm provided coastal service from Castilla to Limon and Cartagena. The service between New Orleans and Havana and Cristobal, and between Mobile and Tela, rewards scrutiny in lush ways indeed. The *Official Guide* demonstrates that New Orleans and Mobile bridged the Caribbean region with the whole Midwest and with central Canada.

Passengers aboard the Panama Limited and other trains often expected to continue their journey aboard United Fruit steamers leaving New Orleans for British Honduras, Guatemala, Cuba, the Canal Zone, Costa Rica, Colombia, and Panama. The schedule of the Panama Limited influenced the sailings and arrivals of the small white liners, and the schedule of No. 7 influenced the schedule of connecting trains. The wealth of detail in the July 1929 *Official Guide* almost overwhelms. The fastest way from Champaign-Urbana to Lima in Peru? The *Official Guide* suggests that the business traveler avoid No. 7 and instead take the Daily Fast Mail, then a Wolvin Line ship to Puerto Mexico, then a train to Salina Cruz, then a United Fruit Company ship to Panama, then No. 7 of the Panama Rail Road Company, then a ship again. But vacationers, the *Official Guide* suggests, should work backward from United Fruit Company sailings along railroad routes and schedules. The trains, the *Official Guide* insists, are like the ships: integral parts of the vacation.

A traveler heading south from New York or Lynchburg aboard the Washington, Chattanooga, New Orleans Limited paused in Hattiesburg in Mississippi at 4:33 AM. About two hours later, sixty miles west on a converging route, a passenger aboard the Panama Limited paused in MacComb. About five thousand people lived in Hattiesburg; almost the same number in MacComb. The luxury trains stopped chiefly to take on water and coal, but in southern Mississippi people in two small towns had access to high-speed, luxury travel as well as to ordinary trains spaced evenly all day long. People in both towns lived near the southern end of New York and Chicago to New Orleans routes, but railroad station maps made it clear that they lived at the midpoint of North American–Caribbean–northern South American lines of travel. Neither town was Memphis, not even Jackson or Meridian, but both were infinitesimal jewels on a cosmopolitan string of far larger gems.

The *Official Guide* offers little in the way of railroad maps. Without its companion volume, the 1928 Rand McNally *Handy Railroad Maps of the United States,* it becomes a sort of sorcerer's grimoire, a gigantic compendium of information become arcane. But the atlas makes the grimoire into a sort of alchemical spell book. After an hour or so of intense effort, the *Official Guide* begins to reward anyone struggling to understand the architecture, cultural institutions, and industrial base of Lynchburg and other cities and towns. A bit more study begins to convert the road atlas view of the Republic into another, vastly richer one in which towns now only little known even to well-traveled Americans become prominent. Mac-Comb, Hattiesburg, and Lynchburg float now in the same mists as Tela, Cristobal, Cartagena, and other Spanish Main cities long ago visited by fruit company steamers. But once these three United States places were hubs of regions linked day and night with great cities and small towns.

Between such hubs gleamed other jewels, usually large towns served by single railroads. Like stones on a necklace that become more beautiful together than separately, the large towns partook of urban glamour too.

In 1945 the Burlington Ak-Sar-Ben Zephyr raced across the rural Midwest on a schedule that allowed only one-minute station stops. For example, on May 31 it arrived in Galesburg, Illinois, twenty minutes late from Lincoln, Nebraska, behind twin diesel-electric locomotives named Silver Meteor and Silver Swift, two of the first postwar-specification locomotives delivered to any railroad. The locomotives proved aptly named. Between Oneida and Altona the ten-car train averaged 97.3 miles per hour, its engineer making use of locomotives geared for 118-miles-per-hour maximum speeds. The 31.28-mile trip from Galesburg to Kewanee took twenty-five minutes from start to stop, and the Kewanee stop consumed only sixty seconds. Then the train raced eastward, and beyond Arlington cruised at 105 miles per hour until reaching Aurora, where it paused for one minute, before rolling at around 70 miles per hour into Chicago, where it arrived on time. Ak-Sar-Ben is merely Nebraska spelled backward, and train No. 12, while important to Burlington management, rolled in the shadow of the Denver Zephyr. No. 12 made numerous station stops between Lincoln and Chicago, including many between Galesburg and Chicago, but on May 31 it traversed the 162.2 miles from Galesburg in 140 minutes and arrived on time. Nowadays Galesburg, Oneida, Altona, and Kewanee are all cities lost in flyover land, and many well-educated coastal Americans cannot immediately locate Lincoln on any national map, highway or otherwise. But the two Burlington locomotives pulling No. 12 that day demonstrated that at the end of the war United States railroads intended to further improve rail service not just between the largest cities but between cities and towns nowadays almost impossible to reach by air.

In rural areas, seeing No. 12 charge past at 105 miles per hour meant something markedly different from seeing fast passenger trains thirty years earlier, but not because earlier trains moved more slowly. Something fundamental had happened along the right-of-way.

"Were you ever a boy in a corn field on a hot June day?" asked Sherwood Anderson in a 1904 *Agricultural Advertising* article. "Did the afternoon train, westward bound at forty miles an hour, pass around the corner of the hill and go roaring and screaming off into the strange land that lay over and beyond Brownville?" The ordinary passenger train meant something special to the farm boy, Anderson knew, for he had been that boy himself. "Did something give a savage tug at your heart so that it hurt, as with big hungry eyes you saw all of these people going so blandly and with such careless mien into that wonderful and enchanted land that lay east of Jasperville?" For the typical farm boy, the train meant a momentary glimpse of urbanity: electric lighting, high-fashion attire, newspapers and magazines from far away. As a boy, Anderson knew "such a hungryness to get on that train that he thought he would die of it," and in time the hunger he described so frankly caused him to make his way to Chicago. His column in *Agricultural Advertising* is far more than a potboiler written as he worked on the stories that became *Winesburg, Ohio,* and catapulted him to fame. It is an incisive analysis of why advertising had to reach the entire farm family.

Agricultural Advertising readers produced advertising that appeared in *Ohio Cultivator, Hoard's Dairyman,* and other magazines farm families read carefully. Unless that advertising made farm implements and farm life appear as attractive as the local passenger train and its imagined terminals, upwardly mobile farm children would leave. Anderson warned advertisers that they confronted a powerful adversary in the trains rumbling along the edges of farms, stirring dust and imagination alike. Ever so slowly, farm families acquired what they considered to be urbanities. Rural free delivery brought them daily mail, parcel post offered mail-order shopping and home delivery at lower cost than railway express, telephone lines stretched along poles and fence posts alike, and batteries re-charged by windmill generators powered radios long before elec-tricity crackled along wires to light lamps and power washing ma-chines. The Model T enabled families to drive into town more than once a week—perhaps to shop, more likely to see a Hollywood film—and Rural Electrification Agency efforts had brought power lines to about half the nation's farms by 1941. Historians know the lessening of rural isolation well, and understand television and the interstate highway as ending it. But most know little about the im-pact of train No. 12 in May 1945.

By the close of World War II trains such as the Ak-Sar-Ben Zephyr cruising at 105 miles per hour had become ordinary, something to notice perhaps, but nothing enchanting or exciting. Farm families in prewar sedans and pickup trucks expected to drive at twenty or thirty miles an hour over dirt roads to the nearest station, and there to board No. 12 for Chicago. Many returning GIs had arrived home on No. 12 and similar trains, and the fast train had become only another modern component in lives broadened by travel in Europe and the Pacific. No. 12 and other trains merely reinforced the way small-city, small-town, and rural residents thought of their home places in national geographical contexts. Fast, convenient long-dis-tance travel swept back and forth along nearby rails.

Airliners stripped away that thinking as thoroughly as Allied bombers had laid waste much of Germany, Italy, and Japan. Ameri-cans now think of regions in large-scale terms only: the Midwest, the South, the Pacific Northwest. Terms like *High Plains* and *Mis-souri Basin* mean practically nothing, for vast reaches have become Flyover Land. As airline routes eviscerated railroad routes, cities like Lynchburg and towns like MacComb saw their importance fade.

Most likely, geography vanished as a mainstream high school subject not only because Sputnik-worried educators replaced it with intensive mathematics and physics but also because large numbers of Americans had begun flying, and once jet airliners replaced propeller-driven aircraft, they flew mostly between large cities. As regional identity withered, urban sprawl quickened, often at the expense of regions bereft of passenger train service.

Nowadays only geographers, railroad enthusiasts, and real estate developers care much about the Delaware & Hudson Railroad region. The deep past of the company involves a canal built to bring coal from eastern Pennsylvania by barge to Kingston on the banks of the Hudson, and then south to New York City. The company abandoned its canal in 1899, having already pushed north from Wilkes-Barre and Scranton into the Lackawanna Valley. Tracing the D&H rails north reveals what geologists emphasize about North American mountain ranges and valleys: they run north to south. From Wilkes-Barre, therefore, the D&H built roughly north, to Nineveh in New York, then on through Oneonta, Schenectady and Albany, Saratoga Springs, Ft. Ticonderoga (with a spur to Rutland in Vermont), Plattsburg, Rouses Point at the north tip of Lake Champlain, and finally to Montreal. Over the past century, the company has seen its chief cargo shift from coal to newsprint rolling south from Canada, but it endures as the armature of much heavy transport in a region nowadays increasingly focused on international commerce. The North American Free Trade Agreement already reorients the shipping of raw material and manufactured items, but it promises to transform the Lackawanna Valley and other regions once tightly linked with Canada as railroads begin moving an ever-increasing share of new products along old routes. It promises to reorient some regions away from adjacent large cities as well.

The D&H created a crescent-shaped corridor arcing southwest from Montreal and moving much more than coal. It linked Saratoga Springs, Lake Placid, Lake George, and other resorts with large populations at its Wilkes-Barre and Montreal terminals. But far more importantly, it shaped upstate New York and western Vermont into a region linked not only with Quebec but with southwestern New York and central Pennsylvania. It put Albany in a spectacular posi-

tion: the New York capital sat athwart trains operating not only between New York and Boston and Detroit and Chicago, but between
Montreal, Binghamton, Scranton, and Wilkes-Barre. Year-round
the D&H moved business passengers from the eastern Midwest to
upstate New York and Quebec. But in summer it poured thousands
of vacationers into a region facing a worsening agricultural situation and relying increasingly on tourism to bolster its manufacturing efforts.

Upstate New York and the so-called Southern Tier of New York—
the counties along the Pennsylvania border—grasp today at any
business willing to relocate. Difficulties faced north and southwest
of Albany originate not in the departure of manufacturing for the
American South and offshore so much as in the impact of the airline industry after about 1965. No longer did first-rate rail passenger
service weld two regions into one that crossed national borders and
offered connecting first-class service from New York City and Chicago. As the D&H faced increased airline competition, its Montreal
Limited, Laurentian, and other passenger trains moved less and less
swiftly before finally disappearing. By 1970 upstate New York had
become difficult to access by rail, air, and automobile, as many vacationers discovered. Its inhabitants, increasingly wary of federal and
state efforts to boost the regional economy, began to rue the passing
of passenger train service on the D&H, the Rutland Railroad, and
other lines that once put small upstate cities on a necklace punctuated by Montreal, Albany, Wilkes-Barre, and other hubs.

If upstate New York and the Southern Tier exist chiefly as flyover land, the Tavaputs Plateau reaching across the Colorado-Utah
border might as well be on the moon. Motorists heading west from
Grand Junction in Colorado along I-70 move across sparsely settled
country indeed. Durham, Mack, Ruby, Utaline, fall into the rearview mirror in Colorado; ahead lie Agate, Cisco, Elba, Brendel, and
Green River before the highway heads almost due west into the San
Rafael Mountains. Woodside, Grassy, Mounds, Price, Helper, and
other tiny towns lie along lesser roads angling toward Salt Lake.
For anyone driving the old main line of the Denver, Rio Grande
& Western Railroad, towns like Solitude, Sphinx, and Desert focus
attention on people who enjoy no public transportation at all and

live hundreds of miles from any airport offering scheduled service. Arches National Park is spectacular, but no passenger trains operate from the branch diverging at Crescent Junction to it, or to the town of Potash farther down the line. The seeming desert may not be a desert in precise ecological terms, but it is dry, fiercely hot in summer and bone-numbing cold in winter, and almost empty of people except in the tiny hamlets along the railroad. Even ranchers cannot make a living along the high iron.

After World War II the western railroads operated high-speed long-distance passenger trains across sparsely settled regions like that west of Dodge City. The Atchison, Topeka & Santa Fe Railroad public timetable lists numerous trains moving along the 1,338 miles between Dodge and Albuquerque. In New Mexico the schedule shows some stopping at Springer, Colmor, Wagon Mound, and Shoemaker, and at Las Vegas (New Mexico) and other larger towns too. Ranchers and other high-country residents would not have expected the Super Chief to stop at tiny wood stations painted yellow (the way the Southern Pacific streamliner pauses at the tiny depot in the 1955 feature film *Bad Day at Black Rock*), but they did expect other long-haul trains to provide frequent daily service. From Dodge in western Kansas, across the southeast corner of Colorado, and into central New Mexico, trains across Raton Pass operated parallel with other Santa Fe passenger trains hundreds of miles south. With its subsidiary lines, the Santa Fe operated 13,085 miles of track, crosshatching the vast region between Arkansas and the southern coast of California but reaching northeast to Chicago via Kansas City. Together with its competitors, especially the Southern Pacific, it provided regular long-distance transportation that made Albuquerque a hub. But it made far smaller cities hubs too. Clovis in New Mexico, Pampa in Texas, Kiowa in Kansas, Lamar in Colorado, all enjoyed connecting train service by the same railroad offering multiple routes not only between Chicago and California but also between New Orleans and California. Moreover, the Santa Fe operated fast passenger trains on north–south routes, linking Albuquerque with El Paso, Newton in Kansas with Galveston, and Kiowa with Presidio on the Mexican border. But the terminals and junctions proved less important to thousands of rural people than Sentinel, Lone Wolf, Odell, Crowell, and Rule along the Kiowa–Sweetwater line that terminated in another Santa Fe line linking Clovis with the Gulf of Mexico and steamships.

The finest Santa Fe trains ran fast across vast distances. In the 1940s new diesel-electric locomotives capable of 120 miles per hour amazed onlookers in places that nowadays rarely see a commercial airliner in the sky high above. The demise of frequent, fast, long-distance train service did less to impoverish large cities than it did to isolate small towns and hamlets. In Lynchburg and its vicinity, driving to an airport takes little time in comparison with reaching one on the Tavaputs Plateau or in the vicinity of greater Wagon Mound.

In 2003 financial tremors shook the national airline industry, but news media reported little until the veritable earthquakes of 2004 and 2005. Federal officials targeted the escalating cost of the Essential Air Service (EAS) subsidy program, something that sparked small-town newspaper headlines in Staunton, Virginia, and elsewhere but made scarcely a ripple in metropolitan dailies. Across the United States, the airline industry suddenly confronted a calamity similar to that which afflicted passenger-carrying railroads circa 1970.

Devised in 1978 to subsidize air travel to and from very small regional airports, the EAS program was a response to the aftershock of the creation of Amtrak. In 1971 Amtrak took over responsibility for most long-haul passenger train service, but it did not take over most passenger trains, and not even most routes. Despite government assurances that few people rode long-distance trains and that those who did would find convenient alternative transportation, by the middle 1970s state and local politicians complained to Congress that many voters lived in regions bereft of passenger train service. In 1978 Congress created a program to subsidize the cost per passenger of airlines operating to small, usually rural airports.

Per-passenger subsidies began to rise almost at once. Even discounting what some fiscal conservatives argued in congressional documents was abuse built into the program—Martha's Vineyard airport is considered a rural one, and federal funds subsidize the wealthy summer residents who use the resort field—EAS costs ballooned as more and more counties and small cities built so-called regional airports. By the late 1980s the airports were competing with each other, and with much larger metropolitan ones. The situation Lynchburg faced by the year 2000 was one that developed earlier elsewhere. Rising fuel costs and the increasing price of installing safety-related equipment in very small airliners and at tiny airports exacerbated matters. Between 1995 and 2002 the average per-passenger subsidy paid to airlines serving very small airports in the lower forty-eight states tripled to $229 per flight. In 1996 EAS cost the federal government $22.6 million; by 2003 it cost $113 million. Almost never do transportation experts mention the subsidy program in the context of subsidizing Amtrak. Yet the per-passenger/per-flight subsidy amount varies from $9 at Johnstown, Pennsylvania, to $567 at Lewistown, Montana.

After September 11, 2001, fear of terrorism combined with rising ticket costs to decrease ticket sales at many regional airports. Before the terrorist attacks, many passengers, especially retirees and vacationers with a bit of time to spare, found driving two or three hours to larger airports an attractive alternative to regional airport ticket costs. Airlines entering the subsidy program contract to provide at least two departing flights a day from each subsidized airport. In the twelve-month period ending in June 2002, more than twenty airports reported three passengers or fewer departing per flight. The airport in Alliance, Nebraska, reported a daily average of 2.1 passengers, scarcely more than one per flight. In western Virginia, Shenandoah Valley Regional Airport, a direct competitor with the one at Lynchburg, recorded a decline from 18,947 passengers in 2001 to 6,583 in 2002.

At the current moment, as major airlines struggle to avert bankruptcy by cutting frills and renegotiating union contracts, fuel costs continue to increase and regional airport ridership has failed to return to preterrorism levels. Concomitantly, every United States airport must conform to security regulations. At Alliance, Transportation Security Administration screeners must process four or five passengers a day. What else they do, and how they are paid, is an intriguing question.

Moreover, local airports usually cannot serve groups of passengers, especially on short notice, so groups tend to travel by automobile or chartered bus. The tiny airplanes, many of them carrying only thirteen passengers, often operate with just enough filled seats that a family of four must make reservations well in advance. A sudden business meeting often involves delay for groups of travelers, and even regional sales meetings sometimes force attendees to drive. Small airliners reduce costs, but in the end eliminate most of the flexibility postwar Americans hoped air travel would produce. Some experts suspect that Internet videoconferencing has reduced business travel at small, EAS airports, but the federal government now understands that it can no longer subsidize flights into airports as small as that in Lynchburg.

In 1929 the Chicago, Burlington & Quincy provided Alliance with quality passenger train service operating between St. Louis and Chicago and Billings, Montana, and between Omaha and Deadwood, South Dakota; some trains carried Pullmans, dining cars, and lounge cars, although many provided only coaches. Moreover, trains operated between Alliance and Denver and between Alliance and Casper, Wyoming. While the last operated as a roundabout route away from main lines, it enabled Alliance residents to board a train moving west and then swinging onto another CB&Q north–south main line paralleling the St. Louis–Billings main line that reached east to Omaha and Kansas City before reaching Chicago and St. Louis. The two parallel "Burlington routes," along with their east–west lines, created a focused economic region in the shortgrass prairie zone of western Nebraska and eastern Colorado. The line to Deadwood carried some business people, of course, but its passenger trains operated mostly for vacationers. Advertised as "the Black Hills Detour," it connected Alliance and the rest of the nation with Wind Cave National Park, Black Hills National Forest, Mt. Coolidge, and other resort areas in westernmost South Dakota. Not every train that stopped in Alliance moved rapidly or operated as an express elsewhere: No. 303 departed at 2:05 in the afternoon and did not reach Denver until 10 that night, taking about three hours longer then than it does to drive from Alliance to Denver today. But no one in Alliance bemoaned a lack of trains, and in 1929 Alliance was scarcely on the main line to anywhere. People expected good service, but not the high-speed service of towns located between large cities.

Nowadays Alliance is a jewel of a little town, but no longer on any necklace. If the EAS subsidy does not rise appreciably, everyone in the area will drive for hours to find an operating airport.

On May 22, 1975, train No. 8 of the Southern Railway System left Lynchburg on its last run to Washington, D.C, scheduled to take four hours and fifty minutes to operate over 175 miles. Reduced to a locomotive and a lone coach rambling at thirty-five miles per hour along the edge of the Blue Ridge Mountains, No. 8 rolled as the wraith of fifteen-car streamliners that once paused in Lynchburg on their way to New Orleans. But No. 8 rolled in an eerie twilight too. Four years after Amtrak took over most passenger trains, the Southern Railway ran its own trains, even the lowly No. 8. Perhaps management saw around the curve of time. Just east of Lynchburg, the one-car train coupled onto some thirty special flatcars carrying truck trailers, and rolled toward Washington. In Alexandria the crew switched out the flatcars and rolled the lone coach into Union Station. Southern No. 8 existed in the twilight of privately operated passenger train service, but it rolled too in the very dawn of mixed passenger/intermodal freight. The Southern had been experimenting for a decade: its Brunswick to Atlanta train carried Pullman cars, but often arrived in Atlanta with a half-dozen red tank cars coupled behind the passenger ones. Management glimpsed something special enough to move it to retain control of passenger trains while it tested mixed consists that might support passenger service. If nothing else, Southern No. 8 revealed the enduring attention Southern management paid to the future importance of Lynchburg. It, Alliance, and so many other towns might become extremely inviting if passenger trains connected them at eighty or ninety miles an hour.

Knowing this now sparks deep-pocket investor support for rails-to-trails programs. Real estate developers grudgingly admit that championing rails-to-trails programs really means "rail banking" rights-of-way. Southwest of Lynchburg, along the old N&W main line on which sped the United States Fast Mail, environmentalists recently heard the governor of Virginia extol the economic advantages of turning abandoned railroad routes into hiking and bicycling trails. The mountain region between Lynchburg and Bristol has lost thousands of jobs as tobacco farming failed, then textile mills moved to foreign countries. Already some of its abandoned railroad rights-of-way have become hiking or nature trails, most notably the Virginia Creeper trail between Abingdon and Damascus, on the North Carolina border. Damascus has a population of a thousand, roughly five times its population in the years when branch-line trains connected it to the main line linking Lynchburg and Bristol. The trail brings about two hundred thousand visitors a year to Damascus, which derives about $81,000 per year from taxes on meals and lodging. Indirectly, the visitors support a mountain-bike shop, outfitters, shuttle operators who bring hikers back to cars, and a nascent lodging industry. No one thinks much of the days when N&W trains rumbled to the end of the seventy-five-mile-long line at Elkland, North Carolina. In 1929 the N&W ran only one passenger train a day each way, and the trains took almost five hours to complete their trips, stopping at many hamlets and, for the twenty miles nearest Elkland, moving freight cars along with coaches. Imagining riding trains No. 201 and 202 requires a lot of effort nowadays; it also smacks of heresy. The Virginia Creeper trail is so beautiful and so quiet.

And its northwestern end, at Abingdon, lies adjacent to Interstate Highway 81, a narrow highway so jammed with tractor-trailer traffic that tourists try hard to avoid it. Around the armature of the I-81 corridor spins regional business expressed in motels, gas stations, fast-food restaurants, and discount stores. The rural corridor is not so much suburban sprawl as linear squalor punctuated with brand-new trucking company distribution warehouses. Local business owners and short-distance motorists picture I-81 as it was fifteen years ago, a bucolic, well-maintained highway over which few long-distance trucks operated. No longer do the corridor taxpayers want the highway widened. They want more truck trailers moved by rail, along the adjacent main line of the old N&W, nowadays the Norfolk Southern.

The railroad prospers, and faces new challenges, as its route south of Lynchburg creeps toward track capacity. It can add a second track and take other measures to increase efficiency, all of which make the collateral industrial and commercial real estate potentially more valuable. Meanwhile, twenty miles away from the corridor, people are mostly poor and jobs few—so few that politicians praise the service jobs produced by hiking trails. Anyone driving in the vicinity of Lynchburg, especially southwest toward the historic and scenic Cumberland Gap district, discovers the jarring disconnect between Lynchburg and its satellite towns and the tedious, ugly mess of I-81.

Land-development investors look closely, see the Norfolk Southern routes, and begin to wonder how they might change, and so change the region. Almost beyond doubt, trains will never return to the Virginia Creeper route. But only freight trains hold the promise of sustained economic growth in a beautiful but straitened region, and only passenger trains will make possible the movement of more hikers to trails served by rural, low-volume roads.

Nowadays at least a few investors just ahead of the real estate development curve focus on Lynchburg: local real estate agents admit to more inquiries shaped by the expanding reach of suburban commuter trains operated by Virginia Railway Express, a transit authority. But a handful of national-scale investors think about Abingdon in terms of Bethel, Maine. Rail passenger access to the southwestern corner of Virginia must hinge on trains operating through Lynchburg and Bristol to other cities. Given such rail routes, however, an entire recreational resort economy might be built in a region free of automobile jams and tractor-trailer traffic. An equivalent of the Maine coast or Adirondack Park in upstate New York might enrich its private-industry-based creators in Virginia, and if such an immense park environment developed within easy passenger train access of Washington, D.C., property values in Lynchburg might well skyrocket. The key to it all is managing road traffic and providing an enduring, substantial economic base better than the I-81 corridor mix of motels, gas stations, truck stops, and fast-food eateries. Investors ask consultants to consider such issues. So far only one thing is certain. Another little regional airport will do nothing to advance either the public good or private profit in the region south of Lynchburg. The tracks exist, even if they are very busily moving freight trains, and where the Washington, Chattanooga, New Orleans

Limited once raced, passenger trains may race again. It may be that some would-be land developers, and some landowners, already picture this train of the future as freighted with riches beyond the dreams of avarice.

SOURCES: Anderson, "Business Types"; Boyd, "One Hundred and Fifty Years of the D&H"; Daniels, "From Rumor to Renaissance"; Hemphill, "The Unknown Rio Grande"; Morgan, "Forget the Gods of Old" and "Mr. Pullman Revisited"; New York State Department of Transportation, "A Future for Southern Tier Rail Service?"; "Rising Cost, Falling Ridership"; Stilgoe, "Onshore Force"; Wiley, "Meet the 'Lynchburg Special.'"

SIDETRACKED

High-speed electric automobiles whisk silently along great boulevards while occupants read, play cards, or sleep. At eighty miles an hour, the cars never crunch fenders and never interfere with others converging and diverging. Cars move in great convoys, break into clutches at cities, and cruise individually the last few miles home.

Electronics and snazzy mechanical engineering make such visions serious possibilities. A lot more federal research money now, and metropolitan regions—especially in California—will soon embark on an ecstasy of highway rebuilding. Or so the twenty-first-century visionaries imagine, their hands extended toward grant money.

So they imagined in 1955, and ten years later. The 1973 energy crisis silenced their optimistic pronouncements, but even in the prosperous 1980s they said little. Something had changed.

Nowadays the soothsayers strive for a comeback, basing their hopes on electronic gadgetry and motorist frustration, and on national amnesia. Across Southern California, drivers lobby for electronic toll collection and toll lanes carved from existing arterial highways. People will pay to avoid some traffic and to enjoy some regularity in driving times. People will pay to know a parking space awaits. People will pay to know that miles ahead a massive collision already blocks traffic, and that their itinerary must change. People will pay to apply computer software to making their automobile rides slightly more efficient and perhaps a bit more pleasant. Already first-class airline passengers walk to the head of security screening queues. Why not let first-class motorists drive a little faster and lot more freely?

Swirling beneath the willingness to pay is a deepening vortex of class discrimination, anger, and future energy waste. Astute politicians are wary of high-tech-loving visionaries, whom they may know as warmed-over failures whose new pronouncements can destroy political careers. Something changed in the 1980s that haunts experienced politicians and a tiny cognoscenti—but not most Americans, who remember nothing of it.

United States highway design originated in post–World War II assumptions and in cold war scenario analysis. The Military and Interstate Highway System, to use the official name Americans routinely truncate, reflects Pentagon thinking about the 1930s German autobahns that made blitzkrieg successful. Nowadays few Americans reflect on the late 1930s exchange of German and United States military officers intrigued by highway construction. United States Army officers visited highway building sites across Germany, paying special attention to straight sections useful as fighter plane runways, cloverleaf intersections that sped traffic flow, and rest areas along the limited-access highways that might enable convoys to feed and resupply rapidly. When Hitler introduced the Volkswagen Beetle, the "people's car" had the beginnings of a unique long-distance highway system on which to operate. German military officers arrived in Pennsylvania to watch the new turnpike under construction on the alignment of a never-completed railroad. Just before Pearl Harbor, the American military realized the significance of a Pennsylvania Turnpike operating with no speed limit. Drivers averaging ninety miles an hour presaged mechanized divisions moving at such speed too. During World War II, when American motorists struggled with wartime fuel-conserving speed limits set at around thirty-five miles per hour, military commanders took the lessons of German limited-access highways and air superiority to heart. They convinced a Congress wary of postwar recession to build a highway system useful in the event of atomic attack. But in the late 1940s—indeed well into the 1950s—the Pentagon envisioned thermonuclear warfare as something dependent on manned bombers, especially the B-52. In its first massive effort to shape the United States built environment, the military understood highways and aerial warfare as integral to one another. Road became highway and runway both, and both became military weapons camouflaged as civilian public works.

Military understanding had changed mightily since the late 1930s. In early 1940, four months after Germany attacked Poland in a blitzkrieg involving air superiority and highway-fed armored movement, the federal government had no coherent plan for stepped-up

In the 1970s, as railroads prepared to discard freight-train cabooses, the cars the public accepted as punctuation marks began showing signs of deferred maintenance.

armament production. Nor did it have any plan for moving men and matériel to embarkation ports. After the war, the head of the War Production Board marveled at a nation that had manufactured 124,000 ships, 100,000 tanks and armored cars, 434 million tons of steel, 2.4 million military trucks, and 4.1 billion rounds of ammunition. Perhaps he should have marveled at the national transport victory, too. Even ship-building material began its seaward progress by rail. But from 1940 onward the board did little to authorize railroads to acquire new locomotives or new cars or signaling equipment. Essentially, United States railroads moved a gigantic increase in freight tonnage and an astronomical increase in passengers using locomotives and cars already in service along tracks maintained in no special fashion. Depression woes in fact meant that many railroad companies had been unable to afford routine rolling stock and right-of-way replacement. Yet from its five-year wartime economic experience, the nation learned a great deal about the flexibility of the railroad industry. The United States military hierarchy learned the lesson much more clearly, and thereafter assumed that the railroad industry would rise to any wartime occasion without much government support or guidance, and would do so immediately. Military academies and war colleges still teach cadets that United States railroads prove a powerful secret weapon because they operate far under capacity and are strikingly flexible transport systems.

Concealment of military bungling still masks the extraordinary contribution of the railroad industry to the war effort. After Pearl Harbor, German submarines began torpedoing oil tankers steaming along the East Coast. In four months the U-boats sank fifty-two tankers, and the navy confessed itself powerless to stop them. Almost all coastwise movement of oil stopped, leaving only enough for the military. Essential civilian needs could not be met, and on May 22, 1942, the federal government rationed oil in the eastern states. Few realized that every sunk tanker meant another 210 tank cars needed. In late summer, far inland from the beaches where civilians found oil-soaked lifeboats, corpses, and debris, trackside observers noticed a surge in railroad movement of tank cars. By autumn, about three-fourths of the oil reaching East Coast refineries moved in fast freights of sixty cars each. From the oil fields of Louisiana, Mississippi, Texas, and Oklahoma, steam locomotives decades in service sped the oil north along sixty-six separate routes on the tightest of schedules. Soon the railroads began moving more such trains back and forth between the oil states and Pacific Coast refineries too. In rural places strings of tank cars roared along at mail train speed, and crack passenger trains took sidings to get out of the way. Only troop trains and freight trains of refrigerator cars filled with fresh produce slowed the madcap progress of the tank trains.

Now only specialist scholars and military scenario analysts know much about the superb success of the oil freights tearing along at passenger express speed. But in July 1943 *Railroad Magazine* published a feature article detailing how 72,500 tank cars moved 900,000 barrels of oil a day (boxcars crammed with drums moved another 21,047); other cars moved gasoline, kerosene, and aviation fuel. Most Americans never learned how close the German navy came to defeating Britain and crippling the early United States war effort. What about the 169 petroleum trains charging north over the Missouri Pacific route from Texarkana to Dupo, each taking thirty hours and fifty-five minutes for a run optimistic experts had scheduled for thirty-four hours? What about the experiences of GIs like C. Grattan Price, who in 1942 clocked the speed of his steam-powered Baltimore-bound Florida Special at 115 miles per hour? It departed Jacksonville an hour late but arrived in Washington, D.C., six minutes early. War produced very fast running indeed, but the precarious military situation produced little published history.

It is possible to learn a good deal from photographs of the last days of steam locomotives. Unlike most prewar images, wartime photographs often show black smoke blasting from stacks. In peacetime locomotives emitted far less smoke. In winter they moved beneath clouds of steam exhausted into stacks to increase the draft over coal and oil fires. In summer they moved beneath a clear haze of hot, shimmering air. No housewife hanging out laundry trackside expected soot to soil her drying clothes, and housewives knew how to complain every bit as fiercely as trackside office workers, storekeepers, and others who expected clean-burning locomotives as neighbors. Railroad companies kept engines in tune, and ordered enginemen to make as little smoke as possible. Failure to comply with smoke-abatement directives meant demerits and discharge.

But in wartime maintenance schedules succumbed to movement schedules, and enginemen grimly determined to make time with extraheavy trains disregarded peacetime emission rules. No one watching a hospital train scream inland from Staten Island or a tank train racing north or west complained about smoke blasting from an overworked passenger locomotive. Then after World War II worn-out steam locomotives seemed suddenly old-fashioned, for all that they routinely moved freight trains at seventy-seven miles per hour and passenger trains far faster. Eclipsed by diesels, they began to vanish, and their whistles became whispers of nostalgia. No one asks today about U-boats operating with impunity off New Orleans, Norfolk, and New York or why the War Production Board restricted the building of diesel locomotives.

In the Depression, European and American railroads experimented with diesel-powered, lightweight passenger trains. By 1939 the German National Railways operated thirty-two such trains that cruised on a variety of routes, mostly west of Berlin, linking Basel, Munich, Hamburg, and Berlin, along with smaller cities. However, Hitler preferred traditional trains pulled by very fast steam locomotives, and his opposition slowed the German experiment. Only slightly different from the German trains, United States experimental trains attracted much attention too, especially the Burlington Zephyr.

In 1934 the Zephyr debuted as the train of the future. Its stainless steel, articulated cars and integral locomotive made it seem like a silver snake. On May 26 it carried passengers nonstop from Denver to Chicago, running a thousand miles at an average speed of 78 miles per hour and hitting 112 for miles at a time. Crowds turned out to witness its streak across the rural region, and many commentators remarked that the streamliner had proved itself. Operating on a railroad of secondary importance, atop lightweight rail ballasted with cinders and slag, the train made a strong impression on railroad officials. Despite its air conditioning, wraparound windows, and other amenities, it proved cheap to operate, even at extraordinary speed. The Burlington immediately ordered similar trains for daytime runs between Chicago and Minneapolis–St. Paul, and between St. Louis and Burlington, Iowa, and more trains to accommodate passengers on the Chicago–Denver route.

Other railroads invested in similar equipment. The Union Pacific experimented with its City of Portland, and the New Haven bought its Comet from Goodyear-Zeppelin, a firm hoping to manufacture something faster than blimps. By 1940 the Union Pacific had invested in more articulated lightweight passenger trains. The New Haven took pardonable pride in its bidirectional Comet, which had an integral locomotive at each end, much like contemporary Amtrak Acela trains. Even smaller railroads such as the Gulf, Mobile & Northern had acquired lightweight experimental trains. The GM&N twin Rebels, modern down to art deco aluminum lighting fixtures, swept through the rural South as harbingers of an impending revolution in intercity travel. Other companies, still not convinced that the articulated trains would succeed, built more lightweight versions of traditional trains pulled by steam locomotives. In the summer of 1935, the Milwaukee Road operated its orange-painted Chicago–Milwaukee Hiawatha at 120 miles per hour behind a locomotive capable of sprinting even faster. Good times seemed to lie ahead.

America's entry into World War II stopped all such innovation. Railroads desperately needed conventional locomotives and ordinary trains of interchangeable cars. Wartime munitions and other matériel often moved behind passenger locomotives operating on passenger train schedules, and long troop trains and civilian passenger trains moved behind multiple locomotives. But all through the war, railroad companies studied figures suggesting that streamliners, especially lightweight, diesel-powered trains, had reversed the Depression-era decline in passenger revenue precipitated by the rising ownership of automobiles.

In 1920 United States railroads enjoyed the peak of peacetime passenger rail travel. Nine years later a third of the riders had defected to automobiles. By 1933 ridership had shrunk by another 40 percent. Government and industry statistics demonstrated that by 1933 railroads carried only 42 percent of the passengers they had carried in 1921, even though many Americans could no longer afford automobiles or the cost of long road trips and instead took trains.

Railroad company innovation and an improving economy reversed the passenger decline in 1934. By 1938 it had become apparent that modern trains, lightweight or not, pulled by ultramodern steam locomotives and the first multipurpose diesel locomotives would prosper mightily because they pleased the public. Two years after the streamlined Silver Meteor began operating over the Seaboard Railroad and Atlantic Coast Line between New York and Florida in 1939, the companies had added four similar lightweight trains. A year before Pearl Harbor, railroad companies cooperated in establishing Midwest-to-Florida trains like the City of Miami and the South Wind. Full from the start and earning a 50 percent return on investment, such trains prompted only duplication and triplication within the industry. Company after company abandoned the earlier articulated, single-unit, lightweight trains for ultranew but more conventional, often streamlined interchangeable-car consists pulled by diesel locomotives. In 1940, as war seemed inevitable, railroad companies found themselves facing a new problem. Adding cars to the articulated trains proved difficult, and growing passenger traffic meant the necessity of adding cars. So new diesel locomotives capable of operating in multiples pulled the City of Miami and other streamlined trains that grew longer and more frequent by the year.

While wartime necessity stopped the building of additional high-speed streamlined trains, it encouraged railroads to plan postwar expansion of fast passenger equipment. Companies that entered the war with superb steam locomotives learned to expect more than their designers had anticipated. In 1944 the Santa Fe operated its Grand Canyon Limited and Scout between Kansas City and Los Angeles, 1,788 miles, without changing locomotives. Such unexpected and hard-won triumphs caused railroads to inform locomotive manufacturers that diesel locomotives had to perform considerably better than wartime steam power. In 1946 railroads began taking delivery of passenger locomotives geared for 118 miles per hour. In so doing they precipitated what scholars call a colossal federal government blunder that produced almost unimaginable adverse impacts nationwide.

In 1947 Congress voted to restrict passenger train speed to seventy-nine miles per hour except on track equipped with automatic train control (ATC). Despite railroad industry arguments that ATC did not work correctly and would prove prohibitively expensive on long runs, and despite the railroad industry's superb wartime safety record, Congress condemned Americans to slow-speed rail travel. The United States became the only nation in the world to deliberately limit the speed of its passenger trains.

Five years later the Italians successfully tested the new electric-powered train its builders christened Rapido. Not every component worked perfectly. In one instance, one of the pantographs connecting the train with the overhead electric wires flew apart at 149 miles per hour. But only seven years after the end of World War II, the

Italians achieved speeds envisioned in wartime Germany but by then forbidden in the United States.

Hindsight proves both 20/20 and blind. ATC never works correctly, even now. Urban subways operate with updated versions, and the subway serving Harvard University enjoys such frequent ATC failures that most passengers fail to notice the whooshing of air brakes stopping trains between stations, especially in icy weather. To notice the unscheduled stops, most reasonably smooth, is to wonder why the motorman has run past a red light. Of course the motorman has not. The ATC sensor aboard the train incorrectly processes data and stops the train. In 1947 the railroad industry correctly denounced a device that seemed as likely to precipitate derailments through sudden stops as it did to prevent rear-end collisions. Mentioning that Congress insisted on the technology stops much transportation debate today.

Three industries lobbied against 118-miles-per-hour rail passenger service. The highway, trucking, and automobile industries knew within two years of the end of World War II that the Pennsylvania Turnpike could no longer handle cars averaging 90 miles per hour, let along trailer trucks. The mix of cars and trucks led to disaster, and neither civil nor mechanical engineers could envision highways for motor vehicles capable of cruising at 118 miles per hour. The future of the aircraft and airline industries lay in luring passengers aboard long-distance flights, but most intercity travel involved journeys of less than five hundred miles, something likely to prove extremely unprofitable. But the military clinched the deal. Without a massive civilian subsidy in the form of airport building, airmail tariffs, and, above all, passenger- and mail-carrying airliners, the aircraft industry would charge the direct costs of developing new military airplanes, bombers especially, directly to the military. Taxpayers might not support the postwar air superiority the Pentagon envisioned when they understood its cost. After the Soviet Union obtained the atomic bomb and the cold war began in earnest, the military used the specter of atomic attack to energize the building of the Military and Interstate Highway System. The interstate system in turn subsidized the trucking and automobile-manufacturing industries, and promised to solve the airline industry's problem of the short-distance flight. Americans would drive at 60 to 75 miles per hour to the nearest airport and then fly—but only if Congress slowed passenger trains.

At first, only railroad management and railroad company stockholders complained, along with the builders of high-speed trains; later they were joined by manufacturers confronting the slowing down of fast freight and other time-sensitive railroad service. In the late 1950s and early 1960s a chorus of complaints rose from rural regions, small towns, and small cities concerned about the imminent collapse of railroad service. The Interstate Commerce Commission, caught between dealing with an industry that had acted in monopolistic ways a half century before and a surfeit of new data impossible to process in the years just before computers, bumbled larger issues involving both service abandonment and profitless service maintenance. Federal and state regulatory agencies simply could not imagine the national rail system withering under government-subsidized competition. Agencies processed data so slowly that circumstances had usually changed by the time they rendered decisions, but as early as 1948, when Charles R. Cherington published his densely argued *Regulation of Railroad Abandonments,* a few analysts understood not only the untenable position in which Congress had placed the industry but also the trap encircling the Republic. The trucking industry and the airline industry combined could not meet the demands of a fast-growing economy, let alone a major war.

Deterioration in railroad passenger and freight service might restrict more than GNP growth, analysts argued. As *U.S. Planning for War in Europe, 1963–1964* and other documents recently released by the National Security Archive make clear, they feared it might hamstring military effort in future wars. After the Korean conflict, defense analysts began worrying about a large-scale ground conflict in Asia, especially one involving the Soviet Union or China or both. Their worries led to a fierce military commitment to air power and quick-time, short-term warfare.

Nazi-era German designers had not only produced the autobahns and high-speed, lightweight trains but also imagined larger-scale railroad equipment. While traditional in many respects, the envisioned trains would dwarf all others anywhere. With a track gauge of four meters, sumptuous cars seven meters high and six wide, gigantic locomotives, and extremely gentle curves and grades, the futuristic railroad, it was posited, would operate between Paris and Berlin—and perhaps deep into a vassal Soviet Union—by 1950. Engineers did preliminary studies for an even more colossal system operating on rails nine meters apart, but the four-meter gauge seemed technically feasible. A nation already wedded to superhighways had reimagined rail vehicles at the scale of zeppelins. During the early years of World War II, with Germany apparently poised to rule over Europe forever, the broad-gauge railroad did not seem out of the question.

But as wartime tankers evolved into contemporary supertankers, ocean liners matured into cruise ships too wide for the Panama Canal, and propeller-driven cargo planes became Constellations, then 707s, then 747s and Concordes, both railroad and highway vehicles retained nearly wartime dimensions. Whereas contemporary railcars still seat people four abreast—or two or three in first class—no traveler aboard a 747 thinks much about being crammed nineteen abreast in what seems like a miniature movie theater. A railroad boxcar is about ten feet longer than it was in 1940, and Amtrak Superliner cars are taller than all but the streamlined dome cars of 1940, but surprisingly little else has changed on tracks or highways. Eighteen-wheelers are longer and a bit wider than the articulated trucks that irritated motorists blazing down the Pennsylvania Turnpike in 1941, but they are not much bulkier, although tractors now often pull two small trailers. Had Congress embraced the high-speed passenger trains railroad companies had ordered in 1946, perhaps the next stage would have been railroad technology borrowed from the nation that invented limited-access highways, jet airplanes, and rockets. German scientists spirited into the United States to develop missile weapons and space exploration rockets were not joined by German railroad designers. After Congress limited passenger train speed, no one bothered with Nazi-era German engineering studies every bit as realistic as those that produced the VW Beetles scurrying all over late-1950s United States highways. As late as 1955, the Association of American Railroads convened a committee to study atomic-powered locomotives, but the federal government offered strikingly little help, even though it was funding an atomic-powered merchant ship.

The first oil-gasoline crisis, in 1973, alerted millions of Americans to the simple fact that they were almost wholly dependent on automobile travel to reach work, to shop, to vacation, and indeed to get much of anywhere within five hundred miles. The second crisis, six years later, only deepened national anger over gasoline shortages and rising heating and cooling costs. Politicians worried about saving their careers. Petroleum scarcity, rationing, and price fluctuation paralyzed Congress because it had long ago eliminated alternatives that would have mitigated the crisis. But the crises and indignation mask a vastly more serious problem as little studied nowadays as the wartime destruction of the tanker fleet or the 1947 congressional limiting of passenger train speed. Women began working outside the home.

Until the early 1970s, highway planners did reasonably well in anticipating growth rates in motor vehicle use. Only in the largest metropolitan areas did planners make serious misjudgments. In New York, Boston, and Los Angeles especially, new highways opened and immediately jammed with traffic. By the end of the 1960s, planners had begun thinking ahead, trying to design highways that could be built immediately and widened later. Sparing taxpayers the shock of building highways with six lanes in each direction seemed politically wise, since many urban neighborhoods had begun resisting so-called urban renewal through highway building. In an age when highway designers seriously considered paving the lanes of limited-access highways in pastel colors so that women drivers might negotiate them without collision—according to Carl Stelling in "Designing for the Ladies," a 1958 article on the challenges women faced on divided highways, "an extra, slow-speed, truckless lane would be provided for women who become nervous at high speeds"—imagining the design of intersections of twelve-lane highways for women drivers taxed male imagination. The idea of building such intersections in urban and suburban areas terrified politicians, who saw them as destroying budgets and neighborhoods both. Then suddenly in the middle 1970s highway planners confronted the skewing and wholesale collapse of all their highway building scenarios. Women moved into the workforce in cars that thronged existing highways and defied traditional routing analysis.

Women who drive to and from work tend to do so differently than men did in the early 1960s. As Margy Waller and Evelyn Blumenberg make clear in *The Long Journey to Work: A Federal Transportation Policy for Working Families,* they are far more likely to make stops at grocery stores and dry cleaners and vastly more likely to drop and collect children at schools and day care. Collecting what planners call "journey-to-work" statistics grew far more complex in the mid-1970s, then worsened as the advent of the personal computer produced a significant number of workers able to telecommute some days and drive others. Moreover, women who hitherto had dropped off and picked up husbands at suburban commuter rail stations no longer did so; men drove, and parked in lots that were suddenly jammed. Planners complained that women working outside the home not only produced a staggering number of multiple-car families and complex trip data but created all sorts of parking issues the public blamed on poor planning.

In the early 1980s highway planners and entire regional planning authorities battered themselves against the reality of highway-widening issues they had imagined facing—or rather, imagined their successors facing—forty years down the road. As ecological concerns widened and deepened, metropolitan planners realized the decreasing likelihood of widening many highways, and the futility of widening highways many commuters, especially women who tended to work in suburbs, did not use. Urban planners and historians of city planning rarely speak for the record about the spatial impacts of women driving to work outside the home. They argue for more studies and more precise data collection, but since 1980 they have been reticent about designing highways that lead where errand-running data suggest they must.

The contemplation of choked urban and metropolitan highways goaded planners toward better prognostication methods. Unfortunately for planner peace of mind, the computer-generated scenarios outlined the highway needs of a growing national population, the rising number of women working outside the home, and time consumed by men and women driving many miles on errands. In 2007 the national population is about 301 million; in 2055 the nation will have 417 million people. Highway planning and design guidelines originated when the national population was about 120 million. At the current rate of growth of tractor-trailer truck traffic across the George Washington Bridge in New York City, *all* the bridge traffic will be such trucks in 2015, since the bridge will be continuously covered with trucks. Such statistics imply that automobiles and buses will be routed elsewhere—an implication that is nonsensical unless a parallel bridge is being designed now and construction planned for next week. A United States of 417 million people will know highway congestion beyond the darkest imaginings of all but a few experts. The vast explosion of population will occur in a handful of sprawling metropolitan regions, while—paradoxically—gigantic sections of the forty-eight contiguous states experience almost no growth at all.

Wheeler County in Oregon is roughly twice the area of Rhode Island but is home to only 1,500 people. A motorist sitting in a Providence, Rhode Island, traffic jam on I-95 might ponder Wheeler County. Why are so many people stopped in Providence, and what will traffic jams will be like five or ten years from now? Will any of it spill into the likes of Wheeler County, or will Wheeler County remain as sparsely populated as it is? Census statistics offer answers, but the answers displease almost everyone.

Such questions preoccupied many Americans in the late 1930s and then again in the 1960s. The Depression-era imagination focused on small aircraft, chiefly the autogiro (a hybrid helicopter/fixed-wing plane), that would alleviate urban boulevard congestion. The subsequent moment concentrated on a variety of land-based inventions, mostly driverless cars. In time, 1960s dreamers derived some instruction from the 1930s visionaries, and eventually they learned defeat.

Invented in the 1920s in Spain, and perhaps simultaneously in Russia, the autogiro is best glimpsed now in the film *It Happened One Night*. Essentially a hybrid of airplane and helicopter, it featured a large propeller overhead and a second giving horizontal thrust. The United States licensee produced only about thirty of these aircraft. In the 1930s a few of the United States autogiros carried airmail, but most achieved prominence when used by journalists hurrying to important news sites. The *Detroit News* used one for aerial photography, and in 1931 Amelia Earhart reached 18,415 feet in one as a stunt. Highly maneuverable and, most importantly, capable of landing and taking off almost vertically, for a short time the autogiro seemed a commuter's dream come true. In the end, however, they used too much space in landing.

After World War II military interest shifted to helicopters. A few inventors tinkered with gyrocopters—one-person, vertical-takeoff-and-landing machines tricky to fly reliably. Another civilian contingent tried to perfect one- and two-person traditional airplanes that offered possibilities to people with large backyards but not enough acreage for runways. By the late 1950s the tinkering had shifted focus to rural places, and by the 1960s it had devolved into *Popular Mechanics* and *Popular Science* cover stories entitled "Build a VW-Powered Plane for $600" or "Build This 4-Place Cabin Plane for $3500." Despite early 1970s interest in James Bond–like tiny automobiles that sprouted wings, propeller, and rudder to become two-passenger airplanes, the 1973 energy crisis shifted interest toward ultralight, purely recreational aircraft. While many rural Americans, especially professionals, depend on privately owned airplanes using private runways or tiny county or municipal airports, the slow death of 1930s autogiro thinking emphasizes a single salient fact: no inventor could explain how a flock of autogiros or other tiny aircraft might converge on a city at rush hour without daily collisions. Nor could any inventor or any government expert explain how or where all the incoming aircraft would land or how flocks would take off simultaneously. In the face of these obstacles, interest in autogiros and similar flying machines waned and finally died.

Highway traffic jams began refocusing inventor attention in the 1960s. Some of the inventions merely tweaked earlier ones: the monorails at the Seattle World's Fair and at Disney theme parks represent nineteenth-century devices much improved. In 1910, for example, an electric-powered monorail system operated from Barstow in the New York suburbs through Pelham Park to Belden's

Point on City Island. The fifty-foot-long, cigar-shaped cars cruised at thirty miles per hour along the three-mile route, providing reliable enough service until one, carrying a hundred people rather than its usual fifty, twisted the overhead rail and wrecked. Long forgotten by the 1960s, such prototypes scarcely shaped the flow of federal research money to institutions like the Cornell Aeronautical Laboratory. As researchers discovered the unwillingness of Americans to tolerate noisy helicopters and sonic-booming airliners, they turned toward imagining a future of driverless (more or less) automobiles having some aircraft characteristics.

Popular Science featured the "Urbmobile" in a 1967 cover story illustrated with an image of bubblelike cars sweeping above a traditional interstate highway. Long on fantasy but short on facts, the story sketched an automobile that might or might not have flanged steel wheels, that might or might not be able to drive directly to guided highways, and that might or might not be powered by subwaylike electrified third rails. Working from the simple facts that an interstate highway lane chokes at around three thousand people per hour and that a traditional rail line chokes at around forty thousand per hour, the visionaries behind the Urbmobile fantasized about necklaces of bubble cars buzzing along at sixty miles per hour while drivers read or napped. If one car develops mechanical problems, magnetic devices will kill power to the third rail and slow the entire necklace to a safe stop. But near the end of the article researchers admitted that the system would only be possible for Los Angeles, Denver, Houston, and other sprawling cities. In New York, Philadelphia, Boston, Chicago, and similar cities "with really dense central cores," the Urbmobile system simply will not work, since no space exists to park the bubble cars. The system, experts agree, "doesn't approach the efficiency of a commuter train." Possibly bureaucrats at the old Department of Housing and Urban Development glimpsed the futility of the Urbmobile research effort: funding stopped. Given the rapid growth of cities, the rising number of women working away from home, and the developing density of automobile traffic, the visionary dream of a 1985 debut lay shattered by demographics in 1975.

In 1972 *Popular Science* reported that Department of Commerce bureaucrats were aware of the mounting catastrophe facing the interstate system. That year the whole forty-one thousand miles of the original system would be finished, but motorists in urban areas, already fuming about traffic jams, would confront worsening driving conditions. Engineers envisioned a futuristic Century Expressway running between Boston and Washington, D.C., as a 150-miles-per-hour route open to ordinary automobiles but not trucks. In 1965 studies had already revealed motorist dislike of trucks, especially big trucks, and engineers planning a highway that, in the words of one *Popular Science* reporter, will "separate the men from the boys" asserted that no trucks would irritate drivers merging from 80-miles-per-hour lanes into the high-speed, long-distance ones. But for commonsense questions the experts had few answers. Fog and snow would cause "beauts" of accidents, in the words of one Century Expressway designer, and no one really expected Detroit automakers to invent engines capable of sustained 150-miles-per-hour operation. By 1968, when the New York State Department of Motor Vehicles allied with the Republic Aviation Division of the Fairchild-Hiller Corporation to produce its prototype "safety sedan"—complete with rearview periscope—most government and industry experts realized that traffic jams meant the end of high-speed highway hype. They shifted their attention toward safety issues, and subsequently toward fuel-saving ones.

But year after year, automobile and mass circulation magazines focused on futuristic highways, for after all, automobile manufacturers advertised heavily. Manufacturers emphasized fast, high-powered cars in campaigns aimed at young blue- and white-collar men. Throughout the late 1960s and into the 1970s, *Motor Trend* featured stories on "sports personal" cars nowadays called muscle cars: Mustang, Camaro, Barracuda, Javelin, Cougar, Firebird. Such cars needed open roads and high speed limits to satisfy their owners, especially those who used them as family cars. Advertising brochures show that similar cars, the 1970 Dodge Coronet for example, competed with "sports personal" models. "Long, one of the longest in its field," the Coronet merely contributed to the downtown parallel-parking crisis and to the growing fervor for high-speed driving.

Only occasionally did reality check the advertising effort. In 1967

Popular Science ran a cover story suggesting that heavy-duty helicopters might diminish traffic jams by lifting damaged automobiles straight up. Tow trucks simply took too long to reach accident scenes and remove wrecked cars. Gradually both general magazine and federal government interest in traffic jams shifted toward very light duty, urban mass-transit gimmicks like the Personal Rapid Transit system—a sort of semiautomated dial-a-bus operation—*Popular Science* profiled in 1971. Such systems seemed somewhat useful in sprawling airports and in theme amusement parks, convention centers, and resorts, automobile magazines admitted grudgingly, but they offered no hope for even suburban-scale travel. But the 1973 energy crisis forced even muscle car magazines away from fantasizing about superfast cars, highways, and ninety-mile-per-hour commutes. A 1974 *Popular Mechanics* feature story suggested putting a highway atop the Alaska oil pipeline, but afterward editors shifted emphasis to fuel economy, and then to the current mix of fuel economy and safety that makes many Americans view muscle cars and SUVs (which evolved from sports personal vehicles) with mixed emotions. No visionary could get past simple issues of traffic flow or deal with parking problems. Even Congress asked for ideas that would speed automobile traffic. But almost no one replied.

Off the record, trucking industry executives wanted commuters aboard commuter trains, preferably lightweight, delicate, trolley-car-like "people-mover" trains operating on rails too flimsy to support freight cars. Rush-hour traffic jams had begun to seriously discommode trucking companies, which responded by increasing efficiency where they could, mostly by operating ever larger trucks but also by installing devices few outside the industry know. The so-called jake brake saves brake-pad wear by diverting exhaust gas into diesel-engine cylinders suddenly free of fuel. But jake-brake exhaust screams from tail pipes, and many communities ban their operation except on fire apparatus. Longer, streamlined trailer trucks, jake brakes, then tractors towing two trailers at a time proved useful on rural long-distance runs, but far less so in cities. Almost all trucking innovation annoyed automobile drivers, and sometimes pedestrians as well, especially in cities. When confronted in the late

1960s by a Congress trying to dampen complaints, the trucking industry admitted what the automobile manufacturers agreed to be true—the passenger train had to keep rolling.

Amtrak originated in 1971, just as motorcar fantasizing was skidding to a halt. This is more than coincidence. Computers had begun to predict motor vehicle traffic growth, and the predictions worried politicians, who in turn harried design professionals. Practicing planners, intent upon preserving not only their self-respect but also their jobs following the disaster of urban renewal, turned against another generation of highways, automated or not. Highway designers confronted not only issues of snow, rain, and fog but rising public ire at traffic jams, long, speeding trucks, and fatal accidents. They fixated on traditional, incremental improvements and complained bitterly, among themselves, then in print, especially in Federal Highway Administration long-range scenarios, about the adverse impact of large trucks on cities and inner suburbs, especially on New York and other very densely populated areas. Even mechanical engineers hopeful about small-scale, onboard-computer-driven equipment that might operate traffic lights shifted focus to creating safer, more fuel-efficient automobiles. Despite continuous generalized lobbying by the automobile, trucking, and airline industries, especially by car manufacturers, Congress created Amtrak simply because the so-called Northeast Corridor seemed unlikely to function without railroad passenger service.

Congress merely spread the cost of a regional railroad service bailout. By creating a handful of long-distance railroad routes along with Northeast Corridor ones, Congress hoped to convince all taxpayers that the quasi-public Amtrak operated a national network. Despite immediate and continual complaints that the bulk of Amtrak funding and vision went to the Boston–Washington corridor, and despite its original assertion that Amtrak would operate no commuter or short-distance trains, Congress persevered in its dual vision of high-speed, frequent service for one densely populated section of the nation, and slow-speed, one-train-a-day service for the rest. If Wheeler County saw two Amtrak trains a day, fine. Providence mattered more: it needed fourteen so that I-95 traffic jams did not destroy access to nearby cities and to adjacent airports.

As early as 1969, the editor of *Popular Mechanics* glimpsed the commuting value implicit in the Penn Central Railroad Metroliner service offered between New York and Washington. While he lamented that faster trains operated in Japan, he saw the United States electric-powered trains as a step toward a sensible, overarching transportation policy. People commuted on Metroliners that reached speeds of 110 miles per hour. Within three years the handful of experts knew a simple fact still rarely cited by historians. Amtrak had to survive simply because regional commuter rail operations had become interstate in scale. Without some federal structure, any one of the regional commuter systems might succeed in ways reminiscent of the 1934 Zephyr. That success would immediately cripple all federal automobile, trucking, and airline lobbying by dramatically increasing real estate values within one region people and news media would see as prototypical. Once the United States motorist glimpsed land travel without traffic jams in one large metropolitan region, airline travel would become long-distance only. The three powerful lobbies understood the failure of the intercity bus industry, and in their corporate memories perhaps recalled the failure of the trolley car industry too. A least a few of their employees knew something of German ideas about colossal railroads. Amtrak represented a simple, indeed elegant means of keeping railroad innovation under the control of a Congress controlled by road and airline industries—and by the military.

But Amtrak notwithstanding, the regional transit authorities began to flex muscle. The Southeastern Pennsylvania Transit Authority (SEPTA) snaked its tentacles out from Philadelphia; the Massachusetts Bay Transit Authority (MBTA) reached southwest from Boston into Rhode Island; the California Transit Authority (CalTrans), if not exactly interstate, sprawled along its own ocean-front corridor; Metro North (a commuter train authority) linked New York City with Connecticut. Other, often smaller systems began expanding too. While Amtrak's Northeast Corridor service began functioning as a commuter line—bringing commuters to and from Trenton and Princeton in New Jersey to New York, for example— many states hitherto not served by Amtrak or served by only a pair of trains daily began seeing opportunities beyond those offered by Congress.

Maine moved surely but steadily in a way that presaged efforts elsewhere. After decades without Amtrak service, it suddenly demanded Boston–Portland trains. Despite much squabbling with the freight railroad that owns the tracks, government agencies made the operation a reality in 2001. But not just a pair of trains connects the two cities. Instead three trains a day each way link the cities. The Downeasters surpassed ridership estimates immediately after beginning service, and despite initial fluctuations in ridership, they pleased passengers: the trains have 96 percent on-time rates and 95 percent customer-satisfaction rates. Many riders commute the 116 miles: the first train leaves Portland at 6:05 and arrives in Boston at 8:50. Many others commute between Boston and intermediate stops, especially Exeter, New Hampshire, seventy-seven minutes from Boston, even at rush hour. But the service is linked to the commuter rail lines Maine is beginning to reactivate around Portland. And it is linked as well to the high-level passenger platform at Bethel, a mile or so from the Sunday River resort.

The Maine effort rewards sustained scrutiny. Unlike earlier efforts by other states, it succeeded in convincing Amtrak to operate multiple trains, not one daily train each way. Moreover, the Downeasters connect—albeit indirectly, Boston having two terminals and having built a gigantic, expensive highway tunnel system while determining to forgo building a rail link between the two stations—with the high-speed Acela trains. A state that advertises itself as "vacationland" at home and in Europe implemented a meticulously scheduled plan while Amtrak struggled to get Acela rolling. Suddenly Maine became far more accessible, but the Amtrak trains serving it connect at Portland with a nascent regional rail network intended to increase property values and help wealthy taxpayers not only commute to Portland but connect for points south.

Very astutely, Maine never asked Amtrak to operate north and east of Portland, perhaps on a route into New Brunswick and Nova Scotia. Maine does little to provide passenger rail service deep into its north woods, although it pays close attention to the condition of freight tracks potentially useful for it. Instead Maine emphasizes, in the quietest way possible, a regional commuter-like railroad that is essentially a recreational-region railroad only partly dependent on Amtrak.

Maine planners were far ahead of most state planners throughout the 1980s and '90s. They knew they needed at least six trains a day to make their concept work, and they convinced Amtrak to provide the trains. What they learned now attracts attention in Virginia, the Carolinas, and even on the Georgia coast, and throughout the Pacific Northwest.

Maine vacationers just looking around glimpse the end of the sidetrack of which Maine residents are so well aware. Maine worked around Congress, finessed Amtrak, and pioneers a new vision of regional passenger railroading derived from historical record. Intended to serve wealthy Maine residents and boost real estate values in environmentally sensitive regions, the Maine vision is not so much focused on urban rail commuting as it is on a resort view of the future.

SOURCES: Burr, *U.S. Planning for War in Europe, 1963–1964;* Cherington, *Regulation of Railroad Abandonments;* Cole, *The Road to Rainbow;* Doughty, *New York Central and the Trains of the Future;* Fales, "How You'll Drive 120 MPH Legally"; Gunnell, *An Atomic Powered Railroad Locomotive;* Hubbard, "Nine Hundred Thousand Barrels a Day"; Lambert, "More Long Islanders Looking to Move Out"; Mischke, "Pages from the Past"; Morgan, "Ninety Miles an Hour Aboard a 4-6-4"; New York State Department of Motor Vehicles, *The Safety Sedan;* Price, "I Remember"; Smith, "The Diesel from D to L"; Stelling, "Designing for the Ladies"; "Super-Highway"; "Testing 6 Sports-Personal Cars"; Thompson, "Definition of a Redball"; Waller and Blumenberg, *Long Journey to Work.*

RESORT

No passenger trains stop at Bethel, Maine. Not yet. But the glistening new station and the high-level platform suggest that leisure may breed more long-distance passenger train experiments than business or commuting.

By the end of the 1950s the airline industry had begun devastating long-haul passenger train service, and coaches and first-class cars grew shabbier every year, with the exceptions of a few railroads determined to make their trains succeed. Railroad companies had abandoned dozen of trains, and the pace of abandonment quickened throughout the 1960s. Urban rioting and crime produced a suburban exodus from downtown residential areas convenient to train stations. Nowadays anyone reading mainstream media stories of passenger train failure will observe the odd morphing of *longdistance* into *intercity*. The change in usage strongly suggests that public-policy argument advanced in skewed ways. When Congress established Amtrak in 1971, most discussion focused on linking cities, not suburbs. Wilderness and resort regions merited scarcely a mention. That clean, fast, friendly passenger trains often lasted longest in the Far West merited none.

Throughout the 1950s and 1960s, vacationers accounted for much passenger train travel, as they had for decades. Trains operated regularly or seasonally between cities and to or through places of leisure, often collecting passengers during one-minute stops in small towns. By no stretch of imagination could anyone call Glacier National Park or the Maine coast *cities*. As airlines purchased more and more news media advertising, however, the media began ignoring how Americans—especially the wealthy—typically traveled. Disneyland became the premiere family vacation, and Disney and the airline industry combined to make flying to California convenient and affordable, the airlines by offering reduced fares, Disney by advertising its park. In time, advertising made Disney World even more desirable among children, and families found discounted ticket prices between most cities and Orlando. National parks became first automobile accessible and then automobile choked, and many resorts, especially those catering to the wealthy, disappeared, often deliberately, into the obscurity the wealthy love.

Most American workers are limited to the standard two-week vacation, in contrast to the six weeks their European counterparts enjoy. So long as Americans must hurry on vacation, air travel holds sway on the long-distance routes that prove most profitable. To most Americans, transcontinental train travel is a joke, not only because they know little about how it once worked or might work in the future, but perhaps also because it offers a half-conscious reminder of how little leisure time they enjoy.

Long-distance driving becomes hectic when undertaken at speed. Many vacationing families discover that the interstate system is really an intercity system that bypasses cities, scenic wonders, and first-class resorts alike. Air travel becomes proportionately necessary as available travel time decreases, but few airlines operate between wilderness areas, national parks, and classy resorts. Well-to-do people escape to places once served by train, many still difficult and expensive to reach by air. Rail travel once offered alternatives to the Disney-type vacations: alternatives involving national parks, forests, grasslands, and other places many taxpayers now find difficult to reach. Parents learn that driving from any coastal city to any one national park, enjoying the park, and driving home is possible in a two-week vacation, but visiting more than one or two parks becomes a frantic chore.

Nonetheless, people try. Often the family car shares the same secondary and tertiary roads as campers, motor homes, agricultural machinery, and other slow-moving vehicles. Often when vacationers approach major parks they find urban-scale traffic congestion. Very frequently, unless they have made reservations well in advance, they find no place to camp and sometimes, indeed, no place to park.

The National Park Service, the United States Forest Service, and other federal agencies despair over the masses of automobiles and other recreational vehicles jamming parking lots. Not surprisingly, they build more lots and more roads, trying to spread visitors over a broader area. As the building of lots and roads continues apace,

The hiker surprised by a freight train realizes that railroads often cross wilderness areas remote from roads.

whole wilderness parks teem with vehicles that destroy any semblance of wilderness experience and any hope of relaxation. Consultants struggling to solve the motor vehicle conundrum may fail to examine the complicity of news media, airlines, and automobile manufacturers as a contributing factor. In desperation they think about a monorail system for Yosemite National Park.

Yosemite once had railroad access, as did most long-established national parks. Part of traveling cross-country on business frequently involved spending a day or two in a national park, and railroads strove mightily to make these minivacations convenient and enjoyable. Business travelers who spent a day or two sampling a park frequently returned on longer vacations, often with family and friends, or timed their next business trip around fishing, hunting, or skiing seasons. Very often, both business travelers and vacationers arrived and departed in first-class style, aboard trains with dining and Pullman cars, but many others made do with inexpensive, so-called tourist sleeping-car accommodations and even coach seats. Trains brought people to Yosemite and other parks, and the Park Service directed people from edge stations into wilderness devoid of automobiles.

When Yosemite opened in 1890 its western edge lay at the end of a two-day stagecoach trip from the San Joaquin Valley town of Merced. The town was situated on the main north–south lines of both the Southern Pacific and Santa Fe railroads. "Midway between Stockton and Fresno" meant little, but "on the main lines between Oakland, San Francisco, Los Angeles and about every point north, south, and east" certainly did. The Yosemite Valley Railroad began operations in 1907, running from Merced to El Portal, on the boundary of Yosemite, where it built a wilderness-style station and a sumptuous lodge. Almost immediately, the two transcontinental railroads began dispatching Pullman cars from Oakland and Los Angeles to El Portal via the Yosemite Valley branch line. First-class and coach passengers boarded wagons, and later open-top motor buses, for transport into the park interior. By 1916, however, more visitors were arriving by automobile than by train, and Yosemite began suffering the first throes of automobile congestion. Train conveyance steadily declined until 1945, when scrappers tore up the rails of the abandoned Yosemite Valley Railroad.

Short lines connected other resorts with main-line railroads. The Lake Tahoe Railway started in 1900 as a narrow-gauge line running south from the east–west Southern Pacific main line over the Donner Pass at Truckee. Twenty-five years later the Southern Pacific bought the line, made it standard gauge, and operated Pullman service from Oakland. Peter T. Maiken reports in *Night Trains: The Pullman System in the Golden Years of American Rail Travel,* that the Southern Pacific timed the night train to arrive at dawn, when the lake seemed almost golden. The company operated a day train from Oakland too, and connecting trains from Truckee for the convenience of long-distance travelers headed for Lake Tahoe, or simply wanting to break their trip in a pleasant place. Until motorists streamed onto its shores, Lake Tahoe was an immaculate gem prized by people who arrived by train and then walked the shoreline or took a tiny steamboat to scenic points around the periphery.

Unlike Yosemite and Lake Tahoe, many other national parks lay far distant from major population centers. Railroads viewed the parks as both long-term destinations and convenient places to break long trips.

In 1901 the Santa Fe Railroad began advertising the Grand Canyon in Arizona as a must-see spot of true wilderness grandeur. That summer it operated the first Pullman cars north along a branch from Williams, a town on its east–west main line. The railroad soon built a splendid hotel on the canyon rim, and quickly discovered that word-of-mouth advertising supplanted the draw of full-page ads in national magazines. In 1929 the Santa Fe inaugurated the Grand Canyon Limiteds, first-class trains between Chicago and San Francisco (with sections to Phoenix) scheduled so that Pullman cars could be detached at Williams and sent on to the Grand Canyon, where they served as temporary hotels. In systematizing what so many passengers already did, the Santa Fe passenger department achieved a service that demanded strict adherence to a custom timetable, since the sleeping cars left one Grand Canyon Limited and joined a subsequent one.

At 10:15 PM on a Sunday, passengers would have left Chicago for Los Angeles and San Francisco, arriving at 10:00 the following morning in Kansas City; 11:45 that night in La Junta, Colorado; and 12:15 the following afternoon in Albuquerque. At 11:00 PM that night the train would pause in Williams to switch out cars for the Grand Canyon. The sleeping cars waited most of the night in Williams, and at 5:40 the following morning began their sixty-four-mile trip to the Grand Canyon, where they arrived at 8:15. At 8:30 that night, their occupants having enjoyed a busy or leisurely day of exploring and dining, the Pullmans rolled back to Williams, where a locomotive switched them onto another Grand Canyon Limited en route to Phoenix via Ash Fork, Prescott, and Wickenburg or on to Los Angeles, San Diego, and San Francisco. While not especially fast, the Grand Canyon Limiteds carried club cars with valets, maids, barbers, bathtubs, and, of course, dining cars, along with a variety of Pullman cars configured with accommodations for single travelers, married couples, and families with children.

Devising a timetable that explained a service terminating in three cities with part of every train stopping over at the Grand Canyon taxed the ingenuity of Santa Fe employees. Passengers could book berths and rooms aboard the Grand Canyon Limiteds in sleepers not detached at Williams, of course. At the Grand Canyon they might want to meet friends aboard the opposing Grand Canyon Limited, which left San Francisco at 10:15 at night; the railroad thus arranged to have both trains switch out sleepers at Williams at about the same time. Finally, passengers might want to go to the Grand Canyon from Chicago or San Francisco not for a day (as a bonus on a business trip, perhaps) but for an extended vacation. In the final instance, the timetable directed their attention to other trains, perhaps the California Limited. But since any passenger aboard any Santa Fe train routed via La Junta–Colorado–Albuquerque might suddenly conceive a desire to visit the Grand Canyon, the company operated two daytime trains, Nos. 11 and 14, between Williams and the Grand Canyon, in addition to the night trains moving sleeping cars. However contorted the 1929 timetable, Santa Fe advertising made clear the proximity of the Grand Canyon to many of its transcontinental trains and the usefulness of a wilderness resort to all sorts of long-distance travelers.

Not surprisingly, other transcontinental railroads soon began to look on the national park system as something that might increase passenger revenue. The early examples of Yosemite and the Grand Canyon transformed coast-to-coast rail travel as coach and first-class passengers alike began choosing destinations based on intermediate wilderness stops.

Glacier National Park is a national park because the Great Northern Railroad saw its potential as a tourist attraction. In 1910 Congress created the park, using the Great Northern main line as its sixty-mile-long southern boundary. The company in turn built all sorts of lodgings for the visitors who stepped from trains operating through what it called "the scenic wonderland." Pullman cars dedicated solely to Glacier National Park service left from Chicago, Kansas City, and Omaha, arriving at Glacier Park station as their destination. Other cars stayed with trains but discharged passengers at a station linked directly with hotels.

Understanding the role of Glacier National Park in 1920s United

States railroading means seeing coast-to-coast rail passenger service in terms not merely of scenery but also of stopover experience in a region still sparsely populated today. Moreover, it involves a consideration of the North, especially the Canadian North, in east–west frameworks. In 1929 the Great Northern Empire Builder departed from Chicago at 9:00 PM, left Minneapolis twelve hours later, paused in Minot in North Dakota after another twelve hours, and four hours later stopped at Glacier Park, twenty-eight hours and 1,100 miles from Chicago. Dozens of towns, each meticulously noted in the 1929 *Official Guide,* slipped past. Read today, the timetable staggers: it extends for three full pages of fine print. The Empire Builder scarcely slowed at Gunsight, Sundance, and Spotted Robe before it stopped at Glacier Park; nor did it stop at Bison, Singleshot, or Hidden Lake after. But slower trains did.

Glacier National Park sat at the junction of a great T. South from it to Kansas City ran Great Northern trains that paused at Great Falls, Billings, Denver, Lincoln, and St. Joseph. The Great Northern operated through Pullman cars from Omaha and other cities far south of the park. But the main line of the Great Northern extended not only southeast from the park to Minneapolis and Chicago but also north (from Crookston in Minnesota) to Winnipeg and east to Duluth. In northern Wisconsin, near the western edge of Lake Superior, the Great Northern touched the territory of the Soo Line, controlled by the Canadian Pacific. From Minneapolis and St. Paul the two railroads operated Pullman service east to Montreal and, by the Boston & Maine, to Boston. Thus a New Englander might travel north, across the top of the Great Lakes, then swing southwest, then take the Empire Builder on to Glacier National Park.

New Englanders might have visited Yellowstone almost as easily, traveling west on the Northern Pacific. For all its fame as the first national reserve—created by Congress in 1872, immediately after the establishment of the first transcontinental railroad—Yellowstone still suffers from identity problems. Part of it extends into Montana and Idaho, but its bulk lies in Wyoming and, like the Grand Canyon, off main-line east–west routes. The Northern Pacific simply built a spur south from Livingston in Montana to Gardiner and, like its competitors elsewhere, erected a wilderness-style log station on a great loop that turned Yellowstone trains back onto the line to Livingston. Thereafter the company advertised itself as the "Yellowstone Park Line," in the hope that harried coast-to-coast business travelers might leave its premiere train, the North Coast Limited, for a minivacation at Yellowstone. Many did, but the suddenly accessible park itself attracted longer-term visitors from across the nation.

Eventually the Northern Pacific operated three gateways to Yellowstone. Gardiner remained extremely popular. In the 1920s, just before the season opened, entire trainloads of college students arrived to work in the lodges, and thereafter a stream of regular and special trains poured into the loop. The company subsequently opened a second gateway station at Cody in Wyoming and a third at Red Lodge, Montana; neither offered the convenience of the Gardiner, but both were more convenient for eastern travelers. In the late 1920s Northern Pacific service included the Yellowstone Comet operating from Chicago. The train split at Billings: one section operated over Chicago, Burlington & Quincy tracks to Cody, and the other went on to Gardiner. The Comet stopped only at St. Paul, Minneapolis, and Fargo before reaching Billings, and it carried what vacationing Americans had come to expect in the way of amenities: dining, buffet, and observation cars, sleeping cars, and bathtubs. From Livingston to Gardner it carried an additional pleasantry: open-air observation cars that made approaching Yellowstone an unforgettable sensory experience. Unnamed special trains, Nos. 3 and 4, operated between Yellowstone and Seattle via Tacoma, Portland, and Spokane, and other trains, even the plodding stop-at-every-town coach-only locals offered connecting service at Livingston.

Park visitors might avoid the Northern Pacific altogether, however, and ride the line that the Union Pacific opened from Idaho Falls to the western edge of Yellowstone. Trains to West Yellowstone carried Pullman cars switched from Union Pacific east–west limiteds at Pocatello and, of course, coaches. While the Yellowstone Express and Yellowstone Special built transcontinental traffic, West Yellowstone soon lay at the northern end of a new route originating in Salt Lake City. Midway between Idaho Falls and West Yellowstone lay the junction of Aston, from which the Union Pacific built a line southeast to the base of a mountain pass more than two miles high; on its far side lay Grand Teton National Park. Union Pacific service to Yellowstone prospered in ways that mystify anyone now turning the pages of old timetables, magazine advertisements, and travel diaries. In the mid-1920s a dedicated Yellowstone Pullman sleeper left Jacksonville in Florida via five railroads before the Union Pacific switched it onto a train at Kansas City. From the south and southeast, and from California, park visitors used the Union Pacific gateway, often without encountering visitors arriving at the northern and eastern gateways operated by the Northern Pacific.

Advertising maps from the 1920s illuminate the importance of the western national parks in rail passenger travel. Would-be tourists and even small children staring at posters in tiny depots might send for brochures from different railroads about wilderness vacations. Union Pacific maps and booklets emphasized that the railroad not only linked cities, small towns, and connecting lines with individual parks but linked the parks with each other. A traveler might want to visit Yellowstone along with Zion National Park, Bryce Canyon, Lassen Volcanic, Crater Lake, Sequoia, and Yosemite. Small-town depot masters and big-city travel agents pored over the *Official Guide* and figured out how would-be customers might enjoy a fast or a cheap ride to one park, then convenient rides to others. In a precomputer age, customers, stationmasters, and travel agents collaborated on many decisions. Passengers who went by the Denver, Rio Grande & Western through Colorado enjoyed detraining during the scheduled ten-minute photography stop in the Royal Gorge of the Arkansas River. Passengers who liked to eat favored the Great Northern and Northern Pacific, both famed for potato and fish cuisine. Others, especially schoolteachers on a budget but with many weeks of summer vacation, might favor slower but far less expensive coach and tourist sleeper trains, as well as "budget tours" of certain clusters of parks. College students bound for summer jobs in the national parks often favored the cheapest long-distance services of all, sacrificing not just luxury but even comfort in coaches rolling toward exquisite summer opportunity. More than most groups, undergraduates in tiny college towns like Galena in

Illinois appreciated the long-distance trains that paused to collect young people en route to wilderness summer jobs.

Vacation travel by rail involved far more than the western national parks, yet nowadays this is difficult to reconstruct. Recent patterns created by interstate highways and airline routes blur the fine distinctions that once reflected important decisions. Many city dwellers moved to particular suburbs not only because they offered convenient commuter train access to central cities but also because long-distance trains bound for vacationland paused at those suburban stations. The Oranges in New Jersey enjoyed summertime Pullman car service direct to the Maine coast, while commuter suburbs a few miles west did not. Choosing a year-round suburban home, and sometimes considering a job offer in a distant city, involved a precise evaluation of work and pleasure rail links.

No long-distance resort rail service better demonstrates the importance of home-base location than the summertime service to northern New England. Convenient connections from downtown New York, Hartford, and Boston meant that fathers might spend long weekends with families away for the summer. Equally convenient service from suburbs meant that families might make several short vacation trips to the same place. Just as few contemporary Americans consider the historical impact of the two-week vacation on highway congestion, airline travel, and resort choice, so do few understand the invention of the corporate executive as enabling the wealthy to vacation at length.

Executives execute orders. In the late 1950s corporate culture overwhelmed much United States thinking and skewed understanding of workplace hierarchy. Few Americans consider the directors who act through executives, let alone trace the creation of executive positions back to the perfecting of long-distance telephone technology. Not only did the telephone allow senior management to move away from factories, mills, and other manufacturing sites, in time creating the office avenues of New York and other cities. It also enabled directors and, far more importantly, owners of large and small businesses to remain in daily contact with trusted employees left behind during business and pleasure trips. To their employees, executives often look like senior authority, but to their employers, often individuals who remain in the background of business culture, they are merely the trusted keepers of order and the executors of new directives. Telephones and the executive class made possible season-long vacations for business owners after the 1890s. Schoolchildren learn about Alexander Graham Bell but little about people other than teachers who enjoy long summer vacations and stay in touch by long-distance telephone. By 1915 the wealthy had perfected the remote resort accessible only by long-distance train.

Year-round passenger trains operating north of Boston to Maine and to the Canadian Maritime Provinces began carrying summer-time tourists in large numbers by 1880. But many of the trains did not operate through Boston, simply because the city lacked—and still lacks—a direct rail link between its two terminals, South Station and North Station. Instead, Pullman cars moving from Washington and New York rolled north along the present Amtrak seacoast route, but diverged in Connecticut at New Haven or New London on a route through Worcester in Massachusetts and Nashua, New Hampshire. North–south travel skirting Boston produced not only a gigantic station in Worcester (now converted into an arena) and a nine-track one in Portland, Maine, but deep fears in Boston. While the city enjoyed heavy commuter train traffic—in the 1890s South Station boasted of being the busiest terminal in the world—and train-to-ship transfer, by the first years of the twentieth century long-distance trains, especially ones carrying very wealthy people, bypassed it. The State of Maine Express operated from Washington over the Pennsylvania, New York, New Haven & Hartford, and Boston & Maine railroads. Serving both Concord in New Hampshire and Portland, the train's summertime consists expanded until "the train" meant multiple sections of first-class cars filled with wealthy people intending to summer in Maine.

Resort travel reinforced techniques railroads learned at Christmastime and, later, Thanksgiving time: trains had to operate in multiple sections to meet demand. A train advertised to depart a terminal at four in the afternoon might operate with several "advance" sections that left earlier; alert newspaper readers watched for advertisements announcing such sections. Then the train departed at the appointed time, followed by several subsequent sections run-

ning as closely spaced as signaling systems allowed. Holiday operations became seasonal rushes by the 1920s. The Santa Fe frequently
operated its Chicago to Los Angeles California Limited in seven sections each way, each separate train carrying not only the name but
eleven sleeping cars, diners, and observation cars. On one occasion,
the train operated with twenty-two sections westbound. Railroad
companies disliked turning away would-be passengers, especially
vacation-bound passengers not in a tearing hurry, since such people tended to find routes on competing carriers. Even the Boston
& Maine, which controlled most north–south travel in Maine, ran
multiple sections of its summertime trains.

For almost sixty years after its debut in 1902, the Bar Harbor Express journeyed north from New York through Worcester to the
Maine coast. Operating over the same or roughly parallel routes
rolled the so-called camp specials of as many as twenty Pullmans
each carrying children to summer camps in Maine and along the
Connecticut River. The New York, New Haven & Hartford Railroad
created the Bar Harbor Express, differed with the Boston & Albany
over its handling of the train, and finally ran it over its own rails
to a Boston & Maine connection. In the summers of the 1920s it
frequently operated in three sections, bringing Pullman cars from
Washington and New York to Mount Desert Ferry and Ellsworth,
and running the remaining sleepers to Rockland. The train carried
private cars belonging to the rich, and one day operated, in addition to its regular sections open to the public, three sections only
for twenty-one family-owned private cars. Long-distance telephone
lines, the creation of an executive cohort, and the Bar Harbor Express made the northern (or eastern) coast of Maine into an exclusive summer resort.

The Bar Harbor Express left Washington, D.C., at 1:00 every afternoon in summer and arrived at Portland at 4:24 the following
morning, its passengers still snuggled in berths, compartments, and
drawing rooms. At Portland the train split. One part rolled on to
Kineo and Waterville, where it arrived three hours later. Another
went to Rockland via Bath, Wiscasset, Waldoboro, and Thomas-
ton; it too terminated about three hours after leaving Portland. Another went westward to North Conway, Crawfords, Bretton Woods,

and Fabyan, and still another on to Kennebago. The final part left Portland for Ellsworth, Mt. Desert Ferry, and Bar Harbor, arriving at 11:45 in the morning. The express left Bar Harbor at 2:00 every afternoon; departures from other resorts were scheduled so that Pullmans would collect at Portland's Union Station and be fed into several southbound sections. The companies respected the wishes of passengers from different resorts who wanted to visit en route based on their home or resort destinations. Consequently, Philadelphia-bound passengers from the deep woods of Maine merged into the flow of Philadelphia-bound passengers from the coastal resorts; that train became a subset of the larger one and carried the name Philadelphia–Bar Harbor Express. Except for the interruption of World War II, the companies enjoyed tremendous success with a train that operated between large cities and the tiniest of wilderness and coastal resort stations.

The Boston & Maine learned from its successes and tailored other trains and even lone Pullman car service to individual resorts. Rockport, a tiny Massachusetts harbor town north of Boston, developed an artists' colony that made it attractive to seasonal visitors in the 1920s. In June 1930 the Boston & Maine experimented with a sleeping car switched from an express train running north from New York via Worcester. Within days the service had burgeoned into five Pullmans and a baggage car departing Rockport at the end of the July 4th weekend. The following year a Pullman dedicated to Rockport left Washington, D.C., on a 4:10 afternoon express; it arrived at the quaint harbor terminal at 7:29 the following morning. On Sunday evening it rolled south at 8:36, after dinner. In the Depression the Boston & Maine launched a new profitable service based simply on the commonsense understanding that passengers had to sleep somewhere and might just as well sleep comfortably en route to a wilderness or resort destination, not to another city.

The smallest of wilderness stations, which ordinarily saw only a couple of coach and freight trains a day, hosted Pullman cars during the summer season. Finding deep-woods Maine resorts like Kennebago and Kineo today is difficult, even with a good map, but they remain resorts dedicated to people who often stay the summer. As Acadia National Park chokes the whole Mount Desert Island region with motor vehicle traffic, the inland resorts in the north woods keep a low profile indeed.

Only people devoted to fly fishing, canoeing, camping, hiking, and other relaxing pursuits in deep forest know much about a vast section of Maine peopled every summer by upper-class families "from away." The sleeping-car service that long ago linked Boston with Minneapolis and St. Paul via the Canadian Pacific also linked the canoe country of Maine with the boundary waters canoeing region of the Upper Peninsula of Michigan, northern Wisconsin, and Minnesota. The Pullman service is long gone, and the tracks to Kennebago are too, but the people who prize their resort areas have kept sprawl at bay in both canoe-focused regions. Just as wealthy, powerful families have kept Washington, D.C., sprawl from swamping Middleburg, Upperville, Warrenton, and other communities along I-66 west of the city, so people who love Kennebago have stopped what most politicians think is unstoppable. When Pullman service to Kineo Station failed, families drove north from Washington, Philadelphia, and New York, and east from Syracuse. Such drives made two-week-long visits rather difficult, but the families asked for neither improved roads nor airline access. Instead they learned how to spend whole summers away.

Such places lay only a little distance from the old Canadian Pacific main-line tracks between Montreal and Halifax that slice east–west across northern Maine. Quebec and New Brunswick lay beyond the Bar Harbor Express, but not beyond the reach of the State of Maine Express. The year-round train connected at Portland with trains bound for New Brunswick and Nova Scotia, and with trains operating to Caribou and Van Buren in far northeast Maine. It crossed tracks with far less elegant Boston & Maine trains like No. 111, which left Boston every morning at 8:30 and arrived at Kennebago eight hours later. No. 111 split in Portland; another part arrived in Rangeley at 5:20 that afternoon. Getting to Kineo Station meant leaving Boston at 1:00 in the morning for a train trip nine hours and forty minutes long. But No. 103 chugged a bit further than Kineo Station in 1929, poking another fifteen minutes through the woods to the Mt. Kineo House, bought in 1911 by the Maine Central Railroad as the way to bring people to Moosehead Lake. Six miles north of the

Canadian Pacific route, Kineo station is barely halfway from the southern border of Maine. North of it lies mostly forest traversed by the Bangor & Aroostook in its long run to Frenchville. And Canada.

Canadians came south on vacation. People from Montreal took Pullmans south to Kennebunkport and Old Orchard Beach in Maine and to Cape Cod. Other Canadians swept south on trains from Quebec and Montreal along the Canadian-owned Central of Vermont, and south through Buffalo. Often, like tens of thousands of Americans, they headed for Florida. In winter the Pullman Company shifted sleepers no longer needed by trains bound for the national parks and the woods of northern Maine, Michigan, and Minnesota to the burgeoning Florida and Cuba markets, and to the steamships leaving New Orleans and Mobile.

The history of Florida as a holiday destination demonstrates the immense power of rail passenger service. The tourist industry boom can be traced back to 1887, when the Atlantic Coast Line Railroad opened the Ponce De Leon Hotel in St. Augustine as a destination for its Florida Special. The Florida East Coast Railway built a line from one Florida island to another until it reached Key West, where it connected with steamships. The combined Havana Special and steamship service offered passengers a forty-four-hour journey from New York to Havana; the Spanish culture, Prohibition-free liquor, and casinos of Cuba attracted thousands of passengers. The fierce competition for speed and luxury of service that developed between the Atlantic Coast Line and the Seaboard Air Line produced both hundred-miles-per-hour trains like the Orange Blossom Special and the Seaboard Florida Limited and a plethora of resort hotels on lines radiating south from Jacksonville.

Travelers wanting to get to a warm climate quickly, enjoy it quickly, and get home again quickly during the busy winter manufacturing and commercial season forced railroads east of the Rockies to create a number of high-speed routes from St. Louis, Omaha, Chicago, Buffalo, and places due north of Florida. Many of the high-speed trains came west across southern Georgia through Bainbridge and Valdosta to Jacksonville. Few snaked along the Florida Panhandle, something that explains why Pensacola, Panama City, and Apalachicola remain less developed than Miami, Palm Beach, and St. Petersburg. The Florida boom enriched cities such as Atlanta, Memphis, and Nashville, and such smaller cities as Montgomery and Birmingham in Alabama and Evansville in Indiana. The quest for trackage rights to Florida resorts preoccupied many Midwest-based railroads. The Illinois Central viewed the Florida boom as a threat to its Panama Limited–focused territory, and in 1909 bought the Central of Georgia a year after getting rights to a route into Birmingham. Its Seminole train offered year-round sleeping-car service from Chicago to Florida, and during the 1920s land boom it also ran the luxurious Floridian in the winter months. Traveling salesmen and other frequent riders quickly tumbled to the impact of Florida development. In wintertime they saw Pullmans painted for the Bar Harbor Express racing south from Chicago. Cincinnati, long a north–south junction, boomed as the Louisville & Nashville and the Southern rolled trains diagonally across the New York–to–New Orleans routes.

Well into the 1920s, no one would have considered these Florida-bound trains *intercity*, although most terminated in places developers called cities. The trains linked a new sort of resort, mostly hotels and long, sandy beaches, much as others provided service to the western national parks and the deep woods of northern Maine or Minnesota. Business began to slow after the 1920s land bubble burst, and it slowed again into the Depression; but it picked up remarkably in the middle 1930s as more and more Americans, especially retirees, discovered that Florida lay not very far at all from Asheville in North Carolina or Evansville in Indiana, and from hundreds of other small cities and large towns where long-distance luxury trains paused for a minute or so several times daily. Ever so slowly, Florida became the midwinter destination of choice for people who lived as far away as Detroit and St. Louis, but it became easily accessible and very desirable for people who lived much closer.

Until the 1950s, many Americans planned two annual vacations, a short wintertime one to Florida (rather than a longer one beyond New Orleans via ship) and a longer summer one, often to wilderness regions. Not owning a car often meant having the funds for more than one vacation, especially if the vacation destination was a city with superb public transit or a wilderness area in which the presence of automobiles seemed to run counter to the intended and expected experience. Gradually, however, both Florida and Southern California fell victim to sprawl produced first by automobiles, then by coastal international airports that connected domestic flights with overseas ones. But elsewhere, wealthy and powerful people protected the seasonal turf they loved as children. When train travel ended, they improved few existing roads and built even fewer new ones, and they built almost no airports. For four decades after World War II they enjoyed an enviable seclusion for weeks and months at a time in places that rarely advertised to attract newcomers. When sprawl threatened, they quietly embarked on restoring what their parents and grandparents once enjoyed.

Into the 1950s ski trains operated frequently in New England, California, and the Pacific Northwest, as well as within the Rocky Mountains. Railroads provided bar cars and dance cars, and sold tickets that put two people in berths for an extra dime. Usually the rowdiness remained good-natured, and travel to and from ski areas seemed far more entertaining than driving—and sometimes skiing. Especially in New England and in the Rockies, the ski trains offered dependable schedules in bad weather and freedom from automobile trouble. Like many concepts from the halcyon days of railroading and their 1950s afterglow, the details of ski trains and resort trains have faded from national memory. They have not, however, escaped the consideration of the real estate developers. Moving skiers from city to ski resorts via fast trains produces little in the way of negative local impact. The skiers sweep in, ski, spend money, and sweep out, no more bothersome to the local inhabitants than were the tens of thousands of visitors who once detrained at Glacier, Yellowstone, and other national parks in the 1920s. In Maine, especially in northern Maine and along the entire seacoast, the powerful residents see rail passenger travel as the solution to the automobile traffic ruining Acadia, Yosemite, and other national parks. North of Portland, rail passenger service will prevent such traffic from destroying Baxter and other parks.

Elsewhere in wilderness regions, similar ideas are taking hold. Residents of Teton County in Wyoming know the ability of trains to order the flow of tourists into adjacent Yellowstone National Park. In 2004 the Internal Revenue Service ranked the county first in per-capita income nationwide; in 2002 its average adjusted gross household income hit $107,694. Perhaps wealthy people living adjacent to a spectacular and increasingly popular national park envision lifestyle deterioration more clearly than others. In any case, they tend to act when they observe a burgeoning threat. Passenger train service would control the flow of park visitors in ways far more effective than more highways or larger airports. Conversely, the trains would give the privileged park abutters convenient access not just to far-off cities but also to other wilderness enclaves likewise inhabited by the wealthy.

Wilderness is closer to many would-be vacationers than many would-be vacationers think. Muddled now by traffic jams, too-short vacations, cheap airline fares to Orlando but not elsewhere, the hazards of driving all night, unpredictable interim motel availability, and the difficulties of transporting canoes, kayaks, and other wilderness equipment, Americans find it awkward to analyze wilderness-as-resort thinking. But adding hundred-miles-per-hour train travel to the perceptual stew clarifies matters, especially if the long-distance trains serve suburbs and offer comfort along with speed. The train itself would be a resort.

SOURCES: Maiken, *Night Trains;* Marshall, *Santa Fe;* Runte, "Yosemite Valley Railroad"; Shaffer, *See America First.*

THRESHOLD

Exclamation points sometimes punctuate the ends of Amtrak trains. Private cars recall an era when the rich traveled in a style far above first class, and savored travel as leisurely but invigorating progress. Lingering on the threshold between places, they enjoyed the immense private rail yachts that still ply North American railroads. Nowadays the wealthy charter cars for weekend or summer-long jaunts, and lucky clients of corporate owners sweep to the Kentucky Derby or Super Bowl, or to wilderness hunting preserves, atop twelve steel wheels. "Travel as travel was and should be" runs the unassuming advertisement, meaning: double beds, showers, chefs and stewards, and a plate-glass proscenium on the passing scene. In Brunswick green, maroon, royal blue, and sometimes burnished stainless steel, the cars trailing Amtrak trains jar the observer into wondering about travel the day before yesterday.

As World War II neared, heiress Barbara Hutton and actor Cary Grant made love aboard Japauldon. Built in 1926 for F. W. Woolworth, the car served the entire family of the dime-store-chain founder, but perhaps pleased his granddaughter most. When she inherited fifty million dollars in 1933 at the age of twenty-one, newspapers lionized the debutante who knew private cars intimately. Her father, Franklin Hutton, cofounded an investment firm with her uncle E. F. Hutton; together they roamed the country in sumptuous private cars. E. F. Hutton had the car Hussar built in 1922 by American Car & Foundry in St. Charles, Missouri, following his marriage to Marjorie Merriweather Post, heiress to the Post cereals fortune. Hussar transported Post clients in extraordinary style, but more often whisked its owners from New York to a palatial home in Palm Beach, or deep into the Adirondacks to a wilderness retreat at Topridge. In the north woods, beyond the end of the Raquette Lake Railway opened to provide swift access for the Vanderbilt, Durant, Huntington, and other railroad financier families, Topridge included sixty-eight buildings. But none surpassed Japauldon and

Hussar in elegance. Japauldon welded the best design money could buy with a Hollywood flair of which the Hutton and Grant pairing was the perfect emblem.

Today Japauldon rolls out of Atlanta under the name Survivor, elegance available for charter. Eight-five feet long, with a railed observation platform gracing its observation lounge end, the car contains a master bedroom with double bed, a double bedroom with upper and lower berths, a fold-down Murphy bed, a convertible sofa, a marble bathtub with shower, electronic gadgetry galore, and full meal service provided by onboard staff. Paneled entirely in wood and fitted with museum-quality furnishings, Survivor is a palpable ghost of Roaring Twenties luxury. Like hundreds of other private cars swaying at the end of Amtrak trains or rolling in trains of their own, it operates under the public radar.

Other charter cars sleep more people in elegance. Amtrak charges private-car owners roughly ten first-class tickets to move a car from point to point at the end of an Amtrak train; five couples each paying first-class fares plus a bit more thus get private accommodation, fine dining, and a taste of luxury about which most Americans know nothing. More importantly, they get superb on-site accommodation, at the Kentucky Derby, at the end of some wilderness spur track, or far along the Oregon or Maine coast. Union Station in Washington, D.C., maintains a special sidetrack for citizens who arrive aboard their own hotels. Those who still travel in their own cars know what a handful of merely very wealthy people know too: not only do the cars make travel exceedingly pleasant, they become private hotels and offices once they reach their destinations. Chartering a private railroad car mandates an intriguing calibration of first-class fares against five-star hotel fees. Folding hotel and restaurant costs into fare calculations transforms any evaluation of total cost into a window opening on another way of visiting cities, national parks, and small towns.

In the early 1980s a number of newspapers, including the *Wall Street Journal,* wondered at the resurgence of private-car ownership. In a 1984 *Wall Street Journal* article entitled "Expensive Toys," Daniel Machalaba interpreted it as being akin to owning ocean-going yachts or isolated islands. He suggested that individuals and

Private-car opulence endures on private sidetracks and in private warehouses; the opulence speaks of a time when the very wealthy understood luxury travel as private.

firms chartering such cars were merely responding to the renewed glamour of the Orient Express in Europe or simply aping the behavior of Old World aristocracy. But many very rich people had always understood private railroad cars as vehicles that enforced relaxation. Newcomers who bought derelict private cars for as little as five thousand dollars and then spent two hundred thousand more on renovations learned what "old money" had known for generations: private-carriage travel relaxed, refreshed, and somehow encouraged wide-ranging meditation, perhaps on the passing scene as potential real estate development. The sumptuous, eighty-foot cars nurtured the rarest of leisure.

Airlines nearly vanquished such leisure in the 1960s. Business travel became harried, and news media focused on the so-called jet set as the new travel celebrities. Both groups shared the same aircraft with economy-class passengers, and despite VIP lounges and a handful of other airline amenities, egalitarianism and brevity swept away older train and steamship distinctions. Jet airliners deified the two-week vacation. No longer could business travelers justify taking passage to Europe, South America, or Asia aboard a fine ocean liner, or enjoying a fine train across the country. As expense-account thinking transformed media notions of expendable wealth, business travelers lamented increasingly frenetic schedules. Vacationers emulating the jet set accepted the compression of two weeks into twelve days bounded by flying time. Only hippies hitchhiking across the country experienced traces of the leisure that once rode rails. Everyone else found themselves trapped in the binary prison: drive or fly. Neither driving nor flying proved conducive to the peculiar leisure and opportunity for scenario-analysis thinking that typified the private railcar travel experience.

The rise of automobile ownership became synonymous with "modern times." Just as the jet airliner shattered the dominance of traditional, time-consuming modes of travel, so automobile ownership deflected personal wealth away from other goods and services. Few American adults away from New York, Boston, and other cities boasting good public transportation networks can imagine life without automobile ownership, let alone analyze its costs and benefits. Automobile advertising supports newspapers; perhaps not coincidentally, few journalists investigate the long-term ramifications of seventy-six-month auto loans, insurance premiums elevated by collision and other riders mandated by lien holders, and the depreciation of vehicles no one expects to last a decade. Half-consciously, automobile owners compare the costs of driving five hundred miles against buying an airplane or Amtrak ticket: unless time impinges, they usually drive. After all, whispers the back of the mind, the car is ready. It should be. It is already owned, even if financed. Do high school or college students ponder what they might do with the personal wealth they will lavish on automobiles, insurance, maintenance, excise taxes, and even gasoline? Probably not. Before Henry Ford popularized the horseless carriage, millions of Americans devoted similar attention to horses (which reproduce in ways automobiles do not), carriages, oats, and baled hay, but with a significant difference: any overland trip more than twenty miles involved a train. Period.

Railroad company advertising before about 1920 consequently jars the contemporary reader, and not just because first-class trains appear so luxurious. The passengers seem so *young*. How did thirty-year-old couples afford travel aboard the Santa Fe de-Luxe? Beginning in December 1911, the de-Luxe operated once a week between Chicago and Los Angeles. The train left Chicago every Tuesday evening at 8:00, and arrived the following Friday morning at 9:00; the eastbound de-Luxe left Los Angeles every Tuesday at 6:10 in the evening and arrived Friday morning at 11:10. The company charged a fare premium of twenty-five dollars; it had learned that young people would pay extra for a good time.

Since inaugurating its California Limited in 1892, the Santa Fe had discovered that first-class service involved far more than high speed. A train operating over 2,265-mile route—a longer journey, the company delighted in pointing out, than that of the slower Orient Express—had to function as a resort. As the Limited barreled over the California border, a flower boy presented every woman onboard with a bouquet of roses, lilies, violets, or other in-season blossoms, and gave every male passenger an alligator wallet. But the key to any successful resort lies in its guests, as the Santa Fe well knew. "On a long journey it is pleasant to know that no over-crowding is permitted, and one's traveling companions are of a desirable class," proclaimed one brochure. "Persons you like to meet—successful men of affairs, authors, musicians, journalists, 'globe trotters,' pretty and witty women and happy children—these constitute the patrons of the *California Limited*." Collecting such passengers proved easier than the company imagined, for as word spread, the passengers selected themselves. The Limited came to be known as a stylish train indeed, and not necessarily because of the new Pullmans, dining car, and buffet-smoker. The "traveling companions . . . of a desirable class" were the real draw.

Creating the de-Luxe involved building on the success of the Limited but angling marketing toward younger people, especially those traveling on business but able to pay the surcharge from their own pocket. Many travelers want only comfort, announced a gold-paper, embossed 1913 brochure, dismissing ordinary first-class cuisine and fellow passengers. Others want all the comforts, plus luxuries. "They are in somewhat of a hurry. They like, too, to be a bit exclusive." The Santa Fe understood that speed might yield precedence to luxury and to the right mix of people sharing luxury across a particular region. Anyone needing the fastest Santa Fe train between Los Angeles and Chicago could grab the Fast Mail or the mail trains operated by competing companies. But for those—especially the young—desiring luxury and good company on an excursion through a sun-washed region, the de-Luxe was an obvious choice. In 1913 *fine train* no longer meant the fastest, at least for the sixty people aboard the de-Luxe.

In one full-color illustration after another, the pamphlet depicted luxuries being enjoyed by people in their late twenties and early thirties. The train carried only compartment and drawing-room Pullmans: no one slept in a berth behind curtains. Each bedroom had its own bathroom, most had doors that opened on the others—making possible travel en suite—and the drawing-room units offered both double beds and foldout beds. The club car provided a smoking and reading section for men. Positioned at the head of the train where no women ever needed to walk through it, the male preserve provided a shower and tub bath, a barber and a porter assigned to clothes care, current magazines, stock market and other telegraphed news reports snatched from cranes in front of depots, and a fully stocked buffet. The train carried a manicurist, a maid to help women bathe and dress, and perhaps more importantly, care for young children, who at night slept in the foldout sofa beds provided in bedrooms. A stenographer took dictation of important mail, typing it directly into letter and telegram format; chefs and waiters provided sumptuous meals in the dining car, and passengers congregated in the observation lounge car at the end of the train, served by stewards. If they chose, they sat or stood on the open-air platform and watched spectacular scenery, or they sat inside, enjoying a luxury newer than electric lighting: air specially cooled and cleaned. The pamphlet in the end proved almost unnecessary; word of the train spread everywhere, and young people delighted in riding it. Travel on the de-Luxe meant one had joined the beautiful young people moving across a discrete region toward a modern, sun-kissed location.

Until the end of passenger train travel, Santa Fe premiere service both created and reflected the glamour of Southern California, and especially of Hollywood. The de-Luxe stopped operating in World War I. In 1926 the Santa Fe created the Chief to relieve pressure on the ever-popular California Limited, and in time the premiere train became the Super Chief, a luxury train still associated with Hollywood stars. Throughout the Roaring Twenties the company upgraded the Chief, changing decor in concert with changing trends, installing indirect lighting, and otherwise integrating ultramodern design with very traditional notions of luxury. In the late 1930s the Santa Fe replaced the train with a streamlined one pulled by diesel-electric locomotives that sliced almost sixteen hours from the steam locomotive schedule. Sunlight reflected from its stainless steel exterior nearly blinded New Mexico onlookers. Inside the cars, Ceylonese satinwood, English sycamore, Makassar ebony, and other rare woods veneered surfaces to relieve eyes watching sun-drenched scenery flash past. Most of the cars carried hand-crafted ornamentation made by Navajo and Zuni artists, and turquoise motifs harmonized the decor from car to car. Passengers reveled in the totally designed environment, while farmers, ranchers, and small-town inhabitants saw the speeding silver trains as slivers of Hollywood fantasy, racing at up to 115 miles per hour.

Dining aboard the Super Chief became a national marvel. In 1936 the dinner menu opened with "Romanoff Fresh Malossol Caviar," hearts of California artichokes, and antipasto; proceeded through swordfish steaks, salmon, and several varieties of steak, accompanied by side dishes ranging from fresh corn on the cob to fresh asparagus; and concluded with a variety of American and foreign desserts. Strawberry shortcake coexisted with English Cheshire cheese and a variety of hot drinks. In the depths of the Depression, some passengers were dining well indeed.

Obscurity nowadays masks many American class distinctions. Electronic media constantly extolling equality subtly convey the message that most people are middle-class, and that the poor and the very rich are few and far off. Yet Americans recognize that catastrophic illness and subsequent job loss almost invariably lead to poverty, and many blue-collar families compete against welfare families for housing. Despite the surfeit of advertising to the contrary, the specter of downward mobility shadows much long-term thinking, perhaps especially when stock-market downturns weaken retirement accounts. Dramatic upward mobility, outside of lottery jackpots, seems far less real as a possibility or probability. But most of the time ordinary living confronts Americans with no more evidence of class distinction than a Jaguar caught in a traffic jam next to a Ford.

The Super Chief, on the other hand, offered a blatant display of class entitlement. Its Depression-era dining car menus surpassed all but a few fine restaurants, and those mostly in New York City. Cuisine historians unravel their significance only with difficulty. The Santa Fe served better meals en route aboard the Super Chief than passengers could obtain anywhere else between Chicago and Los Angeles.

But the Super Chief carried no private cars. The ultrarich attached their cars to lesser trains. The Super Chief served a segment of the population nowadays very difficult to define—Broadway and Hollywood stars, radio celebrities, and political figures—mixing them for days and nights with wealthy people also still hard to characterize. Some of the other travelers merely wanted extremely pleasant carriage over two thousand miles. Others specifically sought casual or intimate contact with the famous, the rich, and people on their way to fame and wealth. In the dining car the chief steward distributed guests among the tables, sometimes precipitating good conversation, short- and long-term love affairs, enduring friendship and business relationships, and quarrels. People mixed beyond the dining cars: in lounges over drinks, in observation cars before plate glass, in barbershops, and—after the war, when the Santa Fe replaced the trains with newer, more sumptuous ones—in second-story, glass-roofed dome cars. They had time to get to know one other.

A great many Depression-era Americans had time on their hands, but comparatively few had time and money both. In the great runup to the 1929 stock market crash, radio frequently reminded listeners that time is money. But as Douglas Rushkoff points out in *Coercion: Why We Listen to What "They" Say*, Americans unwittingly turning to media as children turn to parents soon stopped thinking logically. If time is money, then money must be time. But can money buy time? Or can money perhaps only carve one type of time from another?

Nothing offers a better portal on changes in American leisure than the marketing of Santa Fe premiere trains between 1900 and 1971. When Amtrak took over most of national long-distance passenger train service it confronted vexing issues of class. Should a democratic government provide passenger rail service in multiple classes? Should the taxpayer subsidize caviar and strawberry shortcake? Would Americans mind not having a shower before bed, or in the morning before breakfast? Avoiding and answering such questions consumed thirty years, but the Santa Fe and other companies knew the answers decades earlier.

Ostensibly, exclusivity and ostentation belong nowhere in the Republic. Exclusive suburbs, country and yacht clubs, and universities by definition exclude, sometimes by race or gender or standardized test scores, but far more frequently by class divisions media ignore. Ostentation belongs nowhere in a nation founded on equality, but ostentation drives the entire entertainment industry. Airline travelers sometimes dismiss the great center of the nation as *flyover land*. Immense jets land at St. Louis and Denver, but to many coastal residents, only the coasts matter. In the sparsely populated central states, especially on the High Plains, airliners move so far aloft that no one sees or hears them. But the de-Luxe and the Super Chief moved in plain view, at high speed but almost within touch. At a lonely Kansas or Arizona grade crossing a boy or girl might look up at the silver blur and see Kirk Douglas, Katherine Hepburn, or Marilyn Monroe gazing back.

Once the media created celebrities—the evanescent cohort of people gathered from the stage and cinema, music, fashion modeling, and a variety of subsidiary industries—the traditional rich slipped into a most comfortable obscurity. In the 1970s, when burglars discovered their usefulness, even local newspapers stopped publishing the social notes that informed readers of local luminaries traveling away from home. Birth and anniversary notices disappeared, engagement and wedding announcements appear only in abbreviated format on Saturdays, and obituaries alone memorialize an earlier era focused on people who now never appear in the entertainment pages. Children who somehow elude the grasp of television find almost nothing in print media about the people earlier generations expected to read about daily. The rise of the corporate executive made possible the summer-long vacations by business owners who took the Bar Harbor Express with their families and disappeared for months. Similarly, the rise of the celebrity has made possible the near-perfect disappearance from public view of wealthy people who value leisure and privacy.

Long-distance luxury train travel enforced a state of being utterly different from the so-called *dead time* all but novice air travelers experience. Time aboard the de-Luxe, Chief, and Super Chief moved differently than time aboard lesser trains and—beyond the plate-glass windows—in small towns, great cities, and mountain chasms. In the Roaring Twenties, the heyday of private railroad cars, the rich reveled in downtime only scarcely more luxurious than that others enjoyed aboard luxury trains. For that matter, even schoolchildren reveled in comfort, if not luxury, aboard trains nearly as sumptuous as the de-Luxe.

But those children were preppies. Their existence haunts Fitzgerald's 1925 novel *The Great Gatsby* in ways that give public high school teachers fits: the fictional characters strike contemporary high school students as preternaturally mature. "One of my most vivid memories is of coming back West from prep school and later from college at Christmas time," the narrator recalls, remembering Union Station in Chicago at six in the evening, when "the murky yellow cars of the Chicago, Milwaukee, and St. Paul railroad looking cheerful as Christmas itself on the tracks beside the gate." Unlike the chaperoned children riding trains between East Coast cities and the camps of northern New England, the prep school students rode as adults. Twelve years and older, they rode to and from New England with élan. In those days, children traveled alone and luxuriously, aboard the Pioneer Limited at Christmastime.

The Pioneer Limited north from Chicago has remained Train No. 1 in the memories of many who rode it or saw it flash past as a flagship train of the Milwaukee Road. Leaving Union Station at 6:30

for Minneapolis, it paused at Milwaukee and thereafter only at Red Wing and a handful of other towns. Through what *Gatsby*'s narrator calls "the lost Swede towns" the train raced without stopping, its sleeping-car shades drawn as its passengers slept. Thirteen hours later, its passengers having breakfasted aboard or slept in, it reached Minneapolis.

As early as 1898, when the Milwaukee Road took delivery of new equipment for its new train, local and trade-industry journalists marveled at the experience of traveling in luxury. Interior decor harmonized from car to car in ways one writer decided had never been experienced by many passengers. Women preferred to visit in each others' compartments, but men often chose to gather in the lounge to read, enjoy a smoke and a drink, and sometimes the company of royalty. In 1902 Prince Henry of Prussia took passage aboard one section of the Pioneer Limited, by that time illuminated with electric lights seldom seen outside great cities. Competition forced the Milwaukee Road to constantly upgrade the train: seven trains left Chicago around dinnertime for Minneapolis. The Milwaukee did well in the battle for passenger goodwill by offering convenience, speed, and luxury. By 1914 the Pioneer Limited left Chicago most evenings with fourteen Pullmans, a lounge car, and a dining car.

Five other railroads offered service between Chicago and the Twin Cities. The Soo operated the Twin City–Chicago Milwaukee Express; the Minneapolis & St. Louis–Illinois Central ran the Twin Cities–Chicago Limited, and the Chicago Great Western provided its Great Western Limited. The trains paced the North Western Limited and the Burlington's Minnesota Limited. Overnight travel between Chicago and the Twin Cities proved so heavy and constant that many of the trains operated in multiple sections. The first section of the Pioneer, carrying mail cars, baggage cars, and coaches, departed five minutes ahead of the second, which carried luxury cars only.

Sleeping cars like the Oconomowoc, fitted with three drawing rooms and six compartments that could be connected privately for large families and "parties of friends," made some travelers choose the Pioneer. Minor amenities such as electric clocks, fans, and bedroom doorbells enhanced the deep, genuine luxury of beds, sofas, and private baths. Lone passengers, especially tall men, enjoyed the single rooms and private baths of another car, the Minnehaha, which provided beds six and a half feet long with deep box springs, thick mattresses, and silk spreads. The Minnehaha included an observation lounge with outdoor platform (for viewing the 140 miles of Mississippi River summer travelers enjoyed seeing before or after dinner), writing desks, and an enclosed, intimate women's lounge. For passengers not so interested in the passing scene, club cars like the Chicago, described by Arthur Dubin in *Some Classic Trains*, featured deep, leather-upholstered chairs for thirty-two people, a bookcase of novels and nonfiction facing its "library" section, writing desks, and a "lounging room beyond the buffet from which a steward served snacks and drinks." In the so-called public cars friends and regular travelers gathered, and strangers met other strangers. To encourage such encounters, designers made all furniture except sofas movable; stewards arranged chairs in clusters as groups formed, and separated them as people drifted off to bedrooms or to the dining car.

Food service meant food both extravagant and simple, as well as extraordinary personal service. In 1927 the Milwaukee named a new dining car Dan Healey, in honor of a longtime dining car steward who had died a year earlier. Healey had become an institution in himself, not only for serving nine presidents of the United States but also for remembering the tastes of regular passengers and providing free food to passengers whose taste he deemed needed broadening to include game, European delicacies, and regional fish. Healey and the Milwaukee Road prided themselves on meals besting any served in Chicago restaurants and hotels, but only by providing free side dishes could they convince many serious-minded travelers to experiment. Healey probably knew that many travelers confronted his menus with awe and chose the simplest entrees to be safe. His courtly service put everyone at ease, and his offering for free what he was sure passengers would like in addition to what they had ordered reshaped the palate of many travelers forever. Great Northern stewards and waiters were famous for introducing passengers to potatoes cooked in myriad ways, but Healey and his counterparts and staff focused on a wider range of dinner cuisine—served at ninety miles an hour.

Sleeping-car porters focused on everything else. In ordinary Pullman cars they made up the berths that folded out and up and down from large seats, hung the curtains that provided privacy, and during the night attended to passengers' wants, beginning with shining shoes. On luxury trains they turned down beds, brought food and drink from kitchens to passengers wanting privacy, and performed a thousand other services, from dispatching telegrams to bringing aboard flowers deposited at stations by florists following long-distance instructions. They watched over children and teenagers traveling alone, and often they looked the other away as participants in lounge-car romance strolled back to sleeping cars.

Until well after World War II, luxury train travel continued to advertise stark class division. In 1948 the Milwaukee Road replaced its earlier Pioneers with streamlined, all-room sleeping cars and diners, and into the 1960s the ever-faster train remained profitable. Travelers paid for luxury despite options of fine motorcars and highways and despite far faster airline service. But from the Depression era onward, luxury became increasingly difficult to advertise.

In the 1950s railroads discovered that luxury trains swept through a darkening tunnel of dislike. Motorists delighted with new Oldsmobiles or Lincolns refused to compare apples with oranges, and instead glowered at the streamlined trains racing past. In the postwar years when a new car and a small house on a small lot became what advertisers called "the American dream," the luxury train slithering through the distance smacked of old-money elitism, mass-marketing trickery, or both.

Racy pulp novels like Frederic Wakeman's 1955 *The Fabulous Train* slyly shifted settings backward into the 1930s. Hal, an underemployed college graduate in a Kansas small town, grows desperate to find a good job or enter graduate school. Selling Fords proves almost impossible in the Dust Bowl region, and local women seem less than glamorous. "Ph.D. or Rhoda?" Hal wonders as he waits for customers at the quiescent dealership. Then one day the Santa Fe Chief makes an emergency stop in a town through which it ordinarily passes at more than a hundred miles an hour. While its engine crew works feverishly to repair the locomotive, the passengers de-train to walk along the platform in blistering heat. "There ain't one chair car on her. You either treat yourself to a Pullman or you stay home. And honest to God, two dining cars. And wait'll you see the observation car, where they serve drinks and play cards," a friend bursts in to tell Hal. "And the babes. Hal, there's one blonde walkin' up and down the platform, you can see all the way down to her belly button." The young men drift down to the dusty depot, stare at the passengers, and then, ashamed of their own desperate curiosity, look in the windows at immaculate tables, roses in bud vases, and food they learn is "black bass and cantaloupe sherbert," the rarest, juiciest steaks, "exotic French sauces composed of mushrooms and herbs and butter and divers unpronounceable ingredients," and bowls of black Spanish olives and red raspberries resting on beds of cracked ice set in crystal bowls. Hal and his friends, all college educated and all unemployed or underemployed in a dusty town, gape at "the cargo of exotic humanity."

After the Chief departs, Hal slips into a depression that deepens by the hour, until the following afternoon he considers flinging himself under the westbound Chief. He jumps sideways at the last minute and gazes with longing at a little girl, watched over by a nanny, playing with long paper streamers on the observation car platform. The little girl waves and Hal determines to try his fortunes away from his dusty little town and brand-new Ford automobiles. No automobile will ever match the luxury of the Pullmans.

Like many other authors of 1950s racy fiction, Frederic Wakeman left the advertising industry but never forgot what he learned. *The Fabulous Train* focuses on the abyss between ordinary people like Hal and the people aboard luxury trains. It also emphasizes the staggering power of the close-up view. So long as it speeds through town at a hundred miles an hour, the Chief is scarcely real to onlookers. But when it stops, the whole town seems more grittier than ever by comparison. Everything, even V-8 showroom Fords and pretty girls, fades before the exotics strolling the platform and enjoying themselves in air-conditioned luxury. Advertising, Wakeman knew, might make a Ford desirable, but not if the Chief paused across from the showroom. The stopped train offered a vision more powerful than television.

Four years later Alfred Hitchcock released his box-office hit *North by Northwest*. Nowadays the thriller disturbs undergraduates who view it in film study courses or film festivals, even if they already know it in video format. Cary Grant and Eva Marie Saint still shock the sensibilities of young people. Their affair begins as effortlessly as the streamlined Twentieth Century Limited laps the miles from New York to Chicago. Close examination reveals that censors made Hitchcock dub lines: Eva Marie Saint is clearly telling Grant that she never makes love on an empty stomach, but the voice-over substitutes "discuss" for "make." Who is this confident, sexually free woman aboard the pre–feminist era luxury train? Why does Grant play an advertising man versed in "expedient exaggeration" but never lying? Such questions nag young viewers if they struggle past their awe at the set. Many do not. Too much happens in Room E, Car 3901.

Refitted in 1948 with lightweight cars that retained the splendor of past incarnations, the 1950s Century operated with all the luxuries serious travelers expected and many more. A train secretary, shower, lounge with bar, and other amenities remained after 1948, but radiotelephones, fluorescent lights, and automatic, push-button doors emphasized modernity. Nevertheless, luxury sixteen-hour overnight service between New York and Chicago, even when timed to connect with the Santa Fe Super Chief, no longer appealed as it had in the 1920s, when the Twentieth Century Limited often operated in seven sections chasing other named trains on the same route and preceding many more. As *North by Northwest* opened, the New York Central took the astonishing step of adding coaches to its finest train: the style Hitchcock depicted had begun to fade.

But neither automobiles operating on interstate highways nor competition from airlines instigated the decline of United States luxury trains. Instead, the culprit was the electronic media, especially television. Railroads and government regulatory industries kept long-distance passenger train service operating, but luxuries disappeared. First the barbers and valets vanished, then the ladies' maids, then whole varieties of cars. Tracing the disposal of luxury cars demonstrates that by 1960 luxury cars were migrating from railroads operating in television-rich regions to railroads operating in regions still lacking stations and reception. Millions of Americans stayed home and stared at screens, rather than experiencing glamour, adventure, and the exotics Wakeman described aboard the Super Chief. The New York Central sold Lake Shore and Atlantic Shore lounge cars from its Century to the Rock Island in 1959. No longer could the Central justify barbers and showers and lounges with bars in its premiere train, but the Rock Island running southwest from Chicago to Tucumcari, New Mexico, determined that it might. Television glamour had not yet spoiled the little Kansas towns of *The Fabulous Train* for enjoying luxury train travel. Where television came late, Americans continued to actively enjoy experiences; but eventually they too became passive, sofa-sitting watchers of the blue-light screen.

Television advertising began to subtly shift national priorities in the 1950s. Television skewed not just wants and values but the ability to analyze worldviews objectively. Network television lured more and more Hollywood cinematographers into making television shows: for two decades studios wondered whether movie-going would collapse as quickly as had luxury and long-distance train travel. Local cinemas survived the television onslaught only by shrinking seats and cutting amenities.

The television-Hollywood alliance quickly became a New York–Los Angeles one that stressed and then destroyed older regional ties, especially the north–south advertising link between Dallas and Chicago. Through the 1950s into the early 1960s, sunbathing women readers of racy novels like Wakeman's often wore risqué bikinis designed in Texas and marketed throughout a region reaching north to Chicago. Texas ranching and oil wealth produced self-confident, wealthy people who looked north to Chicago and Canada for recreation and business connections, and to Mexico and the Caribbean for fashion. But such older cultural axes collapsed in the face of New York–based network television news, entertainment, and advertising. Television extolled itself as travel while unconsciously defining real-world travel as short-distance, short-time effort. As media moguls based in New York and Los Angeles worked to ever tighter schedules and accepted transcontinental flying by necessity, television ignored situations it could not penetrate, luxury trains included. The makers of fast-paced television programming succumbed to a fast-paced, homogenized lifestyle that television glorified. Railroads lost not merely passengers devoted to regional style and even regional cuisine but also people who savored time, thought, relaxation, and a few hours or days swathed in luxury.

By the late 1960s America had become home to a vast middle-class peasantry easily led by advertisers. When the peasantry traveled, on business or pleasure, it often drove, using its own labor. If middle-class Americans flew, they carried their own luggage and accepted plastic tableware and microwaved meals, then sandwiches, then finally only snacks. And they hurried, always they hurried. Sometimes they hurried to Rocky Mountain ski resorts and other glamorous places developed with airline industry help, just as they hurried between hotels, and at the end of day stared at the same television shows they watched at home or in the motels at which they paused their cars. In 1970 Reuben Gronau reported in *The Value of Time in Passenger Transportation: The Demand for Air Travel,* that an entire population had learned to value speed of travel over all other considerations.

Advertising supporting the fast-paced programming of television in time made Americans want to speed through their business and pleasure travel alike, especially over long distances. Advertising encouraged Americans, via expedient exaggeration, to spend the time they supposedly saved watching more television, and more advertising. As Douglas Rushkoff explains in *Coercion,* millions of Americans now watch television in the evenings because they work such long hours in such high-stress environments that they are too weary to do anything else. For them, television is a window on glitz if not glamour. Never does the window open on how the rich and powerful really live at home, or how they vacation and travel.

Wakeman's *The Fabulous Train* still resonates today, for all that its raciness now seems tame. Wakeman knew that in tiny plains towns, the mid-1950s did not differ all that much from the mid-1930s. The Chief might still make an unscheduled stop and thrust exoticism onto Main Street; the Ford still had a V-8. By 1980 the Chief was gone, and nowadays small-town people have only televised images of glitz to replace the train's vanished glamour.

Nevertheless, they might watch the rails. Private cars still trail Amtrak trains and sometimes even freight trains. Some people still appreciate the leisurely mode of travel and understand the benefits of having time to think, to get to know business colleagues or would-be lovers—even to see the country. Few observers seem to really *see* Amtrak trains: to notice the private cars at their ends, off-limits to Amtrak passengers. But sometimes the people inside these private cars are looking over a region, often over a period of several days: contemplating how to change it to fit their personal interests, whether that means preserving it from sprawl or limiting access by common, automobile-driving tourists. Along tracks winding through scenic regions, rare observers understand that private-car occupants may want to know how the region looks from the rails, not from local roads.

As of old, private cars and luxury trains still offer the chance for prolonged interaction among like-minded groups and strangers. Americans no longer realize the energizing impact of prolonged chance encounters simply because they rarely enjoy them. The upper classes maintain exclusivity at yacht and country clubs, at private urban clubs, at hunting and fishing camps, and now and then ordinary middle-class Americans learn of these redoubts. But as anyone onboard Amtrak Acela trains may observe, people in first class seem to introduce themselves easily and to fall into conversation. Such encounters happen in first-class sections during international flights, of course, but even large aircraft offer little room for physical movement, and the noise of their engines is not conducive to conversation. The ordering of railroad space is subtly different, perhaps because it exists within a more measured temporal framework and offers a window on the passing scene. Just as ordinary commuter trains produce a relaxed camaraderie over years that helps individuals find new jobs, secure capital, sell houses, and so on, so the luxury train operating not just between cities but between cities, small towns, and wilderness resorts will provide something special for which some people already pay handsomely.

Will provide. Exclusive trains, if not exactly luxury ones, already roll. Acela offers an intellectual feast to any sociology-minded passenger, especially in first class. The train is relatively expensive to ride and its food service exorbitant, for all that the food tends to be good. When the train is not full, business-class passengers drawn to each other by visual cues—similar books, Blackberries or other wireless devices, even upscale shopping bags or European newspapers—often strike up conversations; they may change seats or walk to the snack car together for muffins or sandwiches or wine. The alert eavesdropper discovers that seat changes often lead to the exchange of telephone numbers or business cards. Certain recurrent phrases float through conversations, usually relating to the decided superiority of Acela trains over ordinary Amtrak ones or the freedoms offered by unassigned seats. Strangers remark to one another how discerning Acela passengers are, something that matters more and more as the sun goes down and windows become mirrors that reveal much about what money buys. Perhaps making connections among like-minded others matters a great deal to passengers in their twenties, not only in terms of career or business but socially. Acela rolls like a private club, its tickets the price of entry, and hosts a definable cohort of well-dressed, upwardly mobile men and women in their late twenties. Often they and other passengers voice their fervent wish that Acela operated on other routes as well: to Hyannis on Cape Cod, north to Portland, or southwest to Charlottesville or Williamsburg in Virginia, deep into the North Carolina mountains, or far into the Adirondack Park in upstate New York.

Acela service amply rewards close scrutiny. In the final analysis the trains move only marginally faster than the Metroliners the Penn Central Railroad operated between New York and Washington in the early 1970s. Only near Mansfield in Massachusetts and in western Rhode Island do the Acela trains reach 145 miles per hour; elsewhere they travel at little more than 110 miles per hour, just as the Super Chief and so many other trains did circa 1950. What proves intriguing about Acela has little to do with speed, but with exclusivity and frequency welded to comfort if not to luxury. Most Amtrak cars feature tiny windows and other airliner-like characteristics because 1980s industrial designers intended that trains resemble aircraft. Designers abandoned such thinking when they created Acela: the giant windows, the plate-glass partitions between cars, the wide seats and comfortable footrests, and other amenities immediately make passengers aware that the high-speed trains define a change.

Acela service is not Metroliner service extended beneath catenary to Boston. It is the first evidence that wealthy people might be willing to abandon both automobiles and airliners for high-speed travel over distances between about four hundred and five hundred miles, especially between suburbs, the precise distance Gronau discerned in 1970 as critical in air-travel marketing. Such people will not ride in ordinary trains moving at 125 miles per hour, but will nevertheless be drawn to amenities eerily reminiscent of those boasted by early 1950s streamliners, themselves based on upscale Depression-era trains. The large windows, indirect lighting, and extremely wide seats with generous leg room strike the young as a vast improvement over both ordinary airliners and Amfleet passenger cars. Design historians—and the elderly—recognize these features as 1950s retro despite the electric outlets installed for laptop computers. As metropolitan highways clog, and shuttle-service airline passengers complain about bus-service-in-the-sky inconvenience and rudeness from airline employees and Transportation Security Administration guards alike, marketing firms focus on people who *will pay extra* for short-distance rail services prototyped by Acela. Marketing research shaped the design of Acela equipment, right down to the extension of electrification from New Haven to Boston. Articles in the *Journal of Travel Research* and other periodicals emphasize the growing attraction of amenities other than speed. The attractiveness of rail-based comfort and luxury may chill both automobile manufacturers and airline-industry management: automobiles can scarcely cruise at 110 miles per hour, and airplanes, especially small commuter-type aircraft, can offer no luxuries at all.

Having separated their vacation regions from ordinary places, the rich now savor the exclusivity of some trains and begin to taste other advantages implicit in high-speed, extrafare, relaxing railroad travel. The widening gap between rich and poor in the United States is rapidly becoming a chasm, but most middle-income people prefer to ignore it, believing themselves established on the affluent side of the divide. They seldom question why the United States government directs Transportation Security Administration officers to move first-class airline passengers to the head of security lines, past hundreds of ordinary passengers who pay taxes too. Such favoritism allows the rich to arrive just before flights, rather than two or more hours early, and at busy airports now congests security operations. But airline coach passengers stand mute, defeated by wealth. On toll highways in New York, Massachusetts, and elsewhere, most motorists wait in long lines to pay tolls, while the more affluent use electronic devices to pay as they speed through reserved lanes. The rich have satellite phones, middle-income people have cell phones, and the poor discover almost no public telephones anywhere, even in cities. Just as Wal-Mart squeezes out stores catering to moderate-income people, leaving behind abandoned main streets and the empty boxes of its bankrupt competitors, while very profitable, upscale niche retailers prosper in wealthy communities, just as prices for ordinary single-family houses force more and more middle-income families into buying far out into exurban hinterlands, so Acela demonstrates that the rich and the expense-account-equipped business traveler have shoved Amtrak toward elite service.

Acela links places owned or visited by the rich and, through the Downeasters and other ordinary Amtrak trains, connects the rich with exclusive resort areas. Acela makes real estate developers wonder about high-speed, very comfortable, quite expensive trains operating to the Hamptons on Long Island and to dozens of other wealthy enclaves, even to the Maine coast, exactly as many Acela riders envision. State economic development officials admit, often on Web sites such as those devoted to the Downeasters, that real estate developers and passengers have begun to produce a revolution of rising expectations. Acela prompts scenario analysts, especially those retained by the California High-Speed Rail Authority, to imagine regional commuter rail transit authorities beginning to operate express, extrafare trains, and to rummage through old documents about the parlor cars once attached to Long Island Rail Road expresses. Railroad companies and taxpayers will upgrade existing rail lines and reopen abandoned ones, at first for regular freight and seventy-nine-miles-per-hour passenger service. Then—

and only then—will the first-class trains appear, deluxe in everything but name. The attack on Amtrak must always be understood in part as an attack by people committed to improving rail service regionally, not nationally. State and regional rail transit authorities might be cozened into using taxpayer dollars to restore rail routes of particular interest to the wealthy—and to those who intend to develop real estate for the small but growing number of young people becoming wealthy and wanting something other than televised glamour. *Building a High-Speed Train System for California,* a 2000 report by the California High-Speed Rail Authority, makes it clear that the envisioned ridership differs from that riding urban mass transit.

Interested observers in Vermont, New Hampshire, New York, and California have already realized this and have begun to map the old routes they want to restore for electrified service. Soon their counterparts in other states will discover that on the east and west coasts the rich have already begun abandoning highway travel for Acela and other fast trains. Perhaps the California High-Speed Rail Authority plans are the furthest developed of any state or regional entity, but the triumph of Acela and the documented successes of older luxury trains now come together in tightly argued scenarios. Clogged highways, straitened airline service, and an economic divide combine to make fast, luxurious trains something well-to-do people begin to desire.

SOURCES: W. J. Black, *Santa Fe de-Luxe;* California High-Speed Rail Authority, *Building a High-Speed Train System;* Dubin, *Some Classic Trains;* Gronau, *The Value of Time;* Machalaba, "Expensive Toys"; Morgan, "Ninety Miles an Hour Aboard a 4-6-4"; Rushkoff, *Coercion;* Wakeman, *The Fabulous Train.*

6

EXPRESS

At first a far-off speck of light, then a dark mass surrounding a probing headlight, the train hurtles along the main line toward the small-town depot. Its whistle begins wailing far off, warning that the train will not stop. The post office employee hurries back from one end of the platform, glancing over his shoulder at the small crane from which he has just suspended a large, rugged pouch. He makes sure no bystanders linger on the far end of the platform. The whistle wails, and wails again. Slowing only slightly, the gigantic steam locomotive slams past, and from a specially built railcar behind it, action blurs.

For a moment a man stands framed in a open doorway, a holstered revolver strapped to his waist. Then he heaves out a pouch identical to the one suspended from the arms of the crane. With a single fluid motion he swings up a great curved hook rotating on hinges. As one mail pouch slides along the platform the hook grabs the mail pouch from the crane, and the postal transportation clerk yanks it inside the car as the door rolls shut. It is 1891 or 1928 or even 1951, and this is how first-class mail moves. Swiftly.

Inside the car designated a railway post office, one or more of the thirty thousand railway mail clerks employed by the United States Post Office (now the Postal Service) in 1951 opens the collected pouch and begins sorting its contents, along with through mail from distant places and letters picked up a few miles back. As the train surges on, its engine men concerned only with safety and speed rather than passenger comfort, the mail clerks deftly sort the letters into pigeonholes, then grab and band letters for the next town ahead and stuff them into another pouch. The whistle screams its warning and alerts the mail clerks. The door slides open once again, the clerk leans outward against the safety bar and hook, and launches another pouch into small-town America as the great hook flings another inboard from another mail crane.

In West Texas and Kansas, in 1935, postal patrons expected rapid,

Restored small-town depots across the United States showcase the special doors and platform package wagons integral to express service.

acutely timed delivery of first-class mail. Unlike the local freight and passenger trains that stopped at every tiny town and water tank, unlike even the fast through freights and the long-distance luxury limiteds that usually paused only in large cities, the train most railroad companies and onlookers nicknamed the Fast Mail or the Mail and Express rarely stopped. Many rural dwellers never saw it stopped, or even slowing. The mail clerks aboard it sorted mail as it raced along, and Americans valued the regular, high-speed mail service it provided. Beyond that, it was usually a headlight, a passing roar, and a pair of red markers disappearing in the distance, and perhaps a whiff of coal smoke in the air.

In the depths of the Depression the fast trains demonstrated not only an efficiency that stimulated economic recovery but a nationwide evenhandedness. Across the High Plains, in Midwest farm country, in the timberlands of the Pacific Northwest and the Deep South, in the north of New England, small-town people appreciated the local significance of the mail trains linking great cities and tiny hamlets. The post office hurried for everyone, not just for the citizens of bustling cities.

When a letter positively, absolutely had to be delivered *the same day* up or down the line, it behooved farmers, storekeepers, and perhaps especially lovers to get that letter into the pouch to be hand carried by a local postmaster or other postal employee to the depot mail crane for pickup. Illuminated at night by kerosene lanterns or electric lights, mail cranes derived from the wedding of post office standards with manufacturing innovation. No amount of tinkering solved some problems caused by letters snatched from a standstill at sixty miles per hour or more (coins inside envelopes tended to break free), but the cranes made extremely fast service possible.

Not every letter arrived a few hours later in another small town further down the line. Many traveled across the continent, and many arrived in small towns aboard other mail trains. But always the United States Post Office emphasized the speed of the mail train. In the side of every railway post office car it placed an ordinary mail slot, so that anyone might post a letter directly into the rolling post office momentarily paused at a depot platform. Enthralled children watched as Railway Mail Service employees jumped down from some cars attached to passenger trains, dashed across depot platforms and emptied mail from mailboxes, then rushed back to the post office supplementing the one ensconced in a building a block or so away. The railway post office car attached to so many mail trains provided fast service, but as part of high-speed-mail-and-express-only trains it provided something verging on magic.

Operating as scheduled trains, usually behind high-speed passenger train locomotives and equipped with cars that resembled passenger coaches, mail trains rolled in quasi obscurity. Postal regulations forbade any railroad employee other than train conductors to enter mail cars, so brakemen and other train crew rode in lone coaches attached to the ends of most mail trains. Some railroads sold tickets to passengers in desperate need of quick if uncomfortable passage, but rarely mentioned the service in public timetables. Jolted and vibrated in a day coach lurching at the end of a mail train offered discomfort to be endured only in an emergency, but it introduced a few business travelers to a transport velocity that astonished riders of so-called express passenger trains that operated swiftly and comfortably.

Most important, it suggested to some urban businessmen what observant small-town residents knew. The Fast Mail and Express had vague but powerful implications for business development far from great cities. Its railway post offices and privately operated Railway Express Agency cars carried the potential for ribbons of industrial, commercial, and residential development.

One of the best-kept secrets in both the history of United States industrialization and in the present reorientation of United States real estate development, the smooth functioning of the Railway Mail Service and Railway Express Agency remains obscured by a byzantine mass of maps, schedules, and directives. Almost all the records of the Railway Express Agency, a continent-spanning company offering international service as well, vanished with its bankruptcy in 1975. Teasing out the ordinary activity of the Railway Mail Service and the Railway Express Agency proves maddening, until one applies computer software that integrates train movement, timing, and routing with geographic information systems analysis. Then from the detritus of government record keeping and fragments of

Express Agency records emerges what a number of interest groups understood, however vaguely, in the 1950s, as they lobbied Congress to emphasize highway- and airline-based mail and express shipment. In a way calculated to inflate urban and suburban real estate values and decrease the value of property in small cities, towns, and rural hamlets, special-interest groups championing what became the 1958 Transportation Act derailed the Fast Mail and Express.

Whatever its weaknesses, the century-old Railway Mail Service did much to equalize postal service across regions and stimulate economic development in and between large cities. Its activities grew more and more complex as public expectation of improvement increased. For as long as it moved mostly first-class and bulk mail, especially catalogs and newspapers, it worked extremely well. Only when Congress began nudging it to compete against privately owned express companies in the 1930s did it begin to falter. Railway Express moved even refrigerated packages with aplomb; the post office found moving packages slowed the movement of first-class mail. Parcel-post service led to other service delays, then crisis in the 1960s as the post office, operating its service at a loss, ruined the Railway Express Agency, whose cars helped subsidized the mail trains. Suddenly postal patrons demanded that the government provide package express service equivalent to the vanished Railway Express Agency standard. The post office failed.

Until the first years of the twentieth century, the post office required most rural and small-town residents to pick up mail at local post offices. Only in large cities did letter carriers bring mail to street addresses, a service expedited by Railway Mail Service clerks who sorted urban mail. Although the advent of rural free delivery slowly changed behavior nationwide after 1900, until then many Americans drifted toward downtown—or to a quiet crossroads—first thing in the morning, or soon after the mail train roared through. Businessmen checked their boxes daily, and even more frequently in towns served by several mail trains. Farm families and others living farther from town might check their post office boxes much less frequently, often only on Saturdays. Analyzing such behavior, one can understand how the mail train and post office collaborated to energize small towns. When people came to the hamlet or town or small-city center to check for letters and newspapers (the post office moved no packages), they also visited with each other, shopped, and transacted business in banks and elsewhere.

Railroad depots proved an important "elsewhere," since every depot housed an office of a private express company that handled parcels, crates, and almost any other object requiring time-sensitive shipping. Express companies, amalgamated in 1929 into the Railway Express Agency, offered pick-up and delivery services to street addresses and farms, but many Americans preferred to save local charges and visit the depots themselves. Even after 1912, when the post office launched its parcel-post service (which delivered small boxes along with envelope mail to businesses, homes, and farms), millions of Americans organized their personal and business activities around the schedule of the local Fast Mail and Express. Patterns of industrial, commercial, and office enterprise, including real estate investment, developed in the matrix of the ten thousand mail and express trains.

Federal favoritism ruined the symbiotic mail-express relationship immediately after World War II. As taxpayer dollars subsidized the carriage of parcels below the rates charged by the Railway Express Agency, and far below the actual cost to the post office, more and more shipments moved from express to mail cars. Between January 1949 and December 1950, Railway Express lost about eighty million shipments to the post office, which in 1949 admitted that parcel post operated at an annual deficit of $104 million and that the deficit grew worse each year. Post office employment burgeoned, absorbing many former GIs, but customers found themselves less and less able to ship large or odd-shaped packages, let alone livestock, canoes, and furniture. The post office limited the size and weight of parcels, but federal regulation required Railway Express to accept any item for shipment, even giraffes, as Klink Garrett, a former senior executive, details in *Ten Turtles to Tucumcari: A Personal History of the Railway Express Agency*. As Railway Express lost its most profitable items to the post office by the millions, its employees found themselves handling only objects—including explosive and flammable ones—the post office refused.

The Transportation Act of 1958 strangled the still-healthy long-distance business and real estate development channeled along the routes of mail and express trains. By pouring federal dollars, directly and via subsidy, into the airline and trucking industries, the act shifted taxpayer investment into the handful of metropolitan regions boasting large airports. Forcing the post office to fly more and more first-class mail along with premium air mail eroded the flow of mail via train, something that isolated millions of Americans—and especially businessmen—in what had been "well-connected" towns and small cities. Even into the 1950s, the Missouri Pacific (which operated many mail trains out of St. Louis) and other companies were investing heavily in new mail cars. Suddenly most of those cars sat idle, while the remaining ones moved mostly parcel post, so slowly that rural and small-town customers complained.

Intercity airliners did not stop or even slow down as they flew high above cities, towns, and hamlets withering along railroads. As railroad companies already struggling with diminishing income from Railway Express lost contracts to move railway post offices in dedicated trains and as components of passenger trains, they began eliminating trains in what became a headlong rush by the late 1960s. Around the year 1967 the matrix of railroad-routed high-speed mail and express shipment frayed just enough to precipitate a rapid collapse.

As the post office began moving mail by truck after 1958, and as trucking firms proliferated and competed with Railway Express, the movement of mail and package express, including frozen-food specialty items, began to slow, especially away from metropolitan regions. The Kennedy and Johnson administrations struggled with a worsening situation, but found no way to reverse it.

The Railway Express Agency filed for bankruptcy in 1975, just two years before the remaining United States Railway Mail post office made its last run between New York and Washington, D.C. Neither company nor government service benefited much from early computerization, perhaps because both seemed almost too complicated to computerize. But far younger competitors understood computer-generated scenario analysis from the beginning and quickly skewered a company and service seemingly frozen in the nineteenth century. Few in the 1970s glimpsed the latent power implicit in the Railway Express Agency and Railway Mail Service, or at least no evidence indicates what savvy investors discover decades later by carefully mining the rich ore of dusty schedules and processing the ore into gold.

Nowadays the public sees little United Parcel Service trucks scurrying everywhere in cities and suburbs, now and then dodging Federal Express and Airborne Express vans. Unlike United States Postal Service trucks, which follow regular routes, stopping at each green-painted urban mail storage box or at every rural free delivery box, UPS and other private-carrier express trucks have no daily routes, only patterns ordinarily discernible only to their owners. Most businesses and households receive first-class and advertising mail daily, but not every address hosts a UPS or FedEx truck every twenty-four hours. Legally known as express shipment carriers, the brown and gold or purple, orange, and white trucks seem anything but locally focused. But their heritage runs back to the local railroad depot, be it the immense Cleveland Union Terminal or a tiny wood-frame structure along a branch line.

Pickup trucks take their generic name from the flimsy vehicles farmers and storekeepers altered from Model T automobiles. Replacing the rear seat with a wood box enabled industrious businessmen to drive directly to railroad stations and pick up urgently needed shipments. In so doing they avoided delivery charges by large railroad-company-owned firms like Railway Express and by locally owned parcel delivery firms that operated in small towns and rural areas. A farmer wanted his shipment of newly hatched chicks or goslings as soon as possible, and storekeepers wanted perishable food and seasonal goods—especially at Christmas—immediately too. Picking up shipments at railroad stations spared them delivery charges, but it often meant shaving a few minutes or hours from a delivery process everyone knew as *expedited* or *express.*

First horse-drawn delivery wagons and trucks and then pickup trucks carried parcels, packages, and other express shipments to and from railroad depots. Rarely did they carry freight. Express shipment involved the dropping off, calling for, and pickup and delivery of goods as well as their expedited shipping. Freight involved merely the movement of products loaded directly by shippers and off-loaded by consignees. The distinction remains critical in any analysis of the wrenching spatial and cultural change just now emerging.

At a coal mine, employees of a mining company load a railroad hopper car with coal, and far away employees of a fuel dealer or electric utility unload the car into bunkers. The railroad company merely provides the car and its transportation once full, then removes it once empty. Freight rates reflect the simplicity of railroad company obligation, as does speed: many shippers trade very low rates for slow if certain delivery, especially of bulk commodities. But the storekeeper ordering a second shipment of popular Christmas tree ornaments telephones his order long distance and sets in motion a process different from freight. The ornaments arrive via Federal Express perhaps, not by freight train or 18-wheeler, pretty much as they did in 1935.

In the Depression the ornament manufacturer boxed the order while telephoning Railway Express, which routed a truck to the factory and collected the box. Moved by truck to the local express office inside a railroad station, the box began its journey by rail, often moving from one dedicated express car to another at junctions, until it arrived at the station nearest the storekeeper. From there, another truck delivered the box as one stop in a series of daily runs looping outward from the local railroad station with the arrival of each train. In rush situations, the delivery truck might go directly from depot to customer, and some shippers and consignees requested a telephone call to alert recipients to prepare for arrival of the shipment.

In the minds of individuals and families who traveled often, express shipment merged willy-nilly with baggage shipment, until by the 1930s many people scarcely distinguished between express and baggage services. The day before someone started a long railroad trip, a telephone call to Railway Express brought a man to the door to remove the trunk filled with clothes. When the traveler reached his destination, he found the trunk had been delivered the day previously. In 1900 all but the poorest American travelers expected to manage only hand luggage themselves, and red-capped baggage helpers at urban stations and Pullman porters everywhere assisted with that task. Steamer trunks and railroad trunks flowed into the hands of express companies and traveled as quasi-express shipments, but passengers persisted in calling them "baggage."

In the minds of customers, baggage might be refrigerators. Housewives knew that early electric refrigerators quickly disassembled into three components, the cylindrical coil at the top, the box-like chest, and the metal, legged base. Manufacturers produced such refrigerators so families could ask Railway Express employees to disassemble them, transport them a day ahead to summer homes, and assemble them (and plug them in) the day before families arrived. At the end of summer, housewives reversed the process. The trunk of summer clothes and the refrigerator left together, along with a canoe or rowboat or bicycles, and arrived together. Not surprisingly, most Americans understood *express* and *baggage* to mean about the same thing, since Railway Express Agency employees moved both. Whatever their legal definitions, express and baggage traveled in passenger trains, in special cars behind the locomotive, but some hand luggage not necessary on the overnight train moved in the baggage car too. Passengers aboard luxury trains expected Pullman porters to carry overnight cases to bedrooms and expected to find their hand luggage placed aboard waiting taxicabs at destinations. Women especially did not move baggage, luggage, or anything other than handbags. They no more thought about moving their own baggage than they did about moving coffins.

Corpses, or what railroad companies called *remains,* moved as express. But coffins usually moved by hearse to railroad stations, and undertakers helped express car employees load them, and unload them when they arrived at destinations. Nowadays few railroad museum visitors realize that the so-called baggage wagons that depot masters once pulled alongside baggage express cars stretch just long enough to carry coffins. Lugubrious ballads about widows and widowers traveling in trains carrying the remains of departed loved ones make clear the legal nuances of coffins en route. Like trunks with handles, coffins are clearly baggage, but they are boxes too, temporarily guarded by express messengers. Never are they mail, not even parcel post.

For decades, small and large shipments moved hurriedly via express, chiefly the Railway Express Agency, formed by a consortium of railroads in 1929 from a loose-knit group of competing express companies, including the famed Wells Fargo Company. In a symbiosis whose significance would be difficult to overestimate, the Railway Express Agency and the Western Union Company dominated most of the package and electronic message sending and delivery, their agents working out of most railroad stations, urban and rural. For decades, only Railway Express sold American Express money orders (in the Depression a hundred-dollar money order cost only twenty-four cents) and travelers' checks, causing many customers to cheerfully confuse the two firms. Into the 1950s manned Railway Express cars operated in ten thousand trains covering some 190,000 miles every day. As Garrett explains in *Ten Turtles to Tucumcari*, the local agents and the onboard express car messenger specialized in pets, flowers, and highly flammable nitrate motion-picture film, but they moved just about anything else shipped in haste: vegetables, human remains, dynamite, fresh oysters, automobiles, dishwashing detergent, and animals sent from one zoo to another.

Long before the amalgamation of regional express companies like Wells Fargo, Adams, Southern, and Pacific into Railway Express, the post office had not bothered with shipping packages. It could not compete with private-sector excellence. It carried letters, magazines, and newspapers, and until New Year's Day 1913 nothing much else: on that day it inaugurated parcel post, but for decades the service remained a political boondoggle. Stretched by funding rural free delivery, which it began experimentally in 1897 to bring mail to farm families six days a week, the post office viewed package shipping with suspicion. The express companies had made Sears and Roebuck, Montgomery Ward, and especially J. C. Penney successful beyond imagination. A farm family mailed a letter, often enclosing an express company money order, via the post office, but knew that the great retailers would ship goods via express. Railway Express frightened the post office simply by guaranteeing that any shipment would arrive anywhere in five days. Not surprisingly, almost all long-distance shopping meant mailing or telephoning an order and then either visiting the railroad depot express office or having the local Railway Express agent deliver the package.

Packages ranged from golf clubs (if not in boxes, then with all clubs tied securely) to live bees (shipped in special crates in which queen and bees drank sugary syrup); from live hogs (in special crates that enabled the hogs to lie down) to butter, cream, and dressed meat (carried in refrigerated lockers), and human ashes (moved in safes that carried cash, and treated as shipments of cash); from explosives to whiskey to guns to gold nuggets. Larger packages included prize racehorses, and special shipments ranged from a collection of half a million butterflies to the Smithsonian from Decatur, Illinois, to a meteorite from Paragould, Arkansas, to McPherson, Kansas. All animals moved in cages fitted to provide food and water, and dogs often moved with their leashes so that express messengers could exercise them, and express messengers and agents summoned veterinarians when they noticed animals ill. Ordinary live fish moved in water changed every three hours, but live tropical fish received far more delicate treatment, since the agency had to maintain water temperature according to shipper instructions.

Express company bulletins and other ephemera clarify how shipper instructions dovetailed into company practice. Moving racehorses meant bringing 175 horses from Kentucky to a race in Juárez, Mexico, in 1915. Moving seafood involved constant icing and extremely rapid handling, and moving flowers meant thousands of special movements for special occasions. When a new furniture store opened in Flint, Michigan, in August 1925, the American Express Company delivered twenty thousand roses for the occasion. Moving caged pet parrots required separation from caged shipped cats, whose presence annoyed the birds. For perhaps fifteen years after 1915 (most records are lost), Wells Fargo moved automobiles as both express shipments to auto dealers and as baggage for luxury train passengers who wanted to find their own cars waiting for them at distant destinations. Just as the Eastman Kodak Company located its film-processing facilities on high-speed mail and express routes (before it invented easily removable spool film, Kodak had camera users ship whole cameras for reloading), so other companies discovered how the matrix of mail and express routes made cities like Lynchburg in Virginia spectacular places in which to do business.

Perhaps J. C. Penney understood the relationship of the post office, express companies, and Western Union best. In ways that anticipated experiments by his competitors, he juggled catalog sales and retail stores. Fairmount, Minnesota, proved a superb location for a new J. C. Penney store in 1925, in part because catalog customers who received Penney merchandise extremely quickly guaranteed product loyalty from opening day, something American Express pointed out in its November company bulletin, the *Express Messenger.*

In a way vaguely resembling contemporary disputes about the impact of Wal-Mart on small-town Main Street stores, between about 1890 and 1950 the express system sometimes focused public attention on competition and choice. A farm family or small-town resident might buy locally, but almost all might choose to "mail order" from the great urban catalog merchants or from advertisers in national magazines. Small-town retailers emphasized personal service against the range of items and sometimes lower cost of the catalog companies, but thoughtful Americans understood the personal service provided by the local Railway Express Agency agent too. Almost always one of the most respected businessmen in any small town or suburb, part of an extremely sophisticated company of national and international reach, he spent decades not only receiving and shipping packages but building demand for a service that often functioned better than a well-oiled machine—simply because the agent often anticipated client needs. A good agent not only moved money for bankers, dogs for hunters, and specialty paper and cardboard for printers in a desperate hurry, but constantly visited business owners to solicit business by understanding special needs. As he learned the needs of his customers, the customers often found themselves pleasantly surprised, as when the agent made a special, no-extra-charge delivery to a distraught farmer needing a part for a broken tractor in plowing season.

By the 1940s, however, the post office increasingly dominated the moving of ordinary small packages, leaving Railway Express to move the trunks of summer campers and Scouts heading to jamborees, the surge of Christmastime boxes, and seasonal rushes, especially of fresh fruit sent as gifts, along with all the difficult shipments, especially fresh seafood. Despite successfully entering the airline express market in the 1960s, by 1972 the company, by then renamed REA Express, had watched its overall shipments drop to half of what it moved in 1965. In 1925 so many American Express Company cars moved daily between Washington, D.C., and Cincinnati that the Chesapeake & Ohio Railway dedicated an entire train, No. 101, to fourteen of them. By 1965 the Railway Express Agency moved so little express that its cars scarcely subsidized the passengers in the coaches and sleepers behind. The agency crashed into a series of corporate scandals, deficits, and intense competition from United Parcel Service, Federal Express, and Emery Worldwide, and most railroad companies dumped their remaining passenger trains into the new Amtrak. Only two years after its founding in 1973, Federal Express found itself competing against a bankrupt Railway Express Agency. A firm that once prided itself on its on-time performance and sparkling clean railroad cars, offices, and trucks vanished completely a few months later, and even its records disappeared. In Alvin Toffler's *Future Shock* terms, the nation reacted with amazement or indifference and sometimes annoyance: no longer could it easily ship pets, pianos, canoes, and hundreds of other awkward items. Klink Garrett, who finished his career in upper management at Railway Express, observes that Federal Express prospered by focusing on the on-time performance and personal service that Railway Express once championed, while moving only envelopes and small boxes. UPS, from its beginning in the 1960s, prospered by moving slightly larger boxes. No upstart company moved racehorses or antique tables bequeathed by distant great aunts, let alone items nowadays almost impossible for individuals to ship—windsurfers, surfboards, and personal watercraft, for example. Federal Express and UPS avoided rail transport totally, and moved almost effortlessly into airborne shipping.

Understanding the flow of mail and express via train nowadays means assembling several classifications of data, almost none available in libraries and archives. Much of the government information is virtually unobtainable because officials considered it so ephemeral that they regularly pulped it. A fierce interest in efficiency, combined with efforts at preventing mistakes, forced employees of both the Railway Mail Service and the Railway Express Agency to destroy tariffs, general directions, and schedules the moment they became outdated. But something more than antiquarian or hobby interest explains the surprisingly vigorous acquisition of such documents on eBay and other Internet auction sites, and by secondhand booksellers acting as agents. Assembled, oriented, and analyzed by software focused on mobility across vast regions, the data provide a reasonable sketch not only of a long-gone national landscape and an economy still not accurately understood but also of possible prototypes for the futures currently in the design stage.

Today, regular mail is growing less and less important, although Netflix and other companies demonstrate that locating warehouses near regional post offices means next-day delivery at first-class rates. Faxes and e-mail devastated the overnight document-delivery express business in the early 1990s, but the volume of package shipments continues to grow, driven in part by Internet-based online ordering. Detailed analysis of how objects once moved in a specific region consequently suggests scenarios involving a future beyond Wal-Mart, Netflix, and contemporary express delivery services.

In 1935 some forty-six mail trains arrived and departed Kansas City, Missouri, six days a week; many operated on Sundays too. Analyzing the operation of only a few means finding arcane, ephemeral books, the most important of which are two published by the United States Post Office Department, *General Scheme of Kansas, 1935* and *General Scheme of Texas, 1935*. These now-rare volumes lack much value until collated against two other, even rarer books printed in 1935 by the General Superintendent of the Railway Mail Service: *Schedule of Mail Routes No. 513, Seventh Division, Kansas and Missouri* and *Schedule of Mail Routes No. 294, Eleventh Division, Arkansas, New Mexico, Oklahoma, and Texas*. All are public documents, but only the former originated in the Government Printing Office; private printing companies in Fort Worth and St. Louis produced the latter. None is much use without a copy of *The Official Guide of the Railways* for 1935—a privately produced, ephemeral tome printed on high-acid paper that self-destructs—or without detailed period maps identifying railroads by name. Since some mail trains carried no passengers, the *Official Guide* makes no mention of them. Any inquirer hoping for completeness must also obtain 1935 employee timetables for the several railroads over which certain all-mail-and-express trains operated. Finding the raw material of historical analysis proves almost mind-numbing, since all the documents changed at least yearly, and sometimes more frequently, and employees tended to follow orders and discard them. But the documents enable the sketching of a long-forgotten but extremely efficient mail and express system.

Railway Mail Service route numbers rarely corresponded to train numbers issued by individual railroads. Without employee timetables, contemporary researchers have difficulty learning when mail trains blasted past small depots, depositing and collecting mail on the fly. The Railway Mail Service focused on speed and precise rendezvousing at junctions, where trains met to switch entire carloads of through mail or to exchange one or more pouches. The Railway Mail Service expected promptness at waypoints too, but announced such times to local postmasters and Star Route Rural Free Delivery carriers, assumed railway mail clerks knew the sequence of drop-off/pickup points and whether or not their train was on time or late, and knew that railroads forbade trains to pass waypoints ahead of schedule. What the post office designated the *general scheme* of mail routing, pickup, and delivery in any of its geographical districts originated around and depended on railroad routes and schedules. But this scheme evolved into a complex matrix managed wholly without computers and completely understood by no one, including the postmaster general and the CEO of Railway Express. Nowadays discernible only in documents like the 1938 post office publication *Instructions and Rulings with Reference to Transportation of Mails by Railroads,* the complexity involved minutiae such as the problem of balancing the flow of railway post offices in holiday seasons and the importance of junction cities.

More or less by happenstance, the complexity made Kansas City and other cities surprisingly important, especially in the first half of the twentieth century. Just as Lynchburg proved an exceptionally busy passenger train junction, so Kansas City served not only a broad range of passenger trains but also a swarm of mail and express trains, all of which "worked" some mail in addition to carrying pouches of through letters, sometimes enough to fill entire storage cars. Working the mail meant that clerks sorted letters as the trains moved, "setting up" mail for waypoints (most of them too small to require stopping the train) as well as for points beyond the Seventh Division (Kansas and Missouri). Aboard some trains, clerks sorted mail by street so that city-based mail handlers could move it directly into the hands of individual letter carriers. In a way, the mail and express trains not only made Kansas City important but became the tentacles of something that might be called "Greater Kansas City." Instead of sprawling spatially across rich farm country, Kansas City spread its influence via mail and express trains.

Some trains left Kansas City westbound for a run that the post office designated the Kansas City & Albuquerque Railway Post Office (RPO). Most of those trains operated as segments of Chicago–Los Angeles runs that originated and terminated in Railway Mail Service divisions beyond the Seventh. RPO 7 left Kansas City at 10:00 in the morning along the main line of the Atchison, Topeka & Santa Fe Railroad; it worked mail for Colorado, Kansas, New Mexico, Oklahoma, Texas, Arizona, and California, and as it streaked across the plains its clerks worked local mail via street address for the city of Albuquerque too. At 5:35 it arrived in Dodge City, Kansas, where it paused to load and unload mail, some of it for Bucklin, twenty-seven miles southeast on a branch of the Chicago, Rock Island & Pacific. But Bucklin, a very small town indeed, also lay on the main line of the Rock Island Road, which carried other mail trains focused on Kansas City, mostly ones operating beyond Tucumcari over the Southern Pacific to El Paso. RPO 3 departed Kansas City twenty minutes before RPO 7 and ran roughly parallel west-southwest, giving Bucklin direct access to a national mail train route and tangential access to another extending northwest to Dodge City and from there directly to Chicago and Los Angeles. At 8:32 every weekday morning and at 6:03 every weekday evening, westbound RPOs paused at Bucklin; eastbound service halted at 11:59 and 7:30. But Bucklin also received and sent mail via Dodge City in the north.

Today Bucklin is home to 725 people living in 338 houses. The town covers about half a square mile and is slowly growing: contractors build about one new house each year. The median age of the residents is about thirty-nine years, and the median income $51,400, with a range of less than $10,000 to greater than $200,000. The average house value is approximately $50,000, slightly less than the median income. Bucklin is not exactly easily accessible, but State Highway 54 is certainly well paved and well maintained, as is State Highway 154, which links Bucklin to Dodge City. While a first-class stamp costs the same in Bucklin as anywhere else, real estate is inexpensive; many inhabitants of Bucklin own houses that cost approximately one year's income to purchase. But mailing a letter or package from the village is not exactly simple, although Bucklin boasts a pleasant post office on South Main Street. Mail is carried by truck nowadays, not by mail train.

If mail still moved by train, Bucklin might be remarkably well connected, for the Union Pacific Railroad bought much of the bankrupt Rock Island. Today the main line on the northern edge of the town is still a major Kansas City–El Paso route, and the branch line to Dodge continues to run too, as the Buckhill & Western, a freight-only short line. As in so many small towns in the center of the continent, the post office, stores, and houses of Bucklin abut a highway that parallels a railroad track. Across the Union Pacific main line is only Highway 34 meandering northwest through farm country to Dodge, itself paralleling another railroad, the Buckhill & Western. Bucklin is not on the main road to anywhere, but it is likely to be on the main track to a future already emergent in northern New Jersey, around Houston and Galveston and, especially, near the Port of Los Angeles, where imported goods jam wharves and warehouses.

Manufactured items need to be delivered from factories and from ports of entry. Items manufactured outside the United States arrive at only a few ports and must be distributed from them. The gridlocked confusion of northern New Jersey, apparent to any motorist on I-95 approaching the George Washington Bridge from the south, resembles that of other ports that will be analyzed in a subsequent chapter. But the port concentration that strangles adjacent highways energizes inquiry into distribution networks that once reached everywhere in the United States.

United Parcel Service embraced a new realization two years ago. It increased the upper weight limit of any single parcel to 150 pounds. Interested parties focused on the competition Amazon. com offers to independent bookstores have observed that UPS is a major player in shipping books from regional warehouses and widely scattered secondhand booksellers. But the chief opportunity opening to investors lies not in moving small parcels such as books but in shipping larger and heavier cargo, say household refrigerators.

Often consumers purchase new refrigerators in a hurry, perhaps in the wake of some domestic disaster, as steak and ice cream thaw. Newlyweds tend to accept whatever refrigerator the landlord provides, and buyers of houses often buy refrigerators in situ or have time to pick out specific ones. Redecorating sometimes influences refrigerator purchase. But usually it is refrigerator failure that sends homeowners scurrying to the nearest appliance store. The Web might offer a broad choice in refrigerators someday, but only if on-line ordering means ultrafast delivery.

Refrigerators, washing machines, and other "white goods" move in special boxcars. Hy-Cube cars are taller than most boxcars because appliances are not particularly heavy and most stack reasonably well, if crews follow this-end-up directions accurately. A fifty-foot Hy-Cube boxcar towers over a line of ordinary boxcars by four feet or so of extra height. Just as the height of the typical dishwasher now governs the height of the typical kitchen counter everywhere in the United States, the height of appliances governs the shape of the boxcars designed to transport them. But white goods move as freight, in bulk, in trains rumbling along at forty-five miles an hour. Appliance wholesalers want on-time delivery, but are in no particular hurry.

Stalking United States appliance manufacturers is the specter of Asian competition. Already pioneering in low-voltage appliances for yachts, gigantic recreational vehicles, and wilderness hunting cabins, Asian manufacturers experiment with appliances that might operate off solar-charged batteries, windmills, or other environmentally friendly technologies. But true competition lies in Asian expansion from television and computer manufacturing into mainstream 110-volt appliances. Comfort-zone air-conditioning units (which supplement window and central-air units) may be the beachhead of invasion, but perhaps the great thrust will involve electric stoves. Today Asian-built appliances must move through existing appliance distribution networks, but tomorrow they might not.

Suppose a customer in Bucklin ordered a new refrigerator from a retailer in Kansas City. In 1935 the night mail and express train left Kansas City at 11:55 PM and arrived in Bucklin at 8:32 the following morning. Today, given a similar train operating on the same schedule, a customer might order via the Internet until about 10:00 in the evening. The retailer would move the perfect refrigerator to the express company's loading dock at the Kansas City station, and the following morning an express agent would off-load the unit, deliver it, and set it in place, removing the failed refrigerator and consigning it for recycling. Nothing much futuristic shapes this scenario. Railway Express agents routinely delivered and installed refrigerators; for that matter, they installed the monthly refill bottles of fancy urban dishwashing liquid 1930s small-town housewives enjoyed.

Tweaking the scenario produces an assortment of potential variations on the theme. The local agent might be someone holding a franchise, not a Railway Express employee; after all, the 725 people of Bucklin might not justify a full-time agent. The refrigerator might begin its journey somewhere other than in Kansas City without adverse consequences; if the customer ordered before noon, it might arrive from El Paso by 7:30 the same day. Or maybe private investors will buy the already quasi-privatized United States Postal Service and merge it into some overarching express company. In 1929 the railroad industry created the Railway Express Agency from a half-dozen successful express companies: why not combine UPS, FedEx, and the USPS?

Only at first glance does such a scenario appear outlandish. Few would argue nowadays that moving the mail, especially first-class letters, remains so critical to a free and independent republic that only the federal government can undertake the task. For most Americans and corporate entities, Federal Express provides the security and privacy required for urgent mail delivery. The quasi-public Postal Service has moved with much success away from 1960s difficulties similar to those that destroyed the Railway Express Agency, and now often strikes customers as a private company. Yet despite its accomplishments and tremendous power, its 800,000 employees labor in a workplace shaped by the 1960s restrictions that empowered Federal Express, UPS, and other contemporary competitors. Just as Congress slapped a seventy-nine-miles-per-hour speed limit on passenger trains after World War II, so it hampered post office innovation with the Transport Act of 1958.

As Comarow demonstrates convincingly in *The Demise of the Postal Service?* in the 1960s the post office was more ineffectual than the Hudson & Manhattan tunnel railroad. Political patronage and archaic regulations had almost strangled the department even as it faced stiff private-sector competition. Reform proved partial, leaving control of wages and—ominously—health insurance and retirement benefits in the hands of politicians. Just as 1995–98 changes to the Internal Revenue Service resulted in a precipitous drop in corporate and upper-income audits, so-called reforms still pull Postal Service employees, especially managers, in two ways, forcing them to be both entrepreneurial and bureaucratic. Nowhere is this split more clearly revealed than in the way urban and regional planners think about post offices themselves.

Party-line followers across the design professions champion the location of post offices downtown, on small-town main streets, anywhere they might revitalize business or invigorate "smart growth" efforts. The United States Postal Service, in the eyes of designers, planners, and real estate developers, exists first as a government force that maintains or raises real estate values in "traditional" settings. Never mind that downtown post offices prove poorly accessible by trucks, lack expansion room for automatic devices, and, at least sometimes, lack room for additional employees to accommodate growing business. No one says much about the location of regional distribution hubs by Federal Express, UPS, and competing firms, which choose sites based on accessibility, land cost, and potential for growth. Increasing efficiency in the Postal Service often takes second place to a plethora of half-stated, vague, and sometimes secretive goals of private parties anxious to manipulate public goods for private ends by insisting that post offices be sited according to 1930s memories of Main Street and mail trains.

The Postal Service maintains offices in most municipalities, and in rural areas operates so-called Star Routes along which farmers and other customers can buy stamps, money orders, and so on from rural free delivery carriers. The RFD box mounted atop a post remains an American icon, but it receives little scrutiny from a public that expects to pay extra for Federal Express to pick up an envelope. The Postal Service carrier stops whenever the box-owner raises a red flag, and a Star Route carrier charges nothing extra for picking up a box, bringing it to a rural post office for weighing and postage, then bringing a bill the next day for payment the day after. Federal Express and UPS charge for pickup services, and expect on-the-spot payment from private citizens; neither firms extends credit to individuals in the time-honored way of RFD Star Route service. Rural Americans sometimes marvel at city-only USPS services like special delivery, and urban Americans marvel even more at farm families putting out unstamped letters for pickup. The Postal Service practices widespread spatial discrimination under a pall of so-called universal service; most of the discrimination dates to the mail-train era and its immediate aftermath. As Comarow suggests, only lately do private investors think about picking the profitable parts of the system and leaving the taxpayer responsible for unprofitable rural and wilderness service.

Imagining postal service as it worked in 1895, when private express companies carried all packages and the bulk of expedited mail, and when small-town and rural residents expected to pick up mail at post offices, offers a ready-made scenario for a privatized Postal Service.

If the Postal Service sold stamps only from vending machines as strategically placed as those selling Coca-Cola, and contracted the shipping of packages to strip-mall stores like Mail Boxes Etc. or even Dollar General, it might lay off many employees and pass savings along to customers. Shopping carts fitted with scanners that record the price of each item enable supermarket customers to avoid lines at cashier-staffed and self-checkout registers; grocery store innovation may shape postal operations. Senders might pay lower postage for items delivered to boxes rather than street addresses; recipients might pay less postage on items mailed from gas stations, conve-

nience grocery stores, or other businesses willing to subsidize postage costs in return for increasing customer flow. Whatever Postal
Service unions think of such scenarios, no one doubts that a soft-
drink-like vending machine might have a slot in which a customer
could place a heavy envelope, drop in some change according to an
electronically displayed message, and hear the machine whine or
click as it postmarks the letter. The technology seems available. But
in the end, moving mail proves far more complicated than it looks,
in large part because of hidden subsidies to airline companies. Magazine publishers ship issues from the United States to Canada by international air mail rather than by surface mail, simply because air
shipment is cheaper. Changing almost anything about the system
produces serious anger, and not just from employees fearing closed
post offices. Raising stamp prices, ending Saturday delivery of mail,
even removing less-used urban mailboxes prompts customer protest, and direct-mail advertisers protest most loudly of all.

Some nine million Americans work in the so-called mailing industry. Advertising mail, often dismissed as "junk mail," produces
a huge chunk of Postal Service revenue while prompting some recipients to buy products, sometimes shipped by mail. Essentially,
the USPS subsidizes mailings by nonprofit organizations, most
of which pay only about 60 percent of the rates charged to for-
profit firms. College alumni magazines, hospital fund-raising bulletins, hobby-group newsletters, and much other material travels
extremely inexpensively. Indeed some analysts argue that bulk mail
both subsidizes first-class postage rates and keeps many post offices
from incurring losses that now trouble sixteen thousand small-
town post offices. In the end, junk mail postage is priced according
to decades-old political agreements, and as the nation shifts toward
e-mail communication the Postal Service faces a serious dilemma:
whether or not to continue universal service.

Already many Americans accept rural free delivery and short-
ened post office hours even though they are aware that big-city post
offices stay open later. A first-class stamp buys more or less service
and convenience according to location, and even now express mail
does not serve every post office. Special delivery remains an urban
amenity. But at some point Postal Service losses mean the market

pricing of all postage and the loss of some or all service to certain localities. Does the population of Bucklin, Kansas (725 people), justify a full-time post office, let alone door-to-door mail delivery?

Exploring the symbiotic relationships among a railroad station agent, a Western Union operator, and a Railway Express agent circa 1935 may prove suggestive. Do citizens really need daily delivery of mail? How much will they pay for it in the near future? Could other options—say weekly delivery—prove more efficient? Imagining a transformed Postal Service may involve imagining corollary changes that increase the value of small-town centers, hamlets along railroads, and nascent logistics technologies such as those transforming supermarket shopping.

Throughout the 1990s strange silver boxcars trailed many Amtrak passenger cars. So-called merchandise cars offered a long shot at additional revenue: Amtrak trains would move packages, newspapers, and other time-sensitive lightweight goods under regular contract. The service originated in early Amtrak efforts to duplicate older Railway Express Agency successes, and throughout the 1980s wavered between success and failure. On-time performance problems routinely crippled attempts, and Amtrak ran over too few routes anyway. Its present matrix is less dense than the 1965 passenger train version that proved too thin to maintain Railway Mail and Railway Express Agency service. Beyond that, when the service did succeed, Amtrak faced a problem it only half expected: more express cars meant heavier trains, and thus the necessity for more locomotives. But it is the merchandise cars that deserve the closest scrutiny.

They evolved not so much from old Railway Express Agency cars but from innovative boxcars that appeared in freight trains as early as 1979. Formed as a subsidiary to the Trailer Train Corporation in 1974, the American Rail Box Car Company at first produced fifty-foot-long boxcars fitted with ten-foot-wide doors, one on each side. As more and more shippers used forklift trucks and other mechanized devices to load the cars, materials handling experts realized that as employees filled cars with cargo the loading devices had less and less room to maneuver. In order to speed loading, American Rail Box Car began adding a six-foot-wide door to the left of the larger one, making a sixteen-foot-wide opening for loading equipment. Such innovation not only made boxcar loading far more efficient than the loading of 18-wheeler trailers but made investors think. Clearly such a car might carry express and containerized mail in passenger trains, for machines might load and unload parts of its cargo in a minute or two at any passenger station.

Amtrak and its shippers saw the first merchandise cars as potential alternatives to trucks. In at least some small towns, the one train each way attracted just a bit more than passing notice day after day. Obviously, passengers rode in the coaches, in the dining cars, in the sleeping cars; even children saw them. But the silver boxcars rolled in mystery, and at least some people in the for-profit realm grew thoughtful about the shipping of packages, larger items, even mail. If mail arrived in the silver cars, the post office might remain downtown, albeit perhaps near the abandoned or geriatric railroad depot. Here and there a city councillor or business-boosting activist considered the innovation and envisioned a future quickly discovered to be grounded in the past. Elsewhere, not only in small towns but in large cities that were once hubs of rail passenger service, experts in materials handling, automated warehousing, and time-sequenced delivery glimpsed in the silver cars a potential.

Always the investigation slows at the byzantine sophistication of the old mail and express train matrix. Computer-assisted analysis demonstrates repeatedly that if the matrix existed today, the Internet would make possible extraordinary changes in shipping time-sensitive items. As more people rely on e-mail, even to pay bills, the Postal Service more clearly understands the looming crisis involving flying first-class mail. The volume of first-class mail shrinks and drives up the cost of a first-class stamp in order to pay airline charges, pension contributions, and other costs. Immediately ahead lies a break moment remarkably similar to that created by Congress in the 1958 Transport Act. Just as Congress wrecked the for-profit, taxpaying Railway Express Agency with parcel-post service, then pulled first-class mail from railway post offices, then finally ended domestic air mail, so the Postal Service realizes that flying first-class mail will soon become prohibitively expensive. Utility companies and other firms will respond by charging customers more to receive paper bills delivered by mail, and soon companies will surcharge customers paying by check. Most banks no longer mail canceled checks to customers, and many Americans grudgingly accept it. But all such effort merely postpones imminent catastrophic change that begins to interest long-range investors wondering whether the United States Postal Service might be privatized, perhaps along railroad routes offering services in need of private subsidy.

A matrix of mail and express trains offers an alternative to a retail market dominated by Wal-Mart, shopping malls, high-end urban stores, and Internet sites. If Kansas City and other cities extended their spheres of influence, but not their physical fabric, then living in Bucklin and many other small towns might become highly desirable. People might move to places situated along flows of information and goods alike. Real estate investors examine places like Bucklin now not for what they are but for what they will be—based on what they were decades ago, and on plans made long ago but never realized.

In 1930 the Pennsylvania Railroad, already determined to compete with the fledgling airline industry, began surveying its main line between Harrisburg and Pittsburgh as the first step toward electrifying service. Despite the curving grades that carried track over the Appalachians and steam locomotives pulling trains west of Pittsburgh, the company believed that electrification might produce twelve-hour service between New York and Chicago. The Pennsylvania Railroad undoubtedly thought of its Broadway Limited and other luxury trains in beginning its pre-Depression research. But the company must have realized how well train No. 11, the Fast Mail, might compete with airliners unable to deliver and pick up mail at intermediate cities, or to sort mail en route. A two-cent stamp on a letter mailed in New York before 5:00 on any business day would buy next-day delivery in Chicago, and in Salem, Canton, Massillon, Orrville, Crestline, Bucyrus, Lima, and Fort Wayne too. In 1930 neither the Post Office Department nor the airline industry knew how to deliver air mail, let alone first-class mail, that promptly. But the brand-new Railway Express Agency, amalgamated from a collection of smaller express firms, understood the implications for *next-day* delivery of packages ordered from New York department stores. Mail and express movement, not the transport of passengers, focused railroad executive attention to innovation as late as 1960, and it focused shipper attention forever after that.

The whistle of the Fast Mail echoes now in the minds of readers of a plethora of magazines deserving wider notice: *Parcel Shipping and Distribution, International Railway Journal, Materials Handling Management, Logistics Management, Warehousing Management,* and *Industrial Distribution.* For the historian, the whistle recalls mail and express delivery in a time before metropolitan sprawl and traffic jams, especially those caused by long-haul large trucks. For the investor, especially the venture capitalist scrutinizing high-speed freight trains carrying only UPS trailers between great cities, it produces ideas. It might be possible to bypass local liquor stores, provide prescription medicine or organic produce in exurban or rural areas, supply small manufacturing plants, deliver automobiles, and compete with Wal-Mart Supercenters in ways that reinvigorate downtowns and boost the value of undervalued real estate, especially that away from highways. After all, they have the example of the UPS train before them.

SOURCES: Canton, "Fight for Survival"; Comarow, *The Demise of the Postal Service?;* Garrett, *Ten Turtles to Tucumcari;* Hediger, "New Railbox ABOX Boxcar"; Lamson, "Catching and Throwing the Mail"; Long and Dennis, *Mail by Rail;* Railway Mail Service, *Schedule of Mail Routes No. 513,* and *Schedule of Mail Routes No. 294;* United States Post Office Department, *General Scheme of Kansas, 1935; General Scheme of Texas, 1935;* and *Instructions and Rulings.*

Ordinary freight trains roll along routes still emblazoned with long-gone corporate names; such routes often carried passenger trains on timetables freight trains will soon duplicate.

7

FAST FREIGHT

Cabooses disappeared in the 1970s, a few years after mail trains rolled into oblivion. Freight trains rumbled on, but older Americans saw them as sentences without periods. For generations, the little box-like cars, most surmounted with cupolas and painted red, punctuated the rear end of freight trains. For parents stuck at railroad crossings teaching young children to count freight cars, cabooses marked the end of the arithmetical exercise. A stubby red or yellow caboose rolled past the crossing signals, a denim-clad man waved an apology for the delay from the cupola window, and the train was gone. In daytime a pair of red flags whipped from the ends of the caboose. At night a pair of red lanterns glimmered in the dark.

Today an electromechanical device replaces most cabooses. The Federal Rear End Device, christened "Fred" by railroaders, rides atop the coupler of the last car, constantly monitoring air-brake pressure and transmitting data to the locomotive engineer. Its blinking red light warns following trains that ahead of it rolls a freight train. But Americans in their forties and older see the modern freight train as somehow incomplete without its trailing caboose. In the past it housed brakemen sleeping in bunks, conductors cooking breakfast over potbellied, coal-burning stoves, men swinging down from platform steps, lanterns slung from elbow crooks. Fred replaced cabooses as United States heavy industry changed forever in ways that disconcert middle-aged people.

Engineering experts in the 1970s envisioned trains that needed no humans at all. Unionized employees shook their heads, but research rolled on. Fred had climbed aboard like a hobo in the dark, and had somehow hired on for good; a high-tech revolution had begun to transform transportation, but almost no one noticed anything other than cabooseless trains.

Children don't miss cabooses, for they rarely see one anywhere. What people do notice, often while sitting in traffic, is that freight trains roll faster than highway vehicles and carry 18-wheel truck trailers. By the middle 1990s politicians in many states had begun to consider whether truck traffic ought to be diverted onto railroads in order to ease traffic congestion. As Richard Saunders reports in *Main Lines: Rebirth of the North American Railroads, 1970–2002,* using computer-generated scenarios, railroad management looked ahead and discerned to their consternation that train movement already approached track capacity and, depending on short-term economic ups and downs, would choke sometime before 2010. Converting from double-track to single-track main lines, ripping up sidetracks, eliminating steeply banked, high-speed curves, and abandoning secondary routes to nature trails had produced a situation unknown to most Americans, even to stockholders and shippers. The 2003 nationwide shortage of train crews attracted little media attention, but it confirmed management's understanding and strengthened the hand of those railroad executives who saw the situation as pregnant with opportunity. Railroad companies now move according to a new vision grounded in hard-fact reality, and they intend to prosper, not by bringing back the caboose, but by playing piggyback.

Company public-relations officers use *intermodal freight* to designate rail carriage of truck trailers and international shipping containers. Railroad employees call such carriage *piggybacking,* and freight trains dedicated to such service *pig trains.* Often rolling faster than Amtrak—and far faster than 18-wheel trucks on interstate highways—many pig trains carry not just freight but mail and express. West of the Mississippi, young children on coast-to-coast auto trips might ask parents about the freight trains that parallel the interstate but run at speeds above eighty-five miles per hour. The creaking, swaying freight train of 1980 now outpaces the family minivan.

South of Kansas City long-haul trucks throng I-35. As Larry McMurty eloquently points out in *Roads: Driving America's Great Highways,* the trucks diverge from east–west I-70 for the run south to the Mexican border at Laredo. More than the North American Free Trade Agreement sparked the staggering truck traffic on I-35. NAFTA merely codified a fact known to industrial analysts since the 1980s: Mexico had become a great industrial power, in part by avoiding many of the antipollution, workplace safety, and wage-guarantee laws enacted north of its border. A vast flow of manufactured goods moves into the United States not only through Atlantic, Gulf, and Pacific ports but from Mexico, and while much of the flow bifurcates at Kansas City to the east and the west, much of it continues north into Canada. The highway impact of Mexican and Canadian industrial and population growth is blatant and grim. I-35 south of Kansas City carries a stream of heavy trucks that unnerves automobile drivers and annoys residents, chambers of commerce, and especially tourist bureaus. But the stream threatens the financial health of the trucking industry, too. On I-35, as on I-90 in northern Ohio, I-95 between Connecticut and Maryland, I-40 in east Tennessee, and the interstate highways merging in coastal California south of San Francisco as far as Bakersfield, trucks run into jams that destroy schedules.

Modern fast freight trains, especially pig trains, seem fast streaming across the High Plains, but they madden urban motorists stuck in traffic jams. Silver commuter trains flashing to and from great cities inhabit a perceptual otherworld psychologists study too infrequently. Motorists, even those stopped in traffic, somehow fail to realize the speed and implied convenience of the trains they might board. But they seem to notice speeding freight trains.

Reaching south from Kansas City runs a powerful railroad. The Kansas City Southern (KCS) terminates in Port Arthur, Texas, on the Gulf coast, but in Shreveport, Louisiana, its main lines branch east to Jackson, Mississippi, and Mobile, Alabama, and west to Dallas. Marketing agreements with the Burlington Northern Santa Fe (BNSF) and the Canadian National–Illinois Central extend KCS's reach across the whole of the United States west of the Mississippi, and north from New Orleans to Chicago, and from Chicago north across the whole of Canada. But what fuels KCS's growth lies south: the Grupo Transportación Ferroviaria Mexicana, a large chunk of which the KCS owns, and whose operations integrate with those of the KCS. The TFM rail routes reach south from Laredo and Brownsville and converge at Monterey in Nuevo León to run south to Mexico City via San Luis Potosi and Querétaro. Branch main lines extend to Tampico and Veracruz on the Gulf and Lazaro Cárdenas on the Pacific. The TFM connects with another KCS affiliate, the

Tex-Mex Railroad operating between Corpus Christi and Laredo, just north of the international border. In the near future, KCS may merge all three railroads into a new firm tentatively called NAFTA Rail—a railroad with the potential to reshape the commercial landscape of the middle United States.

From 1998 through the end of 2001, KCS-TFM cross-border traffic grew at an average of 9 percent annually, but in 2002 that growth rate doubled to 18 percent, and in 2003 it grew to 25 percent. Despite the intricacies of accounting in two currencies (the Mexican peso devalued in 2002), cross-border traffic produced a 44 percent growth in revenues in 2003. The rise of Mexico into a global industrial power shipping a massive volume of product to the United States—and through the United States to Canada—is transforming the KCS, but in part because the KCS passed through the 1960 to 1990 period as a most conservatively run railroad. Unlike so many competitors, it invested heavily in track and locomotive maintenance, and so found itself superbly positioned for radical economic change.

The KCS is scarcely backward. It leads its industry not only in safety but in technological innovation that betters its positions with connecting railroads. Its Meridian, Mississippi-to-Dallas main line, recently termed "The Speedway" in company advertising, now boasts more remote-controlled power switches (with more being added) and alignment reconfigurations such as the one at Vicksburg, where the company broadened a tight curve to permit higher speeds. The Meridian–Dallas route moves time-sensitive intermodal freight between the eastern seaboard region served by the Norfolk Southern and the immense western region—including the Pacific Coast—served by the BNSF. The KCS route enables its two partners to avoid the delay-prone rail hubs in Memphis and New Orleans. For KCS stockholders, the Speedway demonstrates how efficiently a well-maintained main line can be upgraded quickly and economically to a higher-speed one that attracts traffic; then further upgraded to one permitting much higher speeds that attract even more traffic, especially that formerly moving via truck. For state, regional, and city planners and for economic development agencies, the Speedway slams home the lesson that a rail connection can emerge from relative obscurity almost overnight and put Meridian, Mississippi, on a high-speed corridor with international connections and implications. The KCS Speedway exists wholly to move intermodal cargo units off Interstate Highway 20. Its pig trains compete directly with trucks. And they win.

Understanding the KCS Speedway in the context of its Mexican connections leads the inquirer to the discovery that the KCS is converting a redundant Kansas City air base into a United States Customs preclearance facility. The KCS intends to use the new facility to expedite the movement of intermodal shipments from Mexico, Latin America, and the Caribbean, and to merge its shipments of new automobiles and light trucks with its intermodal operations. Already the KCS ships Mazda automobiles and Ford pickups built in Kansas City, but its management also realizes how many finished vehicles move north from Mexico, built with parts the KCS rolls south from the upper Midwest. Several trucking firms already contract with KCS to move trailers along the Speedway. Thus brand-new Mazdas and Fords whiz parallel to I-20 faster than speed limits permit motorists to drive the vehicles after purchase.

Watching a KCS Speedway train or examining a map of its route leads one to wonder about the long-term impact on communities and businesses centered on, for example, Memphis and New Orleans. At 10:15 every evening in 1935, the KCS swept Railway Post Office 15 south from Kansas City on its 822-mile run to Port Arthur. At Shreveport, the train halted to move mail to connecting trains on the east–west main line now operating as the Speedway. The brief pause at Shreveport remains a footnote in the history of postal service until some real estate developer—perhaps a warehouse or factory locator—happens to consider the significance of the transfer for municipalities like Poteau or Howe in Oklahoma, Vicksburg in Mississippi, Monroe or Ruston in Louisiana, or Marshall or Longview in Texas. Those places are served by I-20, so perhaps any change might be gradual. But no interstate highway reaches southwest from Shreveport to Lufkin, Texas, for example, although the Union Pacific serves that city. Like Lynchburg, Virginia, Lufkin sits far from congested interstate highways, but on a main line that might make the Speedway not just a fast route but a shortcut of significant implications.

Railroads compete with each other as fiercely as they compete with the trucking and barge industries, but for decades that competition scarcely focused long-range rural, metropolitan, or even urban planning. The KCS Speedway links the Norfolk Southern and the BNSF, to the disadvantage of the Union Pacific. If the Union Pacific acquired the KCS in a merger, Lufkin might be transformed as rapidly as Meridian is transformed today. Too many intellectuals still conceive of trains in terms of boxcars, not "double-stack pigs" outpacing trucks on I-20 and other highways. The boxcar era is gone, although specialized Railbox, Hy-Cube, and other boxcars still move important, high-value freight. Intermodal freight boxes carry much of the present, and will move most of the future.

A year after Southern Railway No. 8 rolled out of Lynchburg as a one-coach train departing a platform built for multiunit locomotives hauling fifteen-car long-distance streamliners, F. C. Margetts, a British transportation expert deeply involved in creating the European piggyback system, warned that piggybacking would either transform North American railroading or that freight trains would almost disappear.

As early as 1961, experts knew the United Kingdom rail network faced calamity, but not until the British Railways Board released *Reshaping British Rail* in 1963 did investors and railroad executives begin to consider rail transport as an alternative to highway building. At first glance the nationalized British rail system scarcely seemed a role model for anything: one-third of its tracks carried only 1 percent of the total ton-miles of freight, nearly half of its freight stations produced only 4 percent of the freight traffic, and most of the rolling stock creaked along in decrepitude. The short runs of most British freight trains had produced a situation in which most of the 450,000 freight cars moved an average of sixty miles a week. A nation roughly the size of the state of New York demonstrated beyond argument that highway freight movement outperformed rail service, especially over short distances. Tractor-trailer trucks, what the British call "articulated lorries," competed in ways that presaged their success in the United States.

But British trucks jammed British roads, especially in cities, and choked ferry ports opening on the Netherlands, Ireland, and France.

As Britain prospered from increased trade with the Continent and with Ireland, its roads and ports began to jam in ways that predictably infuriated motorists and shippers.

Presciently, the British Railways Board realized the potential implicit in intermodal container shipping. Since 1926 British railroads had experimented with containers, and by the 1950s Europeans saw British Rail containers on trains as far east as Italy and Sweden. In 1933 the International Container Bureau began standardizing rail containers, something the postwar International Standards Organization (ISO) accelerated. Despite wartime destruction and postwar problems with shipping to Communist countries behind the Iron Curtain, container traffic increased slowly, and the nationalization of British railroads in 1948 did little to bolster innovation. By 1960 management realized that the containers were too small, that they often merely replaced boxcars in the minds of shippers and railroad executives alike, and that the total volume of shipping meant that containers traveled on flatcars hauled in ordinary, slow-moving freight trains. In order to save itself from oblivion, British Rail focused on intermodal shipping as the best chance to increase revenue. Its directors believed that in so doing they would ameliorate the growing congestion of highways, especially in urban and rural areas attractive to tourists.

By 1965 British Rail had begun to experiment with a new concept in freight trains called "Liner Trains," a name soon changed to "Freightliner." Linking Glasgow and London, the trains operated as semipermanently coupled strings of flatcars on which British Rail loaded the eight-by-twenty- or eight-by-thirty-foot containers it or its shippers owned. Bypassing railroad yards and operating on strict schedules, the trains carried containers as passenger trains carried people. A shipper reserved a space on a given train, brought his container (as a box sitting atop a flat articulated lorry trailer) to either terminal, and a crane swung it aboard a train guaranteed to leave and arrive at specific times. In 1966 the trains carried 27,000 containers; two years later they moved 281,000 and by 1973, 634,500. When the energy crisis spiked the price of highway fuels in 1974, volume shot up to 711,400, and by 1975 the Freightliner trains, operating between twenty-nine terminals linked by seventy-five routes (including ports for Irish and European ferries), had proven a success. ISO-compliant shipping containers and scheduled trains open to any shipper had created an integrated system in Britain, and prompted Spain to establish a nearly identical system.

Eleven years after British Railways inaugurated Freightliner service, Margetts, a former director, envisioned standardized containers moving swiftly across all of Europe. The technology would transcend political division: by 1976 East Germany, Czechoslovakia, and other Soviet-bloc countries had expressed interest in the intermodal revolution. But Margetts saw far further around the curve of time. The Soviet Union moved 80 percent of its freight by rail, much of it over electrified routes; it offered a magnificent opportunity for containerized service itself. But as a land bridge to Asia, its Trans-Siberian Railway opened directly on the manufacturing enterprise of South Korea and China and, via the port of Nakhodka, Japan. Given improved political situations, manufactured goods might move swiftly from Asia across the Soviet Union to western Europe, Britain, and Ireland, and perhaps from the British Isles to Halifax in Nova Scotia.

More than many observers suspect, Freightliner service did much to stimulate the development of the European Union. It focused capital on tunneling beneath the English Channel, and it transformed ferry service across the Baltic and the Irish Sea.

The fragmentation of the Soviet Union and the continued intransigence of North Korea still partially offset the vast manufacturing capability of China. Routing containers from Japan via Nakhodka still competes unfavorably with sending them via container ship. But the extraordinary railroad revolution that began about 1960 in Great Britain continues to shape both private and public policy there and across Europe to South Korea. Operating freight trains as scheduled vehicles onto which any shipper may load a built-to-standards container has not only proved profitable for shippers and railroad companies but also enabled governments to embark on social improvements. In 2005 Britain determined to reduce truck traffic by one billion lorry trips per year. Such decisions depend on an efficient rail system that can easily absorb increased traffic.

Since 1960 many Americans have become familiar with British

and European train service as users of tourist rail passes. College students, vacationers, and senior citizens discover what business travelers find: passenger trains run on time and usually frequently. Without such rail lines and their once- or twice-a-day trains of intermodal containers, remote regions dependent on tourism would be marred by truck traffic. The quaint English or Scottish village, the remote Danish inn, or the river valley German town in which tourists relax, visit historic sites, and shop benefits from both passenger train service and a freight train that passes at the same time each day. A bit of noise, a bit of blur, and the train is gone. The tourist haven becomes quiet, and perhaps the occasional American tourist realizes what is missing: trucks.

By the late 1970s a British firm had perfected a truck trailer equipped with a pair of small lifts that enabled a lone lorry driver to park parallel with a railroad flatcar and slide an ISO container box between vehicles. Blatchford Stack Cranes moved both forty- and twenty-foot-long containers with ease, adjusting for uneven heights between parking lots and railroad sidings. Stack cranes freed shippers from using transfer terminals. In particular, they enabled rural and wilderness shippers to make full use of intermodal cars in low-traffic locations that failed to justify the installation of permanent transfer equipment. Blatchford Stack Cranes offered remote regions in Britain and Europe intermodal shipping and freedom from long-distance truck traffic. One local trucker owning a flatbed truck equipped with such units might move dozens of containers to and from flatcars stopped on an ordinary railroad siding, but the truck itself would never venture far from its home neighborhood.

American railroads began experiments earlier than their British counterparts, but for decades their efforts floundered. In the first years of the twentieth century, the Long Island Rail Road tried moving loaded farm wagons directly into New York City: horses traveled in special boxcars, and once in the city farmers hitched the horses to wagons and proceeded to hawk vegetables on residential streets. Not until 1926 did the Chicago, North Shore & Milwaukee experiment with moving loaded truck trailers aboard flatcars in a manner based on circus train experience. However cumbersome—tractor-trailer drivers had to back up ramps and then along the tops of a line of flatcars, unhitch tractors and drive forward, freeing a path for the next driver in line, a process repeated in reverse at the delivery point—by 1956 truck trailers had begun to move coast-to-coast aboard American freight trains. From the beginning, rail experiments clashed with efforts to move truck trailers on barges and riverboats, an effort begun by Seatrain Lines, Inc., in 1929. The opening of the St. Lawrence Seaway in 1959 profoundly altered the mindset of manufacturers and shippers, who suddenly discovered Cleveland and other Great Lakes cities to be international seaports. For twenty years after 1959, most American transportation experts assumed that entire truck trailers would be transported by rail, river, and sea pretty much as they moved over the road. They would "roll on/roll off" railroad cars, barges, and ships, and perhaps even airplanes, a concept backed by a military anxious to move matériel as rapidly as it did motorized equipment.

Roll on/roll off, quickly designated RORO by its advocates, proved far more time-consuming that anyone first guessed. Loading twenty trailers from the end of the last flatcar in a string meant the first trailer might back three-fourths of a mile along the flatcars, a tricky, slow operation. Then each truck trailer had to be chained down, again a slow and labor-intensive task. When the train arrived at its destination it had to be oriented to permit truck tractors to back up a ramp and remove the trailers one by one. Despite some innovations, especially a hydraulic hitch that moved upward from the floor of the flatcar and securely grabbed the truck trailer, and clawlike devices that picked up entire truck trailers and moved them to and from flatcars, railroad company enthusiasm for moving truck trailers atop flatcars fluctuated.

In the 1950s the New York Central developed its Flexi-Van system, apparently because the low tunnels and bridges east of Buffalo precluded moving truck trailers towering atop flatcars. Essentially a hydraulic-powered swiveling flatbed trailer that shoved containers to and from specially equipped flatcars, Flexi-Van proved an efficient innovation. One truck driver would back his rig at right angles to a flatcar, and in less that two minutes transfer and secure the box. Sending the box alone, minus frame and wheels, offered many advantages. Lowering the center of gravity increased safety and permitted higher speeds, and reducing the profile of the loaded car decreased wind resistance, especially by eliminating air eddying beneath trailers. Shipping only the box meant sparing the bearings on the truck wheels left behind: stationery truck trailers bounced on their springs aboard moving flatcars, ruining wheel bearings designed to bear weight while rolling. Finally, eliminating wheels, rear bumper, and other impedimenta reduced weight and so lowered cost. A handful of Flexi-Vans moved onto Santa Fe, Milwaukee, and Illinois Central rails, but the boxes were useless without the custom-designed truck trailers and flatcars.

Inquiry into United States and Canadian efforts to improve piggybacking after 1955 reveals strenuous if extremely competitive and counterproductive effort. The Pennsylvania and Southern Pacific focused on long-distance trailer-on-flatcar (TOFC) movement, while the Canadian Pacific experimented with a container-on-flatcar (COFC) service it called Portager. TOFC required heavy, specially built flatcars eighty-seven feet long that carried two forty-foot-long trailers. COFC efforts proceeded in fits and starts, especially since Canadian advocates experimented with lightweight, four-wheel (instead of the standard eight-wheel) flatcars. Despite the collapse of Canadian Pacific efforts in the early 1960s, that railroad envisioned matters far more clearly than did most United States firms. From the beginning, it embraced a vision of passenger trains that included a few lightweight flatcars from which standardized containers could be transshipped in two- or three-minute station stops. Small towns and isolated depots in Manitoba, Alberta, and other sparsely populated provinces seemed ideal candidates for transshipping containers in very simple, quick ways, perhaps by using old school buses shorn of their bodies. The Canadian Pacific was familiar with the latest thinking in Great Britain, too. In 1961 it shipped a Portager container loaded with peanuts from Montreal to Liverpool, and brought it home filled with auto parts that then moved by rail to a factory in Ontario. But in the same year the limited-access highway between Montreal and Toronto opened, and trucking firms focused on driving rather than shipping trucks. The reluctance of United States shippers, transportation firms, and government regulators to accept ISO-mandated containers undoubtedly contributed to the slow growth of intermodal shipping of all sorts into the 1980s, but even the Canadians confronted difficulties of scale and integration.

Always the military focus on RORO technology stymied advocates of other systems, especially COFC ones. As late as 1977 one industry expert lamented that United States shippers often insisted on putting truck wheels beneath containers sent by rail, simply because rates proved lower that way. As Seatrain Lines and other freight-forwarding companies experimented with dedicated trains modeled on British Freightliners—Seatrain Lines operated COFC trains from Weehawken, New Jersey, that linked United Kingdom shippers with California destinations—politicians discovered the pain of change. Longshoremen unions, shipping companies, and warehouse firms in New Orleans complained to the Federal Maritime Commission that the dedicated trains had diverted ships from that port to Weehawken. Suddenly a modest experiment—Seatrain Lines chartered one train a week—produced major dislocation in New Orleans and other ports, just as other experiments in moving containers from Long Beach in California galvanized groups elsewhere along the Pacific seaboard. Retrospect suggests that military thinking underlay much railroad industry confusion. A major TOFC company, North American Car Corporation, moved with dispatch toward nationwide RORO service. Its CEO, a general formerly in charge of the United States Army Corps of Transportation, understood the powerful attraction of a truck trailer delivered ready for the road—by rail.

As early as the 1950s a compromise vehicle emerged, a truck trailer fitted with both rubber tires and steel wheels. On the highway, it performed essentially as an ordinary trailer; on the rails, it coupled with identical trailers and, with an adaptor, to any locomotive or freight or passenger car, although its builders preferred that the cars operate in homogenous trains. Invented by the Chesapeake & Ohio Railway as a way of moving time-sensitive freight in passenger trains, so-called Railvans had almost vanished by the 1960s. Not until the 1980s did they reemerge, chiefly as experiments, and by 2000 they had begun operating in once-a-day dedicated trains between San Bernardino, California, and Chicago, with connections there for New Jersey. The Railvan itself morphed into the contemporary RoadRailer; no longer must it carry its steel wheels when it moves over the road. Triple Crown, a private company equally expert in trucking and railroading, operates the fleet that moves over certain routes the company calls "lanes." The BNSF Railroad discovered in its Ice Cold Express service between Southern California and Chicago that refrigerated, air-ride suspension RoadRailers rarely damaged vegetables and fruits. In 1982 the Illinois Central Gulf learned that the close-coupled, air-suspended sinuous trains operated over the curvy, hilly track between Louisville and Memphis at higher speeds than TOFC trains managed. For very time-sensitive, delicate products, and for paper and other tougher shipments, Road-Railer offers an alternative competitive with long-distance trucking. No longer does the railroad company need a special flatcar and terminal: the container uses steel wheels, and drops them when it connects to the eight rubber-tired ones that convert it into a truck trailer. A truck driver need only back his trailer onto steel rails embedded in asphalt to convert it into a railcar. RoadRailer is RORO technology with a twist, and the twist makes it competitive with newer COFC technology.

Over long distances, stacking ISO forty- and forty-five-foot-long containers one atop another proves extremely efficient. Although the Southern Pacific Railroad bought the first double-stack cars in 1981, it was a steamship company, American President Lines, that sparked a revolution by buying its own cars and asking railroads to bid on their operation between Los Angeles, Seattle, and New York via Chicago. By ordering train schedules around ship sailings, American President Lines produced a means of moving ISO standard containers at speeds comparable to those offered by trucking firms. Sea-Land, a global freight company, quickly copied the idea and launched dedicated trains from Tacoma in Washington to Chicago. It found the service so useful it purchased its own rail terminal for New York service, at Little Ferry, New Jersey. As double-stack service spread to other port cities, especially older ones like Boston, Philadelphia, and Baltimore, railroad companies again confronted the low bridge–low tunnel problems the New York Central faced in the 1950s. But by the late 1980s railroad companies foresaw serious profit, and began raising bridges and tunnels—or depressing tracks to accomplish the same gain in height. In some instances, government agencies such as the Port of Seattle, mindful of business lost a decade earlier when ports were bypassed by Seatrain Lines experiments, encouraged railroads to begin double-stack service. By 1986 Burlington Northern operated six trains of double-stack cars between Seattle and Chicago. Today anyone who glances at a mainline track sees double-stack cars, usually in special, fast-moving trains.

Just over a mile long, carrying two hundred containers (each about forty-five feet long), and able to move easily at seventy miles per hour or much faster, double-stack trains offer a special advantage to railroads: they halve the number of trains or lengths of trains. Their chief efficiency lies in fitting two hundred containers on a sidetrack that otherwise holds a train of one hundred. Whatever the other advantages of double-stack technology, limiting the need for more passing sidetracks is perhaps the greatest, although halving train crews cuts costs as well. As traffic booms, no train crews are laid off: others must be hired and trained. Almost certainly the heavy machinery needed to unload the double-stack cars remains the chief disadvantage. At urban terminals the machinery moves with impressive quickness, but no one dreams of unloading a double-stack car at a rural depot. Double-stack containers are not express, even if they move fast.

Consequently, the Amtrak experiment in moving RoadRailers as components of passenger trains intrigued many rail industry watchers, as Cody Grivno reported in a 2003 article describing the units and their use. In 1986 Amtrak formed a subsidiary, Amtrak Express, to improve its movement of express and mail. By 2002 the Amtrak rail yard at Lumber Street in Chicago had three tracks embedded in asphalt for the making up and breaking down of RoadRailer trains to be attached to Amtrak passenger cars. Yet at the same time, Amtrak had moved away from carrying mail and packages in special boxcars. The difficulty Amtrak faces is simple: its trains run too infrequently. Just as a once-a-day passenger train invites few riders, so the same train lures few shippers to desert trucking companies. And Amtrak almost certainly runs its trains too slowly, something that railroad companies discovered in the 1990s when UPS and other time-sensitive shippers suggested innovation beyond anything Amtrak accomplished. Amtrak struggled to make its RoadRailer service profitable and even changed train schedules to suit shippers, in ways that angered passengers and eventually prompted them to avoid trains.

Frequent, reliable, very fast TOFC or COFC service intrigues UPS simply because it intrigues other firms. Slicing a full day from coast-to-coast shipping schedules might give UPS a powerful edge over its many competitors. Railroads consequently experiment when asked, and trial runs of so-called bullet trains demonstrate the feasibility of four-day transcontinental movement of truck trailers and other containers by rail—in freight trains.

In 2003 Fred W. Frailey, editor of *Kiplinger's Personal Finance,* published an hour-by-hour account of one experimental run. His detailed story in *Trains* focuses on four days following the 4:30 AM departure of a test train on March 5, 2002, along the main lines of the BNSF and CSX from Los Angeles via Chicago to Little Ferry, New Jersey, just outside New York City. The readership of *Trains* is chiefly a mix of professional railroaders of all ranks and amateurs deeply interested in contemporary railroading. But it includes another component: investors who read the magazine to help make sense of what they find in company annual reports and other industry documents and what they glimpse in the larger landscape.

Glimpsing the test train meant not blinking. While never running above seventy miles per hour, the train slowed only in a few places, and then not for long. Its owners expected it to operate 3,154 miles in sixty-five hours, with part of it splitting off just south of Albany to run to the UPS central New England sorting facility in Worcester, Massachusetts. It succeeded. But its dash across the continent, along with other experimental high-speed dashes by other trains, produced more proof that existing equipment and track can move freight easily as fast as 18-wheel trucks operated by two-person crews in sleeper-equipped cabs, and with a bit of improvement, far faster.

Overtaking slower trains proved a major difficulty. Even on double-track stretches fitted with switches operated remotely, some other fast freights had to slow in order for the very fast train to pass. Chicago-area track work slowed the train, simply because in fifty-six miles it rolled over eleven crossings of other railroads and through six junctions, and a one-mile section of track limited to ten miles per hour. For a few miles it operated over the Indiana Harbor Belt Railroad (a line that exists chiefly to move strings of cars from one railroad yard to another), which cooperated fully in getting the train to Blue Island Junction, where CSX tracks begin. From Los Angeles to New York, however, the problem of overtaking trains vexed dispatchers. Trains moved west on parallel tracks, and only rarely did the fast train affect them as dispatchers now and then shifted it onto west-bound main lines in order for it to pass slower east-bound trains in a tightly controlled game of dodgems. Frailey articulated the crucial difficulty: no longer did the railroads operate high-speed passenger and mail-express trains that long ago intertwined among the freights. Employees had the skills to manage the movement of a very fast train, but they no longer had the extra passing tracks from the streamliner era.

After the 1970s, eliminating cabooses meant that on long sections of single track not controlled remotely, pulling a mile-long freight train into a passing siding involved someone having to climb down from a stopped locomotive and open the track switch, then wait until the train rolled into the siding before closing the switch and *walking a mile back to the locomotive.* After another train had passed on the main track, the same employee then opened the switch ahead of the locomotive, waited while the engineer pulled the entire train onto the main track, then closed the switch and *walked another mile forward to the stopped locomotive.* What had been accomplished in 1920 with whistle signals, arm waving, and—at night—swinging kerosene lanterns between locomotive and caboose had by 1990 become so cumbersome that railroad companies tried to avoid it. As traffic picked up, railroad executives bemoaned the loss of the double-track mileage reduced to single track following the demise of most passenger train service. BNSF officials determined that the fast freight overtook forty-two other eastbound freights, including several fast freights loaded mostly with UPS trailers. Without cabooses, only the most up-to-date remote control of track switches permitted such overtaking.

Something more important to real estate developers was the fact that freight trains no longer curved around great urban terminals. At Kansas City, Buffalo, and elsewhere, the fast freight rolled directly through cities, usually on elevated or depressed tracks, often past the locations of long-gone passenger stations. Through Utica, New York, a city of 270,000 people, the train scarcely slowed; nor did it slow for Syracuse (732,000) or Rochester (1,100,000). In almost no city east of Los Angeles did the experimental fast freight slow, except for regular thousand-mile safety inspections, refueling, and crew changes, usually in tiny towns. Only the suburbs of Chicago slowed the train.

A consideration of geography will reveal why the CSX was so interested in pleasing UPS. The train moved northeast across the continent, snaked through Chicago, and then rolled east to Albany before rushing south along the Hudson River. A CSX competitor, Norfolk Southern, pursued a more direct west-to-east route from St. Louis to the New York metropolitan region, and offered to move UPS cars free from New York to Worcester for the privilege. A shorter route, probably via Pittsburgh, might prove faster, despite the added cost of moving trains over the Alleghenies rather than along the old "water-level route" following the Great Lakes, Erie Canal, and Hudson River. The fate of very fast freight trains remains in the hands of shippers, especially UPS, which has yet to commit to the sixty truck trailers per train per day on which the BNSF and CSX are willing to set a price. But as the *Wall Street Journal* reported in a front-page story on July 25, 2003, UPS has already achieved one goal: CSX and Union Pacific have combined to operate dedicated trains on a sixty-three-hour schedule.

Two economic factors will determine how many faster freights operate in the immediate future. One is simple: the price of diesel fuel will make high-speed transcontinental truck haulage less than competitive with rail service. The other is complex: Freight trains operate optimally at speeds between sixty and seventy miles per hour; speeds above that produce expensive wear-and-tear on track and schedules. Equipment like RoadRailer might well reduce the maintenance costs, but the scheduling problems may prove intractable. Many parallel lines of long-ago competing railroads have been ripped up or converted to local-service mileage, and even double tracking single-track stretches does little to improve the flow of very fast freights among other such trains, like unit trains carrying coal or grain. Where rails did not become hiking trails, companies began operating some lines as one-way routes, using nearby parallel lines, usually acquired from old competitors in mergers, in ways suddenly profitable. In the late 1990s the Union Pacific converted the old Cotton Belt Route between St. Louis and Texas into a one-way southbound route via Pine Bluff, Arkansas, and used the old Missouri Pacific main line as a one-way northbound route through Little Rock. In *Main Lines,* Saunders explains what tourists discover in the Old Southwest. The former Southern Pacific main line west from New Orleans to Houston is one-way westbound, and the old Missouri Pacific line between the two cities is entirely eastbound. Across east Texas, Louisiana, and Arkansas, increasingly heavy traffic and especially high-speed, critical-schedule container trains flow smoothly—most of the time—in a validation of Union Pacific innovation. Observers may occasionally note that all the trains in a particular region operate only in one direction. Canny investors think about developing real estate along such high-speed rail routes. But railroad management wonders what happens when the one-way routes themselves can no longer accommodate more trains. Double tracking is the only viable answer.

Across most of the middle third of the United States, railroad companies work tirelessly to add automated passing sidings, extend miles of double track, and even lay third tracks alongside heavily used double-track mains. Double stacking ISO containers bought many railroads a grace period of five or so years; now most need double track. But as oil drives up the cost of diesel fuel, another solution shimmers on the horizon.

When the Pennsylvania Railroad studied electrifying its main line over the mountains between Harrisburg and Pittsburgh in 1930, it determined that electrification would shave four hours from the sixteen-hour schedule of its New York–Chicago luxury train service operating over state-of-the-art double track. Depression and war stymied Pennsylvania management, but the findings remain potent: the twelve-hour passenger service would eliminate airline competition between many intermediate stops, if not between New York and Chicago. In 1955, long after diesel-electric locomotives replaced steam for its very fast trains, the company commissioned another study focused on electrifying its route west of Harrisburg. As Michael Bezilla noted in a seminal 1978 article, "The Electrification That Might Have Been—and Might Still Be," some farsighted managers and investors mindful of British piggyback innovations knew the route had approached fast freight capacity. Old electrification studies now offer valuable information for shippers interested in moving freight fast, and for advocates of nuclear-generated electricity as well. Electrification may obviate the need for some double track, but it will succeed best in places lacking space for double or triple track, especially in cities and densely built suburbs.

Venture capitalist interest may well drive the upward spiraling prices offered for what seems at first glance to be mere railroad industry memorabilia. Investors considering opportunities in Rust Belt cities might well profit from reading a scarce document, the New York Central Railroad's *Fast Freight Schedule, November, 1948*. Distributed during the postwar era only to favored shippers and would-be shippers thinking about high-speed freight service, the document has more than historical value today. It explains what a railroad accomplished half a century ago, and might reinstitute, given demand.

Twenty-three years before Frailey's high-speed experimental trip, another author detailed regular piggyback service on the Chicago & North Western (C&NW) west from Chicago to Fremont, Nebraska, a junction with the Union Pacific northwest of Omaha. F. K. Plous recounted the dedicated effort of a company threatened by the flood of freight moving onto the new Interstate 80 after 1969. What was to be done with a multitrack railroad built for high-speed express passenger trains? In 1970 the ten thousand employees of the company bought it from its shareholders, began abandoning rural lines across South Dakota, Minnesota, and other states, and started improving its main line west of Chicago. Nevertheless, the employee-owned railroad could not get past the mid-1960s calamity of converting so much of its double-track mileage into single track. In 1978 train No. 243, part of the C&NW Falcon piggyback service, carried a caboose, avoided the Omaha passenger station, and moved in the very dawn of innovations like coal-carrying unit trains, but it rolled over track no longer in shape for the passenger trains that had raced over it in the 1950s. Its crew had in hand the bits and pieces that so impressed Frailey years later, but even with energy-crisis fifty-five-miles-per-hour interstate highway speed limits, the time had not come. For No. 243—indeed for the entire C&NW Railroad—the gravitational pull of I-80 proved too powerful. Creston and Rochelle in Illinois, and De Witt, Stanwood, Cedar Rapids, Ames, Boone, Grand Junction, and Dunlap in Iowa no longer glistened as jewels along a high-speed rail route. C&NW business worsened. Eventually the mighty Union Pacific bought the company, improved the track, and began to compete head-to-head with I-80 truck traffic.

Nowadays railroad companies, UPS and other shippers, and real estate investors look at RoadRailers, double-stack cars, and fast freight trains with focused attention. The distribution of light-weight, time-sensitive items already begins to move from highways and even from airliners as railroads recall the bygone era of very fast freight trains rolling along track fitted for even faster passenger and mail-express trains. So much freight has recently moved from trucks that railroads have been forced to clear jammed yards and port terminals by hiring trucking firms to move containers over highways. Railroads still experience extreme difficulty competing with first-rate trucking firms for time-sensitive shipments, and it will be years before they will compete favorably for shipments over less than eight hundred miles.

As more and more truck trailers and intermodal containers move onto high-speed freight trains charging parallel to interstate highways, would-be warehouse owners, investors, and consultants hired by overseas companies examine property adjacent to main lines. Potential sites for the new sorts of facilities Roy L. Harmon describes in *Reinventing the Warehouse: World-Class Distribution Logistics* must have access to vehicles that move fast day after day, and long-haul trucking companies can no longer promise such service unless they ship trailers by rail. Congress recognizes a new situation developing: *Planes, Trains, and Intermodalism,* a 2003 report of the

Committee on Transportation and Infrastructure, omits the word *trucks* from its title.

In Rochester and Utica, in Lynchburg and so many other small cities, especially on the High Plains, businessmen are glancing thoughtfully at the fast freight trains knifing across the landscape, especially those carrying UPS and other trucking-company trailers. They know that several hours later the freight train will be someplace else, on time, in a way that invites thought about long-term local real estate, warehousing and distribution, and even manufacturing opportunities unimaginable without fast freight trains. Freight trains that never stop in towns and small cities are the focus of intense analysis nowadays. People who watch people who watch trains may find much food for thought in regions far removed from large cities. Even on open highways west of the Mississippi, 18-wheel trucks rarely roll at more than seventy-five miles per hour; no one imagines them moving much faster in the future. Often trucks irritate motorists as they change lanes to overtake each other or slow down going uphill. Freight trains now and then pass the trucks, and motorists wonder why truck cargoes cannot be shifted from highways, leaving the roads clear for automobiles. Away from the coasts, railroad company television commercials emphasize the highway-clearing impact of fast freight trains carrying truck trailers. The commercials say nothing about a reorientation of warehouse and other commercial activity.

SOURCES: Bezilla, "The Electrification That Might Have Been"; DeViers and Lenz, "Recentralization"; Frailey, "Blank Bullet"; H. R. Grant, "Piggyback Pioneer"; Grivno, "Amtrak's Mail and Express Fleet"; Harmon, *Reinventing the Warehouse*; Howard, "Piggyback and the Portager Dream"; Hubbard, "Will 'Piggyback' Make the Boxcar Obsolete?"; T. Johnson, "Rail Yard Infill"; Machalaba and Chipello, "New Track"; Margetts, "Trains for Tomorrow"; McMurty, *Roads*; New York Central Railroad, *Fast Freight Schedule, November, 1948*; Overbey, "Piggyback"; Plous, "The Flight of the Falcon"; Saunders, *Main Lines*; Sperandeo, "The Bi-Modal RoadRailer"; Stephens, "What to Do with RoadRailer?"; Unites States Congress, Committee on Transportation and Infrastructure, *Planes, Trains, and Intermodalism*.

In a West Virginia freight yard, multiple unit trains of coal await clearance to begin their trips to electric power plants.

BULK

Rumbling through the night, the drag freight rolls as it always has, moving slowly and steadily despite being sidetracked for fast freights and the occasional Amtrak passenger train. Nowadays almost certainly a unit train comprising identical cars carrying identical or similar loads and destined for one or two giant customers, the train of coal, grain, ethanol, chemicals, or corn syrup saves the national highway pavement from destruction and intersections from gridlock.

By the late 1970s interstate highway deterioration could be discerned as a cryptic by-product of the 1973 gasoline crisis. Despite higher fuel costs and fewer Americans driving long distances, interstate highways decayed practically overnight. In a 1978 exposé entitled "Our Crumbling Interstate: A National Dilemma," E. D. Fales advised *Popular Mechanics* readers that decrepit long-distance highways resulted largely from ever-heavier trucks moving at speeds well above the energy crisis limit of fifty-five miles per hour. Despite encounters with experts arguing that deterioration resulted from severe winters, deferred maintenance, and simple aging of highways built twenty years earlier, Fales reported that many thought heavier trucks destroyed pavement.

Fales drove eight thousand miles while researching his article, and discovered that explanations involving poor initial construction and deferred maintenance seemed suspect. I-76, the Pennsylvania Turnpike, appeared in far better shape than the much newer I-80, and U.S. 301 south of Richmond, Virginia, offered a smoother ride than the newer I-95. I-40 across the South produced reports of holes in bridges and very bumpy surfaces, and I-43 in the upper Midwest had a reputation for cracks and potholes. Truckers considered concrete-slab pavement like that on I-90 between Cleveland and Erie a failure. The slabs settled, especially after harsh winters, producing jarring rides that tired drivers and jolted cargo. If harsh winters explained decay, Fales asked, what explained the good roads of Maine, Minnesota, and Montana? Perhaps heat caused I-5 in California to ripple. Maybe I-65 and other new interstates made older ones seem worse by simple comparison, but photographs of shattered pavement on I-81 near Shenandoah, Pennsylvania, did not lie. Almost overnight, something had changed.

Between 1973 and 1981 the costs of interstate highway construction and maintenance doubled. In 1972 the Nixon administration had already capitulated to fiscal reality and begun diverting a small portion of the federal gasoline tax to urban mass-transit systems. The 1973 gasoline crisis subverted the effort still lauded by environmentalists and antiautomobile crusaders. The ensuing sharp rise in housing costs, gasoline prices, and domestic heating costs meant that politicians refused to raise gasoline taxes until after 1983. Far too little money flowed to fuel the Urbmobile or even a city bus, although some was allocated to subsidize rural airports. As Mark H. Rose reveals near the end of his *Interstate: Express Highway Politics, 1939–1989,* the number of all paved-surface road miles built annually dropped from 172,000 in 1970 to only 66,000 in 1979. Apparently computer-driven scenario analysis shaped at least some decision making. In 1982 the National Research Council estimated that between 1980 and 1995, federal, state, and local governments would have to spend $350 billion just to maintain paved highways at minimum levels. The governments planned on spending only $235 billion. By 1986, as potholed reality slowed delivery and damaged cargoes, the national trucking organizations lobbied vigorously for increased highway spending. The heyday of interstate highway building lay in the past, and visions of cruising at 120 miles per hour became pipe dreams or hopes betrayed. In the 1990s federal, state, county, and municipal authorities agonized over the escalating cost of highway maintenance.

Few scholars analyze the very recent past of highway politics, but after 1980 engineering researchers began analyzing the physical realities of road maintenance. In 1983 two Purdue University experts, Benjamin Colucci-Rios and Eldon J. Yoder, raised questions that still resonate in political debates. In *A Methodology for Evaluating the Increase in Pavement Maintenance Costs Resulting from Increased*

Truck Weights on a Statewide Basis, they pointed out that one heavy truck may actually damage a road surface less than two or more trucks carrying the total weight of the heavy vehicle. But about one issue they had "90% confidence": increasing the legal weight limit translated into increased maintenance costs. Older pavements might wear more rapidly than newer ones, but such nuance mattered little in the end. If trucks put more weight on any sort of surface, some government entity would be forced to repair the damage. More trucks meant more damage, but more heavy trucks augured massive damage, especially at the local level.

Across much of the United States, local government means the county, the entity that provides three important services: police, education, and road maintenance. The county sheriff often patrols sparsely populated precincts that enjoy very low crime rates. The officers work with volunteer fire and rescue associations to offer a standard of response time that may shock suburban visitors accustomed to help arriving within five minutes. Rural police and fire assistance may be a half hour or more from someone dialing 911, an eon that explains rural devotion to firearms, sophisticated fire extinguishers, and well-stocked medicine chests. Counties provide public schooling—sometimes in a single building that houses all grades from kindergarten through senior high school; more often in several elementary schools and a lone junior-senior high school. Still called "consolidated schools" from an era when large structures replaced one-room schoolhouses, the public education systems depend on school buses operating over long routes. Police cars, fire engines, and school buses traverse county roads, often gravel ones graded seasonally and repaired after heavy rains. On local roads depend the emergency services and educational operations that bind rural dwellers together.

During the Kennedy administration, as large tractors replaced smaller ones and one well-mechanized farm family did the work that formerly required three or four, vast reaches of rural America depopulated. Fewer families per square mile meant fewer customers for crossroads stores and small-town main street merchants, and many retail businesses failed long before Wal-Mart opened. This mattered little until the late 1970s, when it became clear that fewer families meant fewer taxpayers to maintain the same mileage of county roads.

No historic landscape feature more clearly demonstrates the power of spatial reality to affect local and national politics than the networks of county roads crisscrossing rural America. The roads date mostly from horse-and-buggy days. East of the Appalachians they are contorted, often following valleys rather than crossing hills: the handle of a pail is the same length lying on the rim of the pail as held up, the old farmers said, and since hills tire horses, the more expedient way is the flat one. West of the Appalachians, as airplane passengers may occasionally discern from aloft, the county roads run in a great grid that makes the landscape into a checkerboard of fields and farms. Winding or straight, the roads serve vastly fewer people than they did in 1935, but the people have higher road maintenance standards than ever. Rural dwellers want asphalt pavement, and frequently they believe federal tax dollars ought to pay for it. After all, they argue, the safety of the school bus is paramount, especially on dark rainy mornings when the bus must ford flooding creeks. Rural road maintenance from Maine to Arizona is a sort of public welfare operation, offering nonfarm jobs to county residents employed by contractors frequently active in politics and funding dump truck and heavy equipment dealers. Always the rural road offers at least the potential for profitable traffic, if only a truck laden with harvested grain or chicken feed.

Farmers buy aging 18-wheel trucks and put them out to pasture behind barns, using them mostly at harvest time. Away from the agricultural Midwest, and indeed away from most interstate highways, few Americans spend much time wondering about the paucity of old trailer trucks. But at harvest time, and throughout the year in regions where farmers own their own grain-storage silos, aging heavy trucks rumble along dirt roads, across lightly built bridges, and over thinly paved roads, often converging in small towns boasting one or more grain elevators paying a slightly higher price for grain than those located on railroad routes far closer to many farms.

Large-scale farming means large-scale returns from seemingly tiny cost differentials. A few cents difference in the per-bushel price of grain often prompts a farmer to buy an 18-wheel truck, despite the annual registration and insurance costs of the vehicle. Kansas charges about $1,750 a year to register an eighty-thousand-pound truck, but farmers willingly accept that cost, plus insurance premiums, because the truck offers access to elevators paying a slightly higher price per bushel.

Railroads unwittingly precipitated the surge in rural trucking. After the passage of the Staggers Act in 1980, railroad companies freed from traditional antitrust rate-setting rules began experimenting with efficient innovations initially prized by stockholders and environmentalists alike. Large railroads, called "Class I" companies by industry experts, created hundred-car unit trains to move grain. Loading at automated facilities spread along main lines, the trains provided low-cost transportation, especially to ocean ports. Grain-buying firms benefited from lower transport costs and passed savings along to nearby farmers. Farmers far distant from the new facilities grew jealous quickly, but took years to act decisively. Over twenty years many of them deserted local grain elevators served by short-line railroads, replaced their small trucks that made many short trips to the nearest elevator with old 18-wheelers, and began grinding down rural roads toward loading facilities serving unit trains.

Kansas offers an illuminating example of massive economic dislocation, and nowadays serves researchers as a laboratory. In *Transportation Quarterly* and similar journals, independent examiners confirm the detailed results compiled by Kansas Department of Transportation experts. The short lines spun off as scarcely profitable by Class I railroads at first did well using labor-saving techniques and older equipment, but now suffer from an inability to offer rates competitive with those of unit trains. In the past two years, *Kansas Grain Transportation,* published annually by the Kansas State Board of Agriculture, has reported that many elevators served by short-line railroads now ship grain by truck to Class I loading facilities. Between 1990 and 1999 the truck share of wheat shipped from elevators rose from 37 percent to 47 percent, corn went from 62 percent to 72 percent, and sorghum from 35 percent to 56 percent. Farmer ownership of 18-wheelers becomes only a part of a far larger problem confronting rural counties in Kansas and other agricultural states. Large trucks often operate to grain elevators, and other large trucks often operate from those elevators to state-of-the-art rail-side loading facilities, mills, and animal-feed blenders.

Almost all of the dramatically increased truck traffic originates in a price differential of two cents per bushel.

Buying an aged 18-wheel truck becomes a sensible investment for many young men a few years out of high school or college, although for others it becomes a money-gobbling nightmare. Licensing requirements involving a year's driving experience for the owner of a heavy truck become unimportant when fathers are owner-employers. Initial low purchase prices of used trucks—along with fuel, insurance, and excise-tax costs—strike many young men as reasonable given the seasonal use of the truck. After harvest, some owners surrender registrations for most of the year, while others seek work moving animal feed or fertilizer. Along with rigs bought by large-scale family farmers and the growing number of corporate-owned farms rumble equally heavy, if creaky, trucks owned by young men who rarely risk operating on interstate highways. Like most agricultural truckers, they drive over back roads, surprising tourists and vexing highway maintenance officials.

Computer scenario analysis focuses on the short- and long-term impact of short-line railroad abandonment. Between 1970 and 1979 railroads abandoned 415 miles of track in Kansas; in the next decade they abandoned 815 miles; in the next, 1,246. Railroads gave up 335 track miles in the year 2001 alone, and the future projected by analysts seems grim. After 1990 short-line companies accounted for well more than half the abandoned mileage. Gone is the hope that accompanied the 1980 Staggers Act.

Imagining the economic future of Kansas both with and without four short-line railroads—the Kansas & Oklahoma, Kyle Railroad, Cimarron Valley, and the Nebraska, Kansas & Colorado—has occupied the attention of economists and transportation experts equipped with massive amounts of hard data. Michael Babcock, Eugene Russell, and Curtis Mauler's "Study of the Impact of Rail Abandonment on Local Roads and Streets," a paper presented at the Sixth International Conference on Low Volume Roads (1995), offers a useful introduction to what troubles the Kansas State Board of Agriculture. On the one hand, scenario analysis demonstrates that total transportation costs would prove virtually identical if all four short lines abandoned business and all wheat moved by Class I railroads and trucks. Many farmers would still drive their wheat in small trucks twelve to fifteen miles to local elevators along abandoned tracks, and those elevators would ship it in large trucks to Class I loading facilities. Farmer- and trucking-company-owned 18-wheel trucks might easily operate another hundred miles each way to such facilities, or reach even farther to the great terminal elevators in Salina, Hutchinson, and Wichita loading unit trains routed to export elevators at Houston. On the other hand, farmers in some regions of the state would suffer increased expenses from doubled handling costs as local grain elevators transshipped wheat to main-line railroad loading facilities. In a matrix involving farms, elevators, railroads, and truck carriers, scenario analysis suggests very little adverse impact from short-line railroad abandonment for farmers and other grain shippers.

Only when the question of highway maintenance enters the picture does the analysis shift dramatically. Russell and other researchers using sophisticated models of highway infrastructure deterioration have concluded that abandoning the four short-line railroads would cost $57.8 million annually in increased road maintenance costs.

Because one railcar carries grain equivalent to four 18-wheel truckloads, scenario analysts may wonder about increased tax revenue from diesel fuel sales. Unfortunately, the vast increase in truck carriage of grain would produce only $288,531 in additional fuel tax revenue, half of 1 percent of the $57.8 million in pavement repair costs.

Rephrasing the analysis makes equally bitter reading. In Kansas, grain-hauling trucks owned by farmers, contract truckers, and grain elevator co-ops do about $7.15 per truck per mile damage to the roads they travel. Every mile of short-line railroad abandoned tomorrow would cost $34,000 annually today, and much more in the years ahead.

Of course, trucks move over some roads more frequently than others. A very heavy truck might pass over a dirt road serving a handful of farms only once every three hours in harvest seasons. But less and less often do such trucks move toward local grain elevators strung along short-line railroads. Instead they merge into heavy flows toward state-of-the-art loading facilities built at widely distant points along Class I railroad lines. While such facilities pay property taxes to the municipality or county in which they do business, the revenue fails to cover increased road maintenance costs within the tax district. It does nothing to alleviate road deterioration just beyond tax-district borders.

Kansas highway authorities expect a new paved road to last thirty years, having received substantial maintenance after ten and twenty years. The rise in heavy grain-hauling truck traffic means, first, a much faster rate of pavement deterioration and, second, a far greater cost for building heavy roads better fitted for truck traffic. Across Kansas the $7.15 per-truck-mile annual average cost increases to $8.08 near loading facilities. Abandoning the short lines alone produces a large cost to Kansas state and county government, but it produces a particularly high cost to counties and municipalities hosting a loading facility drawing thousands of truck trips. Truck haulage of grain produces a sort of spatial discrimination across the Midwest and High Plains that angers local, county, and state taxpayers. Experts assembling at the annual meetings of the Conference on Low Volume Roads realize that local roads designated as low volume become high-volume routes in harvest time. So dramatic is the rising social cost of railroad abandonment in the Midwest and High Plains that the Department of Agriculture has begun to analyze it as a national problem. In *Long-Term Trends in Railroad Service and Capacity for United States Agriculture,* Marvin Prater and Keith Klindworth, researchers in the Agricultural Market Service division, conclude that present malpractice bodes ill for the immediate future.

Class I railroads—the largest ones in the nation—charge higher rates during harvest or "bottleneck" periods, often prohibit co-loading of unit trains operated by competing railroads serving the new loading facilities, charge higher rates to destinations off main lines, and interrupt traditional reciprocal car-switching arrangements and joint line agreements with connecting railroads. Moreover, Class I railroads have introduced the so-called super jumbo covered hopper car weighing between 286,000 and 315,000 pounds fully loaded. Only about two-thirds of short-line trackage has rails heavy enough to carry such cars, but national car-interchange agreements require all railroads, Class I and short line alike, to accept standard cars routed from any one railroad. Super jumbo hoppers are extraordinarily economical to operate, and railroads pass along part of the savings to farmers shipping grain in them from modern loading facilities. But they cannot move over some short-line rails, or even over some branch lines owned by Class I railroads, and their very existence may doom much light-rail mileage to the oblivion so evident across much of rural Kansas and western Nebraska.

Trucking companies loathe the super jumbo hoppers, since they dwarf the largest 18-wheelers and increase railroad efficiency beyond anything over-the-road carriers can match. But the immense railroad cars do offer some trucking firms, including rural ones owned by lone men with one old truck, the chance to transport grain from farms to the distant loading facilities served by the new railcars. Trucking company profits drop, and lone operators work longer hours and perhaps defer vehicle maintenance, but as scenario analysts make clear, for a few years longer short-haul truckers will enjoy competitive equality with short-line railroads stymied by Class I railroad indifference.

After that period comes serious trouble, albeit trouble hard to define precisely. Highway maintenance, repair, and rebuilding costs will balloon, producing taxpayer anger and almost certainly greater taxation of trucks. Truck traffic at transshipment nodes already angers motorists, and perhaps will reduce retail property values in the most adversely affected places. Short-line railroads will abandon operation: the first to go will be those dependent largely on grain shipments that farmers can truck to distant Class I railroads, and the next will be those seventy or more miles from main-line railroad competition. Other impacts, particularly collisions between trucks and cars, prove harder to calculate. As trucks jam rural roads converging at grain transshipment nodes, they will move more slowly and produce higher per-trip costs, but perhaps have fewer or less damaging accidents. Scenario analysis focuses the attention of farmers, truckers, and railroad officials, but only recently has it begun to shape the attention of real estate developers and others in businesses seemingly remote from farming and grain haulage.

Short-line railroads and branches of Class I firms haul more than grain. Harvest is the boom period for many such railroads. Increased traffic covers costs and often produces modest profit, but year-long fluctuations in the price of grain cause both farmers owning self-storage silos and local elevator co-ops and firms to ship some carloads at high-price, nonharvest times, often to the great profit of farmers who remain loyal to local business. Across the Midwest and High Plains, trains move yearlong, although sometimes only once or twice a week on some routes. So long as the tracks remain in operation, locomotives serve other industries and can even attract more business.

Some analysts insist that the short-line railroads produce a potential socioeconomic good every day. So long as the railroads operate trains over their weed-grown routes, they serve industries that may expand; they also may attract industries new to their service area. Industries based in lumber products, paper, steel, chemicals, and food almost always choose locations served by rail, especially if they intend to grow. Such industries deal with bulk commodities, either as inbound shipments or as finished products, and often as both. Any inbound or outbound shipment moving more than a thousand miles almost always moves more cheaply by rail than by truck (especially if it starts and ends at a rail-siding business), and a quiet, efficient short line like the Cimarron Valley Railroad may well attract a new industry, especially a high-tech one dependent on bulk freight. A little factory churning out plastic lawn furniture may take delivery of covered hoppers filled with plastic pellets, a wholesale bakery will require covered hoppers of flour and tank cars of corn syrup, and—because ethanol corrodes pipelines and must move in custom railcars—a wood-chip or crop-based ethanol plant needs to receive bulk raw material and ship bulk product. In the databases scoured by scenario analysts, the factory is part of the chemicals-based category, the bakery and ethanol plant components of a food-based one. To the observer, each is only one of the many small manufacturing enterprises blossoming across the rural

United States, often adjacent to sources of supply. But without the railroad these factories might be elsewhere.

The covered hopper behind the new plastics factory looks remarkably like that loading wheat a few hundred yards down the track, or disgorging animal feed at the mill at the next spur five miles south. It looks almost identical to the car unloading fertilizer at a dealership adjacent to the local grain elevator and not very different from the cylindrical tank car offloading propane gas. It looks like the tank cars, put into service in 1978, that move in units of ten and are connected by pipes; one nozzle empties or fills all ten cars. Train enthusiasts and model railroaders notice freight cars spotted at small-town and crossroads rural places, but until recently such cars attracted little attention from investors. Now the latter send analysts, and sometimes arrive themselves, to study rural places undergoing unmentioned but massive change. Farmers in southern Illinois no longer raise many hogs, or almost any other variety of livestock. Instead, they focus on growing corn, which moves via railroad to Texas, to gigantic, high-tech hog-fattening facilities fenced off from prying eyes. In southern Illinois, unit trains operate frequently, suggesting to some investors that underemployed rural populations might readily gravitate to work in well-connected factories.

Only when a grain-hauling short-line railroad lies abandoned do farmers realize that the two cents per bushel they saved by trucking their harvest to a far-off elevator is nowhere near enough to cover the increased costs of truck-hauled fertilizer and propane gas. The railroad that moves bulk grain shipments away from farms moves inbound single-car shipments of fertilizer, propane, and animal feed all year long. Inbound shipments rarely come close to the value of grain, but fertilizer keeps trains moving in spring, and propane shipments pay railroad company bills in the dead of winter. Once the railroad lies derelict, farmers and other county residents confront more than increased costs for fertilizer, fuel, and other heavy items. As taxpayers, they confront the soaring costs of maintaining roads mangled by heavy trucks operating in sparsely settled regions. In the 1990s county commissioners focused on attracting industries to increase tax revenue and provide jobs, and thus learned that many companies prefer to locate along railroad lines.

Rural highway commissioners had begun to divert maintenance and repair funds to routes used by the trucks. While shifting funds from roads used by motorists and school buses provoked local disputes, the short- and long-term consequences of focusing rural road networks on grain-loading facilities meant that long-haul trucks often followed less-favored routes once off interstate highways. For decades the larger agricultural landscape had been laced by short-haul roads linking farms and local-rail-served grain elevators, and by other roads linking farms and small towns with interstate highways. For as long as the latter roads received the bulk of the funding, rural taxpayers, including businesses, enjoyed time-consuming but otherwise convenient access to the national highway system. Traffic flowed, and businesses located along the flow, often on the bypass circumventing crossroads towns. By 1995 diversion of funding had begun to make driving from some farms to grain-loading facilities smooth and fast, especially outside harvest time. Risk-taking entrepreneurs had begun locating retail businesses near the grain-loading nodes, rather than in hamlets along hitherto "main-traveled roads."

Without notice, rural businesses began locating away from interstate highway/local highway interchanges. Long-haul truckers delivering almost anything to rural regions discerned the subtle signs of highway maintenance favoritism. No longer did the best-surfaced highway necessarily lead away from an interstate exit toward a small town fifty or a hundred miles away. In many regions the best-paved, about-to-be-widened highways led from clusters of prosperous farms to new grain-loading facilities remote from towns and even from crossroads hamlets.

Some towns get lucky. Casselton in North Dakota, a few miles from the Minnesota line, sits astride I-94 and only eighteen miles from I-29, a main Canada–Mexico truck route. In 2004 three grain elevator companies combined to open a facility that loads 110-car unit trains on the Red River Valley & Western Railroad, a "short-line partner" of the Burlington Northern Santa Fe. About a half-hour drive from Fargo, Casselton is home to long-time natives and a few commuters enjoying a small-town living experience. Once a junction of railroads, it remains a convenient place for intermodal activity; after all, some truckloads of grain arrive at the new facility along I-94.

Other towns lose out. Crete in North Dakota is scarcely a town at all. Main Street runs parallel to two other very short streets crossed by two others. Not one of the roads is a state highway, and until recently the tiny community focused on Crete Grain, Inc., a century-old firm formerly served by the Burlington Northern Santa Fe. When the owners of Crete Grain attempted to expand their elevator to load 110-car unit trains, they found themselves stymied by abutting structures. They moved their operation to Oakes, about ten miles away and coincidentally conveniently located at the intersection of two local highways, 1 and 11. At Oakes they built a multi-million-dollar high-tech facility consisting of four cylindrical silos 52 feet in diameter and 150 feet tall, split by a slightly smaller central silo fitted with loading and unloading machinery. Trucks arrive, are weighed on an automatic scale, and discharge grain into the four large elevators, each of which holds a quarter-million bushels of wheat, or into the central silo, which holds only 135,000 bushels. Automatic machinery enables the facility to load and weigh a 110-car unit train in exactly eleven hours. Positioned at the intersection of two highways, Oakes is a perfect location—so perfect that a nearly identical grain-loading facility operates only a mile away.

Railroad tracks surround Oakes on three sides. The town of 1,850 people includes retired farm couples and local business people, but its main activity involves the storage and transfer of grain. It is easy to smile at Oakes, with its quiet lifestyle and 13.5-minute average commute time to work; equally easy to picture Oakes in 1929, with trains of the Chicago & North Western; Minneapolis, St. Paul & Sault Ste. Marie; and Northern Pacific companies pausing at its two stations three-quarters of a mile apart. But the trains of 1929 make any thoughtful observer of the new grain-loading facilities wonder about imminent futures involving private investment: the center of business activity and train movement has shifted away from downtown, and the destination of trains isolates Oakes.

The C&NW operated trains through Oakes on its line between Des Moines and Rapid City, between Omaha and Jamestown, North Dakota—the end of the line, a city midway between Fargo and Bismarck, and nowadays located on I-94—and between Chicago and Jamestown. About nine C&NW trains a day stopped in Oakes, none of them particularly fast, most stopping at many other small towns, and all covering vast distances across sparsely populated country. Train No. 50 departed Chicago at 6:05 PM and spent almost thirty-six hours covering the 794 miles to Oakes. No. 54 took some seventeen hours to operate over the 511 miles from Des Moines. The Minneapolis, St. Paul & Sault Ste. Marie Railway, known across its vast territory as "The Soo," ran only two passenger trains a day through Oakes, on its St. Paul and Pollock, South Dakota, route. The Northern Pacific operated two on its St. Paul and Streeter route, two on the Fergus Falls branch line that terminated in Oakes, and two between Jamestown in Minnesota and Oakes. None of the passenger trains in 1929 or today could be called an express, or even a luxury train, and many included nothing other than day coaches and the ubiquitous railway post office and Railway Express Agency cars. Oakes existed as a junction of secondary railroad routes; the Northern Pacific North Coast Limited between Chicago and Seattle passed far to the north.

In 1929 Crete enjoyed only the slow branch-line Northern Pacific trains between St. Paul and Oakes via Fergus Falls. No. 9 clattered out of Wadena, Minnesota, at 1:35 in the afternoon and paused at Crete at 7:56 in the evening, moving over the intervening 143 miles at approximately twenty-two miles per hour; twenty-four minutes and eight miles later, it terminated at Oakes. Presumably anyone in or near Crete wanting faster rail transportation to just about anywhere hitched a ride into Oakes and boarded a faster train.

But the Northern Pacific provided regular and reliable service to farmers using the Crete elevator. For decades, grain followed similar but not identical paths as passengers. Grain moved more slowly and more circuitously until 1980, when the Staggers Act released railroad companies from decades of onerous restriction.

Unit-train transit of grain becomes highly profitable when the train not only turns around quickly but moves rapidly between loading and unloading points. Rapidity results not from high speed but from slow but steady, almost stately progress across distances most people prefer to fly. Old passenger timetables attest to the fact that unit trains of super jumbo cars must move rapidly for owners to recover the high costs of equipment that operates empty one way and sometimes idles after the harvest rush. The more grain unit trains carry, the sooner railroads cover initial purchase costs and begin to make a profit. Class I railroads consequently focus on the export market, and prefer to serve ultramodern grain facilities loading trains that will move such long distances that truck transport becomes uneconomical.

What strikes a well-managed trucking company as marginally economical may strike a farmer or underemployed truck driver (especially one paying off his aging rig) as well worthwhile, especially in the face of little other available work. A farmer with nothing more lucrative to do, especially a farmer working a farm without livestock in a North Dakota winter, may decide to drive his own heavy truck eighty miles to a modern rail loading facility. Almost certainly, however, neither he nor any commercial trucker, even an underemployed one, will move a truckload of wheat from North Dakota to Houston, or even from North Dakota to Kansas. Diesel fuel costs far outstrip the income realized from moving a bulk commodity so far over highways.

The old railroad route maps and timetables suggest something else to government and railroad industry analysts. States unable to build new roads for grain-hauling trucks unwittingly make reactivating or improving a weedy railroad route economical. Grain alone may not cover improvement costs, however, so railroads seek other shipments owner-operator truckers cannot handle. People willing to accept corn or wheat rumbling along in an old truck shy away from propane, liquid natural gas, and chemicals, including fertilizer.

The 1920s train-travel patterns presage future growth patterns across the sparsely settled High Plains. Back then, population and business growth blossomed along main lines, especially at junctions. Growth begat growth. Nowadays analysts, investors, and canny observers see the pattern repeated. The first communities in which investors build high-tech facilities for loading grain into unit trains receive improved track maintenance and more frequent train service. These communities attract more grain shipments, and perhaps other businesses. But communities that fail to attract initial investment in high-tech loading facilities often find themselves locked into depopulation and a downward economic spiral. Even worse, they often must pay dearly for road damage caused by trucks operating nonstop toward distant rail-side loading facilities.

Even in the depressed years of the 1970s, railroads held on to much of their bulk traffic, especially coal. Almost from its beginning, the industry profited from "open-top" cargoes: coal, gravel, sand, and raw ore—loads that stood up to rough handling, slow movement, and exposure to foul weather. Early in the nineteenth century, trains captured much bulk traffic from canals traversed by horse-drawn barges. Earlier on than most people—even history buffs—might suspect, eastern railroads began operating long trains consisting solely of cars carrying one commodity.

Long trains, sometimes experimental but more often ordinary, assisted the rapid growth in United States coal production after about 1850. From 8.3 million tons in that year it rose to 40.4 million tons in 1870, and the total nearly doubled by the end of the subsequent decade. In the beginning, miners worked the anthracite coal of eastern Pennsylvania, but as early as 1843 the Baltimore & Ohio had begun moving soft coal from Maryland. Coal moved across the northeast by the 1870s, and everywhere across the nation by 1880, much of it mined in the bituminous region of West Virginia and Kentucky and thence exported. Cleaner-burning anthracite coal powered factories and heated houses and other buildings, and it fueled railroad locomotives as well. Railroads outside coal-mining areas transported it even further afield: in 1880 the New York Central moved 1.6 million tons. While local freights switched single cars of anthracite coal onto small-town coal-yard sidetracks and factory spurs, most coal moved in seemingly endless trains.

Anthracite coal rolled in dedicated slow trains, often made up of small four-wheel cars called jimmies. While other four-wheel freight cars had vanished by 1850, jimmies survived because they fit perfectly under coal-mine loading chutes. In the late 1830s, some railroads moved trains of twenty to thirty cars; by the late 1850s many operated trains of nearly sixty cars. But railroads had begun to experiment with far longer trains. In 1850 the Boston & Maine ran a sixty-one-car train over a seventy-four-mile route; three years later, the Michigan Central ran a train of a hundred and eighteen cars. The Philadelphia & Reading pioneered much long-train experimentation; when it opened in 1839, its very first train carried eighty cars.

A few months later Philadelphia & Reading moved 101 loaded jimmies behind a single locomotive, albeit one operating largely downhill. By 1845 the Reading operated coal trains averaging 703 tons, an accomplishment of industrial technology almost invariably ignored even by historians, who imagine pre–Civil War railroading in terms framed by Thoreau. In 1879 the Lehigh Valley operated a coal train of an astounding 593 cars with no recorded problems.

Such trial accomplishments did not always translate into ordinary operation. Moving long trains meant lengthening passing tracks and making other capital improvements that sometimes proved uneconomical. In 1891 Lehigh Valley's coal trains usually consisted of 225 jimmies moving coal toward New York for domestic consumption or export. But in 1879 the Lehigh Valley operated a train *one and a half miles long.*

Such experiments produced a frenzy of locomotive redesign, and by the 1880s coal-hauling railroads had dramatically increased the size of their engines. One locomotive now did the work of two. Trains did not immediately become longer, but companies saved the expense of a crew for the locomotive formerly coupled behind the first. As locomotives grew larger, greater tractive effort revealed itself in longer and longer trains, especially those laden with coal. From Pennsylvania and West Virginia to Kentucky, and subsequently in the coal regions of Utah and other western states, long coal trains moved ponderously toward the blast furnaces of Pittsburgh, Birmingham, Gary, and Provo; to export facilities at Norfolk and elsewhere; and to New York and other metropolitan centers of coal consumption.

In northern Minnesota and Wisconsin, other specialized steam locomotives pulled long drags of stubby ore cars filled with dense, heavy iron ore. Dumped into immense so-called lake boats at Duluth and other harbors, ore moved by water to Gary and other southern ports, then by rail to steel mills. The Duluth, Missabe &

Iron Range, the Pittsburgh & Lake Erie, and other railroads devoted almost solely to moving iron ore attracted little romantic attention. The companies operated few passenger trains and served regions rarely traveled by song writers and other entertainers, let alone the educated elite. Their long trains of hopper cars chugged along at twenty or twenty-five miles an hour, irritating motorists caught at grade crossings. But they freighted the raw bulk material of United States industrial growth. Simply because the spot lay halfway between Pennsylvania coal and Minnesota iron ore, the United States Steel Company sited its mills in the sparsely settled region of Indiana that it named Gary. Steel mills required a steady supply of raw coal and ore, but no one cared how fast the crude cargo rolled through the night—only that it arrived regularly.

Stockholders, however, cared very much about how profitably such bulk cargo rolled, and boards of directors struggled constantly to shave costs. In 1876 accountants employed by the Erie discovered that new locomotives pulling coal trains twice as heavy as those operated in the previous year reduced operating costs per mile from nine cents to five. Railroad companies not only pioneered most business management techniques nowadays accepted as standard but also created sophisticated accounting systems to monitor and suggest innovation. After 1900 number crunching prompted changes in the hauling of coal, ore, and other bulk products, and even produced a new railroad.

Financier Henry Huttleson Rogers built the Virginian in the first years of the twentieth century expressly to move coal across the Appalachians from West Virginia to a brand-new, company-owned export pier at Norfolk, Virginia. Rogers specified heavy rail, massive bridges, gigantic hopper cars, and the most powerful locomotives, but he could do little about the 2 percent grade eastbound between Elmore and Clarks Gap in West Virginia. By 1915 the company operated steel coal cars that each carried 120 tons of coal atop twelve wheels. From 1909 on, the Virginian purchased some of the most powerful steam locomotives American manufacturers built. Its ordinary gigantic locomotives had the equipment of two ordinary heavy locomotives working beneath stupendous boilers. Such engines had two pilot wheels, eight coupled drive wheels, another eight drive wheels, and two trailing wheels; each locomotive weighed 342 tons. To cope with the increased coal traffic following the outbreak of World War I in Europe, the Virginian experimented with a gigantic locomotive three times the size of the heavy locomotives used by most other railroads. Moving seven million tons of coal a year through Clarks Gap required most trains to have three monster steam locomotives, generally one leading and two pushing the long trains. Given a forecast that coal traffic would double within a few years, and knowing that the long coal trains inching over the single track could be neither lengthened or speeded up behind steam power, Virginian management determined to electrify 134 miles of track and replace the steam locomotives.

The box-shaped electric locomotives, each fifty-one feet long and weighing 212 tons, usually operated in groups of three. The Virginian management considered them discrete units—and so publicized them as the largest locomotives in the world. In September 1925, with much fanfare, the Virginian moved an eight-thousand-ton train of sixty-two cars using two of the three locomotives. Powered by electricity generated from its own coal-fueled power plant, the Virginian had a surefire winner in the new motive power.

The boxcab electrics doubled the speed of coal trains over the pass. No longer did the trains roll at fourteen miles an hour. By 1927, the first year of full operation under electric power, the company moved almost 12 million tons of coal. Despite a drop in tonnage during the Depression, coal traffic remained profitable, and during World War II surged to almost 13 million tons. Three years into peacetime, that figure rose to 15.5 million tons, and the company began replacing its first-generation electrics with units that stretched 150 feet and weighed 517 tons. One new electric soon moved a three-thousand-ton coal train up the grade at thirty-five miles an hour: it moved a ten-thousand-ton coal train at forty-five miles per hour on level track. In 1957 the company bought more heavy electrics capable of operating at sixty-five miles per hour, and until 1962 enjoyed immense success.

Merger with the Norfolk & Western ended the Virginian electrification, since most coal traffic shifted to the gentler grades of the N&W. A smoke-choked tunnel nearly three-fifths of a mile long prompted the N&W to choose electrification in 1912, although its grades made electrification a profitable choice too. By 1915 the company was boasting that electric locomotives moved coal trains through Elkhorn Tunnel in three minutes rather than seven and eliminated the danger of suffocation to crews operating smoke-belching, slow-moving steam locomotives in tunnels. N&W electrics performed almost flawlessly, moving fifty-four million tons of coal in the year 1943 alone, and saved vast sums in operating expenses. But immediately after World War II the N&W built a new grade and tunnel beneath Elkhorn Mountain that eliminated the need for electric locomotives. Heavy steam locomotives rolled coal trains through the new double-track tunnel at speed, and soon captured the coal traffic of the Virginian as well.

High-tech innovation in the poverty-stricken Appalachians passed without much comment, but electrification on the Virginian and N&W convinced the management of other railroads that unit trains operating between mines and large clients might be profitable enough to offset the postwar flood of freight to the trucking industry. In 1960, the year the last regularly scheduled passenger train operated behind a steam locomotive (between Durand and Detroit on the Grand Trunk Western), several railroads began moving coal in unit trains that had been operating since the 1850s.

Unit trains originated in the railroad industry's effort to tap the cheaper, low-sulfur coal regions of Wyoming and other western states. Strip-mined coal poured into hopper cars at a lower cost than coal moved from underground mines, and electricity-producing companies, especially those along the Great Lakes and the Ohio River, wanted the cheapest coal possible. The 1970 Clean Air Act accelerated the unit-train concept, since the federal government mandated that all coal-fired power plants switch to low-sulfur coal. From strip mines in Virginia, Wyoming, and elsewhere, unit trains began moving cleaner-burning coal to power-generating customers, supplanting the fading steel industry. The 1973 and 1979 gasoline crises only accelerated the momentum of the unit-train concept.

In September 1966 the first Santa Fe unit coal train left the York Canyon mines in New Mexico on its 1,082-mile trip to Fontana, California, about fifty miles east of Los Angeles. Between a Kaiser Steel coal mine and the sprawling Kaiser Steel mill, the brand-new train shuttled mostly along the main line of a long-established railroad. But the Santa Fe had built fifty-seven miles of heavy track away from its main line at French, New Mexico, to tap the new Kaiser mine in the northeast corner of the state. Only a short time earlier, the Southern Pacific had abandoned its 114-mile Tucumcari-to-French branch line. By pure coincidence, the Santa Fe was thus the only railroad able to reach into York Canyon and the new mines fitted with equipment that loaded each hopper car in sixty seconds. The company bought eleven new locomotives and 101 massive hopper cars for the Kaiser unit-train service, and soon operated one of the first, and longest-routed, precision-scheduled unit trains in the nation.

A unit train moving coal consists of some 100 to 110 identical cars owned either by an individual railroad or by a client, usually a power-generating company. The train shuttles between mine and client, always an integral unit, always full one way and empty the other. The dedicated train moves on a regular schedule and produces a regular, predictable profit from contracts negotiated annually or at longer intervals. It generates income as steadily as it moves, and the more efficiently it moves, the more profitable it proves for both the railroad company and the purchaser of the coal it carries. But just as the long pre–Civil War trains of the Philadelphia & Reading rarely enter university history courses, and the high-tech Appalachian experiments of the Virginian and N&W existed far from the eyes of most express train passengers, coal-carrying unit trains operate from remote mining regions to power plants usually located away from close public scrutiny, often across sparsely settled rural or wilderness regions. If bystanders occasionally notice the ribbonlike trains of silver or yellow or black coal cars, they probably fail to recognize them as both generators of economic value and indicators of spatial and economic changes immediately ahead.

Bulk transport using standardized, integral trains operating over fixed routes on predictable schedules suggested all manner of innovations by 1965. Developments in mainframe computers, software, and integrated logic circuits implied that dreams might come true, perhaps sooner than expected. No doubt union leadership shivered every time the industry adopted another cybernetic component.

Automatic train operation debuted in New York. In January of 1962 a robotic subway train began shuttling between Times Square and Grand Central Terminal. Union opposition delayed the inaugural run: until a motorman manned the robotic train, the Transport Workers Union threatened to close down the entire New York City subway system. Within weeks, however, the shuttle train had begun to prove itself. The prototype for the automatic "people movers" now whisking terminal-changing passengers beneath airports in Atlanta, Dallas–Forth Worth, Pittsburgh, and elsewhere, the New York City shuttle train moved a bulk cargo most railroaders by then ignored. People.

In Canada, far from cities and beyond the gaze of all but the most intrepid hikers, automatic train operation had already proven itself. On the Quebec, North Shore & Labrador, eighteen-car trains of iron ore routinely operated twenty-four hours a day, seven days a week behind robotic diesel locomotives. Over the 5.7-mile route moved four trains. At any given moment, one train moved slowly under loading chutes, another moved slowly across unloading devices, and two rolled along the main line, passing each other at a midway passing siding. The QNS&L saw the robotic trains as short-term experiments, for the company had long-range plans involving automation in a wilderness area beset by harsh winters.

Earlier experiments in the United States, especially the 1955 demonstrations of automatic train operation on the New Haven between New Rochelle and Rye Beach in New York, prompted ongoing research by the Union Switch & Signal Division of the Westinghouse Corporation. By 1962 General Electric had begun demonstrating a robotic trolley car named Tomorrow, one of the prototypes of the cars that now operate on the Bay Area Rapid Transit system in San Francisco. But most research focused on moving freight robotically.

By 1969 the new Muskingum Electric Railroad in southwest Ohio had proven that automatic train control and electrification welded into smooth, extremely economical operation of bulk material. Hauling coal from mines to the Muskingum River generating plant of the Ohio Power Company, the railroad used the latest in 25,000-volt, 60 cycles per second, alternating current power distribution already proven in Europe and Asia. Such electric power simplified the equipment needed in substations and locomotives, eliminated the need for special transmission lines paralleling the contact wire touched by the locomotives, and permitted very lightweight catenary overhead construction, saving initial outlay for copper and subsequent maintenance. Two trains, each with a new locomotive and fifteen cars, operated as automatically as a home washing machine, cruising at fifty-five miles per hour, loading and unloading while moving at slow speed, and easily sweeping up the 2 percent ruling grade.

Not until 1983 did Amtrak change its power distribution system to 25,000 volts, but the lessons of the Muskingum sank deeply into railroad management thinking. In a sealed-off area, with instruments probing the track ahead for debris and other hazards, an electric locomotive operated with less human attention than a toy train moving at the whim of a child adjusting its speed transformer. While ordinary diesel-electric locomotives could operate automatically, as the QNS&L proved, all-electrics moved far more reliably and at lower cost. By 1975 the QNS&L had electrified much of its four-hundred-mile main line and begun automatic train control as effective as the Times Square shuttle subway.

For all intents and purposes, Amtrak Acela trains might operate today without engineers. Passengers might worry about emergencies: despite autopilot equipment that enables an airliner to take off, fly, and land without human help, few passengers would trust their lives in a drone aircraft, and life on the ground seems as valuable as life aloft. Bulk haulage of grain, coal, ore, forest products (especially wood chips), newsprint, and other commodities offers glimpses of what already shapes Oakes in North Dakota, and suggests imminent automatic-operation innovation.

A unit train of a standard length, often 110 cars, loads automatically and proceeds to a single destination for automatic unloading, but an engine crew still operates its locomotive. Standardized train length means standardized length of passing sidings. Precision scheduling means a steady, uninterrupted flow of trains; and fast, regular service means a railroad company needs only a few trains to move gigantic amounts of bulk cargo. Standardized service means reduced costs for shippers. The unit train taught railroad management to think in terms of an industry no longer operating as a common carrier but as a contract carrier to large clients. But in the longer run, the unit train focuses management attention on components of the railroad not yet standardized, including the ordinary diesel-electric locomotive still unable to compete with all-electric units. High horsepower is fundamentally easier to design and build into an all-electric locomotive like the Amtrak Acela.

After the Staggers Act of 1980, railroads began exploring the potential implicit in merging old-fashioned mail and package express service with modern unit-train technology. Among the grain, coal, and ore trains it is easy to miss pioneering unit trains like the Burlington Northern Santa Fe Ethanol Express moving biofuel from the Midwest to a refinery in Watson, California, or the first "grocery" unit trains of raw foodstuffs other than grain. Between Florida and New Jersey the all-orange refrigerated Tropicana Orange Juice unit train rolls like clockwork. Eighty unit trains of coal roll out of Wyoming every day, putting many small towns on superb freight tracks that might one day carry something else. Outside the railroad industry little attention accrues to robotic trains that make the Urbmobile seem antiquated. Quebec and New Mexico are remote, and even in Ohio such trains operate behind chain-link fences and "no trespassing" signs. But many vacationing long-distance motorists note with despair the truck traffic on many interstate highways and the wretched pavement stretching endlessly ahead.

It might be instructive to follow unit trains of grain to the small town of Kalama on the Columbia River in Washington. A thriving, beautiful town in a spectacular wilderness setting, Kalama is home to an ultramodern marine shipping terminal. Unlike the older ports of Elizabeth, New Jersey, and Norfolk, Virginia, Kalama's marine terminal scarcely interrupts daily life and indeed is almost invisible. But it is immensely profitable. Day after day, unit trains arrive and depart at the five facilities loading ships departing for destinations around the world. Kalama, then, is Oakes on a slightly grander scale, with boutiques and marinas and sumptuous mountainside houses blossoming from unit-train-generated wealth.

It is not Crete. Nor is Prince Rupert, in British Columbia, transshipping not only bulk commodities but thousands of containers at the far end of a transcontinental rail line that reaches to New Orleans and to Halifax. Nor is Port MacKenzie, a brand-new seaport two miles from Anchorage, transshipping wood chips, limestone, and coal.

Such ports are the new ends of the line. New container ships, especially the gigantic ones owned by the Danish firm Maersk, which carry thirteen to fifteen thousand twenty-foot-long containers at a time, and bulk carriers transporting coal, oil, and grain are far too large to pass through the Panama Canal, let alone fit into older harbors with low bridges and shallow channels. High-tech and prosperous, the new ports demonstrate the astounding impact of behemoth ships and unit trains rolling bulk commodities on global trade, reshaping investment and the North American landscape. Railroads know that mile-long, slowly moving unit trains frustrate motorists stuck at grade crossings, so they replace crossings with overpasses. As grade crossings vanish, railroads note increased potential for high-speed freight trains, automated operation, and even passenger trains. Innovation may arrive first along routes modified for the oldest cargoes of all, but ones headed from new transshipment points to new deep-water ports.

SOURCES: Babcock, Bunch, et al., "Impact of Short Line Railroad Abandonment," and "Impact of Short Line Railroad Abandonment"; Babcock, Russell, and Mauler, "Study of the Impact of Rail Abandonment"; Colucci-Rios and Yoder, *A Methodology for Evaluating the Increase in Pavement Maintenance Costs*; Drury, "Tank Train"; "Electrification: In the Future"; Fales, "Our Crumbling Interstates"; Josserand, "Tomorrow"; Kansas State Board of Agriculture, *Kansas Grain Transportation*; Middleton, *When the Steam Railroads Electrified*; "Muskingum Electric Railroad"; "Muskingum Electric: Trains on Their Own"; O'Neil, "Quebec, North Shore & Labrador"; Prater and Klindworth, *Long-Term Trends in Railroad Service*; Rose, *Interstate*; Santa Fe Railroad, news release, R-33-2, August 27, 1966; Sonstegaard, "Competitive Access to North American Rail"; Transportation Research Board, *Low-Volume Roads*; J. H. White Jr., *The American Railroad Passenger Car*.

Approaching a grade crossing at 70 miles per hour, the commuter train deflects attention from the unpaved service road paralleling it, but that road indicates space enough for adding another track when patronage increases.

TRANSFER

Predicting sometimes fails. The most meticulous analysis of census data proves no guarantee of future birth or death rates, and the stock market performance over decades may suggest little about its behavior tomorrow. Even demographic and economic data rooted in geography and existing real estate development sometimes trick analysts, and what seems surefire sometimes backfires, as the New York, Westchester & Boston Railroad (NYW&B) learned in the 1920s. Only a few relics remain of perhaps the most visionary, best-built passenger railroad in the United States, one intended to carry almost no freight at all.

The East 180th Street Station of the New York subway system ought to interest patrons, but most rush in and out of the handsome structure, unaware of its clouded history. Its facade fails to intrigue, and inside few glance at the adjacent abandoned platforms and tracks used to store older subway trains. The No. 2 and No. 5 trains pause at active platforms, operating between Dyre Avenue in the North Bronx and downtown, and people bustle in and out. Few notice the caduceus molded into the station facade. But the symbol of Mercury, the Roman god of speed, still dignifies a subway line punctuated here and there by extraordinarily massive, ornate stations built in a quasi-Mediterranean style. The nearby Dyre Avenue station, now housing also a police station and a convenience store, resembles that on East 180th Street. The massive, ornate, timeless, vaguely modern architectural style, and the disused tracks adjacent to active ones, suggest that something special happened in the Bronx, but only temporarily. Fragments endure, reminding twenty-first-century investors that predictions fail.

In early 1929 disaster stalked the Harlem Board of Commerce. It published *Three Plans for the Relief of Traffic Congestion in New York City,* a cogent, assertive, and perhaps disingenuous plea for relief from motor vehicle traffic. The board wanted an end to ferry boats serving upper Manhattan, and so proposed what became the

Triborough Bridge, to "divert thousands of motor trucks away from lower Manhattan," across the upper part of the island, then across another proposed bridge opening on New Jersey. The board hoped to channel rail commuters through the upper end of the island, to which purpose it proposed moving the terminal of the New York, Westchester & Boston Railroad from the Bronx. Trains would operate through tunnels under the Harlem River, then through tunnels connecting with all but one of the Manhattan north–south subway lines, and terminate at a new station near the intersection of 125th Street and St. Nicholas Avenue, the site of the Eighth Avenue Subway Line, already under construction. If suburban trains of the New York, New Haven & Hartford Railroad moved through the NYW&B tubes as well, commuters from Connecticut might reach the upper end of Manhattan as easily as commuters from the Bronx and Westchester County.

Couching the proposals in language that managed to suggest the whole city would benefit, the board obscured its deep interest in attracting office, manufacturing, and commercial enterprises northward. "The present congestion in Grand Central Terminal and 42nd Street will be greatly relieved, the distribution of Westchester County commuters taking place practically the entire length of 125th Street," it concluded. "It would further tend toward the distribution of business and manufacturing establishments, bringing many hundreds from lower Manhattan to the Bronx and other uptown sections, relieving downtown congestion." The Chrysler Building slowly rising toward the sky, the Empire State Building already announced, and other office towers terrified the business community based in the northern end of Manhattan. Unless suburban commuters had a new railroad terminal far north of Pennsylvania Station and Grand Central Terminal, lower Manhattan would prosper as its buildings grew taller. It would prosper at the expense of the rest of the island.

As the board emphasized on the last page, demographic and traffic experts had located the "pivotal point, or hub, of the teeming millions in and around New York" at about 112th Street and Fifth Avenue. For decades the point had been moving northward, but by 1929 it had moved almost three miles north of the northernmost bridge leading onto Manhattan. The two proposed highway bridges would relieve congestion in lower Manhattan and incidentally bring commuters, motor truck traffic, and long-distance motorists across the north end of the island, freeing it from a future as an area of low-income housing. But the key proposal involved relocating a railroad terminal placed where the finest 1900-era expertise predicted commuter traffic would materialize. Something had derailed the predictions on which the builders of the NYW&B invested millions.

Stretching north and east from a terminal at East 132nd Street and Willis Avenue, at the southern edge of the Bronx and adjacent to an expanse of freight yards, the NYW&B eventually reached as far as Port Chester to the northeast and White Plains to the north, branching at Mount Vernon toward its two suburban terminals. Between 174th Street and Mount Vernon, its trains operated on a four-track main line, totally free of grade crossings; beyond the suburban junction, they moved on double tracks. Bridging depressions on massive steel-and-concrete viaducts and burrowing under the Bronx and Pelham Parkway in a four-thousand-foot tunnel, the railroad struck both laymen and experts as extraordinary. Not only did its builders use the finest material, they dignified its route with elegant stations. But most importantly, they electrified every inch of the right-of-way, making possible extremely fast trains, both local and expresses, operating at twenty-minute intervals in off-peak times and more frequently during rush hour.

The NYW&B carried 2,874,484 passengers in 1913, its first full year of operation, and by 1928 moved 14,053,188. However, traffic never grew at the rate its investors envisioned. Although real estate development burgeoned across the suburban region it served, the railroad suffered intense competition. Once the New York, New Haven, and Hartford opened its Hell Gate Arch Bridge in 1917—the gigantic structure Amtrak's Boston–New York service uses today—potential NYW&B riders had yet another quick way to lower Manhattan. Within four years after its inauguration, NYW&B management confronted riders' suggestion that city-bound trains divert at Port Morris from the new right-of-way onto the tracks across the Hell Gate Arch Bridge. Passengers wanted direct service either to

Pennsylvania Station or to Grand Central Terminal, not the subway transfer facility they condemned as inconvenient.

Twenty years later, the NYW&B was still using its original terminal, and its timetable covers explained how to get there. "To reach the New York, Westchester, & Boston Ry. Via Third Ave Elevated Line, change cars at the 123rd Street Elevated Station and use covered passage way direct to Harlem River Station," the directions begin. Via the Lexington Avenue subway, "take express to the East 180th Street joint station with the 'Westchester' or via the Pelham Bay Park extension at Hunt's Point station. Direct connection with 180th St. and Harlem is made via Willis Avenue taxis crossing Harlem River and running through 123rd Street to Fort Lee Ferry." No matter how much New York City improved its elevated and subway lines, NYW&B riders accustomed to spacious, comfortable, high-speed trains found public transit cars crowded, noisy, dirty, and slow. The Harlem River Station seemed a greater abomination with every passing year, and increasingly passengers found ways to commute on other railroads or by automobile. Instead of enhancing commercial activity and property values at the north end of Manhattan, the NYW&B terminal seemed to have no impact at all.

In addition, government intervention condemned the NYW&B to bankruptcy from the start, although at the beginning no one glimpsed the impact of local ordinance. In 1916 New York enacted its first zoning laws, restricting the growth of commercial development north of 59th Street. In the last decades of the nineteenth century and up until 1916, the center of business activity had moved slowly but certainly northward. The inventors of the NYW&B assumed that by around 1950 it would arrive at 125th Street, approximately across the river from the Harlem River Terminal. NYW&B inventors and investors alike envisioned increased patronage as the suburban region grew more populous and the focus of Manhattan commerce moved toward the new terminal. Escalating ridership might pay to extend NYW&B tracks under or over the Harlem River, directly into the new center of Manhattan enterprise. But three years after its trains began operating, NYW&B management confronted the impact of a zoning ordinance that made the upper half of Manhattan largely an awkward mix of residential and warehouse neighborhoods increasingly clogged with trucks. Instead of moving north as it had been doing, white-collar enterprise had begun to build upward, making the area near Pennsylvania Station and Grand Central Terminal thronged with pedestrians, especially in rush hour. In the meantime, in the suburbs NYW&B riders learned to drive their automobiles to competing railroads that operated into the two great terminals of Manhattan.

The 1920s suburban commuters driving to railroad stations other than NYW&B ones behaved almost exactly as grain shippers behave in the High Plains today. They used automobiles as grain shippers use trucks, and they produced the same controversies over highway alignment, improvement, and maintenance. Far more importantly, however, they altered highway planning in Westchester County and transformed real estate investment. A community enjoying high-speed, frequent, comfortable electrified commuter service over fenced tracks isolated from highway crossings discovered would-be residents and businesses moving to similar communities whose trains reached Grand Central Terminal or Pennsylvania Station. By the 1930s suburban real estate developers everywhere in the United States knew the paralyzing lesson of the NYW&B.

The short life of the NYW&B deserves more than passing mention, for it illuminates a profound change in the trajectory of American urbanism. Other railroads deposited Manhattan-bound commuters away from the two great stations. The Erie and the Lackawanna used ferry terminals in Hoboken; and until it built its tunnels beneath the Hudson, the mighty Pennsylvania diverted commuters to the Hudson & Manhattan, nowadays rebuilt by the Port Authority and operating between Manhattan and Newark. The Baltimore & Ohio; the Reading; the New York, Ontario & Western; the Lehigh Valley; and other railroads never swept into Pennsylvania Station and Grand Central Terminal. Social historians, urban planners, and political pundits still ignore parameters imposed by steel-and-concrete investors more than a century ago. Engineers on the payroll of profit-minded investors shaped the public realm in ways that still vex city and regional planners, urban designers, and politicians today and that profoundly threaten the modern real estate development, trucking, and automobile industries.

A year before the Harlem Board of Commerce publicized its concerns about street congestion and the uselessness of the NYW&B passenger terminal, the Regional Plan of New York and Its Environs documented a broader crisis. *Transit and Transportation and a Study of Port and Industrial Areas and Their Relation to Transportation* remains a landmark in urban planning history. The fourth volume of the Regional Plan traces patterns of growth within contemporaneous context, and then predicts likely events. Illustrated with maps keyed to tables and charts, the volume emphasizes that a "policy of drift" has permitted private-directed growth at public expense, producing extremely unbalanced urban and suburban development. More importantly, especially for any contemporary reader musing on sprawl, revitalizing cities, creating high-paying office and industrial jobs in urban areas, or simply caught in automobile and truck traffic near or in New York, *Transit and Transportation* warns that ignoring engineering issues imprisons taxpayers, property owners, and especially politicians. Above all, it demonstrates beyond doubt that late 1920s experts analyzed data that let them see around the curve of time.

"The present serious difficulties in Manhattan exist at a time when only a small proportion of the buildings exceed ten stories in height," warns the foreword. "The real problem is what is going to happen when the land in Manhattan is put to its full use." *Transit and Transportation* is not really a planning document, but it is an analytical one. Decades before the rise of computers, the engineers retained by the Committee on the Regional Plan used desk calculators and pencils to outline what would happen in the immediate and distant future. Theirs is one of the finest early scenario analyses, and one of the last made public in ways that reached special-interest groups and citizens alike.

Retrospect made the analysts skeptical at once. Simple engineering realities produced gigantic social consequences. The Long Island Rail Road, a subsidiary of the Pennsylvania, enjoyed tunnel access beneath the East River into Pennsylvania Station. Direct service, even service requiring changes at Jamaica, caused a boom in suburban residential development in western Long Island, and enriched the Pennsylvania. Commuters reveled in the direct service to lower Manhattan so coveted by NYW&B commuters north of Long Island Sound. But analysts discovered a geopolitical secret buried in Long Island schedules and ticket receipts: the Long Island Rail Road provided such excellent service that New York City had delayed building subway or elevated rapid transit lines in the easterly part of Queens.

Moreover, since the Pennsylvania Railroad realized its massive new Manhattan station would be overwhelmed if New Jersey commuters used it in numbers approaching those from Long Island, commuters from south of the Hudson River discovered fares intended to make them shift in New Jersey to the rapid-transit "tube trains" of the Hudson & Manhattan. The arrangement worked splendidly, not only to eliminate potential congestion in Pennsylvania Station, but to boost revenue on the H&M, which the Pennsylvania controlled. But since Pennsylvania competitors provided free ferry service from their Hoboken terminals across the Hudson to Manhattan, many commuters preferred the ferries to paying an additional fare to the H&M just to save a few minutes. Bit by bit, analysts assembled seemingly fragmentary and conflicting data into a pattern of commuting that linked rising suburban property values on Long Island with New Jersey commuter willingness to use free ferries that took longer than H&M trains. Pennsylvania Railroad commuter tickets offered a glimpse at corporate power skewing the growth of the metropolitan region.

Some data outlined puzzling issues. Certainly, wealthy commuters avoided the H&M transfer and chose Pennsylvania commuter trains operating to and from Pennsylvania Station. Those commuters simply walked to their places of employment, enjoying total freedom from the subway rides that irritated NYW&B riders. Such riders undermined the entire methodology of commuter study. For the Regional Plan analysts, purchase of monthly tickets defined railroad commuters, although in a pinch the analysts applied the definition to all passengers riding trains inside the zone in which railroad companies offered reduced-fare tickets. "Commuted-price tickets," often sold by the week or month, not only gave commuters their name but seemed a simple way of identifying regular riders. But the prosperous Pennsylvania commuters using Pennsylvania Station suggested a new commuter pattern.

In one of its few deviations from hard-data analysis, *Transit and Transportation* stated that there were "quite a number of commuters coming daily from points between the one- and two-hour zones and a few that come from still greater distances." Such commuters merged seamlessly into the larger pool of long-distance passengers, and proved nearly impossible to isolate. The passengers enjoyed comfortable, fast trains, including dining cars and club cars in which to enjoy an afternoon drink, and often walked to both their local stations and Pennsylvania Station. The time they spent aboard trains operating beyond the one-hour zone had to be weighed against amenities and their not having to ride a subway train, trolley, or bus to an urban station, or even a trolley to their local one. Such passengers appear to have included NYW&B commuters who learned to drive to New York, New Haven, and Hartford stations for trains running directly to Grand Central Terminal. Almost all who did not walk used local stations with ample free parking for their automobiles. In 1946 the long-distance railroad commuters produced unending difficulties for planners and real estate developers. Many of these long-distance commuters spent less time each day traveling than people who used subways or a combination of subway and ordinary commuter trains. Typical commuters might spend ten minutes on a subway train to reach a H&M tube train or to reach a ferry leaving for New Jersey; others might spend twenty minutes on a subway train headed for the NYW&B terminal. But such commuters also had to walk to the subway station and then sometimes wait for a train; if they arrived on the platform just as a train departed, they might wait an additional three to eight minutes. The waiting time would vary, but the commuter had to allow for the longer period in order to consistently make the scheduled departure of the commuter train. Some commuters learned to calculate total commute time in each direction, and at least some determined to work within walking distance of Grand Central Terminal or Pennsylvania Station and commute via long-distance train. Higher transportation charges (partially offset by the absence of subway fares) and comfort might tip the scales in favor of such a decision, but the opportunity to live in pleasant and often less expensive places may have provided more incentive. Those places became the exclusive, high-property-value suburbs so evident by 1960.

In 1929 Regional Plan analysts found themselves mired in what had become conventional wisdom. "It is generally conceded that families should be encouraged to live as far as possible outside the congested centers where land is cheaper and where their environment, while it might be less exciting, would be more wholesome," they admitted in a report entitled *Transportation*. Bowing to what women's magazines had concluded forty years earlier and had hammered home with dedication, the analysts glimpsed not only the realpolitik of suburbanization but its engineering implications.

Unless New York built more railroad terminals on Manhattan, upper-middle-class families would tend to locate along the long-distance lines running from Pennsylvania Station and Grand Central Terminal. Corridors of wealth would reach south into New Jersey, north along the Hudson River, and eastward toward Connecticut. For a decade or two, Long Island would accommodate the families of men did not earn quite enough money to commute long-distance. Then the city and its immediate neighbors would confront either impossible congestion or a sort of centrifugal shattering. In 1929 the term *sprawl* was not yet in currency, but undoubtedly there were concerns about an impromptu, unplanned spinning off of downtown capital into diffuse suburban and exurban space. "Excitement" might leave lower Manhattan, jump over a zone jammed with trucks and over a drab residential ring, and take root in a zone of large-lot homes inhabited by the households of long-run commuters.

Between 1914 and 1924, Grand Central Terminal commuter traffic increased by 9.8 percent over each preceding year. In general terms, based on surveys at all New York rail terminals, commuter traffic doubled every nine years, and total railroad passenger traffic doubled every thirteen. Since 1918 the price gap between monthly commuter tickets and regular round-trip ones had been increasing, but by 1928 analysts knew that many riders bought monthly books and used them only twelve to eighteen times before giving them to family members or friends. Ticket sales alone produced only part of a larger picture; passenger counts made clear the inadequacy of ticket sales as indicators. Actual counting of passengers demonstrated that projected growth rates might be too conservative, and that without immediate steps the region would confront, first, traffic jams and flight of real estate capital, then the loss of middle-income families and the businesses dependent on them. Accordingly, the Regional Plan analysts suggested building more railroad terminals on Manhattan and linking at least some of them with a belt line used by commuter trains. Such construction would increase property values away from lower Manhattan, certainly above 59th Street, and would open huge adjoining regions to suburban residential development focused on Manhattan.

The analysts studied the movement of express and freight, too, and paid special attention to the role of piers and warehouses. Transshipment between steamships and barges and railroad cars—and trucks—received as much scrutiny as passengers striding toward Hudson River ferries. While commuter patterns remained relatively stable between 1918 and 1928 as ridership grew, freight movements altered dramatically. Fuel oil began replacing coal, for example, and analysts envisioned scenarios in which coal would become far less important within two decades. Declining coal traffic would free coal yards and other facilities for redevelopment, but it would adversely impact the Lackawanna, Lehigh Valley, and other coal-focused railroads that also provided commuter service. Beyond coal, the chief problem of transportation—excluding "transit" involving people—lay in the movement of food into New York and manufactured goods into, from, and across the city and its region, increasingly by trucking companies that kept inadequate records.

Lack of data complicated the problem. Since 1914 no agency had collected totals on express and freight movements, and only fragmentary data hinted at changes between 1899 and 1924. Imports of hay had dropped as motor vehicles replaced horse-drawn ones, and coal moving to New England did so increasingly by rail, rather than by ships or barges leaving from Hudson River wharves. Throughout the 1920s, building material arrived by all three modes of transport, and the building boom that produced such commuter congestion problems in turn exacerbated the movement of building material into lower Manhattan. The amount of food entering the city increased year by year, but more and more of it arrived as time-sensitive, refrigerated cargo, and much of it moved by truck. Outbound express and freight made up only about a fourth of the total tonnage of inbound shipments, but it proved of very high value, consisting almost entirely of manufactured goods. Most departed as time-sensitive shipments as well. Motor truck traffic increased dramatically year by year, and the city needed to build some sort of airport for the growing numbers of airplanes, dirigibles, and other flying machines that seemed likely to multiply but prove useless in mitigating commuter jams. A lack of data about the movement of material was worsened by vague and sometimes inaccurate information about the transfer of goods. Some food arrived by train and moved from warehouses to trucks to grocery stores, but some moved directly from railroad cars to trucks. Some fuel oil moved from railroad cars to distributor storage tanks, but some flowed from tank cars directly into factory storage tanks. Certainly the movement of express and freight interfered with the movement of people, but it also threatened to overwhelm street traffic, especially away from the skyscraper district. The Harlem Board of Commerce perceived the threat of motor truck congestion all too accurately, as did the Regional Plan analysts.

At some point, Manhattan would suddenly begin to hemorrhage jobs, capital, and especially innovative new companies. Public schooling and other social goods would suffer, gradually at first, then dramatically. One plausible solution emerged from the success of the Railway Express Agency and other railroad industry affiliates. Engineers retained by the Regional Plan suggested building a miniature freight subway beneath Manhattan, with extensions to New Jersey, Long Island, and the Bronx. Trains would bring merchandise to stores and, more importantly, remove ashes, trash, and garbage; they would move purchased items to close-in residential neighborhoods, toward suburban ones, and directly to Railway Express Agency facilities for transfer to high-speed long-distance trains. Subterranean freight trains would eliminate much local-delivery truck traffic, speeding trolley car and bus schedules and making motorists happier, all the while broadening the influence of New York City retail enterprise.

Chicago had enjoyed such a subterranean freight railroad since 1906. When investors in a nascent underground telephone cable company realized that the small construction tunnels might carry miniature freight trains, they began building larger tunnels secretly. After squabbling over franchise rights with politicians, they received the right to operate trains through sixty miles of interconnected tunnels, most below central Chicago. Forty feet below city streets, running in steel-and-concrete arch-shaped tunnels pushed through clay soils, fifteen-car trains pulled by electric locomotives soon linked almost every major building with every railroad company freight house.

Trains cruised at fifteen or twenty miles an hour, exchanged cars in a freight yard beneath a wholesale grocery warehouse, and sometimes operated directly into department store basements. Marshall Field became a major customer immediately, receiving merchandise round the clock and dispatching hundreds of thousands of packages for transshipment—to the Railway Express Agency. Candy manufacturers were delighted with the rapid shipment of product to long-distance railroad trains, especially via the Illinois Central Railroad, whose Central Station stood directly above the narrow-gauge tracks. While Marshall Field had its own spur tracks and loading platforms, other businesses used elevators that plucked individual cars upward from tunnels. In its first decades, the company proved successful and profitable, even trendy.

The Illinois Tunnel Company, later renamed the Chicago Tunnel Company, impressed United States legislators and foreign dignitaries. At hotels such as the august Palmer House, Mae West and other celebrities descended to glimpse high-tech urbanity and perhaps be photographed within it. The company built a special tunnel to serve the Field Museum of Natural History, demonstrating its ability to reach across as-yet-undeveloped land toward valuable customers, and for decades seemed an eminently sensible means of minimizing street congestion.

But while New York Regional Plan engineers were admiring it in the 1920s, the Chicago railroad had begun to confront the impact of fuel oil replacing coal. By the late 1920s its motor truck subsidiary had drawn away much time-sensitive merchandise as underground haulage of coal and ash slipped. Between the late 1930s and 1943 the building of city subways eliminated six miles of Chicago Tunnel Company tunnels, cutting off all access to downtown department stores. As late as 1954 new leadership experimented with moving mail between the main and branch post offices, but the loss of the department store connections ended in bankruptcy and, in 1959, abandonment.

While a few miles of tunnel today carry high-voltage electric lines and fiber-optic cables, most of the system lies empty. In surprisingly good condition for century-old tunnels (despite some water damage caused by a 1992 pile-driving mistake that diverted the Chicago River through it into basements whose owners had long forgotten the trains), the system exists in limbo. Perhaps it waits, as Greenbush waited a half century after the last trains left the salt marsh terminal for Boston. Perhaps it waits in vain, perhaps not. But it does not disappear from urban design thinking. After all, such a system might at least remove trash, garbage, and recyclable products. Even if the system delivered only half or perhaps even a quarter of the merchandise arriving by truck, removing most trash might make it feasible.

Since 1929, urban designers have understood that moving people often collide with moving goods. While 1960s visionaries gobbled up federal funds in studies of automated people-moving devices like the Urbmobile, almost none focused on the goods–people collision depicted so acutely in *Transit and Transportation*. Even the 1970s energy crisis did nothing to stimulate sensible—or even wacky discussion—and today few experts know much about the movement of goods, garbage included, as a modifier of urban life, let alone as a generator of urban design and real estate profits. UPS and FedEx are well versed in the fine points of package moving, but who knows why a single convenience store or delicatessen is serviced by six different bakery trucks every day? Designing a city above a freight, merchandise, and refuse subway railroad still remains an abstraction, although planners studying the movement of people grudgingly admit that goods-transfer congestion impedes downtown people movement.

In 1928 packages dropped down chutes beneath the Marshall

Field store, moved along a conveyor belt, and dropped again onto tables from which men sorted them into the little cars of the Chicago Tunnel Company. After arriving at the proper freight house or Railway Express Agency depot, the packages moved up conveyor belts for sorting. What happened then around the clock happens around the clock now in Memphis, at the national hub of FedEx. Given simple barcode and robotic technology that already routes FedEx and UPS packages and envelopes, the Chicago Tunnel Company activity might function with extremely few employees: perhaps almost none. A robotic underground freight railroad would decongest city streets and dramatically improve urban sanitation. Certainly it would reduce air pollution. But the nature of business, especially wholesale business, still precludes serious planning for such improvements.

While the FedEx driver delivering an envelope at an address may also pick up a package for shipment, the bakery truck driver delivers product and takes orders for more. In hundreds of thousands of small firms, delivery drivers work also as salespeople, and they move goods only one way. Possibly the bakery truck returns at the close of day with a few loaves of day-old bread on board, but most delivery trucks return totally empty of merchandise but with order books on board.

Dedicated delivery trucks are not common-carrier vehicles. Generations of regulations restrict the operation of common carriers open to hire by any shipper. Some of the regulations are starkly simple: an 18-wheeler that carries poisonous chemicals to a factory may not roll down the street and accept a load of cookies for movement a thousand miles away. Health and safety concerns make up only a small portion of regulations; the bulk of government effort focuses on regulating rates and services for the public good, ostensibly by ensuring competition. Thus a bakery-owned truck cannot transport household belongings, apples, or newspapers later in the day. Such items must move either in trucks owned by their manufacturers or purchasers, or aboard UPS, FedEx, or other motor freight common-carrier vehicles.

Just as no owner of an automobile may drive to the end of a queue of taxicabs and begin his own taxi business, no owner of any truck, even a pickup, can set up shop as a trucking company. The metal taxicab medallions and masses of stickers and cryptic initials decorating the sides of cabs and common-carrier trucks attest to the host of arcane regulations governing their use. Politicians who speak glibly of deregulating the motor freight industry know perfectly well that deregulation can proceed only so far before chaos develops. Economists who study the motor freight industry know its remaining regulations as perhaps the most byzantine of any industry.

Regulations govern the cost of trucking dog food, but not other animal food; dog food moves at a cost 10–35 percent greater than cat food. Prepared frozen meals including chicken, turkey, and fish move free of regulation; meals including a hamburger patty move under regulated tariffs that increase costs 20–25 percent. Lobbyists for some trucking companies oppose restrictive tariffs, but other lobbyists champion them. Into the debate move unions and non-union associations, shipper and consumer alliances, and representatives of railroads and other competitors. Always watchful and always proactive, local and state politicians monitor regulation of motor freight rates, for they understand that regulation and deregulation have sharp geographical consequences.

Congress began regulating railroads in 1887, when it created the Interstate Commerce Commission (ICC) to oversee safety concerns and rate setting. Schoolchildren still learn how hundreds of thousands of farmers organized through the Patrons of Husbandry to lobby Congress; the "Grangers" figure prominently in Frank Norris's famous 1902 muckraking novel *The Octopus,* and in other works pitting rural families against rapacious railroad barons charging all the market will bear. Federal regulation of railroad rates not only produced tens of thousands of specific rates for specific products between specific places but also made almost any innovation, from abandoning a line to building a new route, a political issue, almost invariably at the local level. Into the 1970s the railroad industry confronted regulatory ferocity when it tried to abandon money-losing passenger train service or transport truck trailers via express train. The regulation and deregulation of railroads, and subsequently of the trucking industry, prove that national policy often originates in measures as localized as New York City changing its zoning to benefit real estate developers owning property near Grand Central Terminal and Pennsylvania Station.

The Motor Carrier Act of 1935 brought the trucking industry into the jurisdiction of the ICC. From its birth after World War I through the last years of the Depression, the long-distance trucking industry moved over rough roads that produced tough, often rough behavior. Few graduate students read A. I. Bezzerides' 1938 novel of the industry, *The Long Haul,* although many old-film aficionados know the Raoul Walsh film based on it. In the 1940 epic *They Drive by Night,* starring George Raft and Humphrey Bogart, tough truckers in frail trucks blunder off roads into criminal behavior, and into federal regulation. The heavy hand of formal education keeps *The Octopus* in print, but *The Long Haul* has slipped into an oblivion as near total as that of the NYW&B.

From 1940 until the 1960s the ICC stymied motor freight innovation and stifled competition. Any trucking firm that produced the necessary paperwork to demonstrate its pre-1935 operations received a federal certificate permitting subsequent operation, but after 1935 entrepreneurs found creating a new trucking firm almost impossible. Instead, investors would try to buy an existing firm and expand it, often paying hundreds of thousands of dollars for a permit to carry a particular product over the road between two cities. Expansion and merger produced regulatory rate conflicts that drove many owners to distraction. If a trucking firm owning the right to move a product between Pittsburgh and Detroit acquired a firm with the right to move the identical product between Detroit and New York, the ICC required that the product continue to move via Detroit, not over highways running directly from Pittsburgh to New York. As John R. Meyer, Merton J. Peck, and other noted economists pointed out in a seminal 1959 book, *The Economics of Competition in the Transportation Industries,* ICC regulation of the trucking industry restricted national economic growth while guaranteeing the prosperity of some cities and businesses along certain routes. After twenty years the ICC had seemingly lost sight of the motor freight industry as one fundamentally different from railroads. The ICC saw long-haul trucking as railroading on rubber tires, and its view shaped the creation of the Interstate Highway System. Highway designers understood ICC tariff and route regulations to predict future growth in truck traffic, and designed accordingly.

It mostly escapes general notice that interstate highways are situated where they are in large measure owing to an ICC fixation on trucks as de facto trains that ought to follow predictable, unchanging routes—routes that make cities prosperous.

The ICC restricted railroad innovation until the 1970s. Order 321 ICC 582, Grain in Multiple-Car Shipments—River Crossings to the South, a 1963 ICC decision derisively remembered in the railroad industry as "the Big John case" from the nickname applied to the innovative railroad car involved, reveals federal regulator unease over the invention of extremely large grain hoppers that could be coupled into unit trains that would immediately reduce shipping rates and enrich farmers and railroads. Engineering invention was a cause of concern for ICC officials, since any invention offered the potential for making the railroad industry suddenly more efficient than the barge and trucking industry.

Long after the de facto deregulation of the trucking industry— begun in 1975 by the Ford administration and continued by the Motor Carrier Act of 1980 at the insistence of Jimmy Carter—difficulties persist with roads owned and maintained by government, and tariffs involving dog food and other products. Deregulation slashed the power of the Teamsters and other unions. While the industry as a whole still pays higher wages than most others and so attracts many rural young people into a seemingly romantic life on the road, overall its upper-limit average wages have dropped about a tenth over the past decade. Competition not only drives innovation and efficiency but also drives down wages; lower wages have helped keep the trucking industry viable in a time of railroad innovation.

Buying a used 18-wheel truck and becoming an owner-operator common or contract carrier is not a simple process, but neither is it especially difficult or hard to finance; even buying a small licensed trucking firm is straightforward. Entrepreneurs need only the vehicle and appropriate licenses and permits. The road is free, except for road-use taxes, and the road leads anywhere. On the other hand, individuals can buy used railroad locomotives and even learn to operate them, but no railroad company will accept their operation. Even short-line railroads are big business compared with one-truck owner-operators who sleep behind the seat.

The floor of an 18-wheeler trailer sits four feet above the road, a constant reminder that trucks evolved to load and unload from railroad boxcars with a standard floor height. Today, in a quasi-deregulated business environment, scrutinizers of urban warehouse districts, rural crossroads, and exurban parking lots often notice 18-wheel trucks unloading part of some cargo into the beds of pickup trucks backed against them. While railroad companies focus on long-distance unit trains and solid consists of intermodal containers, many very large long-haul motor freight carriers now compete with UPS and FedEx Ground, each of which moves packages up to 150 pounds. But no longer do large-truck drivers necessarily seek out warehouses with loading docks. Often they rendezvous with business people who own only pickup trucks, or who rent a U-Haul box truck and transship freight, or who run businesses in residential districts and ask that truckers deposit heavy freight on front lawns despite zoning regulations. What seems like innovation indicates a fast-deepening poverty, a sort of mercantile scruffiness. Trucks roll everywhere, not only jamming roads and parking lots but defying any rational response by highway and other planners.

The idea of regulating the motor truck industry originated in part through congressional awareness that physical constraints might make trucks the predators of urban prosperity. The Harlem Board of Commerce wanted to improve passenger access to the northern end of Manhattan, particularly via the NYW&B. It and the Regional Plan Association were well aware that truck traffic had begun to strangle much of upper Manhattan, and even parts of the Bronx and Brooklyn. The situation was serious enough to prompt congressional action: the 1935 Motor Freight Act, aimed in part at proportioning truck traffic congestion among cities.

Despite its best efforts, the ICC failed. By the middle 1950s trucking companies had pulled huge volumes of lucrative freight traffic away from railroads, often because railroads either refused to innovate or discovered ICC opposition to innovations it deemed unfair to the trucking and airline industries. Interstate highway construction at first kept pace with growing truck traffic, but manufacturers, freight forwarders, warehouse firms, and consignees discovered massive congestion on and abutting their real estate. The ICC set many rates without regard to regular, predictable traffic delays. The arbitrary rates assisted established shippers and receivers only into the 1960s. Then many new shippers and receivers began relocating to cities and suburbs free of truck congestion, and demanding lower rates. Trucking firms realized far greater profits from high-speed, fast-turnaround trips, and so favored rural and exurban clients as much as they could under regulation. As more shippers and receivers moved away from center city, then even suburban areas, rural-area congressmen pressured the ICC to set rates based on open roads and vast, sprawling parking lots and loading docks.

While Kennedy and Johnson administration experts viewed the lines of 18-wheelers waiting to off-load at single urban freight elevators as an imminent economic calamity, they were only too conversant with the power of the Teamsters and other unions. Despite Kennedy's insistence that the United States needed an integrated national transportation plan, neither he nor Johnson did much to anger unions. But Ford and Carter moved with dispatch, and despite the 1982 recession, by the mid-1980s the impacts of the 1980 Motor Carrier Act and the 1980 Staggers Act began to be obvious. Between 1981 and 1986 intermodal shipment of truck trailers by railroad companies grew 70 percent.

Unit trains of truck trailers or containers speeding along well-maintained tracks now pass so frequently through much of the Midwest and Far West that few locals pay them much attention. But unlike hopper cars of coal or corn, the containers are individual items moved and monitored differently. In the late 1960s the railroad industry began experimenting with bar coding all its cars and locomotives. On January 1, 1970, every piece of rolling stock carried a machine-readable label similar to the bar-code labels nowadays found on every grocery store item. The industry envisioned the project first as an accounting/information system. Computers would track the whereabouts of every car and locomotive, reducing paperwork and providing data useful in increasing efficiency. In some semiautomatic classification yards, the labels might enable computer-driven switching and makeup of freight trains. The second projected use of bar codes—never widely publicized—involved automated control of trains: the labels might precipitate a new era in which optical scanners recognized entire trains and fed data into computers regulating speed and routes. But just as supermarket chains have found bar codes useful for inventory control and speeding checkout, yet have so far found the labels useless in automating the bagging of disparate groceries, so the railroad industry found the label system unsatisfactory in the long run.

Dirt, especially rain-washed dirt, and snow obscured the sophisticated labels and eventually prompted the replacement of the entire system with other systems that simply read serial numbers painted on car sides. By 1980 the industry had essentially automated its car-monitoring system, but a decade earlier had discovered that moving truck trailers and containers expeditiously did not guarantee that the trailers and containers *arrived* expeditiously at their final destinations. The trailer, automatically monitored during its rail trip across the nation, moved away from an intermodal railroad yard onto highways and local roads and into an informational black hole. Despite advancements in subsequent years, particularly in Global Positioning System monitoring, truck drivers still determine many short-haul truck movements and often must decide to detour on long-haul routes as well. Just as rural highway commissioners find themselves surprised by overnight conglomerations of heavy grain-hauling trucks, so urban, suburban, and metropolitan planners and real estate investors discover mysterious gaggles of trucks suddenly descending upon particular locales. The lack of data concerning short-haul truck movements, especially following transfer from railroad trains, that vexed Regional Plan experts in the 1920s endures today.

In the absence of information, real estate developers choose boldly but cannily, accepting very high risks. In aging cities such as Boston and Baltimore, New York and Indianapolis, Chicago, St. Louis, Denver, and Seattle, and others with increasingly vibrant downtown business districts generating "excitement," inner ring zones jammed with trucks are now scorned. Passed through quickly by suburban commuters aboard trains, moved across far less quickly by suburban commuters driving their own cars, the ring zones grow more jammed and more rundown by the day. Long-haul truck trips terminate in them, and inside their confines railroads transfer trailers and containers from flatcars to trucks that often jam parking lots. In old coastal cities, such transfer often mixes with transfer between ships and planes and trains, producing the gridlock so evident to I-95 motorists approaching the George Washington Bridge from the south. Almost everyone, from environmentalists to politicians to artists, is enthusiastic about "revitalizing downtown," but almost no one is interested in the ring zones separating downtown from suburbs. No longer the industrial zone of manufacturing, not even a zone of warehouses and freight forwarding firms, the ring caters almost entirely to intermodal transfer and to the transfer of long-haul truck cargo. Among the clogged highways and local streets live the poor, squeezed between gentrified downtowns and high-value inner suburbs easily accessed via commuter trains.

Public transportation means, of course, vehicles that transport groups of people. Goods, however, tend to move privately, and these movements are difficult to track and defy analysis. Real estate developers embrace the dichotomy directly. They assume that where passenger trains once ran, they might, indeed will, run again, and they invest accordingly, especially downtown. Recently the federal government awarded New York City another $150 million for its ongoing East Side Access Project, a rerouting of Long Island Rail Road passenger trains through the new tunnels near 63rd Street in the vicinity of Grand Central Terminal. Renewed passenger train access translates into tens of thousands of people transferring between trains and places of work, shopping, and recreation; such transfer drives up property values, and developers know that. Developers assume, too, that local delivery of goods that conflicts with the movement of people drives people away. In this assumption they are in accord with Regional Plan analysts and the Harlem Board of Commerce. Consequently they concentrate on old passenger train routes into cities and leave the question of freight and trash subways to financiers thinking about automating the transfer of goods. No one knows exactly how people and goods flow into, around, and from cities. It is clear, however, that expediting the flow of people now means segregating the flow of goods to ring zones that will soon strangle downtown expansion.

Real estate developers scrutinize the example of the NYW&B not because they know it offers a window on local zoning ordinance transforming the development of a vast metropolitan region, nor because it demonstrates that commuters will drive from one commuter train station to another they believe offers better service. Instead they examine the NYW&B because it terminated in the Bronx next to freight yards.

Investing in almost any urban downtown, especially one blessed with stable or rising property values, requires significant capital. Property immediately adjacent to downtown usually bustles with trucks, warehouses, and related businesses serving downtown and suburbs. If more and more truckborne freight moved via rail, not beneath downtown but adjacent to it, large quantities of ring-zone real estate might suddenly become available for reuse. From the bottom of the pot in which the stew of the old and new Motor Carrier Acts, the Staggers Act, and other government regulations simmers now bubbles up the example of the NYW&B. Thinking ahead is hard, and scenario analysis sometimes fails. But an extraordinarily profitable real estate investment boom might have happened in upper Manhattan in the 1930s, especially if the locale had been freed of truck traffic and made accessible to commuters.

Many cities have such locales today, laced with railroad tracks to be sure, but also crammed with trucks and truck-dependent businesses. If the trucks might be eliminated or nearly so, and their freight handled more or less robotically in very condensed neighborhoods, developers might be able to transform regions near downtown. Almost all real estate developers realize the short-term consequences of the massive population growth immediately ahead, and they realize that almost all of that growth will occur in metropolitan places. The only sort of space with any potential for solving the coming housing crisis—and at a profit—is the ring-zone warehouse district adjacent to downtown.

Over the past decade, Harvard University has quietly acquired a gritty neighborhood of warehouses, freight-forwarding companies, and even a railroad yard. Few academics—indeed almost no white-collar people—ever visited the neighborhood just beyond the Harvard Business School in Boston. Harvard expects rail and truck traffic to move away from its newly acquired property in Allston, and it intends to build a new campus after it demolishes the old buildings. The truck-based businesses will indeed move away, but now shippers and politicians insist that the intermodal rail transshipment yard remain. Harvard waited too long. It bought the last rail/truck/warehouse conglomeration abutting downtown Boston, at very inflated prices and from investors who knew the long-term property value of a neighborhood most white-collar people found—and still find—invisible, even as they sit in traffic jams caused by trucks entering and leaving its last functioning businesses.

Then Harvard discovered something scenario analysts began studying in the late 1970s, the Grand Junction line. An active freight railroad over which switching locomotives move commuter train cars late at night, the track indirectly connects the northern suburbs of Boston with those to the west and south. This indirect link between North Station and South Station bisects the campus of the Massachusetts Institute of Technology and crosses the Charles River, but the Boston-area intellectual elite scarcely see it. Scholars studying mental mapping discover that few questionnaire respondents even know the bridge exists. News media mention the line annually, when elephants parade from a circus train stopped adjacent to MIT laboratories, but for almost everyone the track proves invisible.

Now it is a nightmare. With almost no modification other than a concrete platform, commuter trains from north of Boston might terminate not at North Station but at a new stop at the southern edge of the new Harvard campus. Even worse, that southern edge abuts a very active commuter rail line whose passengers might choose to detrain in Allston rather than at South Station, a mile east in downtown. Even as the realization dawns that sending passenger trains over the Grand Junction track would link Wellesley College, Boston University, Harvard, MIT, Tufts University, and north-of-Boston beaches, real estate developers close the trap on Harvard. If the university indeed creates an entire new campus across the Charles River from its existing one, if it encourages spin-off commercial and scientific development, might it not create a new locus of commuter train service? Canny developers knew the answer by 1980 and sold only some of the property, at inflated prices, to Harvard. The rest they retained, assuming that the combination of Harvard growth, predicted by analysts anticipating the moves of large institutions, would combine with rail access to shift much capital away from downtown Boston. This is the lesson of the NYW&B. Passenger- and freight-train access to a point near the downtown of a vibrant city can destabilize growth in downtown. But when the moment is right, it can also radically enrich long-term investors by shifting capital to a new nearby location invisible to almost everyone.

SOURCES: Arcara, *Westchester's Forgotten Railway;* Harlem Board of Commerce, *Three Plans for the Relief of Traffic Congestion;* Homberger, *Historical Atlas of New York City;* John R. Meyer, Merton J. Peck, et al., *The Economics of Competition in the Transportation Industries;* Moffat, *Forty Feet Below,* and *The "L";* Mortimer, "ACI . . . Have You Got It?"; New York, Westchester, and Boston Railway, *Westchester Timetables;* Regional Plan Association, *Transit and Transportation and a Study of Port and Industrial Areas;* Westcott, "Midnight Local."

OVERHEAD

In 1979 the Muskingum Electric began proving that General Electric remote sensing technology then undergoing testing on Bay Area Rapid Transit (BART) equipment in San Francisco worked well. The massive coal trains operated under simultaneous continuous and intermittent automatic train control, but not under human supervision. When loading and unloading, and at the ends of the lines, the robotic locomotives received automated radio signals. Only eight commands proved necessary: stop, creep (one-third of a mile an hour), 4, 15, 35, and 50 miles an hour, and north and south. Except when automatically changing speed away from ends of the line, the trains moved under intermittent control. Every five thousand feet one of two paired sensors embedded beneath the rails radioed the locomotive to proceed; if the second sensor received a response from the locomotive within two seconds, the train moved ahead another five thousand feet to the next pair of sensors. While other sensors activated track switches so the trains could pass onto double track from single track, and opened and closed hopper car bottom doors during unloading, the fail-safe electronic sensing system struck all but electrical engineers as NASA-like wizardry. The control system sent messages to the locomotives, but the locomotives actively signaled the sensors too. Automatic train control could move heavy trains in wilderness settings, in all sorts of weather, efficiently and safely.

Such operation made few headlines outside railroad industry journals and magazines read by train enthusiasts, but it affected the long-range thinking of many technically minded real estate investors. Readers of a 1967 *Popular Mechanics* feature article on the new Great Slave Lake Railway operating into the sub-Arctic from Peace River in Alberta, learned that tall microwave towers, radios, and telephones meant no poles and wires marching beside the new tracks. Long trains of lead ore moved behind diesel locomotives operated by engineers, although the wireless communication net-

On rainy days, tourists find the New Orleans light-rail system especially pleasant.

work necessary to automatic train control already existed. Like the cutting-edge subway cars delivered the same year to Cleveland, a city suddenly boasting that its new rapid-transit rail line made it the only city in the United States with high-speed rail service between its downtown and airport, Great Slave Lake Railway equipment still required onboard engineers. But the new Cleveland equipment included the rudiments of far-reaching change. The cars permitted radio-sent cab signals so motormen no longer had to watch ahead for colored light signals beside the track, and sensor-driven equipment that stopped the trains if operators ran past red signals. In 1967 such equipment had been planned for new subway lines in Chicago and Boston, and uneasy unions felt a presentiment that the Muskingum Electric confirmed a dozen years later.

Labor unions stymied automation for decades after 1960. *Trains* editorialized in October 1978 that railroads, like building elevators, had built-in guidance systems: elevators had become automated and railroads might be. Yet after eighteen years of effort, Congress prohibited the railroad industry from adding staffing and work rules to its nationwide contract negotiations. Both the United Transportation Union (UTU) and the Brotherhood of Locomotive Engineers (BLE) successfully lobbied Congress to stymie industry automation initiatives, especially those involving bankrupt railroads. The industry asked Congress to permit bankruptcy trustees to change work rules—but not wages and benefits—on bankrupt lines. Congress refused. The BLE labeled the idea "a time bomb," and in 1978 unions still controlled Congress.

Automation inflected much industry effort after the 1970s energy crises and the success of the Muskingum Electric and other new-built railroads, just as it directed federal research funding. Eventually, it also shattered labor union alliances. The UTU accepted the concept of radio-controlled locomotives directed by conductors, while the BLE rejected the idea. In a last-ditch effort to halt the yard locomotives switching cars remotely (but under the control of a UTU employee on the ground), the much-diminished BLE merged with the Teamsters. Not until the Chicago, Rock Island & Pacific and other huge railroads had entered bankruptcy—often after having been abandoned by trustees unable to make them operate long enough to pay creditors—did Congress finally understand that the greater public good meant changed crew staffing laws and operating rules on all railroads. Cabooses disappeared as crews diminished and conductors rode in locomotives; short lines began working tiny, all-task crews; and dozens of automatic devices, particularly the handheld freight-yard locomotive controller, changed railroading in a multitude of ways.

Urban railroading divided subtly into two categories. As Cleveland and other cities began extending existing subway and trolley lines, and as Calgary and even Los Angeles began building all-new rapid-transit lines, real estate values began changing adjacent to short-ride infrastructure improvement. Not always did upgrades drive up the value of adjacent land; perhaps the examples of the New York, Westchester & Boston and similar lines remained potent. At the same time, Amtrak and urban freight trains were growing shorter and shorter, or sometimes even vanishing altogether. In 1980 the last freight train moved along the old New York Central West Side freight line—the so-called High Line—in Manhattan, abandoning a miles-long, double-track structure. The juxtaposition of modernizing, expanding rapid-transit lines and the withering of long-distance passenger train service and inner-city freight service in the context of railroad automation prompted tremors in real estate investment. In hindsight, 1980s real estate newspaper ads demonstrate the impact of upgrades and other changes along railroad tracks.

By 1990 railroad annual reports began emphasizing the laborsaving advantages of automation. Buses, in contrast, needed drivers. As W. D. Volkmer told *Electric Line* readers in a 1998 article, "Ten Years of Light Rail Progress," urban politicians had realized that light-rail and other rapid-transit rail vehicles needed fewer operators: one person might operate a three-car train. In the immediate future, they reasoned, rail vehicles might need no onboard operators at all, as BART demonstrated. The equation was simple. As the wages and benefits of a bus driver increase in proportion to the number of passengers carried aboard the bus, building an automatic (or semiautomatic) rail-based rapid-transit system becomes more economical, then the only possible alternative for cash-strapped cities and states. *Fixed-guidance systems,* to use the federal term for urban mass-transit systems operating on rails or under permanent overhead power transmission lines, might not be justified in neighborhoods with low population density. As Zachary Schrag demonstrates convincingly in *The Great Society Subway: A History of the Washington Metro,* real estate developers realized that changed zoning laws might make such systems linear generators of higher-density housing stock, office space, and retail development. Against the initial cost of building such systems, especially their protected rights-of-way, investors balanced the wages of bus drivers.

Across most of the United States, trains operate within very permeable corridors. At tens of thousands of grade crossings, automobiles and trucks collide with moving trains, most frequently plowing into the middle of trains, not locomotives. Flashing lights, ringing bells, illuminated gates, and the ear-splitting howl of locomotive horns fail to prevent such collisions. At lesser-used crossings, only signs warn motorists; elsewhere the right-of-way is scarcely protected from wandering livestock and other interruptions. Farmers and hunters routinely move along and across tracks despite signs announcing "no trespassing." When Thoreau said that he crossed the railroad as though it were "a cart path in the woods" he voiced the attitude of subsequent generations of rural and wilderness people. Along unfenced and poorly fenced tracks, automatic train operation proves difficult to implement. Only a traditional locomotive engineer, hand upon the throttle and eye upon the rail, offers safe operation.

But rapid-transit routes typically operate within enclosed rights-of-way. Subways offer the best example of rail routes awaiting automation.

Until just after World War II, only three cities boasted what William Middleton terms "heavy-duty subway operation." In his history of rail-based mass transit, *Metropolitan Railways: Rapid Transit in America,* he explains that for decades Chicago, Hoboken (whose "el" was once considered the largest iron structure in the world), and other cities relied largely on electric-powered trains operating atop elevated structures. Noise and visual blight made els seem old-fashioned in the 1930s, but maintenance costs condemned most by

1940, although some subway lines still operate over short stretches of elevated structure. Only New York, and to a slightly lesser degree Boston and Philadelphia, operated integrated subway systems that shaped urban growth and real estate investment. Throughout the Depression, planners in many transit-poor cities confronted more than financial difficulty. They realized that private automobile ownership reduced transit system ridership, especially in outlying regions feeding downtown rapid-transit systems. Financial strictures and declining patronage led to little construction, but indirectly precipitated downtown automobile traffic congestion, the destruction of buildings to make way for parking lots, and finally the building of highways through central city areas. Heavy-duty subway operations in the three eastern cities molded planning efforts and some construction, but in the end failed as models for smaller, less densely built cities.

Typical small-city subway operation involved trolley cars moving over suburban streets toward cities, then rolling down ramps into tunnels leading downtown. Boston and Philadelphia operate such light-duty subways today, but such systems once seemed an ideal compromise between surface-street trolleys and heavy-duty subway operation. After World War I, many cities choked with trolley cars used abandoned canal beds as the core of light-duty subway systems. Between 1927 and 1956 the Rochester, New York, subway system operated in tunnels located in the abandoned Erie Canal. The present Newark, New Jersey, system, now upgraded to heavy operation, opened in 1935 in tunnels located in the bed of the former Morris & Essex Canal. But the strangest example of subway building endures in Cincinnati.

In 1927, seven years after construction began, the city of Cincinnati had built four miles of tunnels in the bed of the abandoned Miami & Erie Canal, the first of twenty miles intended for immediate completion. But the city made what transit experts now recognize as a classic error: it built a multilane boulevard, now called Central Parkway, directly atop the tunnels. Motorists consequently flooded downtown, and in the Depression worked stopped for good on what might have been a superb light-rail subway. No trains ever operated in the tunnels fitted with rails, station signs, and even benches.

Cincinnati opted to improve automobile access to downtown, and finally located I-75 directly through the heart of the city, along the alignment reserved for future trolley cars moving between suburbs and downtown tunnels.

Eerily, the tunnels remain today. During the Cold War the city debated using them as air-raid shelters, and later its water department located mains on their floors, but few Cincinnatians even know of them. As late as 1946, however, a group of investors tried to use them as a freight subway serving sixteen manufacturers, and the city council passed an ordinance permitting such use. However, when three large potential customers, all breweries, became concerned that diesel locomotive exhaust might contaminate foodstuffs and ended their support, the project died. What Regional Plan experts envisioned in New York in the 1920s, and what Chicago businesses already enjoyed in their electric-powered freight subway, Cincinnati scorned. The result was a "pickled" downtown. The city remains one of the few seemingly unable to break free of automobiles, trucks, and buses, although it persists in producing plans for light-rail systems, often using existing tunnels.

At the opposite end of the spectrum, Newark managed to destroy one of the finest light-rail subway systems in the world. By 1911 trolley cars operating along two main streets that intersected in central downtown brought traffic nearly to a standstill during rush hour. Between 5:15 and 6:15 every workday, 562 trolleys moved through the intersection. When the Lehigh Valley Railroad proposed abandoning the Morris Canal, private interests bought the right-of-way, and amid infighting and chicanery the Hudson & Manhattan Railroad began building its line under the Hudson River to Newark. By 1916, however, Public Service Coordinated Transport, a consolidation of hundreds of small trolley lines carrying 451 million riders annually, had opened its grandiose Central Terminal to reduce street congestion. Each business day the two-level terminal served some 2,600 trolley cars operating to and from Jersey City, Perth Amboy, and other cities within a radius of fifty-five miles. About fifty-five thousand riders poured through the terminal daily, shopping in its grand concourse that never closed, and forcing Public Service to install prepayment fare collection devices. The state-of-the-art terminal attracted experts worldwide, for it demonstrated how meticulous design might create a terminal in which trolley cars moved almost as efficiently as heavy subway trains.

Increased automobile use not only lessened ridership on Public Service trolleys but further jammed streets on which the trolleys operated. Throughout the 1920s Newark debated building a subway, and during the Depression carried forward its Roaring Twenties plans, focusing the system on the new Pennsylvania Railroad station, which served long-distance and commuter trains, including those operating into Pennsylvania Station in New York, and the Hudson & Manhattan electric trains operating under the Hudson River to lower Manhattan. Despite a connecting subway link to the gigantic Public Service terminal, ridership flowed via subway to the new Pennsylvania Station, which became the de facto transit center of Newark almost overnight.

By 1961 only two platforms in the Public Service terminal remained in use, both for buses operating over rails abandoned by streetcars since 1938. Four years later the buses vanished, and the owners converted the lower level of the great terminal into space for air conditioning equipment and other utilities serving offices built onto the upper level. Almost everyone forgot about the tunnel linking the terminal with the city subway. But in 1978 wreckers demolishing the terminal building broke the tunnel roof and discovered streetcars stored in dust, abandoned since the 1930s. A few years later Public Service Electric & Gas had built a new corporate headquarters on the 5.3 acres once covered by perhaps the finest light-rail terminal in the world. Nowadays only transit experts know that the Newark terminal proved the model for the present Port Authority bus terminal in Manhattan. The Public Service terminal disappeared into oblivion.

Buses helped destroy streetcars. Manufacturers advertised buses as flexible. Buses might overtake and pass each other, pull to the curb at the will of drivers, and swerve around double-parked cars and trucks, especially trucks unloading goods in front of stores. Most importantly, buses might operate over different streets in times of severe traffic congestion. Over decades, this flexibility became a trait prized by unthinking Americans, especially in California cities where buses vanquished streetcars. Despite persistent conspiracy theories that bus manufacturers bribed city councils, especially in Southern California locales, to pass ordinances that restricted streetcar operation or forced trolley companies to maintain blatantly unprofitable fare structures, Van Wilkins, whose 1990 *Electric Lines* article, "Who Really Killed the Streetcar?" offers a convincing analysis, and other experts agree that streetcars facing urban traffic congestion simply moved too slowly to please many riders. Those riders who could choose other transit options usually did, eventually leaving behind the poor, whose last-resource vehicle often proved a bus.

Streetcar companies experimented with buses from the 1920s onward, and in the 1930s Public Service tested them in regular service. Between 1934 and 1937 it tried Dodge railbuses that operated over roads on rubber tires; at any grade crossing such a bus could turn onto tracks, lower steel wheels, and proceed independent of trolley-line power. Especially on lightly patronized trolley car routes, the railbus idea seemed attractive, even if the buses provided a bumpier ride than trolleys. The railbus might serve locales away from tracks, might shortcut on and off rails, and might whisk past jammed downtown streets on reserved rail rights-of-way. In the end, it also might eliminate the need for the overhead electric wires that powered trolley cars. As other private urban transit companies experimented with hybrid buses—the Boston Elevated Railway Corporation operated seventy-two generator-electric buses for twenty-two years over city streets, replacing three-inch seat cushions with nine-inch ones to make the ride resemble streetcar smoothness—Public Service abandoned its rail buses. Company accountants argued that a bus might as well be a bus, operate over highways, and avoid expensive private rail rights-of-way.

All-electric buses fascinated operators of many urban transportation systems, and this interest partially explains experiments with hybrid electrics in Boston and elsewhere. In 1913 Merrill, Wisconsin, experimented with buses powered from overhead wires, but the Philadelphia experiment begun ten years later marked the first large-scale effort. Built by Brill and formally christened "Railess Cars," the little buses each seated twenty-eight people, with room for about as many more standees. Until 1935 the buses came with solid rubber tires, but during the Depression a switch to pneumatic tires provided smoother riding and eliminated the need for nine-inch cushions. Trackless trolley operation proved relatively successful in Philadelphia and other cities. The buses, each with two poles reaching up to double electric wires, moved silently, accelerated and slowed as gracefully as any streetcar, swerved around double-parked vehicles, and pulled to the curb for boarding and discharging passengers. In the 1920s Detroit, Salt Lake, New Orleans, and other cities began experimenting with trolley buses.

Westinghouse Electric produced an extensive report on the innovative buses in 1935. As a manufacturer of components used by most builders, it had a vested interest in success, but more importantly, it wanted to demonstrate the efficiency of the buses. *Trolley Coach: Application and Performance Data* makes dense reading: much of the report is highly technical and much focuses on economics. Trolley buses required far less maintenance than those powered by gasoline or diesel engines; they also used little electricity and reduced road repair costs associated with streetcar operation. Trolley buses could swerve around double-parked cars, but they negotiated construction sites just as easily, whereas any road repair work involving streetcar tracks meant streetcar companies paying for overnight effort simply to keep cars in operation across ditches, gravel, and other impediments that trolley buses crossed effortlessly. *Trolley Coach* remains ignored, however, even among transportation historians, although it examines the larger significance of all-electric buses operating under fixed overhead wires.

Westinghouse engineers discovered that abutters loved the silent buses that produced no pavement vibration. Streetcars required heavily built, well-maintained track to move quietly, and usually they squealed around curves. Trolley buses provided passengers with near-silent rides and moved alongside pedestrians, storekeepers, and residents just as silently. The buses accelerated far more quickly than did diesel buses, thus easing vehicular traffic, and their double-stream front doors swallowed and disgorged multiple streams of riders at a time, making stops much briefer. Suburbanites accepted trolley bus installation with better grace than they did the construction of streetcar lines or the imposition of diesel bus routes, because they scarcely heard the electric buses. Urban residents embraced them wholeheartedly, except along streets with high-speed streetcar service. Westinghouse determined that, for economic and environmental reasons, trolley bus lines might serve as feeders for streetcar routes or pioneer traffic creation on new routes until streetcars replaced trolley buses. While the trolley buses could not carry nearly the flow of passengers managed by streetcars, they nonetheless assured merchants and real estate developers of a fixed route.

During the Depression the business community learned the downside of bus route flexibility. Surface-transit ridership did not always shrink or vanish; often it merely changed alignment, sometimes by only a parallel street or two, and often by the machinations of corrupt city councils. A flow of streetcars or even trolley buses along a city street meant a more-or-less assured flow of potential customers. Passengers window-shopped from trolleys, and signaled motormen to stop so they could get off and examine stores featuring especially inviting windows. Except at rush hour, retail streets thronged with slowly if steadily moving trolleys or trackless trolleys became retail gold mines as window displays lured would-be shoppers from streetcars. Merchants invested heavily in so-called trolley-street stores, because they knew trolley and trackless-trolley routes to be virtually permanent. Moving tracks and overhead wire meant extraordinary capital expense, and only rarely did transit companies or transit authorities choose such action.

Buses did not so much destroy window shopping as destroy store owner confidence that their buildings faced a permanent stream of traffic. In order to expedite passenger flow, and sometimes to assuage city councils acting to favor merchants on less-traveled streets, bus companies and transit authorities diverted buses from established routes. Rush-hour commuters often benefited from reduced transit time, but shoppers sometimes preferred slightly longer transit times to moving along streets with unfamiliar stores. In the Depression, as public transit authorities acquired bankrupt street railway companies, more than retail merchants learned how flexible buses made bus routes writhe and bend. Landlords and real estate developers discovered that buses did not necessarily remain on abandoned streetcar routes. Instead they often moved along parallel but low-value streets, making abutting property suddenly far more valuable. Buses might be routed practically anywhere, making entire neighborhoods suddenly bereft of short-distance and commuter pass-through traffic. Just as the 1910-era replacement of clogged downtown streetcar routes by subways transformed real estate values by boosting value around subway stops and lowering it at points midway between stations, so the replacement of streetcars by diesel buses taught urban landowners a nasty lesson.

In Dayton, Columbus, and Toledo, in Rockford and Peoria, and even in Fitchburg, Massachusetts, replacing streetcars with trolley buses reassured abutters that traffic would still flow in the established directions that maintained property values. Where diesel buses replaced streetcars, entire sectors of cities might lose most public transit. Silent-film aficionados might ponder the many sequences in which comics run afoul of Los Angeles streetcars labeled "Watts." Until the late 1930s, Watts enjoyed some of the finest streetcar service in greater Los Angeles, in part because longer-distance routes passed through the neighborhood. New bus routes circumvented Watts, and African Americans found getting to and from work harder by the year.

The jitney fad also hurried the demise of streetcar service, and had an adverse impact on early trolley bus and diesel bus experiments as well. A brief, almost unstudied, and now forgotten fad in the 1920s, jitneying involved automobile owners picking up would-be streetcar and bus passengers and driving them downtown for less than transit fares, then ferrying them home in the evening. Jitneying produced crises in many cities, but the phenomenon has been closely studied only in Birmingham, Alabama. Despite rapidly passed city ordinances forbidding the practice, police in the end did nothing if driver and passengers claimed to be friends. Moreover, city governments often confessed failure if jitney drivers operated across municipal lines, especially when state governments regulated the fledgling motor bus industry as poorly as they did trucking. By 1917 entrepreneurs had bought used motor buses and begun driving their own routes, diverting fares from streetcar lines operating on parallel or adjacent streets. Antijitney legislation endures today—

automobile insurance explicitly fails to cover passengers carried for hire—but transportation historians rarely give the temporary fad much attention. However, many motorists paid for their cars by carrying commuters for pay, and in so doing contributed to the Depression collapse of privately owned transit companies. The latter had invested millions in infrastructure improvements ranging from the Newark terminal to thinly traveled trolley lines reaching across regions not yet suburbanized.

Trolley buses helped private companies and public transit authorities confront automobile ownership, jitneying, Depression-era ridership drops, and suburban sprawl while reassuring developers and property owners that passengers would move along permanent routes. Westinghouse and other firms worked together to build buses that operated under diesel power on the outskirts of cities and under overhead-wire electric power as they neared downtowns. Such hybrid buses eliminated the tunnel fumes that infuriated riders, particularly in summer when ventilator units failed to rid bus interiors of smoke. But diesel-electric hybrids came too late to save many trolley subways. Usually cities that abandoned streetcars late discovered that electric buses might operate well in paved-over tunnels. Cambridge, Massachusetts, began running silent, clean buses in a short subway, but Rochester and Newark abandoned their tunnels just a few years too soon.

A full bus might remove fifty motorists from the highway, and so remove fifty cars, but the bus sat stuck in traffic as did any other over-the-road vehicle. In the late 1960s General Motors Corporation demonstrated a diesel-powered bus that operated on roads and railroads alike. Fluke, however, consigned the new rail bus into the oblivion that consumed its 1930s ancestors.

In the summer of 1967, the GM model SDM 5302, a standard forty-nine-seat, air conditioned, suburban-service (meaning fitted with forward-facing, reclining upholstered seats) bus equipped with vertically movable steel wheels, operated in tests over Philadelphia Suburban Transportation Company tracks in the vicinity of Bryn Mawr, Pennsylvania. Company president Merritt H. Taylor immediately proclaimed it a success, suggested it might restore rail service along abandoned tracks in southern New Jersey and elsewhere, and even interested the Port Authority of New York and New Jersey. Designated the Hy-Rail Test Bus, it made several ceremonial trips with journalists aboard, then made test runs on other commuter railroads, then served as a featured attraction at a national conference of railroad executives. Then, in autumn, the bus rendezvoused with fate in Washington, D.C.

Snow flurries brushed the vehicle as it waited in front of the New Senate Office Building for dignitaries to board. Once full, it cruised easily to Baltimore & Ohio tracks near Union Station and began a demonstration run. Two hours later, in a driving snowstorm, it managed to reach Silver Spring, Maryland, six miles away, where passengers departed in disgust. Not until it reached a grade crossing in Gaithersburg could its driver maneuver it from the rails. Despite being equipped with sanders, the rail bus had crawled twenty-one miles in four hours, delayed an untold number of freight and passenger trains, and convinced Taylor to retain his high-speed electric trains. Americans expected railroad trains and streetcars to operate in bad weather, including the likes of the storm that dumped a foot of snow on the national capital during the Hy-Rail Test Bus demonstration.

Not surprisingly, then, Edmonton and Calgary in Alberta focused on light-rail vehicles (LRVs) in the middle 1970s, only a few years after the Hy-Rail Test Bus debacle. Both cities required fast, reliable rapid transit in snowstorms, and both had learned from the struggles of Boston and San Francisco. In 1959 Boston converted an abandoned commuter rail line to a high-speed trolley line. Conversion of some streetcar routes to trolley buses had left the Metropolitan Transit Authority with a surfeit of trolley cars, and the new Highland Branch proved an inexpensive but amazingly successful innovation. San Francisco, finally moving toward building its Market Street extension of the Twin Peaks tunnel opened in 1917, wanted to buy brand-new streetcars in an era when manufacturers no longer built them. While Toronto determined to maintain its existing streetcar fleet and extend its lines by buying large fleets of used streetcars from Kansas City, Cleveland, Birmingham, and Cincinnati as those cities converted to buses, San Francisco and Boston determined to use federal funds to buy state-of-the-art streetcars from Germany. When the Nixon administration vetoed this idea as exacerbating a worsening balance-of-payments problem, the Urban Mass Transit Administration forced both transit systems to find a United States manufacturer, which they did: a firm that built helicopters. The manufacturer responded by building a prototype car that literally fell apart during testing. United States transit systems officials in Pittsburgh, Shaker Heights, and other cities watched with dismay. The Standard Light Rail Vehicle project seemed only to delay a solution to replacing aging streetcars. In time the firm delivered 170 cars to Boston and 100 to San Francisco (some purchased after Boston refused the balance of its order), but the fiasco delayed innovation by almost a decade. Edmonton and Calgary officials absorbed the lesson and ordered reliable cars from Germany.

Light-rail transit is essentially a euphemism for ultramodern streetcars operating along city streets, sometimes in subways, and usually over reserved but not grade-separated tracks away from downtown. Suspension innovations enable cars to ride only a few inches above the pavement, making entering and exiting easy and fast. Undercarriage design makes cars extremely quiet and able to accelerate and brake rapidly. Multiple-unit control, a century-old invention, enables one person to operate multiple-car trains, even during rush hour. For many cities, particularly small ones with dispersed populations and serious highway congestion, light-rail transit seemed futuristic in 1970 and eminently sensible a decade later.

Calgary opened its first brand-new light-rail transit line in 1981, a second in 1985, and a third in 1987, proving to United States transit officials that people in a small, anything-but-densely-built city would forsake their cars, even on sunny summer days. The German-built streetcars operating largely in expressway median strips and divided boulevards, and along downtown retail streets, transformed urban-design thinking almost overnight. Nevertheless, Americans today often know little of the light-rail revolution that followed the Calgary triumph, and upper-class suburbanites in expensive cars often know the least. Despite subsequent successes elsewhere, electronic news media tend to ignore new light-rail systems as one-of-a-kind experiments or somehow trivial. Newspapers pay more attention. Light-rail riders often read newspapers.

Pie-in-the-sky urban transit efforts ended in Pittsburgh in 1974, when the state of Pennsylvania refused to fund its share of an elevated, automated transportation system called Sky-Bus. Despite the fact that 87 percent of the design work had been completed under federal grants, local citizens argued that the Sky-Bus system would never work in bad weather. Instead, the Penn Central Railroad offered its Panhandle Bridge across the Monongahela River to the city, a consultant reported that streetcars could use the bridge after inexpensive and fast improvements, and in 1985 LRVs began running among older Pittsburgh streetcars. The fifty-five German cars assembled in Pittsburgh advanced the revolution in thinking Calgary and Edmonton had begun. United States urban transit authorities saw success, at a surprisingly low cost.

San Diego's effort built upon the successes of Canada and Pittsburgh. In Southern California, officials abandoned the idea of specialized buses operating between freeway lanes; the futuristic vehicles had vanished before the example of Calgary LRVs. San Diego crated a light-rail system from scratch, bought Siemens-Duewag U-2 LRVs, and by 1981 operated cars between San Diego and San Ysidro on the Mexican border. Patronage grew far faster than anyone expected, forcing the purchase of more cars and, within two years, the double tracking of the main line. In 1986 the system opened a second route to Euclid, and its plans for a 140-mile system no longer elicited "Tijuana trolley" jokes.

Almost unnoticed, the West Coast had become the epicenter of light-rail system innovation. While the San Francisco region emphasized its automated BART system, cities to the north and south moved rapidly toward lower-cost systems using European LRVs. The pace of change flummoxed practicing architects and urban designers and bypassed the curricula of graduate design schools. At a fundamental level, the rapid acceptance of light-rail transit on the West Coast contradicted the commonplace assumption that California, Washington, and Oregon would never abandon the private automobile as the generator of metropolitan design and form.

In Portland, Oregon, grassroots opposition to more freeway building surfaced first in a 1972 referendum. Municipal officials attended a 1976 light-rail conference in Philadelphia, but few other attendees, including would-be United States LRV manufacturers, paid them much attention. Almost certainly the Portland representatives gave San Diego participants the courage to proceed with plans for the line to San Ysidro, and the two cities thereafter supported each other despite the derision of national and eastern experts. In 1976 Portland determined to rebuild an existing freeway with two light-rail tracks, and six years later began laying new track on a former trolley car right-of-way to the suburb of Gresham. Bombardier, a Canadian company with a plant in Vermont, just across the Quebec border, provided the new cars, forestalling complaints about public transit authorities "buying foreign." In Pittsburgh and Portland, citizen opposition to both freeways and high-tech mass-transit alternatives reoriented urban transportation thinking.

Bad weather, especially snow, focused light-rail thinking elsewhere in the country, however, in commonsense ways. In the 1970s Buffalo embarked on a subway-building idea much like that Edmonton envisioned, hoping that fast, frequent trains would revitalize a stagnant downtown. Common sense and perhaps a desire for massive amounts of federal grant money nudged Buffalo toward a traditional subway scheme, but federal authorities insisted that the project be downsized to focus on light-rail. Once service began in 1985, low ridership disappointed city officials. Completing the six-and-a-half-mile-long line in 1987 increased patronage, but the Buffalo experience caused many other transportation authorities to wonder at the moderate-weather successes in San Diego, Portland, and elsewhere on the West Coast.

In 1987 San Jose began service on the first leg of its light-rail system directed toward Silicon Valley, and a year later began operating vintage trolley cars on dedicated downtown tracks intended to spur tourist visits. Balancing high-speed commuter and shopping movement and antique trolley cars intended to enthrall tourists immediately changed public and investor attitudes toward central San Jose. As late as 1991 commentators remembered when downtown San Jose resembled "Buffalo with palm trees," a cutting remark about urban blight that in addition emphasized the enduring inability of Buffalo to make underground light-rail transit a generator of urban reinvestment. By then, however, Los Angeles had been operating its

Metro Blue Line for a year, providing unnerving information on the long-term impact of light-rail system building in larger, older cities.

The Metro Blue line operates along a right-of-way abandoned by Pacific Electric Company trolley cars in 1961, down the median of Long Beach Boulevard now replanted with palm trees. Part of it runs through a subway tunnel under downtown, and part of it operates over new alignment near Long Beach made available after the Union Pacific built a new intermodal terminal and access track nearby to handle increased ocean container traffic. It ends in the Long Beach Transit Mall. Los Angeles County accepted not one cent of federal money: all $877 million came from sales taxes on local purchases. Into the 1960s the Pacific Electric terminated at Main Street and Sixth in Los Angeles, an area that had become ground zero of skid row by the 1980s, pushing the de facto center of downtown activity to Flower and Seventh. Officials deflected the path of the subway from the old Pacific Electric terminal area to a new station at Seventh, where it connects with the new heavy-duty, third-rail-powered subway line, Metro Red. Much of Metro Blue's open-air route lies through some of the poorest and most crime-ridden neighborhoods in the region. Instead of avoiding the area, the Los Angeles Transportation Commission planned at the beginning to police the line heavily, and to lace it with remote cameras. Fares do not begin to cover operating costs, but the line serves two groups: poor people commuting to low-paying inner-city service jobs, and middle-class passengers commuting between the ocean and downtown. Yet unlike the San Diego, San Jose, and Portland lines, Metro Blue attracts little publicity. Indeed, many Los Angeles inhabitants scarcely know it exists.

The line's obscurity originates in its hidden nature. It neither traverses a well-known, easily identifiable corridor nor seems likely to make one surround its fast, clean, Japanese-built LRVs. Its cars can be coupled together to make long trains at rush hour, it operates safely with low fares, and it most certainly reaches downtown. But it exists in a perceptual limbo in part because it operates along sixteen miles of an existing freight railroad corridor. Close scrutiny by the get-out-and-look method reveals that Metro Blue cars whisk along a corridor evolving so subtly that its present condition is slightly unnerving.

For sixteen of its twenty-one miles, the line shares a corridor with an active freight railroad. In the late 1970s an underutilized freight railroad corridor connecting with an abandoned high-speed trolley corridor seemed the ideal ribbon along which to build a new light-rail line. From the design stage on, however, Los Angeles County Transportation Authorities (LACTA) encountered one difficulty after another, reminiscent of difficulties that had hampered similar efforts in Baltimore and other old eastern cities. The corridor proved barely wide enough for three tracks, two new ones for the Metro Blue system and the still-active one used for freight. Moving the freight track to one edge of the corridor only worked away from stations and bridges, and produced the need for spur tracks to cross Metro Blue rails so the railroad could service corridor clients on the opposite side. Center-platform stations required the most careful design work, since the platforms pushed Metro Blue tracks away from each other. Widening bridges worried highway officials, who saw lengthened bridge abutments as additional obstructions to motor vehicles, and angered abutting landowners who lost frontage. Moreover, along the rail corridor ran dozens of utility system lines, many almost as difficult to move as the water mains weaving through the empty subway tunnels in Cincinnati. Eventually, LACTA negotiated sixty agreements involving relocation of gas mains, electric cables, and other services installed below or above the corridor. About two miles of Metro Blue track rise into the air over heavy-traffic freight spurs. At two locations, the so-called flyovers lift LRVs over crossings of other freight railroads too. What appeared simple to visionaries looking at ordinary maps became extremely difficult to implement once designers began studying existing conditions.

Underlying all Metro Blue design and construction was a scenario understood by the Southern Pacific Railroad and glimpsed by a handful of close observers. In the middle 1980s the "underutilized freight line" carried twelve trains a day, most of them serving the ocean shipping facility but some switching cars to and from corridor customers. As observed by many light-rail advocates, freight traffic in the corridor had been dropping for years. But while the number of trains remained roughly the same, the trains had become longer and individual cars moved more cargo. Sometime in the late 1970s the long-term decline in both numbers of trains and numbers of cars per train leveled off. By 1920s and World War II standards, the line worked far below capacity. But longer trains, and especially longer trains carrying much longer individual cars, tricked many casual onlookers into believing that most of the time the corridor remained idle. Only the railroad company suspected that freight traffic might boom, especially between its Long Beach intermodal facility and the rest of North America.

In the sales and construction agreement signed in 1985, LACTA agreed that its entire construction process would focus on aligning Metro Blue tracks so that the freight railroad might easily double-track its own operation. Five years after Congress passed the Staggers Act, the Southern Pacific understood the potential for massive growth in intermodal shipping to and from ocean terminals. It sold off about half of its sixteen-mile corridor, but it retained almost all its existing use-value and all its potential for growth.

Anyone riding LRVs in Calgary south of downtown discovers that the cars exit the third suburban tunnel into a freight railroad corridor. The LRVs operate between freight tracks: the heavily used ones on one side carrying about ten unit grain and sulfur trains a day on the Canadian Pacific main line from Calgary to Fort Macleod and Lethbridge, the spur one serving local industries on the west side of the LRV tracks. At many places the two railroad routes squeeze tightly, especially at LRV stations sandwiched between LRV and Canadian Pacific rights-of-way. Away from downtown, where short platforms restrict train length, LRVs can operate in five-car trains to speed rush-hour traffic. At the grade crossings south of Calgary, LRVs, especially coupled in multiunit consists, move across highway traffic essentially as ordinary trains. But in Calgary, then in Los Angeles, Baltimore, and elsewhere, LRVs do not share track with freight, commuter, and long-distance passenger trains.

In Sacramento, which designed its light-rail system from the beginning around a philosophy emphasizing minimal cost, trains first operated largely over a single-track route, only part of which was signaled. The system lacked automatic train stop technology, used tie plates salvaged from abandoned freight railroads, and put its first routes in abandoned and disused freight railroad corridors located along a right-of-way purchased for a never-built freeway. The system seems "green" indeed, not only because its builders spent relatively little money, but because it has had scarcely any impact on its corridor environments. At rush hour, lone operators guide trains consisting of four eighty-foot cars; in off-peak hours the same personnel operate single LRVs. Economy guided the creation of the Sacramento system, but the old freight railroad corridors guided its route locations.

Light-rail transit is just that: light rail. Even the heavier rail and roadbed construction used in traditional subway tunnels cannot bear the weight of modern freight and passenger trains, nor can long-distance trains negotiate the sharp curves and narrow tunnels used by LRV and traditional subway cars. Light transit operates in a conceptual limbo only just now beginning to worry and even alarm urban planners, investors, and environmentalists.

Installing light-rail in existing railroad corridors, no matter how disused or even abandoned, usually eliminates the potential of such corridors to carry long-distance trains again. In most metropolitan areas, freight service seems unlikely to return to downtown or adjacent neighborhoods. But where such service exists, it is likely to endure, and perhaps even increase in an era when manufacturing continues to decline but warehousing experts foresee a growing need for urban delivery of valuable goods by rail to eliminate truck congestion. Environmentalists and waste industry experts musing about shipping urban trash by rail pause whenever light-rail advocates ask about using freight corridors, but as yet rail-based solid-waste removal lacks the grassroots support enjoyed by light-rail systems. But restoring passenger service, especially electric-powered commuter rail service operating eighty or a hundred miles outside cities, raises issues simmering since the Muskingum Electric reoriented railroad industry thinking in the 1970s. Once converted to light-rail, corridors lose their potential to serve distant commuters.

Massachusetts recognized the trade-off in the middle 1970s, when the conversion of abandoned commuter railroads to light-rail seemed less and less a good idea. The state benefited from experience most others lacked. The Highland Branch had once transported riders only a few miles from downtown before rejoining a main east–west route reaching far from the city, but its traditional commuter trains operated mostly over main-line tracks terminating on ample capacity South Station platform tracks. In the 1960s trolley cars zipped along its refurbished surface rails, then dove below ground into already crowded trolley subway tunnels. As traffic increased on the upscale Highland Branch, even three-car LRV consists did little to alleviate the tunnel congestion caused by single- and multiple-car consists operating through the tunnels en route to it and other aboveground lines.

Very quietly, the transportation authority abandoned one streetcar route and part of another, trying to free up tunnel space for politically influential Highland Branch riders. The truncated route served a mostly African American part of Boston; the abandoned route served a gritty industrial area that lost value as it lost accessibility, despite being across a river from Harvard University.

Improved LRVs and better signals did little to alleviate light-rail subway congestion, which worsened through the 1980s, forcing thoughtful Massachusetts Bay Transportation Authority riders to realize that the extension of the Red Line heavy subway to Braintree had occupied two of the three available tracks that long-distance commuter trains serving the South Shore and Cape Cod might use. In the 1990s, as the MBTA gloried in the overnight success of two of three long-abandoned commuter routes and planned the opening of another, expert consultants pointed out the limits to further growth imposed by the single track snaking south of the city. At the southern edge of Boston, the lone commuter rail route wends its way between two two-track subway routes, one route on either side. Commuter trains already operate two-level cars to meet public demand. When trains begin operating to and from Greenbush, the lone track will be at capacity, two-level cars notwithstanding. Only electrification will boost its capacity by enabling trains to operate faster.

The only other choice confronting Massachusetts transportation planners seems almost obscene. Part of I-93, notoriously jammed with traffic, will become a railroad right-of-way.

While the situation south of Boston involves the 1970s extension of a heavy subway line into suburbs along an abandoned railroad alignment, light-rail systems pose identical issues everywhere. LRVs prove useful in transporting people, especially commuters, within a radius of about twenty miles from downtown areas. Beyond that zone, however, more-traditional commuter trains prove faster, more comfortable, and in the long run more economical, especially when they share the rails with long-haul passenger trains and, usually in · the wee hours of the morning, with freight trains.

Then, too, traditional commuter trains serve well-to-do commuters who like living in leafy suburbs but want very fast access to downtown. However vague and circumspect their voiced desires, they want to travel nonstop through inner suburbs and industrial warehouse zones, and they really prefer to move at speeds above sixty miles an hour. Seventy-nine miles an hour strikes them as a very nice speed indeed.

Looming now as a massive political debacle exacerbated by technical limitations often created by newly built light-rail systems, the coming clash between long-distance and LRV commuters became noticeable in 1977. Federal courts in Pennsylvania and elsewhere determined that all Amtrak trains rolled by definition as intercity rather than commuter trains. Despite the fact that, for example, standing-room-only crowds boarded the Boston-to-Washington Night Owl in Baltimore for the short commute to work, Congress and federal courts persisted in the belief that no commuters rode the system. Amtrak's New York–Philadelphia and Philadelphia–Harrisburg trains precipitated the court cases, simply because the law creating Amtrak specifically prohibits operation of "commuter and other short-haul service in metropolitan and suburban areas." Long-view scenario analysts and real estate investors knew by 1980 that light-rail transit would fail to accommodate long-distance commuters.

Light-rail systems fail under intense ridership pressure, especially when cars fill at the end of the line and irritate would-be passengers who cannot board at subsequent stops. Even operating as multiple-unit trains, LRVs cannot carry enough passengers or move quickly enough to compete with heavy commuter trains. Moreover, LRVs often operate over downtown city streets. While their presence indeed boosts downtown property values, their center-city terminals cannot accommodate large increases in numbers of trains without blocking street traffic. A typical nineteenth-century urban railroad terminal can move many times the number of passengers onto traditional commuter trains usually moving over grade-separated routes and making no stops until they are fifteen or more miles away from downtown. In an ideal world, LRVs would service riders within fifteen miles of downtown and not clog downtown streets, and commuter trains would carry suburban residents. But many cities have planted new light-rail transit lines in disused railroad corridors once used by commuter trains and freight trains. Building light-rail systems often eliminates the option of restoring commuter rail and freight service.

In 1998 the *Economist* produced a special report on commuting that dovetails almost perfectly with a 1978 *Environmental Action* report on Amtrak. In 1978 few experts thought much of light-rail transit; in 1998 the *Economist* scarcely mentioned it. In two decades automobile traffic jams had increased in density and scale, and ridership pressure on urban mass-transit systems had increased dramatically. But in the United States and elsewhere, prosperity had inclined an ever-growing number of individuals and families to buy more than one automobile, and often cars for suburban teenagers. Metropolitan growth covered hundreds of thousands more square miles, and large city downtowns had bolted upward in hundreds of new office towers. In many American metropolitan regions, great numbers of commuters spent at least two hours a day commuting between home and work.

Raw figures are the grist of both data analysts and long-range investors. In Massachusetts alone, 551,000 commuters spend at least forty-five minutes every morning and another forty-five minutes every evening moving back and forth between home and work. For travelers using the Southeast Expressway, forty-five minutes translates into approximately fifteen miles; for riders on the Green Line light-rail routes, about nine miles; for riders on the new commuter rail lines south of Boston, thirty-five miles. Forty-five minutes aboard an Amtrak Acela train operating west of Boston means about a hundred miles, but few commuters can afford to commute via Acela. Yet such time-space equations now shape the bottom line in almost all analyses of downtown Boston commercial real estate ventures and govern housing prices far outside the city. Everywhere around Boston—and around Baltimore, Atlanta, Indianapolis, Houston, Seattle, and dozens of other cities—real estate developers hire analyst firms to recast historic data in scenario-focused ways.

Paradoxically, traditional and brand-new light-rail lines pose serious problems for prospective developers of urban warehouse districts often jammed by trucks but accessible by rail. Redevelopment often depends on reusing railroad tracks as light-rail connectors to downtown. But converting ordinary freight railroad tracks to light-rail means slicing off a section of railroad corridor that formerly extended far from the city center. Thus the warehouse area becomes a profitable zone of residential and perhaps even commercial and office development, but also a blockade that keeps traditional commuter trains from reaching into the far suburbs beyond it. City planners may maintain that some old railroad corridors are wide enough to accommodate single traditional train tracks next to the pairs of light-rail tracks, but most single track strangles commuter train flow.

Light-rail systems isolate downtowns and inner residential, commercial, and industrial rings. Almost invariably—perhaps most notably in Baltimore and Sacramento—they strike taxpayers as necessary and local real estate developers as stable. Only as metropolitan regions choke with highway traffic do municipalities realize that light-rail systems occupy the very corridors essential to reactivating intercity rail routes and the commuter train service that causes downtown and suburban property values to skyrocket. Only when light-rail trains clog tracks at grade crossings at rush hour do riders understand the impossibility of automating light-rail systems in ways that resemble decades-old mining railroad experiments and contemporary airport people movers.

Light-rail systems represent a failure of regionwide scenario analysis. Their opponents often seem fixated on automobiles and buses, but at public hearings it becomes clear that some light-rail opponents want weedy railroad corridors kept open for passenger railroad use in the not-so-distant future. Environmentalists rarely distinguish among opponents of light-rail systems, even as they realize that they misjudged how quickly hiking trails would morph into railroads again. But as Buffalo demonstrated a decade ago, a system without commuter rail links to far suburbs is likely to fail. Light-rail systems only exacerbate the crisis facing metropolitan regions desperately in need of passenger trains.

SOURCES: Baldwin, "Getting to the Trains in Time"; Bente, "The Airporters"; Brownell, "The Notorious Jitney"; "Buses on Rails"; Cheney, "Boston's Electric Buses"; "Commuting"; Comstock, "Slow Train to Great Slave"; Corns, "Ohio's Robot Railroad"; Frank, "Philadelphia Trackless Trolleys"; Gibson, "Rail Transit Returns to Calgary"; Halperin, "The Trolley Coaches of St. Joseph, Missouri"; "Labor, 1978"; Lustig, "Los Angeles' LRVs"; Mannkoff, "The Seventh Wonder of the Traction World"; Matoff, "Sacramento"; McSpedon, "Building Light Rail Transit"; Middleton, *Metropolitan Railways;* Nelligan, "Amtrak Has No Commuters"; Pence, "Cincinnati's Sleeping Subway," and "Dayton Trolley Buses"; "Pittsburgh: One Problem, Two Solutions"; Schrag, *The Great Society Subway;* Transportation Research Board, *Light Rail Transit;* Volkmer, "Light Rail Rolls in L.A.," "Story of Trolley Coaches in the Crescent City," and "Ten Years of Light Rail Progress"; Westinghouse Electric & Manufacturing, *Trolley Coach;* H. S. White, "People Movers"; Wilkins, "Who Really Killed the Street Car?"

CONCLUSION

Contractors work along the old right-of-way leading to Greenbush. Dozens of buildings have vanished to make room for the new passenger train yard and for the huge parking lot adjacent to it. Bridges have disappeared, and some have already been replaced. A lengthy tunnel stretches beneath the seventeenth-century town center of Hingham, and seawall work reaches along part of the right-of-way in Weymouth. Elsewhere along the line, especially deep in the woods, cut brush, surveyor tape, new roadbed, ballast, and rails mark further changes ahead. The train is coming back, and local officials confront demands for realigned roads and zoning changes, shuttle buses, road traffic control, and enduring if now scattered protests from abutters who never dreamed trains would race twenty feet from their back doors.

The county newspaper features a weekly column entitled "Greenbush Update." Every few days the paper addresses problems ranging from floodplain amelioration to the sound of whistles to the demand for condominiums. Activity along the Greenbush line strikes locals as important, and indeed it is locally important. But the route was and will be only a branch line jutting off from a main track that once linked Boston and Cape Cod. Intended to move several thousand commuters a day, and to connect wealthy Bostonians with the marinas and harbors along its route, it will save time and traffic jam frustration for Boston-focused residents of quaint coastal towns and leafy suburbs.

It will transform all sorts of other activities as well. It will enable people to shop in Boston, going and returning after and before rush hour, and it will bring overnight beach guests from the city. Its stations will reorient traffic, shifting much from north–south roads onto east–west routes that end at beaches. It will produce all sorts of minor effects too. Perhaps enterprising high school students or retirees will earn a few dollars driving people to the station if the parking lot fills up before the last inbound rush-hour trains. The prospect of jitney service already worries the handful of taxi cab operators licensed in the towns. Auto repair shops adjacent to stations intend to prosper: commuters will drop off their cars for oil changes and repairs, and pick them up after work. Change floats along across the Greenbush line, sometimes as silently as the sea gulls, sometimes as noisily.

Grasping the scale of the railroad industry in 1930 now challenges more than a few academics. Kansas City Union Station opened in 1914 as the third largest in the nation. Only Grand Central Terminal and Pennsylvania Station in New York surpassed it. Its North Waiting Room alone stretched longer than a football field and nearly as wide. Its restaurants served both grand and simple meals, and its Grand Hall became a place of citywide celebrations. But passengers and visitors never saw its third level. There moved hundreds of carts carrying mail, express, baggage, and food rolling directly to the eight loading platforms, each 1,400 feet long. Through World War II the immense station throbbed with activity almost impossible to imagine today. Approximately half of all military personnel at one time or another walked through its Grand Hall as three hundred trains arrived and departed every twenty-four hours. Then almost overnight its energy began to dwindle, until by 1964 it moved only seventy trains a day, not enough to justify its costs and nowhere near a challenge to its train- and passenger-moving capabilities. In the early 1970s only six trains operated from the station, and Kansas City, along with so many other cities, entered a long era of downtown inactivity.

In Savannah, the joint Seaboard–Atlantic Coast Line depot its owners called a union station vanished to make way for a freeway ramp, and the Savannah & Atlanta station housed an antique business after 1990. The grand Central of Georgia Railroad station became the city visitor center, its tracks bereft of trains, which moved to a little Amtrak station located near the junction of rail lines hauling ever greater amounts of freight. Savannah toys with building some kind of antique trolley car line to attract and move tourists, but as in Kansas City and San Jose, light-rail transit produces little in the way of innovative passenger terminal thinking. Commuter trains might operate into Savannah, but even if they followed the

The engineer sees the long, uninterrupted ribbon of steel, and almost never encounters the equivalent of a highway traffic jam.

tracks of container trains serving the busy wharves, they would have no place to terminate.

Savannah booms in part because of a record trade deficit, one usually reported in billions of dollars but easily calculated visually in the tens of thousands of containers moving from ships in Savannah, Los Angeles, and other port cities. Despite worries about the strength of the dollar and the Chinese trade surplus, moving containers is almost as profitable for railroads as moving grain and other bulk commodities—and sometimes even more so. But containers moving to and from port cities by truck jam highways, especially those used by commuters. Timothy Lomax and other researchers at Texas A&M University assert that between 1982 and 2002 jammed urban traffic went from consuming 700 million hours to 3.5 billion. Even given the explosive population growth in metropolitan regions, especially along the coasts, the figures sober the most optimistic advocates of highway building. The typical Los Angeles motorist spent ninety-three hours stopped in traffic jams in 2002. Around Washington, D.C., the typical motorist spent sixty-seven hours annually. The 187 percent average increase from 1982 to 2002 augurs ill for further highway building efforts, even if cities could find land fit for new highways, since the growth rate surpasses almost any highway building capacity in the country. But no analysts can yet relate booming port-city trade-deficit container movement by truck to details of traffic jams, even in Savannah and similar smaller cities to which upper-income people move in search of high-quality living.

Statistics alert many educated newspaper readers to issues already worrying real estate investors and chain-store retailers, but they prove difficult to analyze against each other. The fact that metropolitan Boston commuter trains board 141,000 passengers every workday and that 225,000 passengers board the light-rail system most certainly matters to someone somehow, but proves almost useless in imagining how an annual growth rate of 10 percent might exacerbate existing highway congestion near suburban stations. How do the 426,000 passengers boarding the heavy-duty subways figure in any analysis of how commuter rail passengers move around Boston after they exit trains? In the end, accumulating mountains of statistics often leads to conclusions similar to those of the Regional Plan experts in New York before World War II.

At a small urban scale, drawbridges offer extraordinary insights into how pedestrians reach train stations. Older cities often replace movable bridges as harbor and river traffic decreases. If some waterborne commerce endures, especially by pleasure boat, highway planners replace drawbridges with fixed bridges arching over water. Motorists transition easily: they push accelerator pedals slightly and cruise over the new bridges. But pedestrians dislike the hills that replace level, albeit intermittently movable, pavement. Replacing a movable bridge with a fixed arch bridge deflects pedestrian flow, especially on streets where rush-hour walkers hurry. Adjacent to South Station in Boston lies a political nightmare, the rusting, decrepit Northern Avenue center-pivot swing bridge pedestrians refuse to abandon for a nicely arched fixed bridge a block away. Distance from South Station or even walking time from South Station no longer suffices to inform real estate developers who know that walking effort often spells the success or failure of real estate development near urban railroad terminals.

At a suburban scale, the parking garages disfiguring small towns in New Jersey and eastern Pennsylvania announce commuter rail success. No longer do ordinary station lots accommodate the cars of commuters. Environmentalists ought to cheer the success of trains, but no one says much about the unsightly garages urbanizing small-town centers. The slightest improvement in schedules causes some commuters to shift allegiance from one station to another on an adjacent line. Automobile traffic to and from suburban train stations confuses public officials. The old suburb–city highways that produced ribbons of tawdry retail development no longer carry most commuter traffic. Often that traffic now moves past the homes of the wealthy, who complain about traffic, noise, and air pollution jamming tertiary roads leading to commuter train stations. Suburban design and planning nowadays prove harder to analyze and practice, even in university graduate schools of design, than urban design. Part of the problem lies in the growing penchant of suburbanites to use any Amtrak suburban stop as a way of reaching another suburb.

Passenger trains operating between eighty and a hundred miles an hour profoundly influence understanding of metropolitan regions and metropolitan lifestyles. Assume the train as a given, and suddenly many small satellite cities, often with very low real estate values, become attractive to real estate investors. Generally, such cities have both operating and abandoned railroad lines, chunks of derelict property abutting underused downtowns, and an inventory of well-built, easily restored period architecture. While increasingly irrelevant as manufacturing centers, such small cities strike investors as ripe for plucking. The most desirable ones—certainly the ones receiving the most careful if camouflaged investment analysis—lie about eighty to a hundred miles between major cities. High-speed passenger train service would transform such locales.

Cities on the edge of wilderness or rural areas might be transformed too. In the 1980s well-educated young married couples discovered Portland, Maine, as a down-at-the-heels but proud small city boasting not only a fine stock of inexpensive period housing but also active freight railroads. As much real estate changed hands, new energy poured into the school system and other municipal departments, and nonprofits established new museums and other cultural amenities. Demands for passenger train service to Boston materialized in ways scenario analysts recognize as predictable, and not just in Portland, but in cities roughly 120 miles from Chicago, St. Louis, Atlanta, Houston, and Portland, Oregon.

Massive real estate transformation produces massive investment return. On a medium scale, Portland provides a fine example. On a very small scale, New Bedford in Massachusetts offers an example of a run-down but finely built seaport community, but difficult to access by highways, being discovered by well-educated young homebuyers and real estate investors. The transformation in New Bedford mirrors that in Portland: rising house prices, a much-invigorated waterfront and Whaling Museum, and then, suddenly, a demand for fast commuter train service to Boston. But large-scale change seems most likely to occur away from coastal New England and metropolitan New York, in places like Albuquerque.

As railroads improve their rights-of-way by laying heavier rail, installing sophisticated signal systems, and building double or even triple tracks, they open the prospect of fast passenger trains linking small rural towns with downtowns. The fast trains might link the towns with larger metropolitan regions, but far more likely, the trains will sizzle through warehouse districts and inner suburbs, perhaps connecting here and there with light-rail systems. The trains will need downtown terminals, and terminal traffic will generate business development within the walking distance Regional Plan analysts recognized in the 1930s. Such trains will operate first over existing, well-maintained freight lines, exactly as Albuquerque officials intend to use Burlington Northern Santa Fe tracks north and south of the city. But almost certainly, urban real estate investors will demand such service on many disused and abandoned routes as well.

Urban investors recognize that the first cities to reinvent commuter rail operation over a 100- or 120-mile radius from downtown will grab human and economic capital from cities perhaps 150 miles away. Beyond about 75 miles from the seacoast and the shores of the Great Lakes, and away from the arid regions where even cattle ranching proves nearly impossible, cities tend to be about 150 to 200 miles apart, a distance dating to long-vanished steam locomotives and 1890s train travel. Train service once linked them as jewels on necklaces, but the trains moved over vast distances, linking cities in part because they lay on the path to somewhere else. Now investors realize that Amtrak might be supplanted by something less national and less public-spirited. Regional railroads focused on particular cities would cause such hub cities to boom while not necessarily offering service to cities 150 miles or more distant. At ninety miles per hour, commuter trains would focus capital of all sorts, but especially financial, in definable and stable ways. The first city with such service radiating from it would draw riders and capital from within the potential commuting zone of other cities. In the guise of reducing rush-hour automobile congestion, many downtown property owners see radial commuter rail service as a way of gathering in entire populations and reducing the value of inner-ring suburban real estate.

Highway congestion will worsen as the national population increases almost wholly in coastal strips seventy-five miles wide and in perhaps fifteen inland metropolitan regions. Given the worsening congestion and booming population, even the trucking industry realizes that change lies just over the hill. Factories indeed relocate to rural places, in part to benefit from the predictable truck schedules that translate into lower shipping costs, but as manufacturing moves offshore, the great port cities jam with containers moving from ships to trucks. New rail lines now snake away from Elizabeth, New Jersey, and inland from the Port of Los Angeles, but only a few thoughtful observers notice the impact of such lines a thousand miles inland.

The Internet plays an important if shadowy role in the movement of upper-income people to places served by some kind of rail service. Beautiful, trendy, inexpensive-to-live-in places—Leadville, Colorado, is a useful example—that lack high-speed Internet access stumble in the race to prosperity and power. Throughout the 1990s, information technology specialists argued that only when about 40 percent or more of American households enjoyed high-speed cable Internet access would online ordering flex its muscle. The Christmas 2004 shopping season proved the specialists right, but the proof that connection causes change still shapes little news media reporting of people and freight movement. Most shoppers, especially those in metropolitan regions, more or less understand that online shopping has transformed the retailing of everything from books to antiques to DVDs. Often the backroom of a traditional business proves the power of online ordering, as clerks fill orders to be shipped via UPS and FedEx. Sometimes stores close, often suddenly, either in the face of invisible competition or because backroom business has so outperformed ordinary retail that owners locate to cheaper real estate. Scenario analysts tend to agree that the Internet will suddenly transform the national transportation system.

Almost certainly it has, often in negative ways. The difficulties airlines now confront almost certainly originated elsewhere than deregulation, no-frills competition, and terrorism. Business travel began decreasing in the last years of the 1990s, as did the volume of first-class mail: the Internet fueled both revolutions. In positive ways, online shopping explains the proliferation of UPS, FedEx, and other express trucks. FedEx especially distinguishes its services by painting its logo in different colors on different trucks. Online shoppers know the difference between FedEx and FedEx ground, and anyone walking through busy downtown or suburban neighborhoods discovers different FedEx trucks serving adjacent addresses. The combination of online shopping and high-speed express delivery gives shoppers choices undreamed of only ten years ago. But however difficult balancing negatives and positives appears, scenario analysis involves projecting from data and situations known only in fuzzy ways. The Internet, and perhaps cell phones, will transform the landscape by transforming ground transportation. Almost certainly, they will accomplish that transformation by altering railroads.

In September 2006 an Austrian Railways train set a new record for speed beneath catenary. It operated at 221 miles per hour, breaking the 1955 record of 205 miles per hour set by two French Railways electric locomotives.

Serious money moved in that direction by 1985, and vast amounts of capital move so now. Landownership records remain the last decentralized, noncomputerized database in the United States. Blind realty trusts own structures and land, but no one penetrates the trusts to the individuals who create and run them. Tracing the changes in ownership of land near a railroad junction means time-consuming work in a registry of deeds, but it usually confirms the argument of this book. While some land remains, decade after decade, in the hands of trusts waiting for something, much has changed hands recently, often for much higher prices each time. Local real estate agents know that some owners simply deflect any buyer, but that knowledge is difficult to extract from strangers. Consulting firms, especially those retained by trust officers of banking institutions and attorneys charged with increasing the value of funds in their care, generally prove close-lipped on the subject.

When the analysts access historical documents, especially those pertaining to the operation of a railroad rather than its financial status, archivists, librarians, and scholars glimpse something of the research effort that focuses so much intellectual energy. Often the analysts must approach railroad enthusiasts and their historical societies to learn the answers to seemingly arcane questions. Gradually, the more thoughtful of these enthusiasts, especially those connected in nationwide Internet groups, realize that the inquirers have agendas beyond history, nostalgia, and intellectual curiosity.

Consultants and analysts and investors-at-large may contact their graying professor to ask about lectures they heard twenty years ago. They inquire about my own *Metropolitan Corridor: Railroads and the American Scene,* which appeared in 1983, and often their questions reveal research, at least well begun and sometimes completed. The questions range from purely historical ones to inquiries about my present research, but answers come only when the questions are put in the frameworks that teach the asked. One involves a never-built connector railroad intended to link two metropolitan New York lines. Another involves a half-imagined chain of wilderness inns resembling one along a Swiss railroad. Other questions look forward. If commuter trains run on time, Professor, evening after evening, would commuters use cell phones to order take-home meals from restaurants located near stations? Bit by bit the questions reveal where so much now-hidden late-1990s dot-com-boom money went. It went to wait for the train.

All anyone else can do is look around, especially at railroads and where railroads once operated.

MIT erected buildings over the lightly used Grand Junction line and it owns other air rights above the track. Its buildings rise over trains and are constructed so that the single track can be widened immediately to double track. Such architectural evidence of assumed future change is everywhere along railroads, but only the observant notice it. Across the entire United States trains are moving faster now, and often much more frequently. Where trains rarely operate, or where the right-of-way lies bereft of rails and ties and trains, rewards scrutiny too.

Anyone who stands and looks around may glimpse the signs of railroad resurgence. Often in the quiet, long-ago whistles echo faintly, announcing the train again.

SOURCES: Hamilton, "Savannah Scrapbook"; Hansen, "Give the People a Monument"; Lomax, 2004 *Urban Mobility Study*.

NOTE ON SOURCES AND NAMES

While much of the material underlying this book can be obtained from any good public library, some of it lingers in obscurity. The New York State Department of Transportation's *Special Report on Railroads* (April 1976) includes a perceptive article by Raymond T. Schuler, Commissioner of Transportation, about the long-term impact of downgrading the main line of the Erie-Lackawanna Railroad running through the southern half of New York. It is the sort of document only sustained academic inquiry—or great good luck—rescues from dust. Examined over decades, railroad industry press releases often suggest at least the outlines of large-scale change ahead. One 1970 release notes that three railroads, the Seaboard Coast Line, the St. Louis–San Francisco, and the Union Pacific, had organized to operate the longest daily scheduled freight train, 3,311 miles from Florida to the Pacific Northwest. Not for decades did real-estate investors realize the impact of that experiment. Railroad company annual reports offer much data about present operating conditions and intentions for future development. Some source material includes railroad and railroad-related industry data not intended for the public. *Trolley Coach: Application and Performance Data,* an in-house report by the East Pittsburgh Works of the Westinghouse Electric and Manufacturing Company, explains much about the present diesel-engine bus industry. Underlying this book, too, are weekly Internet reports aimed at industry officials and investors. One of the best such reports is *Weekly Rail Report,* produced by David Mears and available free to any inquirer. Valuable unpublished works like "Railroad Postal Routes from 1867 to 1961," by Herbert H. Harrington, a philatelist who mined the archives of the Boston Philatelic Library (now at Boston University) to delineate mail train routes over decades, make sense of ephemeral but critical government documents like *Instructions and Rulings with Reference to Transportation of Mails by Railroads,* a 1938 publication of the Office of the Postmaster General. *Directions for*

Using Fleming Mail Catcher and Deliverer (1898) published by an Erie, Pennsylvania, manufacturer of robotic devices that enabled mail trains to pick up and deposit mail without stopping, describes equipment that changed post office standards from those specified in its 1886 *Mail-Bag Crane*. Such sources the reader may find listed at the end of each chapter and in the bibliography of this book, but many similar ones of extremely narrow significance are omitted. Readers interested in the recent history of the railroad industry might begin with Richard Saunders's magisterial *Main Lines: Rebirth of the North American Railroads, 1970–2002*. Those intrigued by railroad operations that shape larger changes might buy the latest copy of any enthusiast magazine, perhaps especially *Trains, Railfan & Railroad, Model Railroader,* and *Railroad Model Craftsman*. Finally, this book derives from long-term reading of special-focus, non-railroad-industry magazines like *Transmission and Distribution*. The electricity-generating industry has its own agenda concerning electrifying railroads, but that and many other topics are beyond the scope of this book. The best source of information remains close scrutiny of railroad operations and real estate investment along railroad corridors. Railroading is dangerous: it is best to observe from a distance.

Mergers make the use of former railroad company names problematic. Here old names designate companies and routes as they existed, and contemporary names designate present postmerger corporations and lines.

BIBLIOGRAPHY

Abbey, Wallace W. "Railroads and the War." *Railroad History* [Millennium Special volume] (2000), 81-88.

Anderson, Sherwood. "Business Types." *Agricultural Advertising* 11 (April 1904), 39–40.

Arcara, Roger. *Westchester's Forgotten Railway: An Account of the New York, Westchester & Boston.* New York: Quadrant, 1972.

Armstrong, A. H. *The Future of Our Railways.* Schenectady, N.Y.: General Electric Co., 1920.

Babcock, Michael W., James L. Bunch, et al. "Impact of Short Line Railroad Abandonment on Highway Damage Costs: A Kansas Case Study." *Transportation Quarterly* 57 (Fall 2003), 105–21.

———. "Impact of Short Line Railroad Abandonment on Wheat Transportation and Handling Costs: A Kansas Case Study." *Transportation Quarterly* 57 (Fall 2003), 87–105.

Babcock, Michael, Eugene Russell, and Curtis Mauler. "Study of the Impact of Rail Abandonment on Local Roads and Streets." *Conference Proceedings: Sixth International Conference on Low Volume Roads,* 1995, 110–19.

Baldwin, Deborah. "Getting to the Trains in Time." *Environmental Action,* August 26, 1978, 4–9.

Bente, Bruce R. "The Airporters: Cars for Cleveland's New Airport Rapid." *Headlights* 29 (December 1967), 4–10.

Bertolini, Luca, and Tejo Spit. *Cities on Rails: The Redevelopment of Railway Station Areas.* London: Spon, 1998.

"Better Move, A." *Boston Herald,* September 16, 2005, 30.

Bezilla, Michael. *Electric Traction on the Pennsylvania Railroad.* University Park: Pennsylvania State University Press, 1980.

———. "The Electrification That Might Have Been—and Might Still Be." *Trains* 38 (March 1978), 30–34.

Bixler, Herbert E. *Railroads: Their Rise and Fall: A Personal Observation.* Jaffrey Center, N.H.: The author, 1982.

Black, Archibald. *The Story of Tunnels.* New York: Whittilsey, 1937.

Black, W. J. *Santa Fe de-Luxe: Third Winter Season, 1913–14.* Chicago: Franklin, 1913.

Borrone, Lillian. "Sparking the Globalized Trade and Transportation Connection: Supply Freight System Responses to Global Trade Demands." *Transportation Research Record,* no. 1906 (2002), 5–16.

Boyd, Jim. "One Hundred and Fifty Years of the D&H." *Railroad Model Craftsman* 42 (August 1973), 38–45.

Brown, Kevin V. "Build This 'Flying Volkswagen' for Less Than $600." *Popular Mechanics* 129 (May 1968), 120–24, 176.

———. "Build This New 4-Place Cabin Plane for $3500." *Popular Mechanics* 131 (May 1969), 112–17, 208.

Brownell, Blaine A. "The Notorious Jitney and the Urban Transportation Crisis in Birmingham in the 1920s." *Alabama Review* 25 (April 1971), 67–89.

Burr, William, ed. *U.S. Planning for War in Europe, 1963–1964.* NSA no. 31. Washington, D.C.: GPO, National Security Archive, 2005.

"Buses on Rails—a New Concept?" *Headlights* 30 (January 1968), 2–6.

California High-Speed Rail Authority. *Building a High-Speed Train System for California.* Sacramento: CHSRA, 2000.

Canton, Steve. "Fight for Survival: How Long Can Railway Express Stay in Business?" *Railroad* 53 (December 1950), 20–30.

Carstens, Hal. "The Shawangunk Carrier." *Railroad Model Craftsman* 45 (February 1977), 4, 106.

Cheney, Frank. "Boston's Electric Buses." *Rollsign* 23 (October 1986), 10–24.

Cherington, Charles R. *Regulation of Railroad Abandonments.* Cambridge, Mass.: Harvard University Press, 1948.

Christopherson, Ed. "Bold Proposal: A Bridge for Alaskan Oil." *Popular Mechanics* 141 (January 1974), 106–8, 182.

Cole, Henry G. *The Road to Rainbow: Army Planning for Global War.* Annapolis: Naval Institute, 2002.

Collucci-Rios, Benjamin, and Eldon J. Yoder. *A Methodology for Evaluating the Increase in Pavement Maintenance Costs Resulting from Increased Truck Weights on a Statewide Basis.* West Lafayette, Ind.: Purdue University, Dept. of Highway Engineering, 1983.

Comarow, Murray. *The Demise of the Postal Service?* Bethesda: National Academy of Public Administration, 2002.

"Commuting." *The Economist,* September 5, 1998, 1–18.

Comstock, Henry B. "Slow Train to Great Slave." *Popular Mechanics* 128 (July 1967), 110–13.

Condit, Carl W. *The Port of New York.* Chicago: University of Chicago Press, 1980–81.

Corns, John B. "Ohio's Robot Railroad." *Trains* 39 (March 1979), 22–28.

Crossley, Robert P. "Those Fast, New Trains." *Popular Mechanics* 131 (May 1969), 98–99, 205.

Daniels, Wayne M. "From Rumor to Renaissance: The Delaware & Hudson." *Railroad Model Craftsman* 43 (November 1974), 33–34.

DeGraw, Ronald. "Ohio's New Electric Railroad." *Headlights* 30 (January 1968), 8.

Department of Agriculture. *Open-Country Poverty in a Relatively Affluent Area— the East North Central States.* Washington, D.C.: GPO, 1971.

———. *Rural Poverty in Three Southern Regions.* Washington, D.C.: GPO, 1979.

DeViers, Jon B., and Gary Lenz. "Recentralization: Intermodal Shipping Centers Have the Potential to Transform America's Inner-City Industrial Areas." *Urban Land* 58 (June 1999), 69–73, 94–96.

Doughty, Geoffrey H. *New York Central and the Trains of the Future.* Lynchburg, Va.: TLC Publishing, 1997.

Drury, George H. "Tank Train." *Trains* 38 (October 1978), 16.

Dubin, Arthur D. *Some Classic Trains.* Milwaukee: Kalmbach, 1964.

"Electrification: In the Future." *Headlights* 32 (November–December 1970), 10–17.

Ewing, Reid, Rolf Pendall, and Don Chen. "Measuring Sprawl and Its Transportation Impacts." *Transportation Research Record,* no. 1831 (2004), 175–83.

Fales, E. D. "How You'll Drive 120 Mph Legally." *Popular Science* 187 (October 1965), 98–101, 186.

———. "Our Crumbling Interstates: A National Dilemma." *Popular Mechanics* 145 (July 1978), 66–69, 118.

Fantel, Hans. "New Low-Cost System Lets You Tape TV Pictures at Home." *Popular Mechanics* 122 (October 1965), 117–19.

Faulkner, W. D. "The Story of Trolley Coaches in the Crescent City." *Electric Lines* 5 (May–June 1992), 8–12.

Fifer, Valerie J. "Transcontinental: The Political Word." *Geographical Journal* 144 (November 1978), 438–49.

Fitzgerald, F. Scott. *The Great Gatsby.* New York: Scribner's, 1925.

Fleming Mail Catcher and Deliverer Company. *Directions for Using Fleming Mail Catcher and Deliverer.* Erie, Pa.: Fleming, 1898.

Frailey, Fred W. "Blank Bullet." *Trains* 63 (February 2003), 32–43.

Frank, Joseph H. "Philadelphia Trackless Trolleys." *Electric Lines* 5 (January–February 1992), 23–25.

Garrett, Klink. *Ten Turtles to Tucumcari: A Personal History of the Railway Express Agency.* Albuquerque: University of New Mexico Press, 2003.

General Electric Company. "Can Technology and the Environment Peacefully Coexist?" *Wall Street Journal,* September 19, 2005, A10–A11.

Gibson, Alan J. "Rail Transit Returns to Calgary." National Model Railroad Association *Bulletin* 47 (June 1982), 34–39.

Gilmore, C. P. "How You'll Drive the Amazing Urbmobile." *Popular Science* 191 (October 1967), 75–78, 208.

Grant, Bob. "This Car Really Flies." *Popular Mechanics* 136 (June 1975), 87–91, 176.

Grant, H. Roger. "Piggyback Pioneer: Any Idea to Boost Revenues Was an Idea That the Great Weedy Couldn't Refuse." *Trains* 46 (January 1986), 31–34.

Griswold, Wesley S. "How to Drive in a Crisis." *Popular Science* 185 (September 1964), 43–45, 182–83.

Grivno, Cody. "Amtrak's Mail and Express Fleet." *Model Railroader* 79 (March 2003), 71–73.

Gronau, Reuben. *The Value of Time in Passenger Transportation: The Demand for Air Travel.* New York: Columbia University Press, 1970.

Gunnell, Bruce C. *An Atomic Powered Railroad Locomotive.* New York: Association of American Railroads, 1955.

Halperin, R. J. "The Trolley Coaches of St. Joseph, Missouri." *Electric Lines* 3 (September–October 1990), 28–31.

Hamilton, Andy. "Savannah Scrapbook." National Model Railroad Association *Bulletin* 47 (August 1982), 24–29.

Hansen, Peter A. "Give the People a Monument: Kansas City Union Station." *Trains* 59 (April 1999), 62–73.

Harlem Board of Commerce. *Three Plans for the Relief of Traffic Congestion in New York City.* New York: Harlem Board of Commerce, 1929.

Harley, E. Thomas. "U.S. Railway Freight Electrification." *Electric Lines* 1 (July–August 1988), 12–13.

Harmon, Roy L. *Reinventing the Warehouse: World-Class Distribution Logistics.* New York: Free Press, 1993.

Harrington, Herbert H. "Railroad Postal Routes from 1867 to 1961." Unpublished typescript, 1964. Photocopy, Boston University Library.

Hediger, Jim. "New Railbox ABOX Boxcar." *Model Railroader* 56 (September 1979), 58–59.

Hemphill, Mark W. "The Unknown Rio Grande." *Trains* 45 (July 1985), 24–35.

Hicks, Clifford B. "They'll Tell You How You'll Vote." *Popular Mechanics,* 122 (October 1964), 105–10, 116, 122.

Homberger, Eric. *Historical Atlas of New York City.* New York: Holt, 1994.

Howard, F. H. "Piggyback and the Portager Dream." *Trains* 37 (April 1977), 44–51; (May 1977), 45–51.

Hubbard, Freeman. "Nine Hundred Thousand Barrels a Day." *Railroad Magazine* 34 (July 1943), 8–45.

———. "Will 'Piggyback' Make the Boxcar Obsolete?" *Railroad* 69 (February 1958), 28–31.

Hungerford, Edward. *A Railroad for Tomorrow.* Milwaukee: Kalmbach, 1945.

"Italian Electric 'Rapido' Does Amazing 149.04 m.p.h." *The Whistle Stop* 2 (December 1952), 35.

Joachimsthaler, Anton. *Die Breitspurbahn Hitlers.* Freiburg: Eisenbahn-Kurier Verlag, 1981.

Johnson, Stanley W. *The Milwaukee Road Revisited.* Moscow: University of Idaho Press, 1997.

Johnson, Todd. "Rail Yard Infill." *Urban Land* 62 (June 2003), 40–51.

Josserand, Peter. "Tomorrow: Trains with Brains?" *Railroad* 74 (April 1963), 19–24.

Kansas State Board of Agriculture. *Kansas Grain Transportation.* Topeka: Kansas State Board of Agriculture, 2003.

Koester, Anthony J. "The Fun of Finding Yesterday." *Railroad Model Craftsman* 47 (August 1978), 90–91.

Kotkin, Joel. "The Great Plains." *Wall Street Journal,* August 31, 2006, A19.

"Labor, 1978." *Trains* 38 (October 1978), 3–6.

Lambert, Bruce. "More Long Islanders Looking to Move Out, a Survey Finds." *New York Times,* December 1, 2005, A31.

Lamson, Ted. C. "Catching and Throwing the Mail." National Model Railroad Association *Bulletin* 37 (October 1971), 14–15, 41.

Levy, Mark R. *The VCR Age.* London: Sage, 1989.

Light, Jennifer S. *From Warfare to Welfare: Defense Intellectuals and Urban Problems in Cold War America.* Baltimore: Johns Hopkins University Press, 2003.

Lomax, Timothy. *2004 Urban Mobility Study.* College Station: Texas Transportation Institute, 2004.

Long, Bryant A., and William J. Dennis. *Mail by Rail: The Story of the Postal Transportation Service.* New York: Simmons-Boardman, 1951.

Lustig, David. "Los Angeles' LRVs." *Railroad Model Craftsman* 59 (March 1991), 65–73.

Machalaba, Daniel. "Expensive Toys: Private Rail Cars Are Back on Amtrak." *Wall Street Journal,* November 12, 1984, A1, A21.

Machalaba, Daniel, and Christopher J. Chipello. "New Track: Battling Trucks, Trains Gain Steam by Watching Clock." *Wall Street Journal,* July 25, 2003, A1, A16.

Maiken, Peter T. *Night Trains: The Pullman System in the Golden Years of American Rail Travel.* Chicago: Lakme, 1989.

Mankoff, Al. "The Seventh Wonder of the Traction World." *Electric Lines* 3 (July–August 1990), 30–35.

Margetts, F. C. "Trains for Tomorrow." *Trains* 36 (April 1976), 40–45.

Marshall, James. *Santa Fe: The Railroad That Built an Empire.* New York: Random House, 1945.

Matoff, Tom. "Sacramento." *Electric Lines* 3 (July–August 1990), 14–19.

McMurty, Larry. *Roads: Driving America's Great Highways.* New York: Simon & Schuster, 2000.

McSpedon, Edward. "Building Light Rail Transit in Existing Rail Corridors: Panacea or Nightmare? The Los Angeles Experience." *Electric Lines* 4 (January–February 1991), 19–25.

Meikle, Jeffrey L. "Industrial Design Speeds Forward." *Railroad History* [Millennium Special volume] (2000), 62–72.

Menzies, Ian. "The South Shore—200,000 People Within 10 Minutes of an Unused Rail Line." *Boston Globe,* February 11, 1974, 20.

Meyer, John R., Martin J. Peck, et al. *The Economics of Competition in the Transportation Industries.* Cambridge, Mass.: Harvard University Press, 1959.

Middleton, William D. *Metropolitan Railways: Rapid Transit in America.* Bloomington: Indiana University Press, 2003.

———. *When the Steam Railroads Electrified.* Milwaukee: Kalmbach, 1974.

Mierzejewski, Alfred C. "High Speed Motor Trains of the German National Railway, 1920–1945." *Railroad History* 175 (Autumn 1996), 57–68.

Mischke, Charles P. "Pages from the Past: The Pelham Park Monorail." *The Whistle Stop* 2 (December 1952), 34–35.

Moffat, Bruce. *Forty Feet Below: The Story of Chicago's Freight Tunnels.* Glendale, Calif.: Interurban Press, 1983.

———. *The "L": The Development of Chicago's Rapid Transit System, 1888–1932.* Chicago: Central Electric Railfans Association, 1995.

Morgan, David P. "Forget the Gods of Old." *Trains* 38 (October 1978), 58–59.

———. "Mr. Pullman Revisited." *Trains* 25 (January 1965), 20–23.

———. "Ninety Miles an Hour Aboard a 4-6-4." *Trains and Travel Annual* 1 (1953), n.p.

Morris, Bill. "How Copters Can Solve Traffic Jams." *Popular Science* 190 (April 1967), 94–97.

Mortimer, Kenneth. "ACI . . . Have You Got It?" National Model Railroad Association *Bulletin* 33 (April 1968), 7.

"Moving Mail on the MoPac." Terminal Railroad Association of St. Louis Historical and Technical Society *Bulletin* 49–50 (Winter–Spring 1999), 2–31.

"Muskingum Electric: Trains on Their Own." *Headlights* 34 (January–February 1972), 10–12.

"Muskingum Electric Railroad." National Model Railroad Association *Bulletin* 34 (April 1969), 12–13.

Mysak, Joe. *Perpetual Motion: The Illustrated History of the Port Authority of New York and New Jersey.* Santa Monica: General Publishing, 1997.

Nelligan, Tom. "Amtrak Has No Commuters." *Trains* 37 (June 1977), 44.

Nelson, John W. "Look Again." National Model Railroad Association *Bulletin* 49 (June 1984), 39–44.

New York Central Railroad Co. *Fast Freight Schedule, November, 1948.* New York: New York Central Railroad Co., 1948.

New York State Department of Motor Vehicles. *The Safety Sedan: Summary of Final Report.* Albany: Department of Motor Vehicles, 1968.

New York State Department of Transportation. "A Future for Southern Tier Rail Service?" *Special Report on Railroads* 3 (April 1976), 1–4.

New York, Westchester, and Boston Railway. *Westchester Timetables.* New York: New York, Westchester, and Boston Railway, November 1, 1937.

Norfolk Southern Corporation. *Annual Report 2005.* Norfolk, Va.: The Corporation, 2005.

Official Guide of the Railways and Steam Navigation Lines of the United States, Porto Rico, Canada, Mexico, and Cuba. New York: National Railway Publication Co., 1929.

Olson, Mancur. *The Logic of Collective Action: Public Goods and the Theory of Groups.* New York: Schocken, 1965.

O'Neil, Thomas. "Quebec, North Shore & Labrador Railway." National Model Railroad Association *Bulletin* 41 (October 1975), 31–34.

Overbey, Daniel L. "Piggyback: Where Do We Go from Here?" *Trains* 46 (February 1986), 40–47.

Pence, Herbert. "Cincinnati's Sleeping Subway." *Electric Lines* 3 (March–April 1990), 18–21.

———. "Dayton Trolley Buses." *Electric Lines* 4 (November–December 1991), 17–20.

Pennypacker, Bert. "When Steam Achieved Metroliner Speeds." *Railroad Magazine* 61 (May 1970), 21–25.

"Pittsburgh: One Problem, Two Solutions." *Headlights* 31 (September–October 1969), 2–7, 16.

Plous, F. K. "The Flight of the Falcon." *Trains* 39 (February 1979), 22–30.

Poorvu, William J. *The Real Estate Game: The Intelligent Guide to Decision-Making and Investment.* New York: Free Press, 1999.

Prater, Marvin, and Keith Klindworth. *Long-Term Trends in Railroad Service and Capacity for United States Agriculture.* Washington, D.C.: Department of Agriculture, 2000.

Price, C. Grattan. "I Remember." *Trains* 37 (February 1977), 46–47.

Railway Mail Service. *Schedule of Mail Routes No. 294.* Fort Worth: Babcock, 1935.

———. *Schedule of Mail Routes No. 513.* St. Louis: Curran, 1935.

Rand, McNally & Co. *Handy Railroad Maps of the United States.* New York: Rand McNally, 1928.

Regional Plan Association. *Transit and Transportation and a Study of Port and Industrial Areas and Their Relation to Transportation.* New York: Regional Plan Association, 1928.

Reutter, Mark. "Building a Better Iron Horse." *Railroad History* [Millennium Special volume] (2000), 38–61.

"Rising Costs, Falling Ridership Rattles Rural Air Program." *Staunton News Leader,* August 30, 2003, 1.

Rose, Mark H. *Interstate: Express Highway Politics, 1939–1989.* Knoxville: University of Tennessee Press, 1990.

Runte, Alfred. "Yosemite Valley Railroad." National Railway Historical Society *Bulletin* 39–40 (1974), 10–13.

Rushkoff, Douglas. *Coercion: Why We Listen to What "They" Say.* New York: Riverhead, 1999.

Saunders, Richard. *Main Lines: Rebirth of the North American Railroads, 1970–2002.* Dekalb: Northern Illinois University Press, 2003.

Scammon, Richard M. *Study of Population and Immigration Problems.* Washington, D.C.: GPO, 1962.

Schrag, Zachary. *The Great Society Subway: A History of the Washington Metro.* Baltimore: Johns Hopkins University Press, 2006.

Schwieterman, Joseph P. *When the Railroad Leaves Town: American Communities in the Age of Rail Line Abandonment.* Kirksville, Mo.: Truman State University Press, 2001.

Shaffer, Marguerite S. *See America First: Tourism and National Identity, 1880–1940.* Washington, D.C.: Smithsonian, 2001.

Smith, Vernon L. "The Diesel from D to L." *Trains* 39 (April 1979), 22–29.

Sonstegaard, Miles H. "Competitive Access to North American Rail." *Transportation Quarterly* 57 (Fall 2003), 61–67.

Sperandeo, Andy. "The Bi-Modal RoadRailer." *Model Railroader* 49 (July 1972), 62–63.

Stelling, Carl. "Designing for the Ladies." *Landscape Architecture Magazine* 63 (Winter 1958–59), 84–86.

Stephens, Bill. "What to Do with RoadRailer?" *Trains* 62 (May 2002), 32–39.

Stilgoe, John R. *Metropolitan Corridor: Railroads and the American Scene.* New Haven: Yale University Press, 1983.

———. "Onshore Force." *Cambridge* [U.K.] *Architecture Journal* 18 (2006), 92–101.

———. *Outside Lies Magic: Regaining History and Awareness in Everyday Places.* New York: Walker and Co., 1998.

"Super-Highway." *Life,* July 29, 1940, 56–59.

Swain, Stafford. "Scenery of the Canadian Shield." *Railroad Model Craftsman* 47 (January 1979), 56–63.

"Testing 6 Sports Personal Cars." *Motor Trend* 20 (January 1969), 24–42.

Thompson, E. L. "Definition of a Redball." *Trains* 26 (June 1966), 25–27.

Toffler, Alvin. *Future Shock.* New York: Random House, 1970.

Transportation Research Board. *Light Rail Transit.* Proceedings of a National Conference on Light Rail. Washington, D.C.: National Academy Press, 1975.

———. *Low-Volume Roads.* Proceedings of a Workshop Held June 16–19, 1975, in Boise, Idaho. Washington, D.C.: Transportation Research Board, 1975.

Union Pacific Railroad Co. *Map of the Kansas City Terminal Area Showing Junctions and Interchange Points.* Omaha: Union Pacific Railroad Co., 1972.

United States Congress. Committee on Transportation and Infrastructure. *Planes, Trains, and Intermodalism: Improving the Link between Air and Rail.* Washington, D.C.: GPO, 2003.

United States Post Office Department. *General Scheme of Kansas, 1935.* Washington, D.C.: GPO, 1936.

———. *General Scheme of Texas, 1935.* Washington, D.C.: GPO, 1935.

———. *Instructions and Rulings with Reference to Transportation of Mails by Railroads (Steam and Electric) Issued by the Second Assistant Postmaster General.* Washington, D.C.: GPO, 1938.

———. *Mail-Bag Crane.* Washington, D.C.: GPO, 1886.

Urban Mass Transportation Act of 1962. H.R. 11158. Washington, D.C.: GPO, 1962.

Usselman, Steven W. *Regulating Railroad Innovation: Business, Technology, and Politics in America, 1840–1920*. Cambridge: Cambridge University Press, 2002.

Vardy, T. L. "Something for the Freight Yard." National Model Railroad Association *Bulletin* 43 (April 1978), 62–64.

Volkmer, W. D. "Light Rail Rolls in L.A." *Electric Lines* 4 (January–February 1991), 8–11.

———. "Story of Trolley Coaches in the Crescent City." *Electric Lines* 5 (May–June 1992), 8–11.

———. "Ten Years of Light Rail Progress." *Electric Lines* 1 (May–June 1988), 8–13.

Wahl, Paul. "Personal Rapid Transit." *Popular Science* 199 (November 1971), 72–77, 136.

Wakeman, Frederic. *The Fabulous Train*. New York: Rinehart, 1955.

Waller, Margy, and Evelyn Blumenberg, *The Long Journey to Work: Federal Transportation Policy for Working Families*. Washington, D.C.: Brookings Institution, 2003.

Warren, Elizabeth, and Amelia Warren Tyagi. *The Two-Income Trap: Why Middle-Class Mothers and Fathers Are Going Broke*. New York: Basic, 2003.

Westcott, Linn H. "Midnight Local." *Trains and Travel Annual 1953*, n.p.

Westinghouse Electric and Manufacturing Company. *Trolley Coach: Application and Performance Data*. East Pittsburgh: Westinghouse, 1935.

White, Howard S. "People Movers: Mass Transit's Wave of the Future or Just Another Boondoggle?" *Headlights* 35 (November 1973), 3–5.

White, John H., Jr. *The American Railroad Freight Car: From the Wood-Car Era to the Coming of Steel*. Baltimore: Johns Hopkins University Press, 1993.

———. *The American Railroad Passenger Car*. Baltimore: Johns Hopkins University Press, 1978.

Wiley, Aubrey. "Meet the 'Lynchburg Special.'" National Model Railroad Association *Bulletin* 41 (January 1976), 7–10.

Wilkins, Van. "Who Really Killed the Streetcar?" *Electric Lines* 3 (January–February 1990), 20–21, 38.

Wurst, Nancy Henderson. "On Rail's Trails." *Chicago Tribune*, January 11, 2004, 12-2, 12-5.

Young, Andrew. D. "San Jose Light Rail." *Electric Lines* 4 (July–August 1991), 14–15.

INDEX